Last Order
ANGEL REBORN

1

STORY & ART BY YUKITO KISHIRO

BATTLE ANGEL ALITA:
LAST ORDER
Angel Reborn
1

Story & Art by
Yukito Kishiro

English Adaptation by Fred Burke

Translation/Lillian Olsen
Touch-up & Lettering/
Susan Daigle-Leach & Adam Symons
Cover & Graphics Design/Sean Lee
Editor/Annette Roman

Managing Editor/Annette Roman
Director of Production/Noboru Watanabe
VP of Publishing/Alvin Lu
Sr. Director of Acquisitions/Rika Inouye
VP of Sales & Marketing/Liza Coppola
Publisher/Hyoe Narita

GUNNM LAST ORDER © 2000 by
Yukito Kishiro
All rights reserved.
First published in Japan in 2000 by
SHUEISHA Inc., Tokyo.
English translation rights in the United
States of America and Canada arranged by
SHUEISHA Inc. The stories, characters, and
incidents mentioned in this publication are
entirely fictional.

Printed in Canada.

Published by VIZ Media, LLC.
P.O. Box 77064
San Francisco, CA 94107

10 9 8 7 6 5 4 3
First printing, June 2003
Second printing, May 2004
Third printing, June 2005

store.viz.com

CONTENTS

PHASE 01:

THE FIRST THING I REMEMBER...

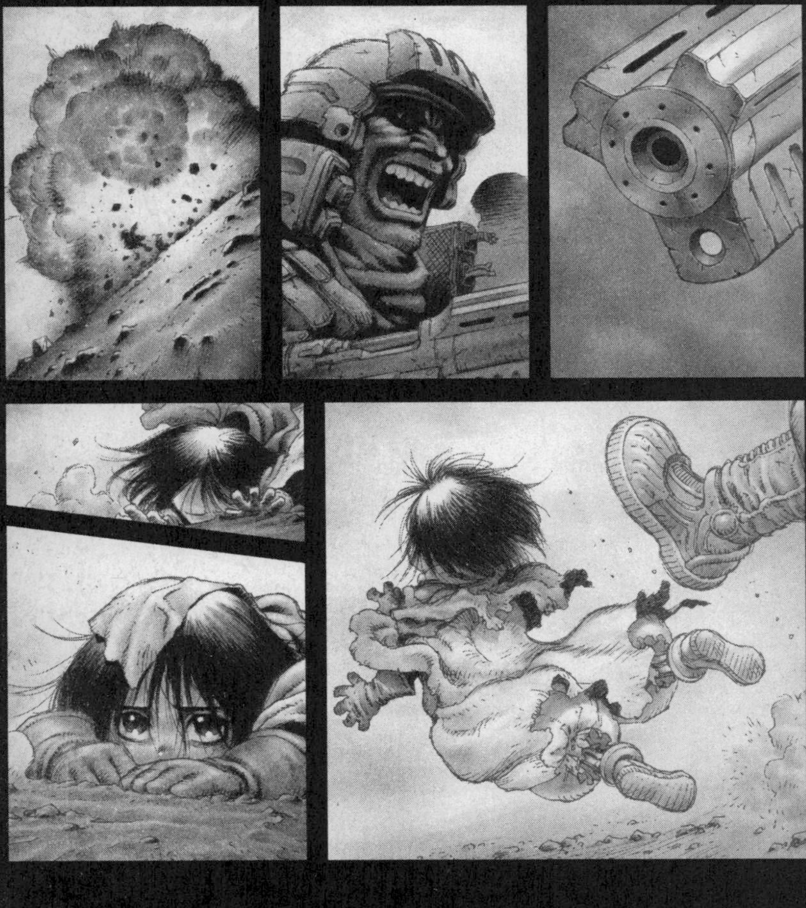

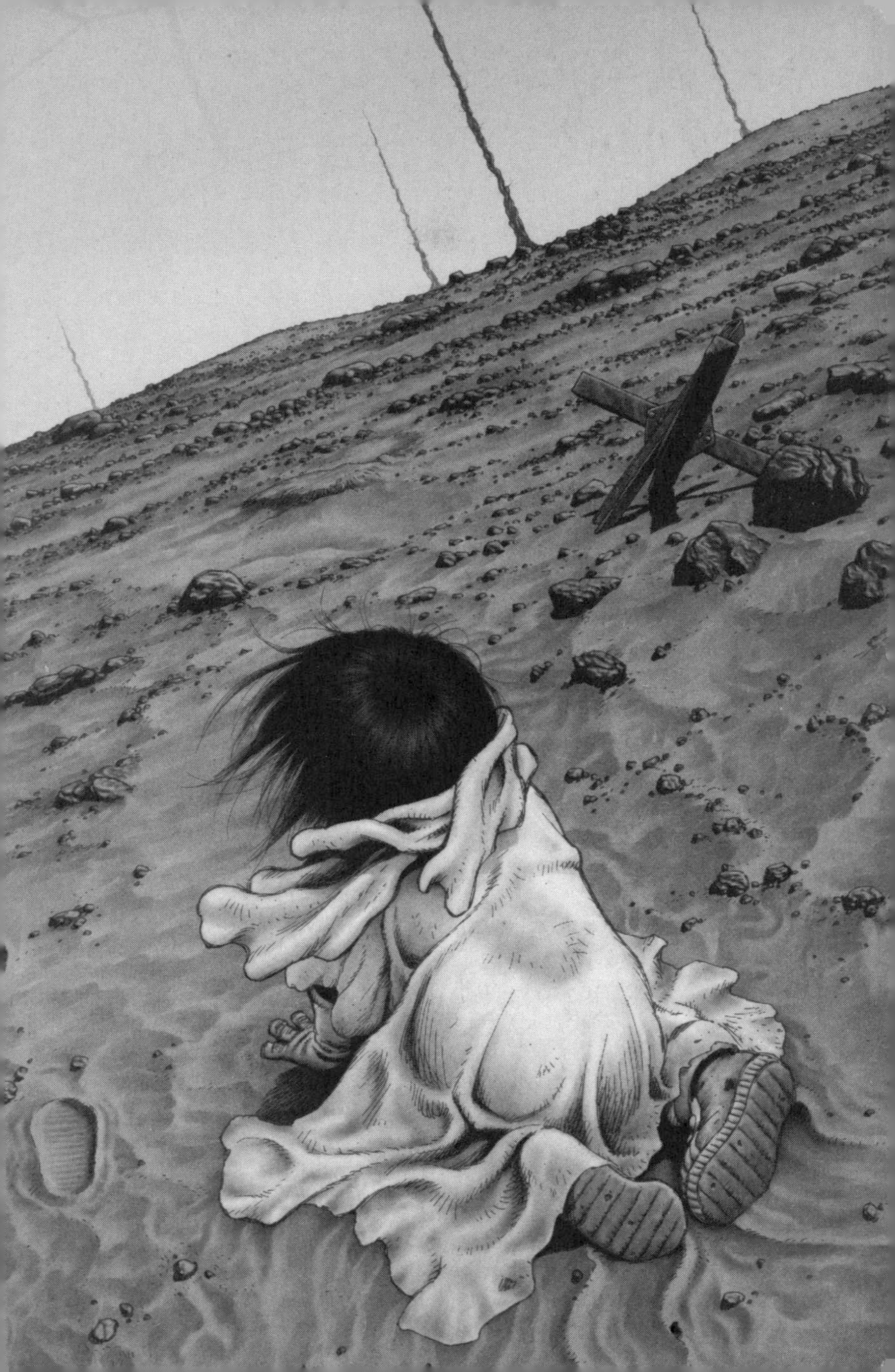

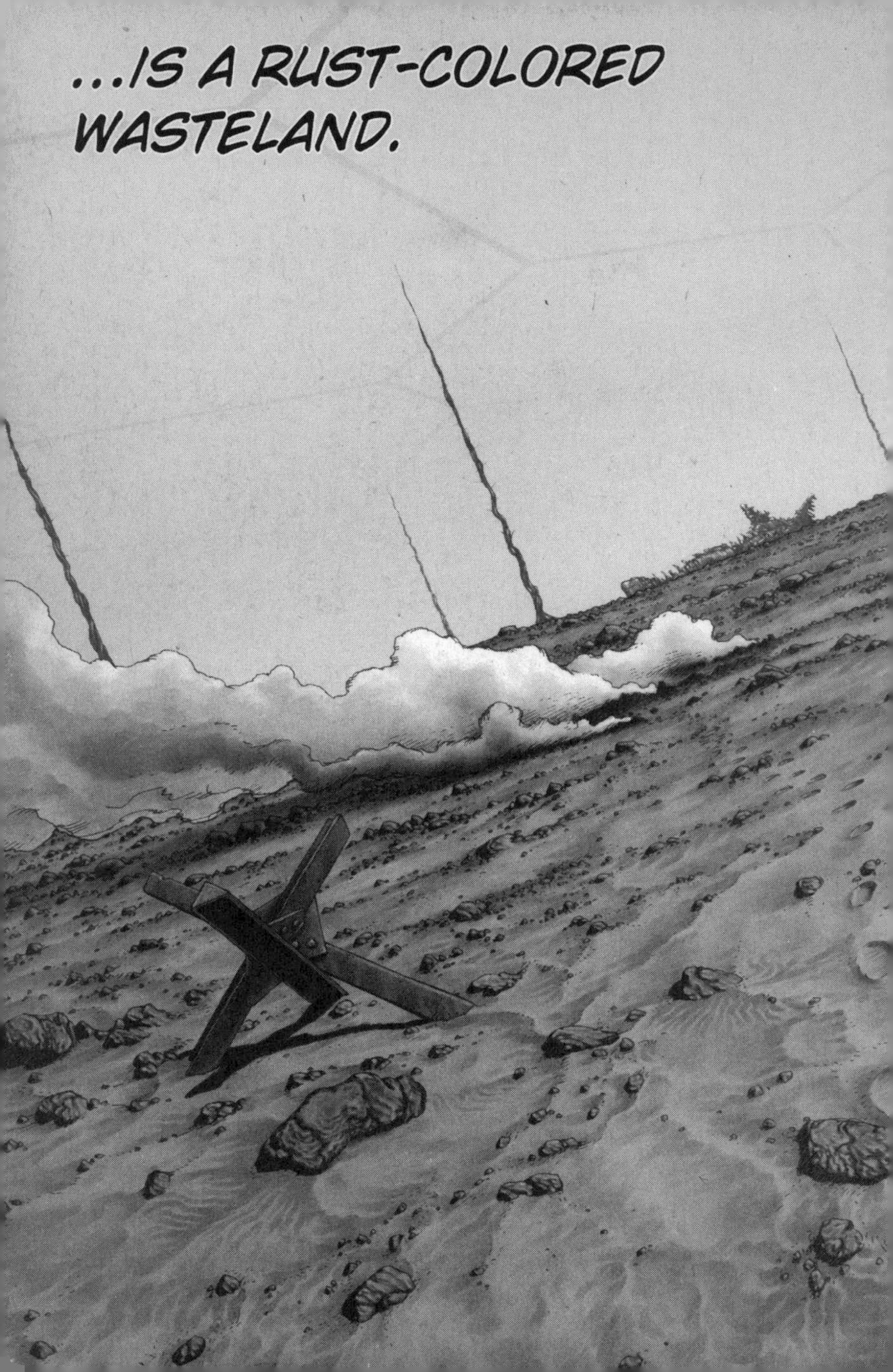
...IS A RUST-COLORED WASTELAND.

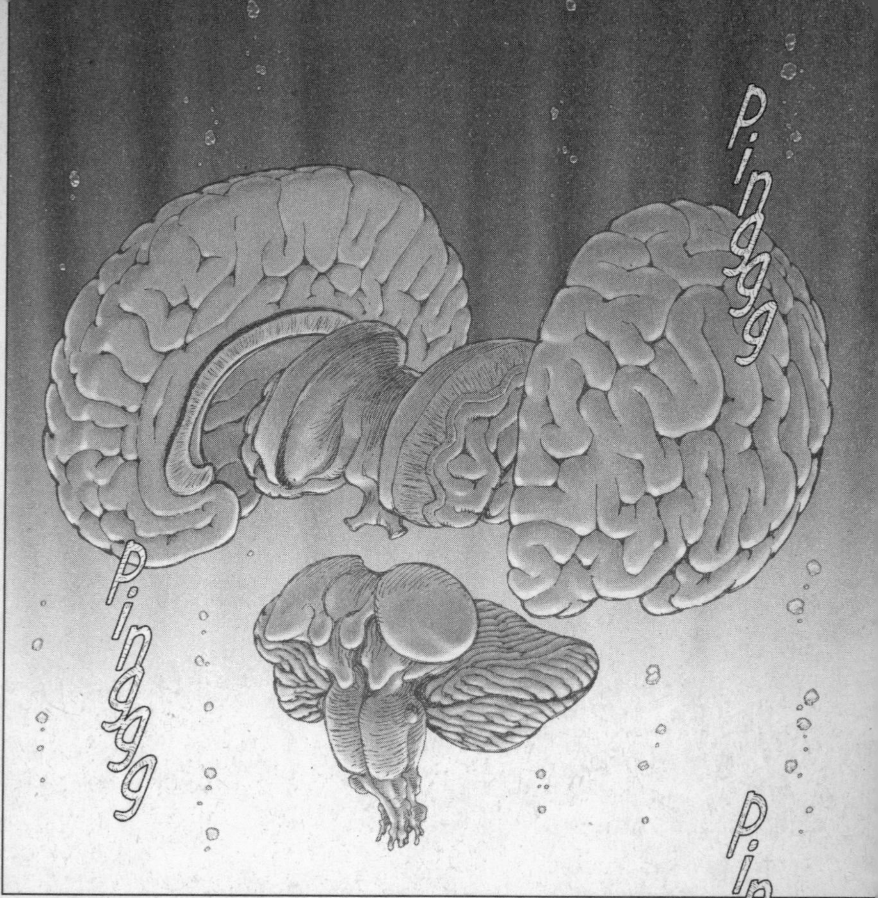
Pinggg
Pinggg

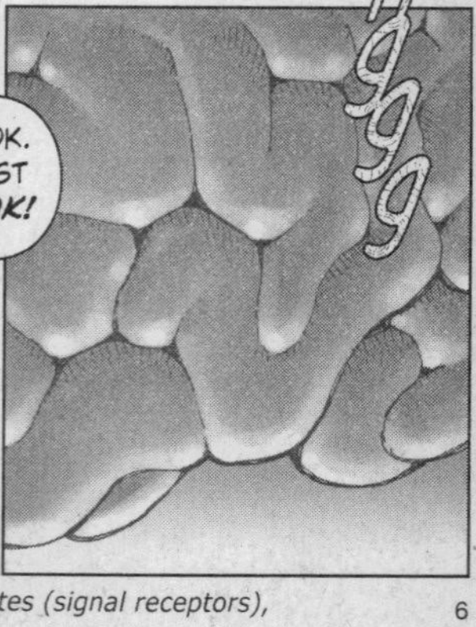
Pinggg
LOOK. JUST *LOOK!*
THE NEURONS* HAVE RESUMED THEIR FIRE DANCE.

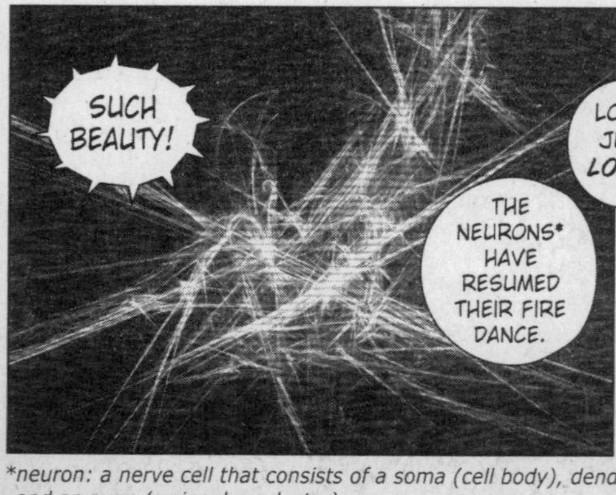
SUCH BEAUTY!

**neuron: a nerve cell that consists of a soma (cell body), dendrites (signal receptors), and an axon (a signal conductor).*

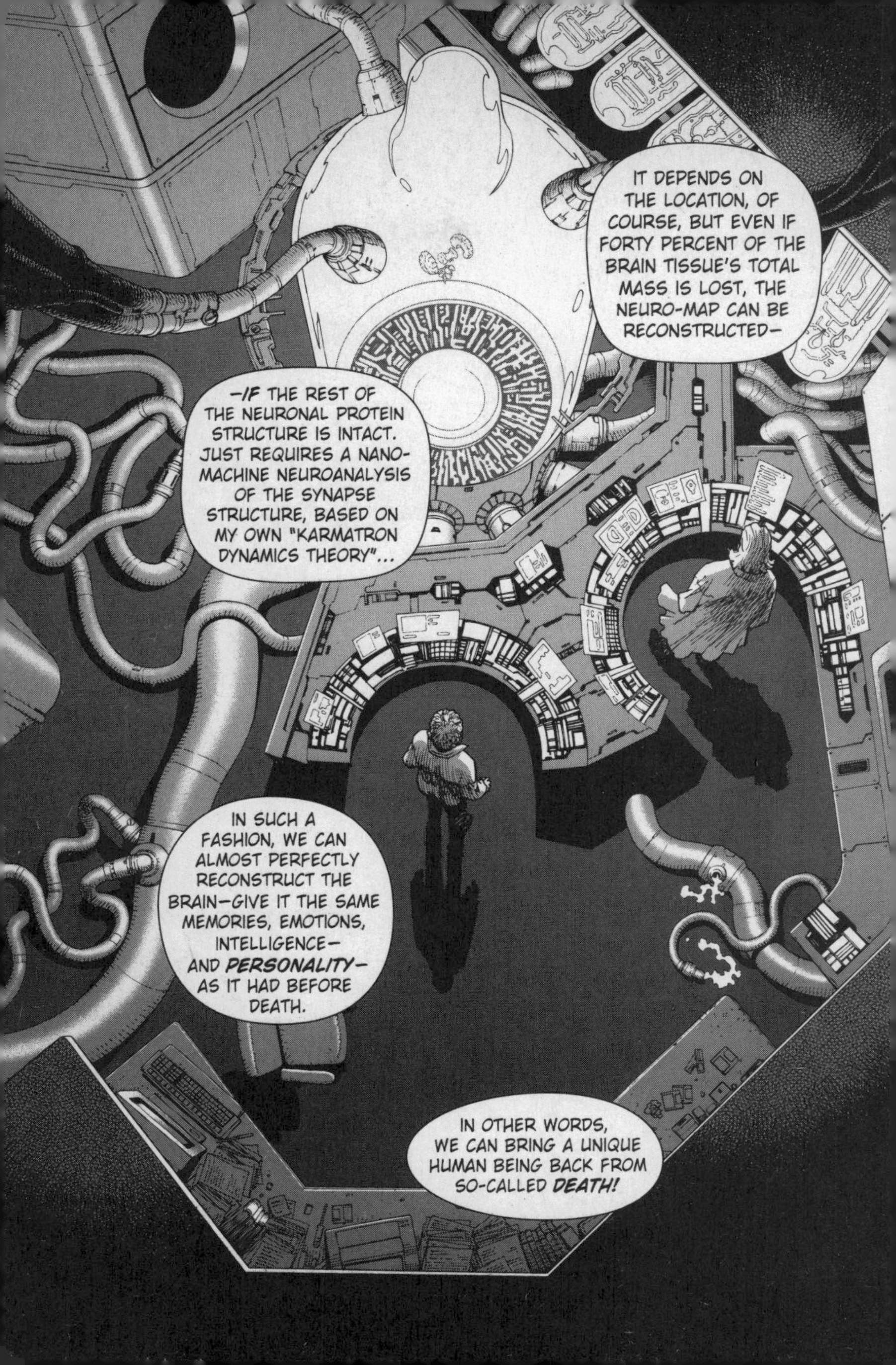
IT DEPENDS ON THE LOCATION, OF COURSE, BUT EVEN IF FORTY PERCENT OF THE BRAIN TISSUE'S TOTAL MASS IS LOST, THE NEURO-MAP CAN BE RECONSTRUCTED—
—*IF* THE REST OF THE NEURONAL PROTEIN STRUCTURE IS INTACT. JUST REQUIRES A NANO-MACHINE NEUROANALYSIS OF THE SYNAPSE STRUCTURE, BASED ON MY OWN "KARMATRON DYNAMICS THEORY"...
IN SUCH A FASHION, WE CAN ALMOST PERFECTLY RECONSTRUCT THE BRAIN—GIVE IT THE SAME MEMORIES, EMOTIONS, INTELLIGENCE— AND *PERSONALITY*— AS IT HAD BEFORE DEATH.
IN OTHER WORDS, WE CAN BRING A UNIQUE HUMAN BEING BACK FROM SO-CALLED *DEATH!*

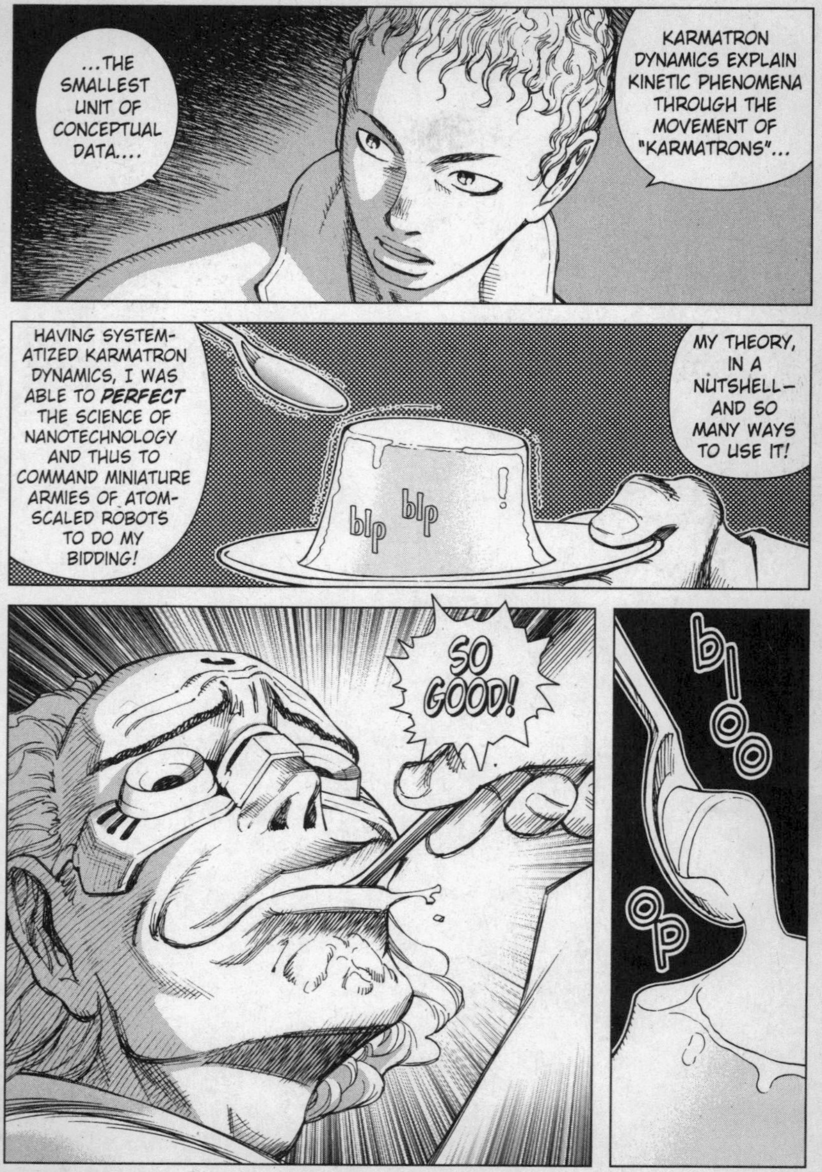
KARMATRON DYNAMICS EXPLAIN KINETIC PHENOMENA THROUGH THE MOVEMENT OF "KARMATRONS"...
...THE SMALLEST UNIT OF CONCEPTUAL DATA....
MY THEORY, IN A NUTSHELL— AND SO MANY WAYS TO USE IT!
!
blp blp
HAVING SYSTEM-ATIZED KARMATRON DYNAMICS, I WAS ABLE TO ***PERFECT*** THE SCIENCE OF NANOTECHNOLOGY AND THUS TO COMMAND MINIATURE ARMIES OF ATOM-SCALED ROBOTS TO DO MY BIDDING!
bloooop
SO GOOD!

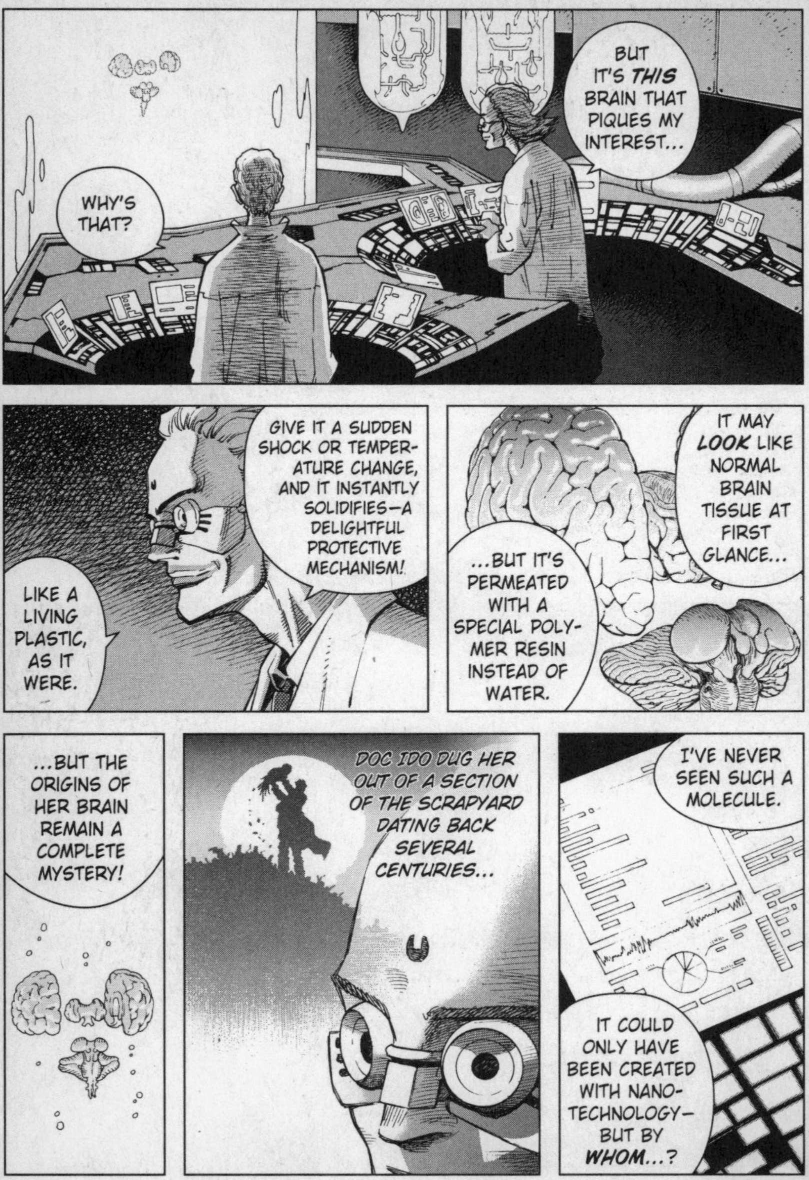
BUT IT'S ***THIS*** BRAIN THAT PIQUES MY INTEREST...
WHY'S THAT?
IT MAY ***LOOK*** LIKE NORMAL BRAIN TISSUE AT FIRST GLANCE...
...BUT IT'S PERMEATED WITH A SPECIAL POLYMER RESIN INSTEAD OF WATER.
GIVE IT A SUDDEN SHOCK OR TEMPERATURE CHANGE, AND IT INSTANTLY SOLIDIFIES—A DELIGHTFUL PROTECTIVE MECHANISM!
LIKE A LIVING PLASTIC, AS IT WERE.
I'VE NEVER SEEN SUCH A MOLECULE.
IT COULD ONLY HAVE BEEN CREATED WITH NANOTECHNOLOGY—BUT BY ***WHOM***...?
DOC IDO DUG HER OUT OF A SECTION OF THE SCRAPYARD DATING BACK SEVERAL CENTURIES...
...BUT THE ORIGINS OF HER BRAIN REMAIN A COMPLETE MYSTERY!

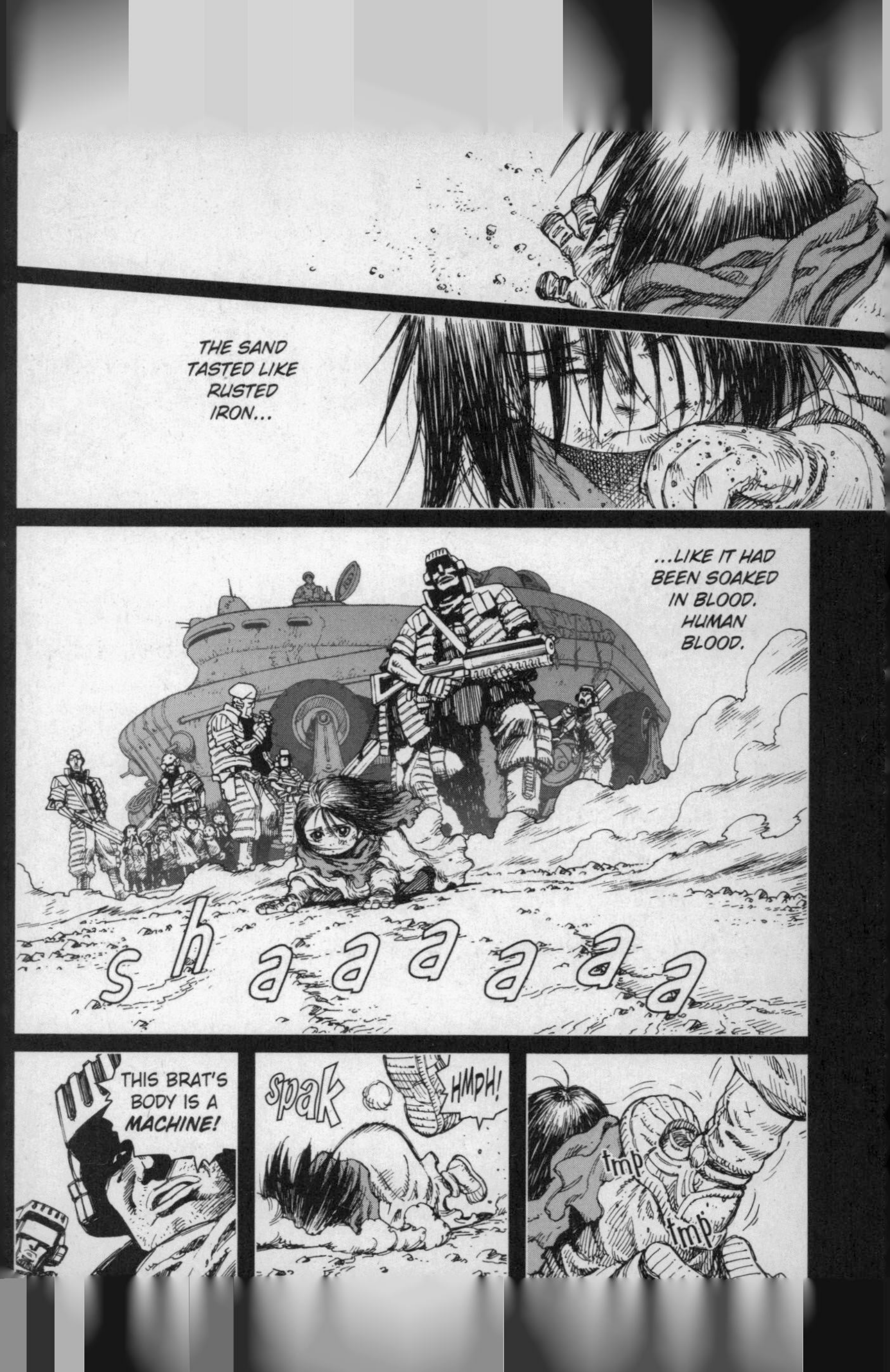
THE SAND TASTED LIKE RUSTED IRON...
...LIKE IT HAD BEEN SOAKED IN BLOOD. HUMAN BLOOD.
shaaaaaa
THIS BRAT'S BODY IS A MACHINE!
spak
HMPH!
tmp
tmp

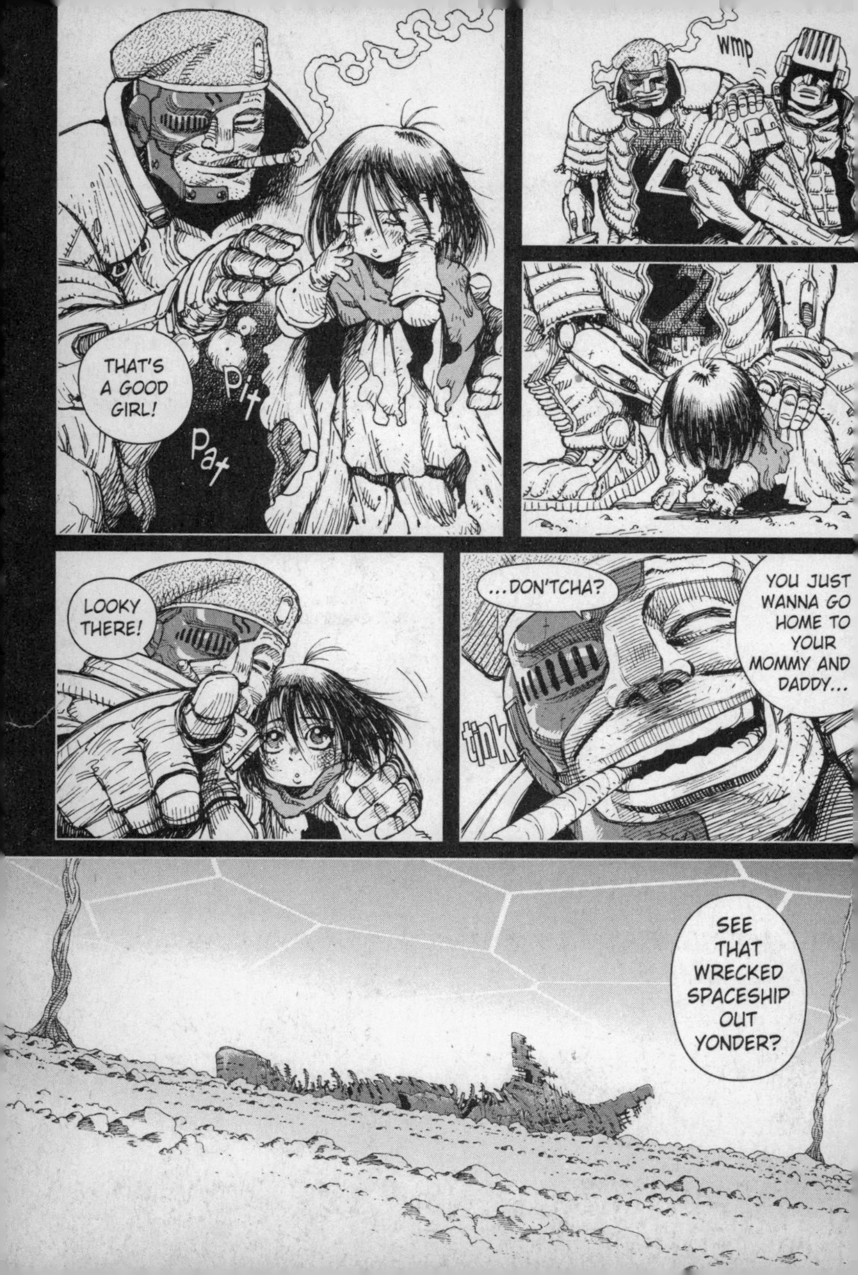
wmp
THAT'S A GOOD GIRL!
Pit
Pat
YOU JUST WANNA GO HOME TO YOUR MOMMY AND DADDY...
...DON'TCHA?
tink
LOOKY THERE!
SEE THAT WRECKED SPACESHIP OUT YONDER?

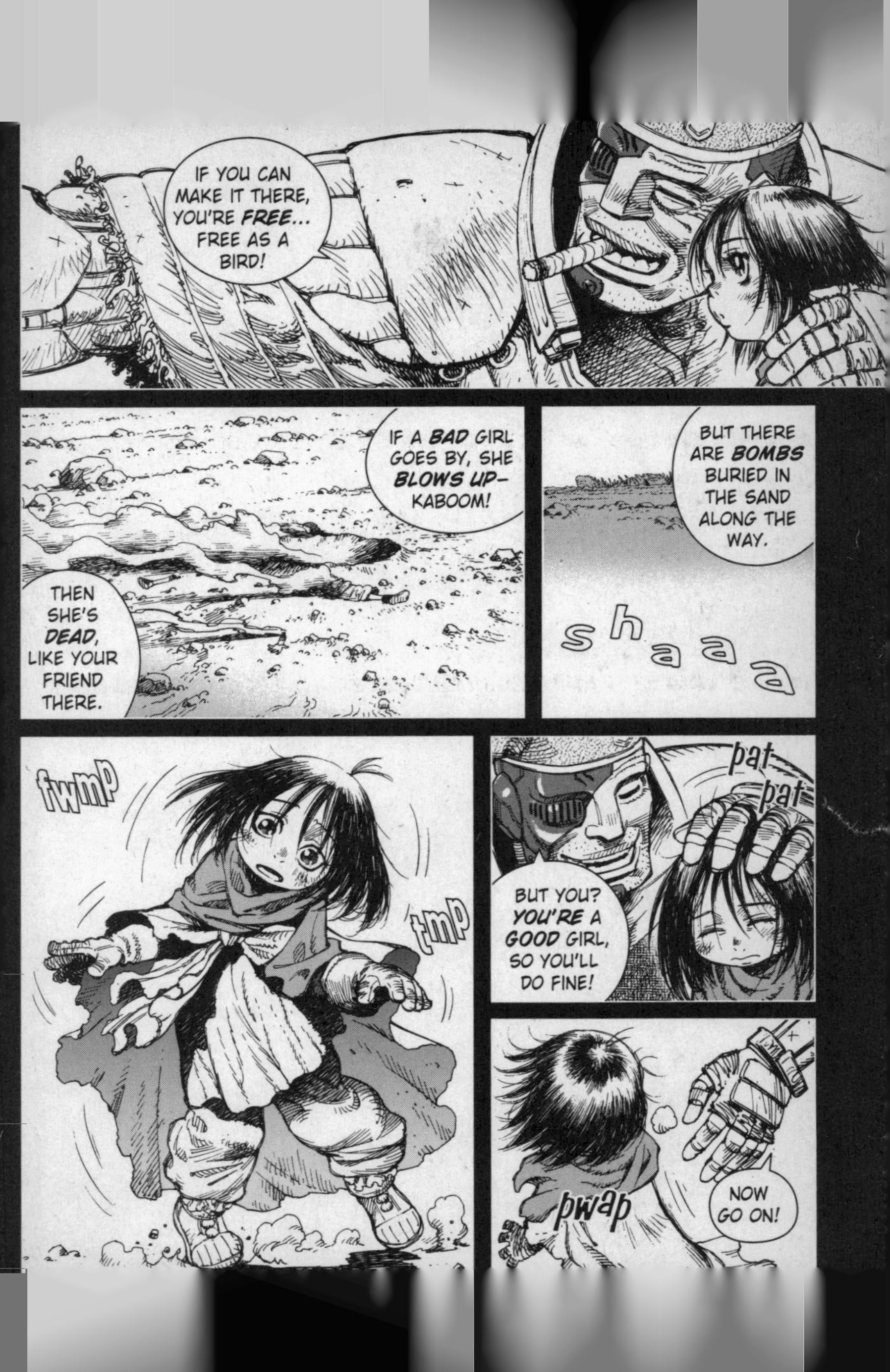
IF YOU CAN MAKE IT THERE, YOU'RE **FREE**... FREE AS A BIRD!
BUT THERE ARE **BOMBS** BURIED IN THE SAND ALONG THE WAY.
shaaa
IF A **BAD** GIRL GOES BY, SHE **BLOWS UP**— KABOOM!
THEN SHE'S **DEAD**, LIKE YOUR FRIEND THERE.
pat pat
BUT YOU? **YOU'RE** A **GOOD** GIRL, SO YOU'LL DO FINE!
NOW GO ON!
pwap
fwmp
tmp

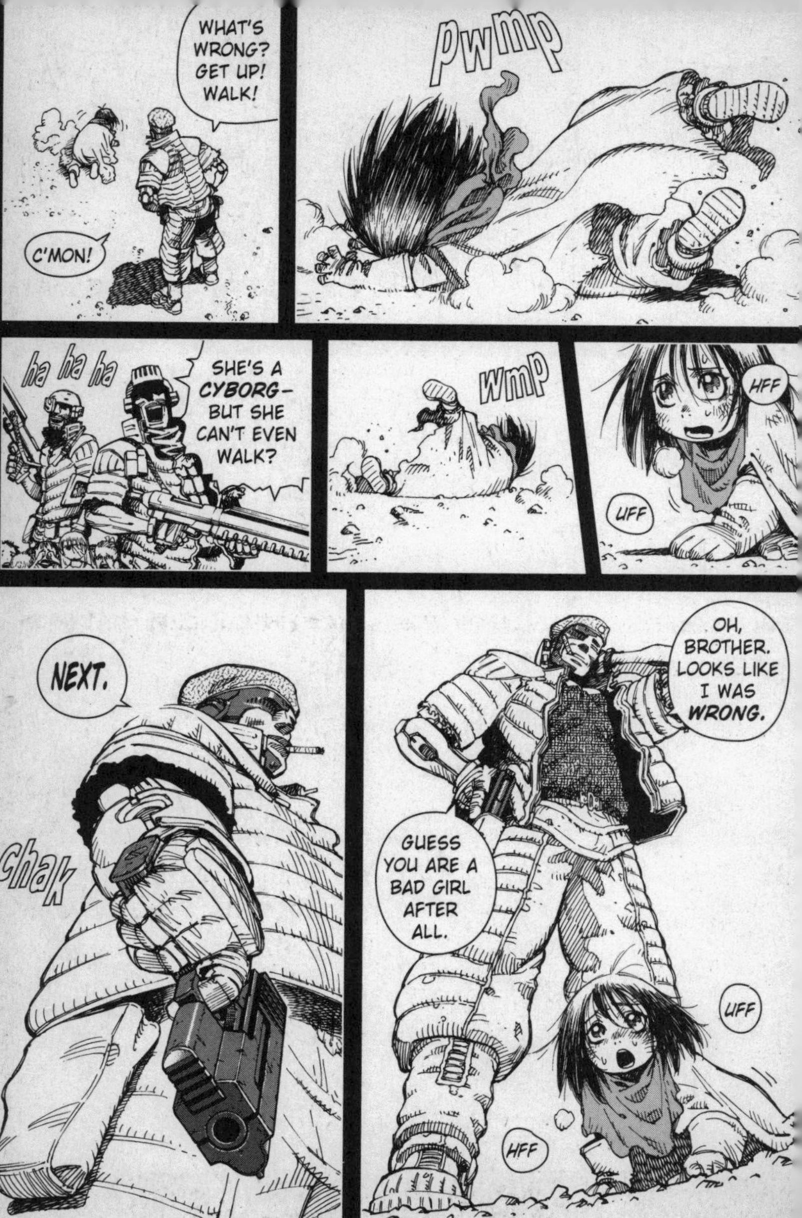
WHAT'S WRONG? GET UP! WALK!
C'MON!
pwmp
ha ha ha
SHE'S A CYBORG-- BUT SHE CAN'T EVEN WALK?
wmp
HFF
UFF
NEXT.
chak
OH, BROTHER. LOOKS LIKE I WAS WRONG.
GUESS YOU ARE A BAD GIRL AFTER ALL.
UFF
HFF

BLAM

NO! STOP!

thwump

BUT SHE CAN DO IT! I'LL GO WITH HER!

HER BODY— IT ISN'T WELL! CAN'T YOU SEE?

FINE. WORKS FOR *ME*.

FSST

fwooo

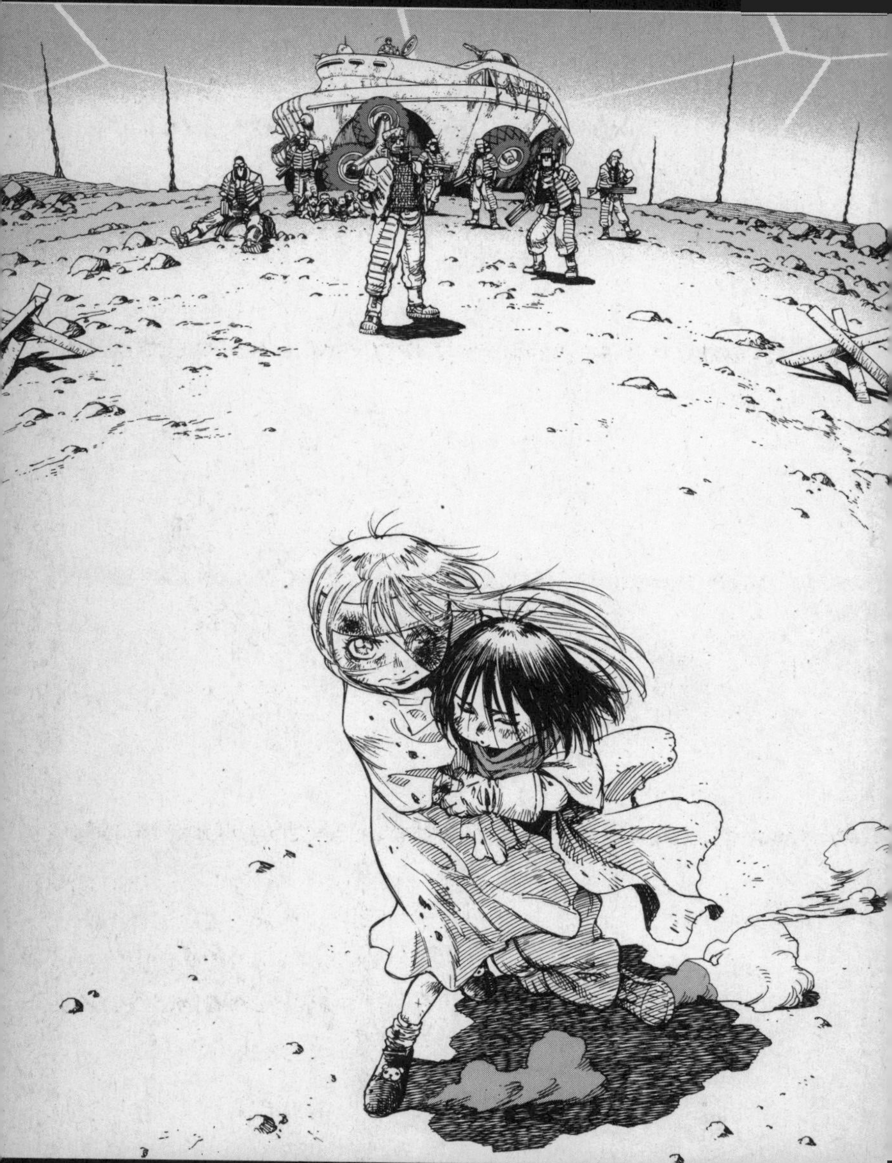

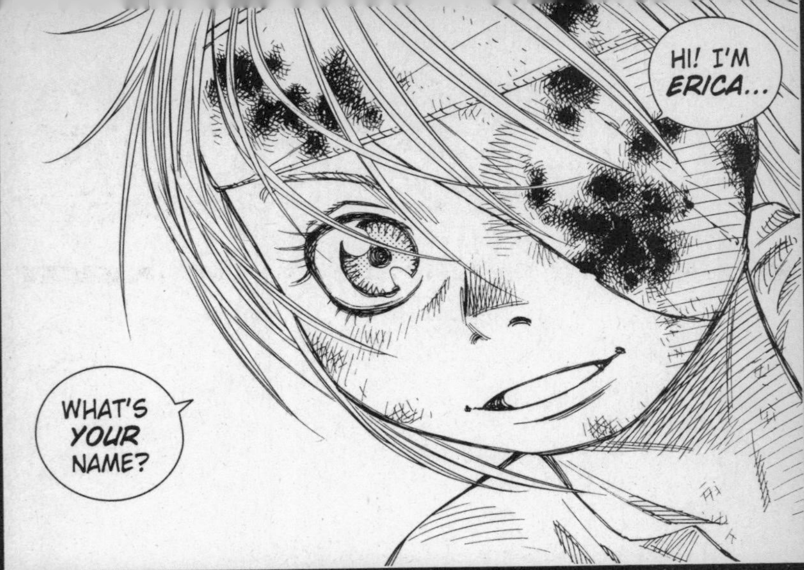
HI! I'M *ERICA...*
WHAT'S *YOUR* NAME?
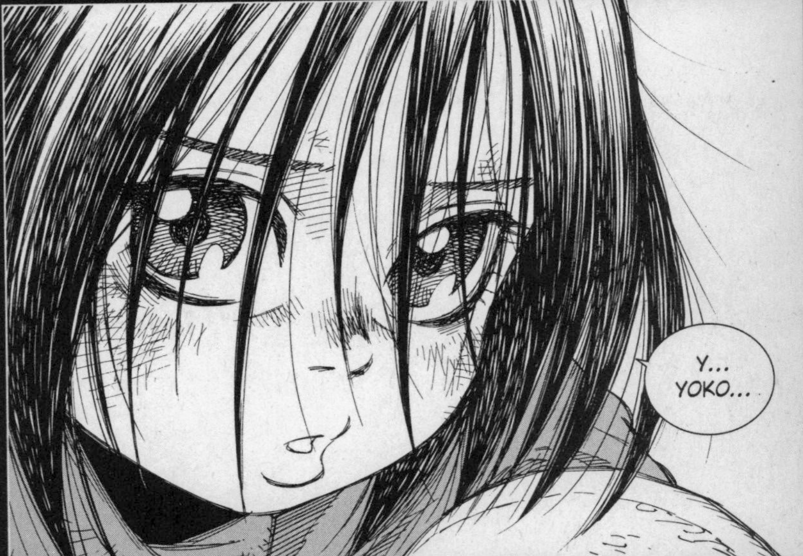
Y... YOKO...

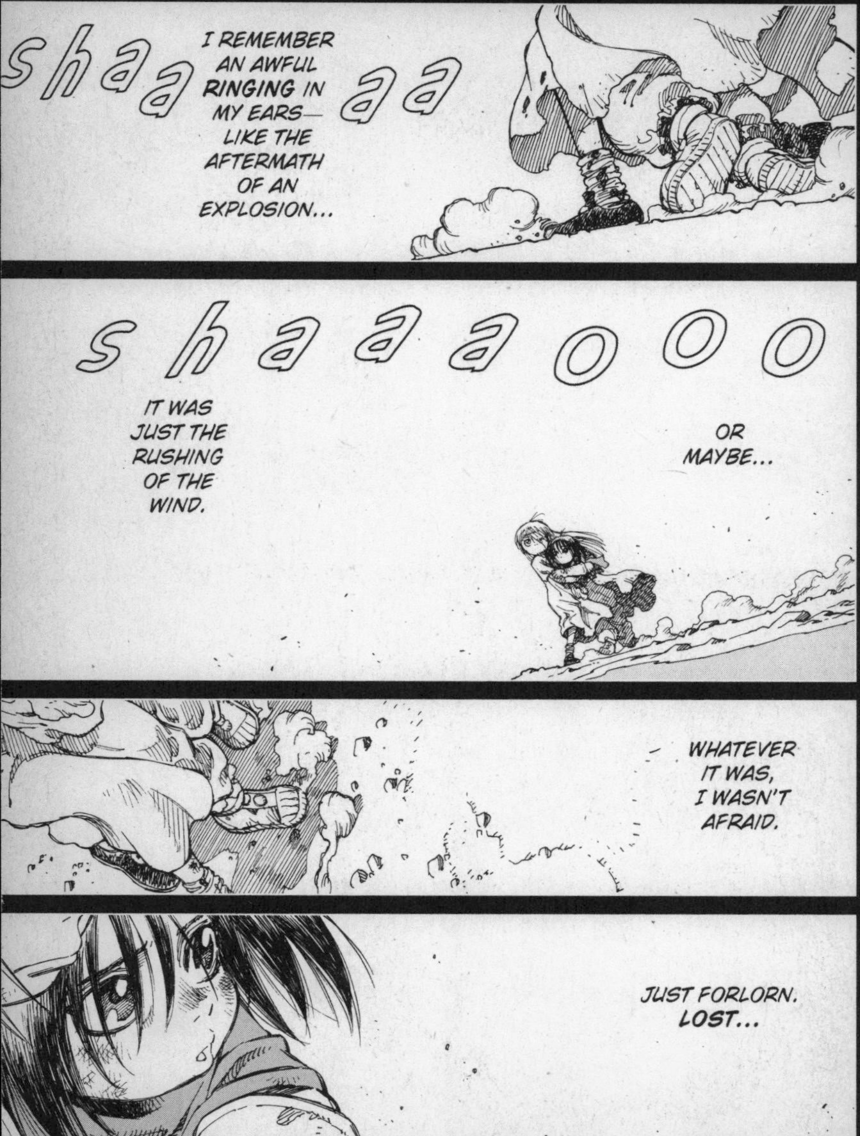
shaaaaa
I REMEMBER AN AWFUL RINGING IN MY EARS— LIKE THE AFTERMATH OF AN EXPLOSION...
shaaaooo
OR MAYBE...
IT WAS JUST THE RUSHING OF THE WIND.
WHATEVER IT WAS, I WASN'T AFRAID.
JUST FORLORN. LOST...

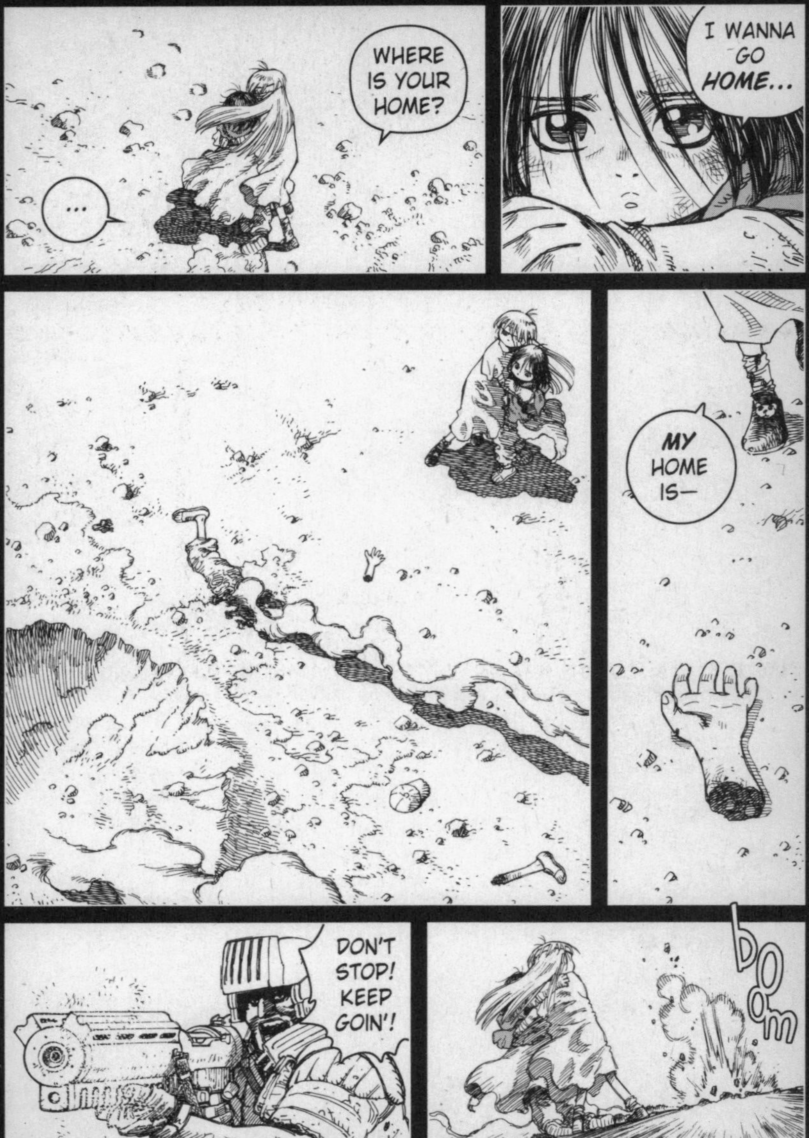
I WANNA GO HOME...
WHERE IS YOUR HOME?
...
MY HOME IS—
BOOM
DON'T STOP! KEEP GOIN'!

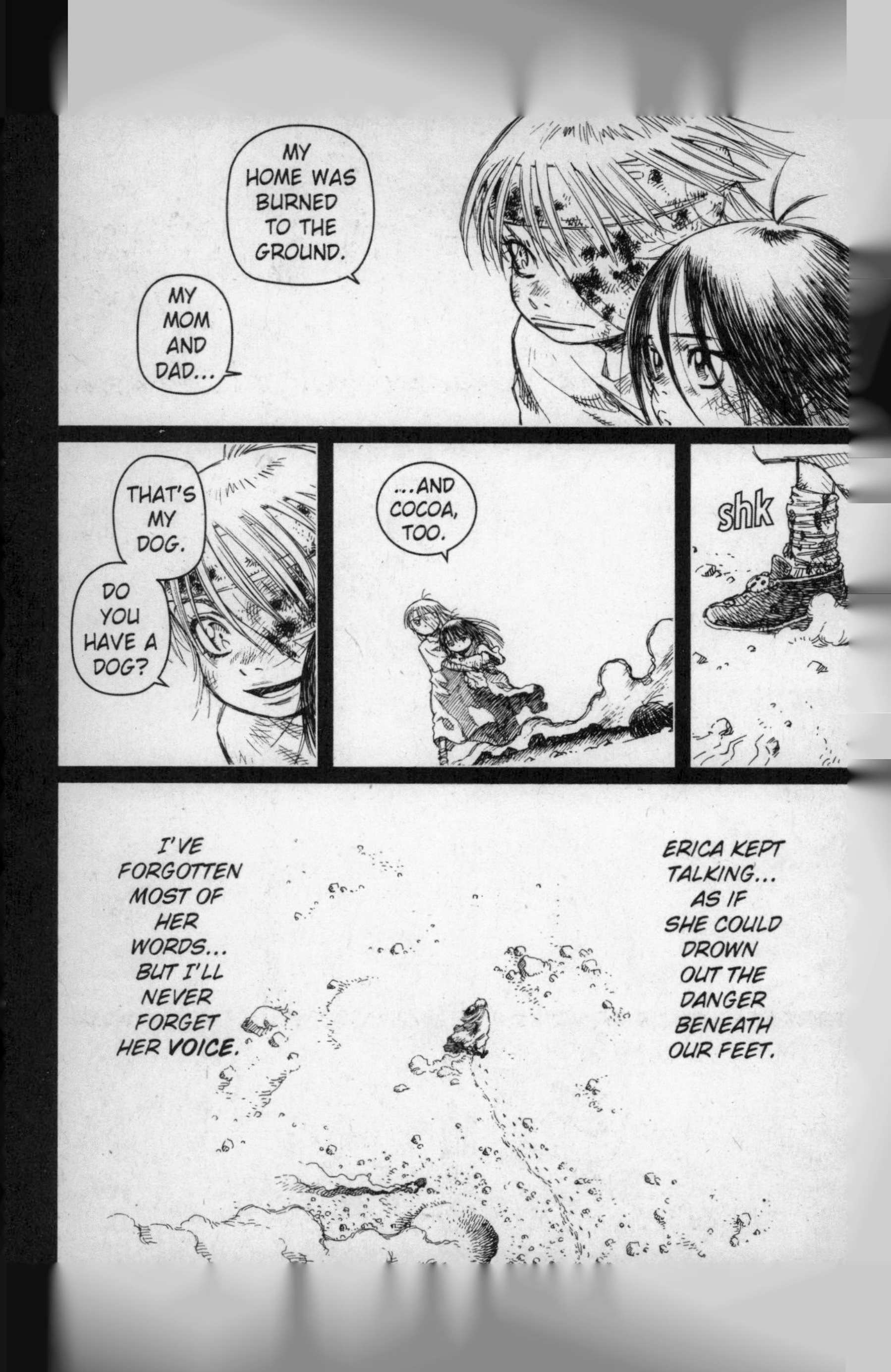
MY HOME WAS BURNED TO THE GROUND.
MY MOM AND DAD...
shk
...AND COCOA, TOO.
THAT'S MY DOG.
DO YOU HAVE A DOG?
ERICA KEPT TALKING... AS IF SHE COULD DROWN OUT THE DANGER BENEATH OUR FEET.
I'VE FORGOTTEN MOST OF HER WORDS... BUT I'LL NEVER FORGET HER VOICE.

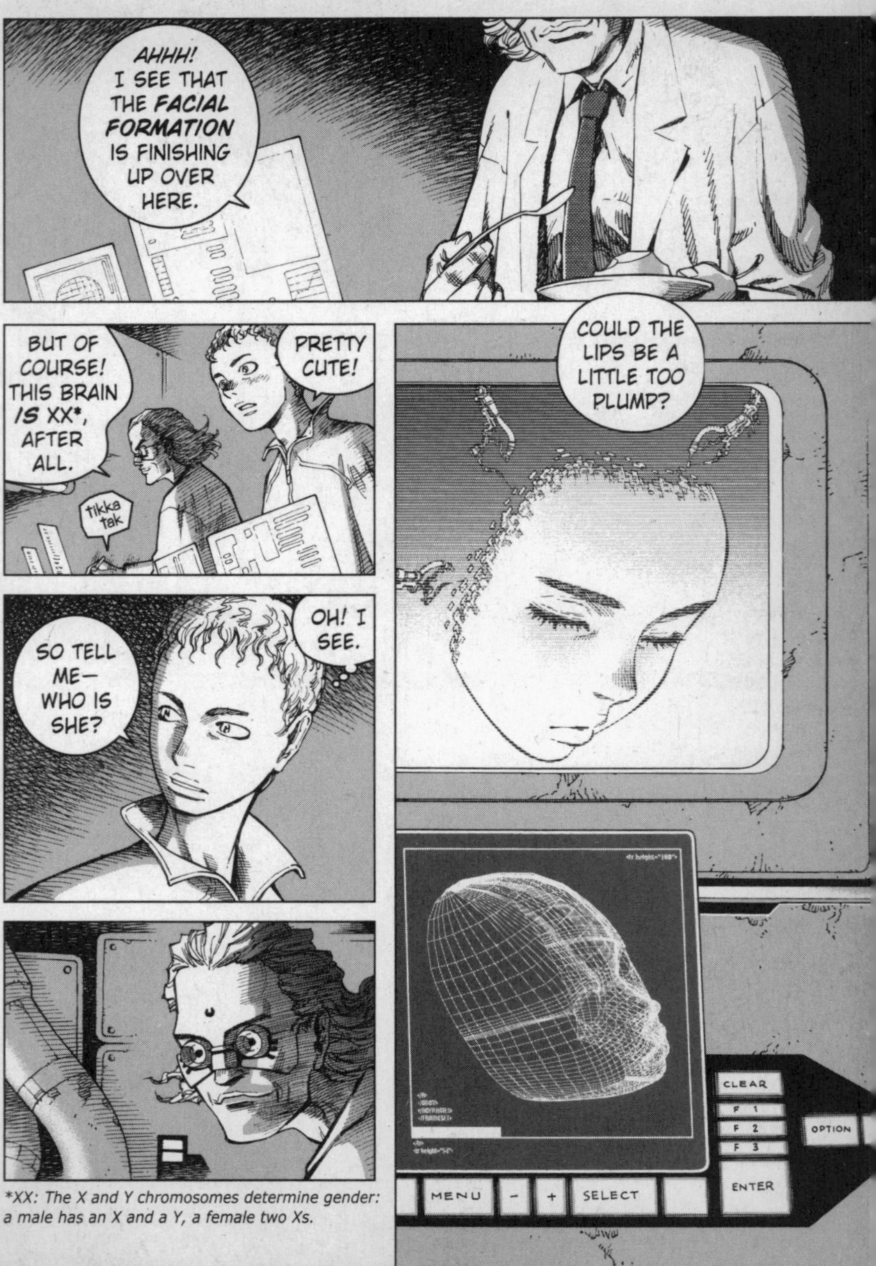
AHHH! I SEE THAT THE FACIAL FORMATION IS FINISHING UP OVER HERE.
COULD THE LIPS BE A LITTLE TOO PLUMP?
CLEAR
F 1
F 2
F 3
OPTION
ENTER
SELECT
+
-
MENU
PRETTY CUTE!
BUT OF COURSE! THIS BRAIN IS XX*, AFTER ALL.
tikka tak
OH! I SEE.
SO TELL ME— WHO IS SHE?

*XX: The X and Y chromosomes determine gender: a male has an X and a Y, a female two Xs.

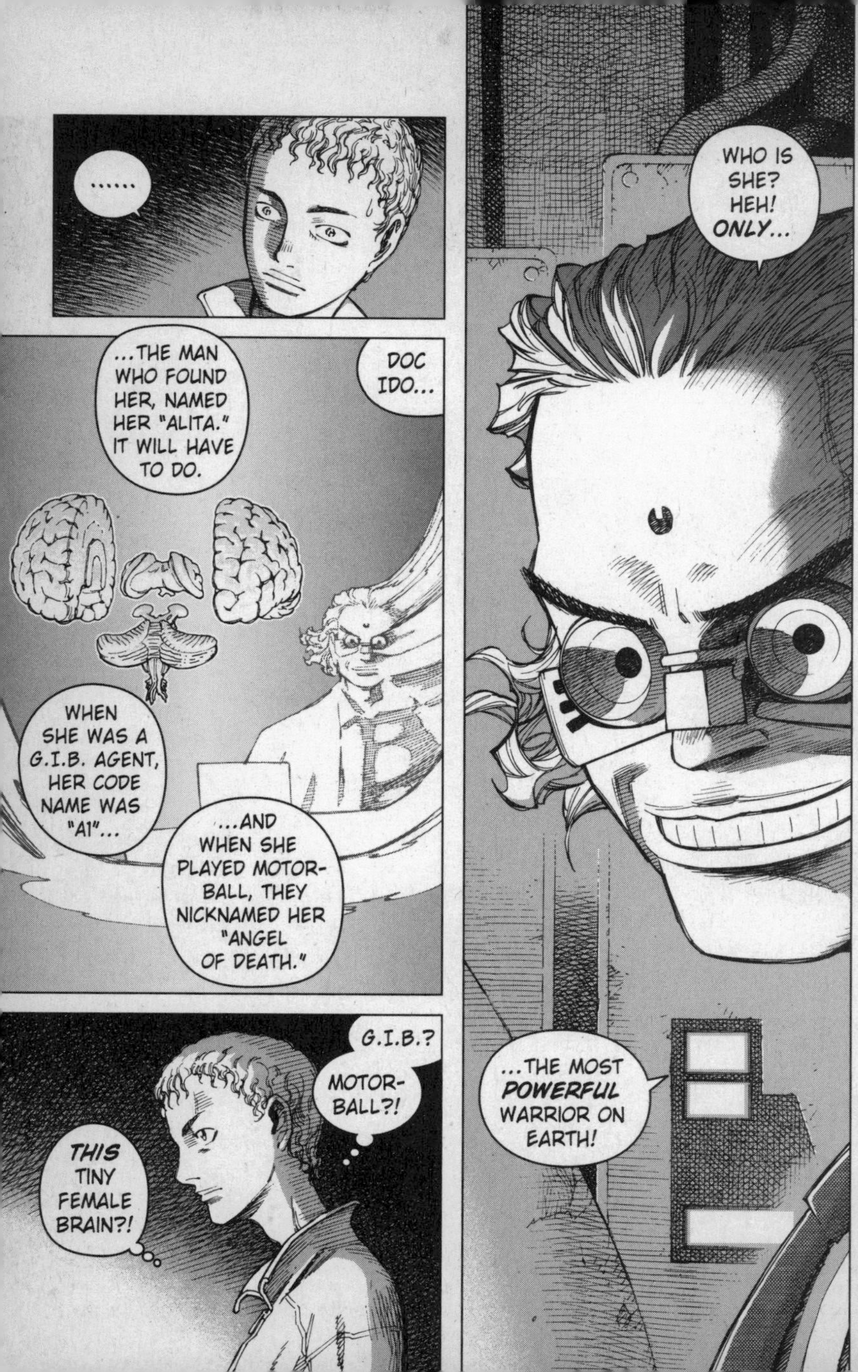
WHO IS SHE? HEH! ONLY...
...THE MOST POWERFUL WARRIOR ON EARTH!
......
DOC IDO...
...THE MAN WHO FOUND HER, NAMED HER "ALITA." IT WILL HAVE TO DO.
WHEN SHE WAS A G.I.B. AGENT, HER CODE NAME WAS "A1"...
...AND WHEN SHE PLAYED MOTOR-BALL, THEY NICKNAMED HER "ANGEL OF DEATH."
G.I.B.?
MOTOR-BALL?!
THIS TINY FEMALE BRAIN?!

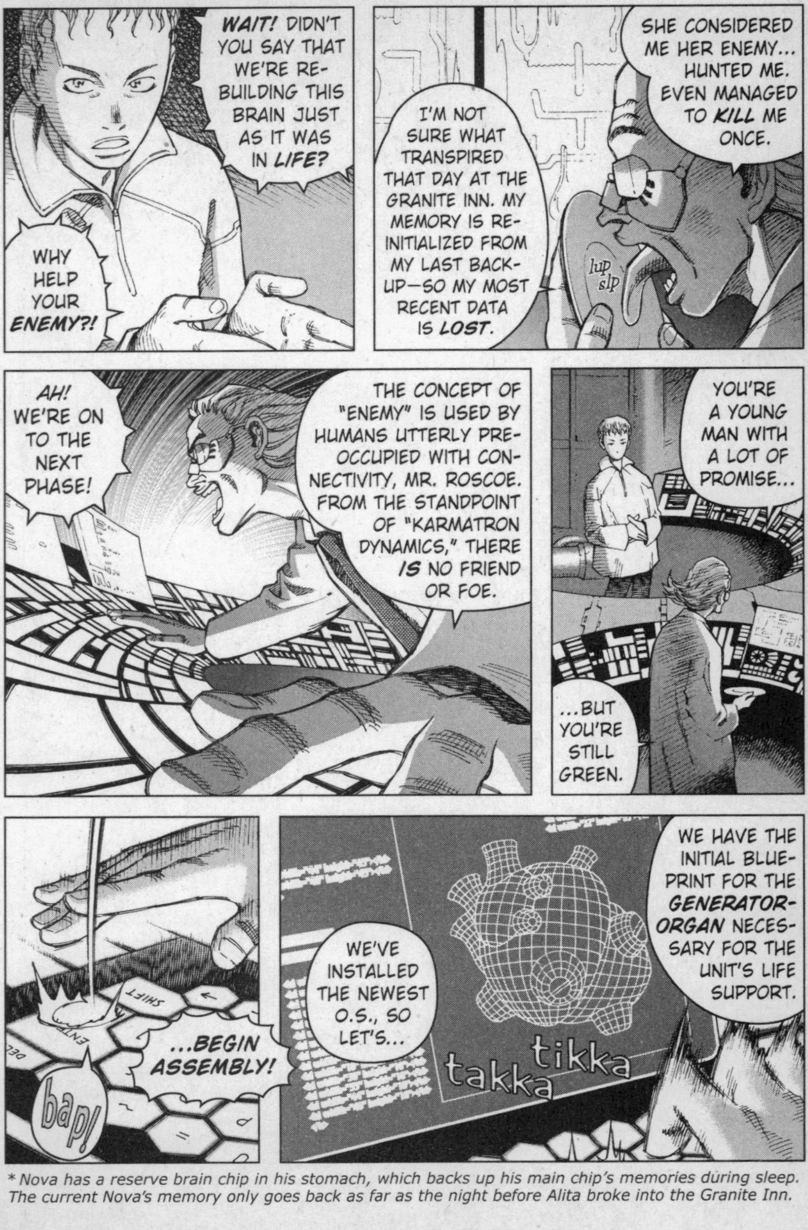
SHE CONSIDERED ME HER ENEMY... HUNTED ME. EVEN MANAGED TO KILL ME ONCE.
I'M NOT SURE WHAT TRANSPIRED THAT DAY AT THE GRANITE INN. MY MEMORY IS RE-INITIALIZED FROM MY LAST BACK-UP—SO MY MOST RECENT DATA IS LOST.
lup slp
WAIT! DIDN'T YOU SAY THAT WE'RE RE-BUILDING THIS BRAIN JUST AS IT WAS IN LIFE?
WHY HELP YOUR ENEMY?!
YOU'RE A YOUNG MAN WITH A LOT OF PROMISE...
...BUT YOU'RE STILL GREEN.
THE CONCEPT OF "ENEMY" IS USED BY HUMANS UTTERLY PRE-OCCUPIED WITH CON-NECTIVITY, MR. ROSCOE. FROM THE STANDPOINT OF "KARMATRON DYNAMICS," THERE IS NO FRIEND OR FOE.
AH! WE'RE ON TO THE NEXT PHASE!
WE HAVE THE INITIAL BLUE-PRINT FOR THE GENERATOR-ORGAN NECES-SARY FOR THE UNIT'S LIFE SUPPORT.
WE'VE INSTALLED THE NEWEST O.S., SO LET'S...
tikka takka
...BEGIN ASSEMBLY!
SHIFT
bap!

Nova has a reserve brain chip in his stomach, which backs up his main chip's memories during sleep. The current Nova's memory only goes back as far as the night before Alita broke into the Granite Inn.

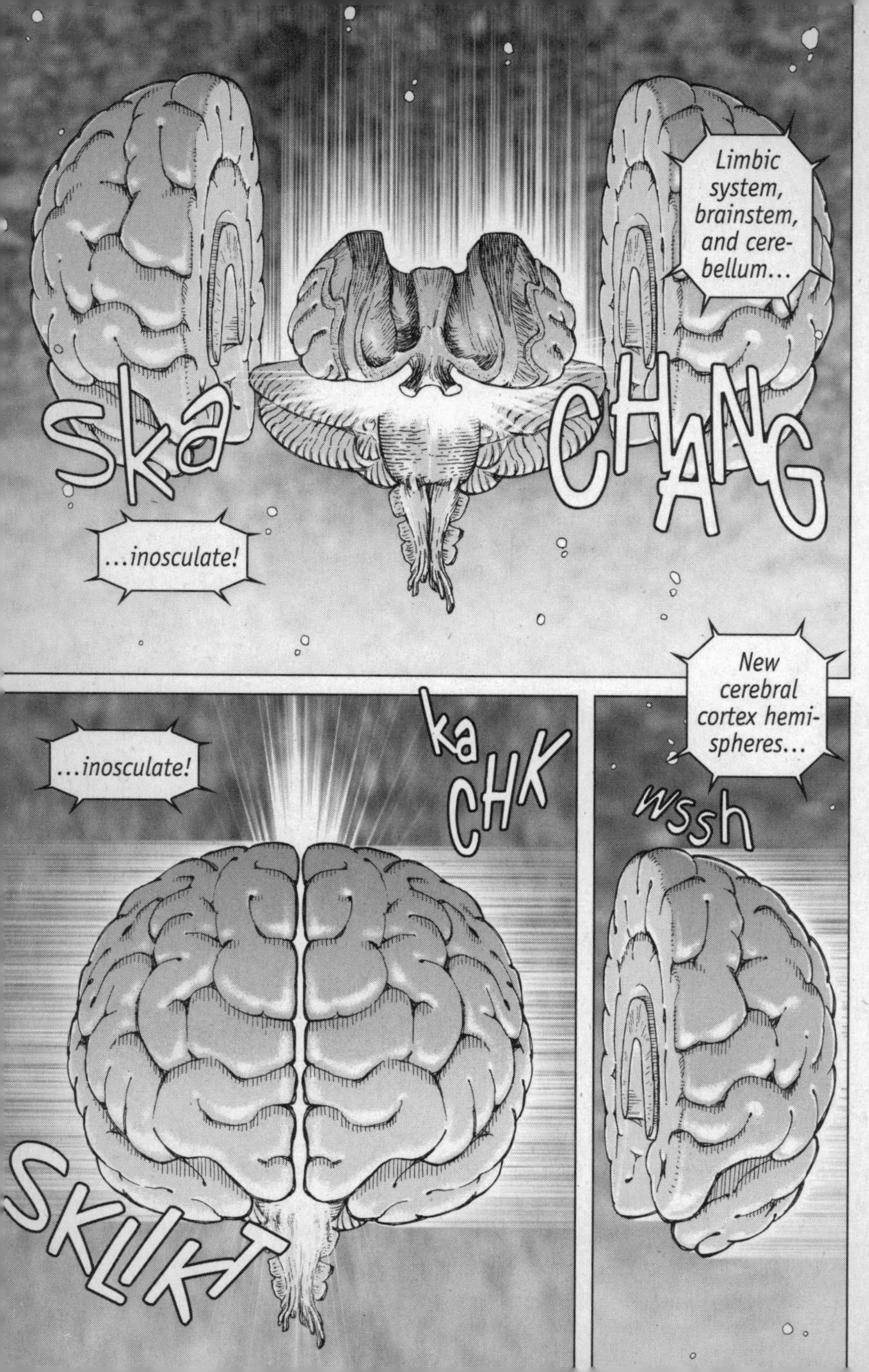

Limbic system, brainstem, and cerebellum…
Ska CHANG
…inosculate!
New cerebral cortex hemispheres…
wssh
ka CHK
…inosculate!
SKLIKT

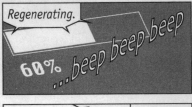

Regenerating.
...beep beep beep
60%
Complete.
Dopamine levels normal.
100%
breeep
Eyeballs inosculated.
SNAP
Spinal nerves constructed.
flwrrr
wrp
shllwippp
Peripheral nerves fabricated.

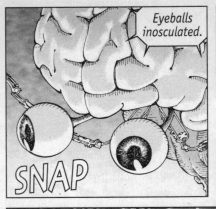

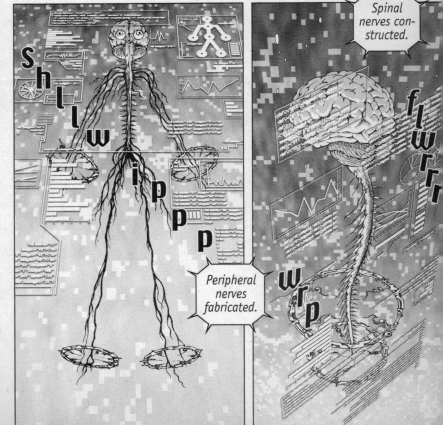

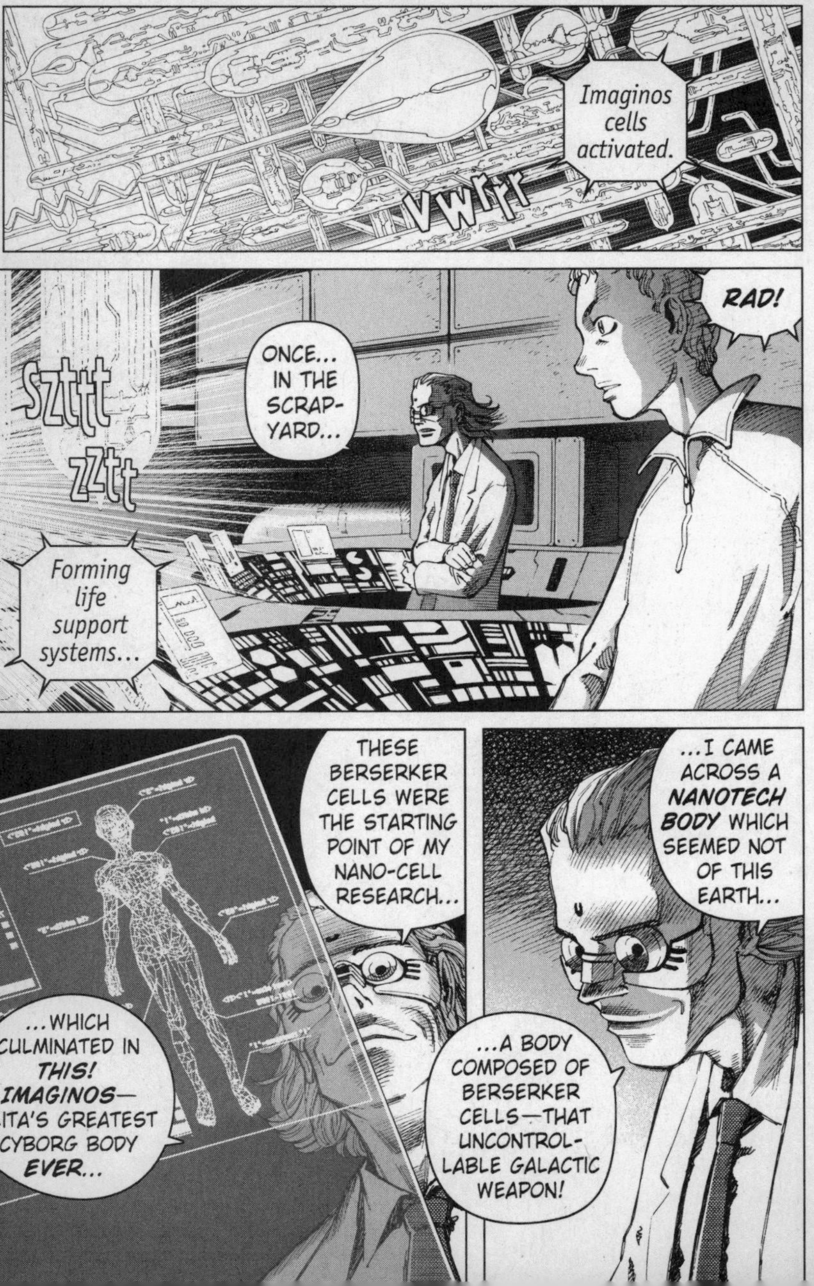
Imaginos cells activated.
VWRRR
RAD!
ONCE... IN THE SCRAP-YARD...
SZTTT
ZZTT
Forming life support systems...
...I CAME ACROSS A NANOTECH BODY WHICH SEEMED NOT OF THIS EARTH...
...A BODY COMPOSED OF BERSERKER CELLS—THAT UNCONTROL-LABLE GALACTIC WEAPON!
THESE BERSERKER CELLS WERE THE STARTING POINT OF MY NANO-CELL RESEARCH...
...WHICH CULMINATED IN THIS! IMAGINOS—ALITA'S GREATEST CYBORG BODY EVER...

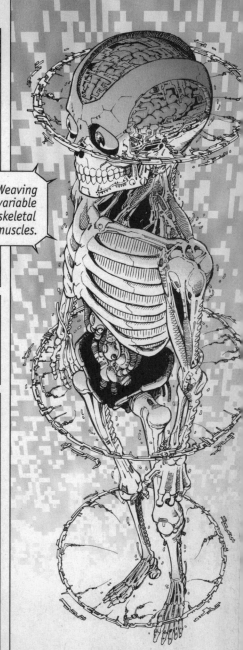

shoom

Weaving variable skeletal muscles.

THE KARMATRON DYNAMICS WORK ON THE *MICRO* LEVEL HAS ALREADY REACHED PERFECTION.

BUT...

...ON THE *MACRO LEVEL,* THE RECONSTRUCTION IS STILL FAR FROM COMPLETE.

Shwip

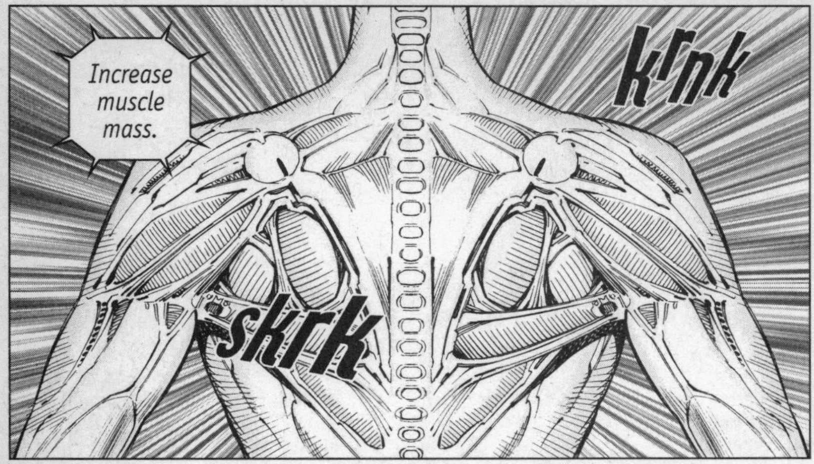
KRNK
Increase muscle mass.
SKRK

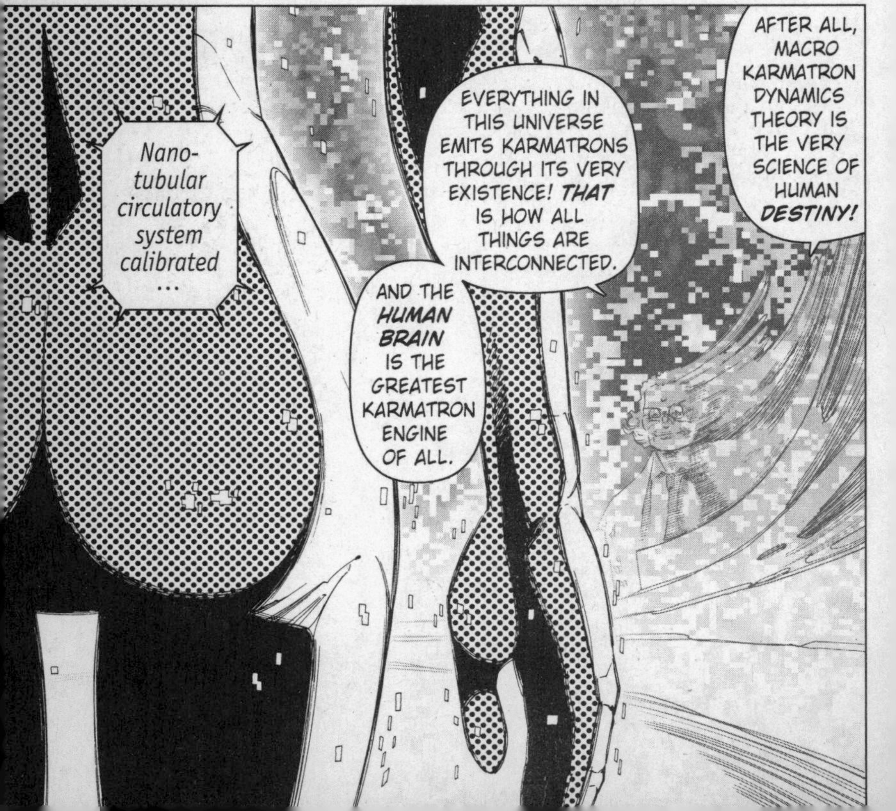
AFTER ALL, MACRO KARMATRON DYNAMICS THEORY IS THE VERY SCIENCE OF HUMAN *DESTINY!*
EVERYTHING IN THIS UNIVERSE EMITS KARMATRONS THROUGH ITS VERY EXISTENCE! *THAT* IS HOW ALL THINGS ARE INTERCONNECTED.
AND THE *HUMAN BRAIN* IS THE GREATEST KARMATRON ENGINE OF ALL.
Nano-tubular circulatory system calibrated...

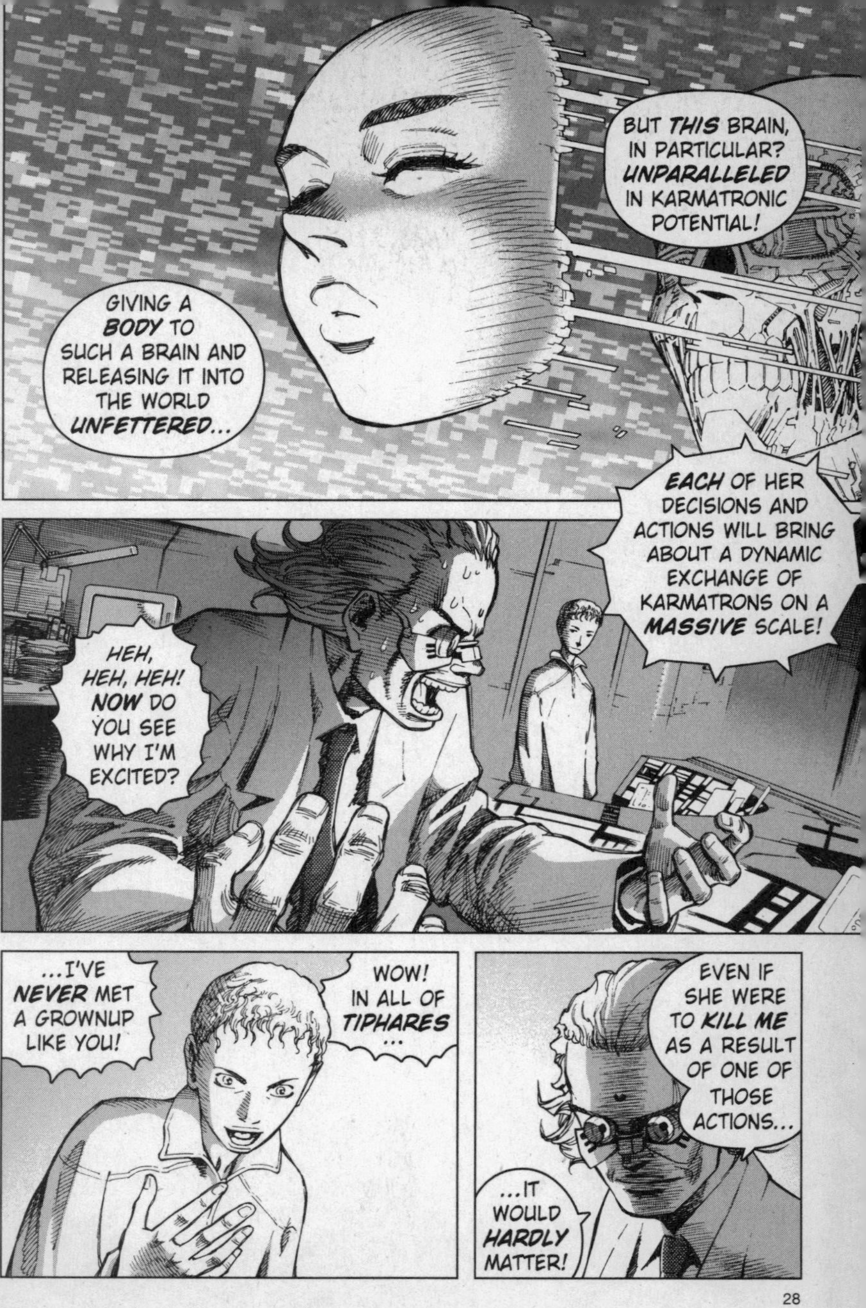
BUT *THIS* BRAIN, IN PARTICULAR? *UNPARALLELED* IN KARMATRONIC POTENTIAL!
GIVING A *BODY* TO SUCH A BRAIN AND RELEASING IT INTO THE WORLD *UNFETTERED*...
EACH OF HER DECISIONS AND ACTIONS WILL BRING ABOUT A DYNAMIC EXCHANGE OF KARMATRONS ON A *MASSIVE* SCALE!
HEH, HEH, HEH! *NOW* DO YOU SEE WHY I'M EXCITED?
EVEN IF SHE WERE TO *KILL ME* AS A RESULT OF ONE OF THOSE ACTIONS...
...IT WOULD *HARDLY* MATTER!
WOW! IN ALL OF *TIPHARES*...
...I'VE *NEVER* MET A GROWNUP LIKE YOU!

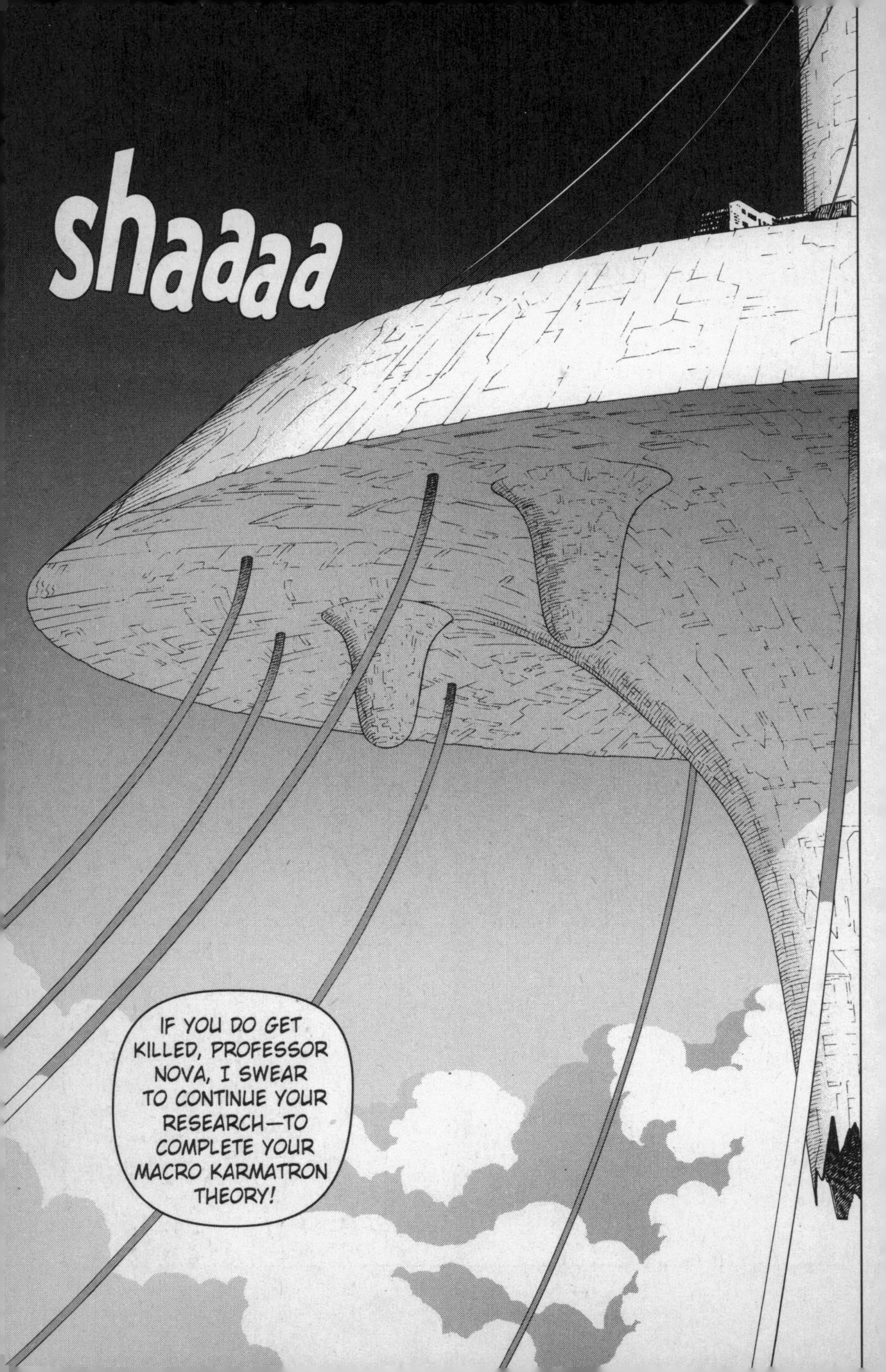
shaaaa
IF YOU DO GET KILLED, PROFESSOR NOVA, I SWEAR TO CONTINUE YOUR RESEARCH—TO COMPLETE YOUR MACRO KARMATRON THEORY!

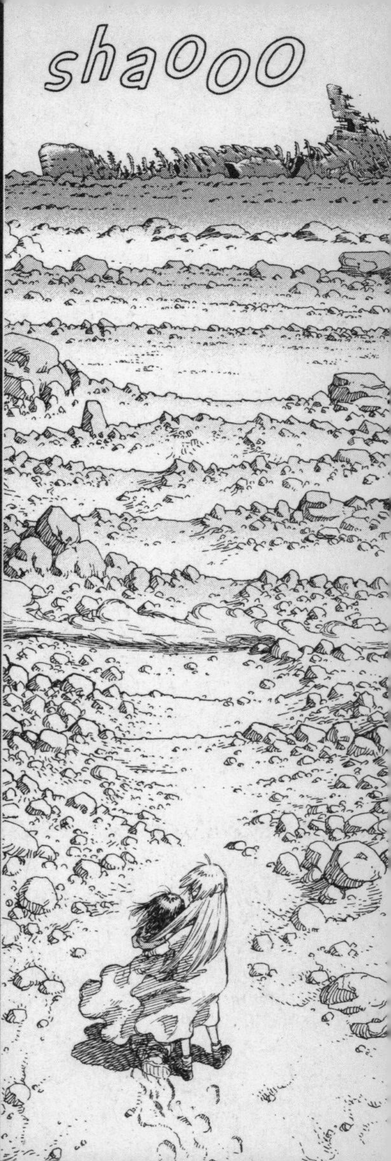
shaoooo
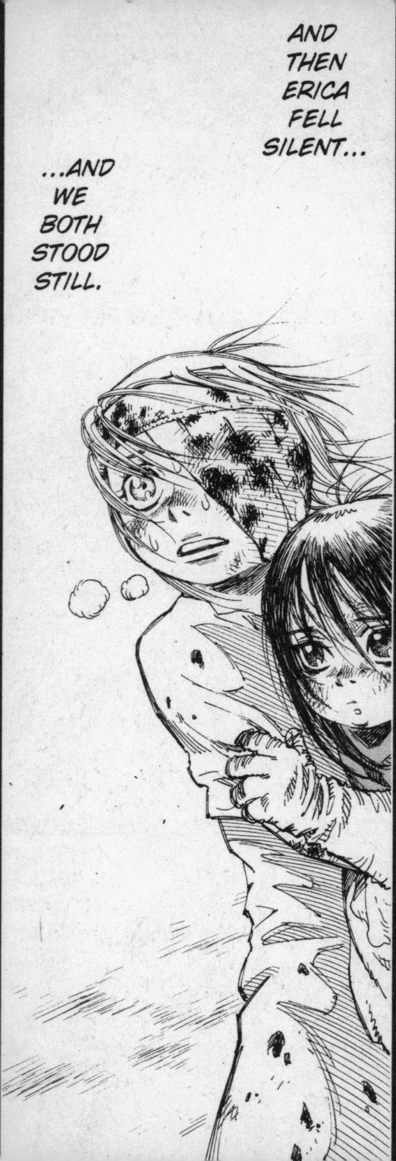
AND THEN ERICA FELL SILENT...
...AND WE BOTH STOOD STILL.

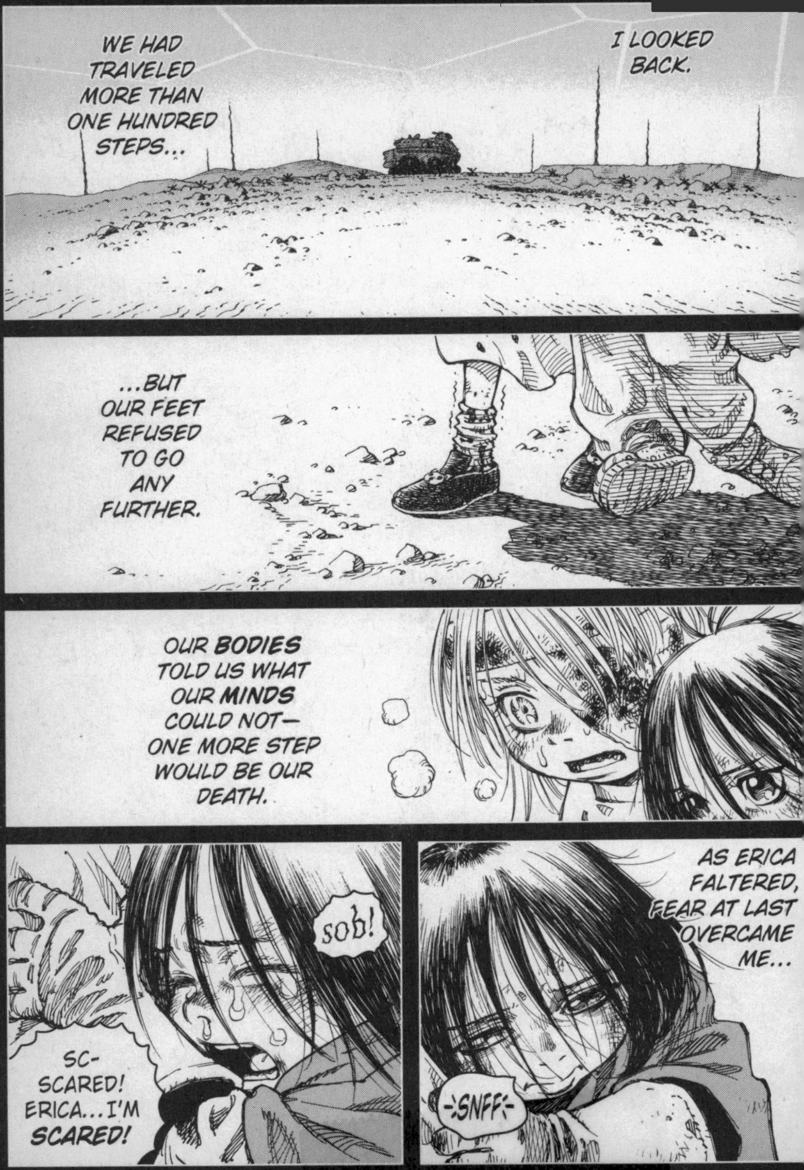
I LOOKED BACK.
WE HAD TRAVELED MORE THAN ONE HUNDRED STEPS...
...BUT OUR FEET REFUSED TO GO ANY FURTHER.
OUR BODIES TOLD US WHAT OUR MINDS COULD NOT— ONE MORE STEP WOULD BE OUR DEATH.
AS ERICA FALTERED, FEAR AT LAST OVERCAME ME...
-SNFF-
sob!
SC- SCARED! ERICA...I'M SCARED!

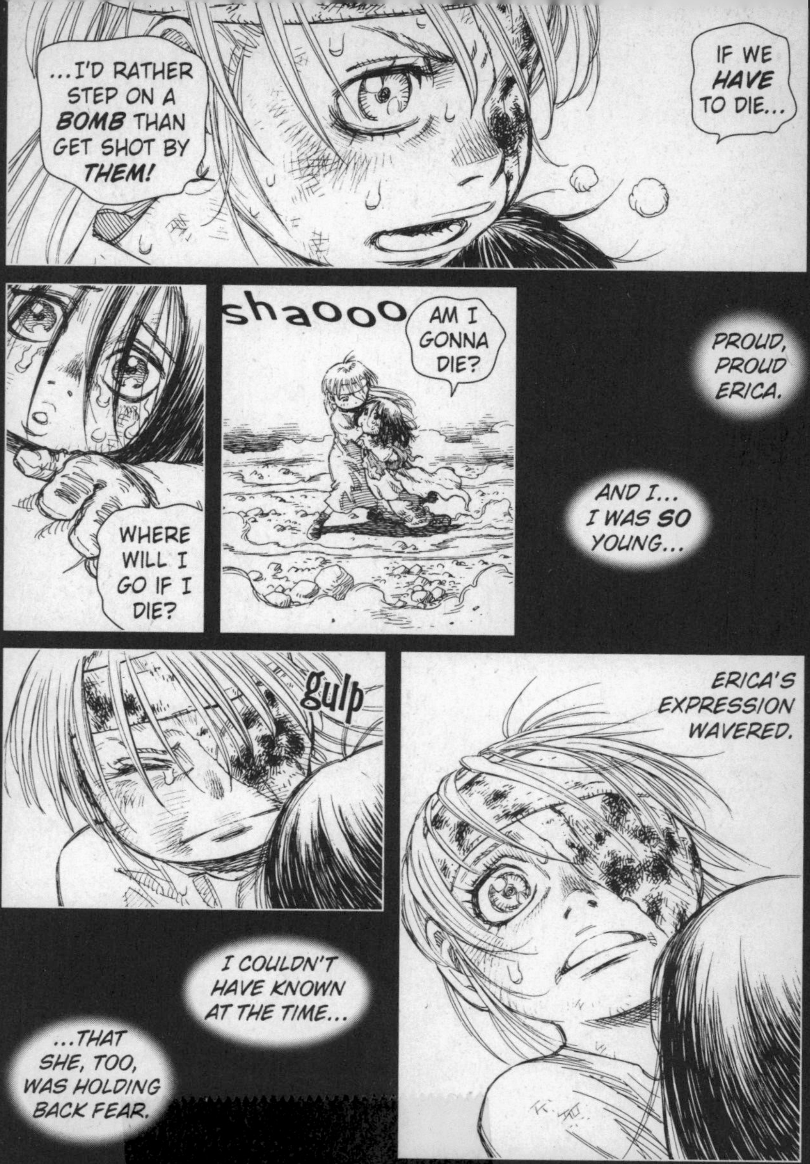
IF WE HAVE TO DIE...
...I'D RATHER STEP ON A BOMB THAN GET SHOT BY THEM!
PROUD, PROUD ERICA.
AND I... I WAS SO YOUNG...
shaooo
AM I GONNA DIE?
WHERE WILL I GO IF I DIE?
ERICA'S EXPRESSION WAVERED.
gulp
I COULDN'T HAVE KNOWN AT THE TIME...
...THAT SHE, TOO, WAS HOLDING BACK FEAR.

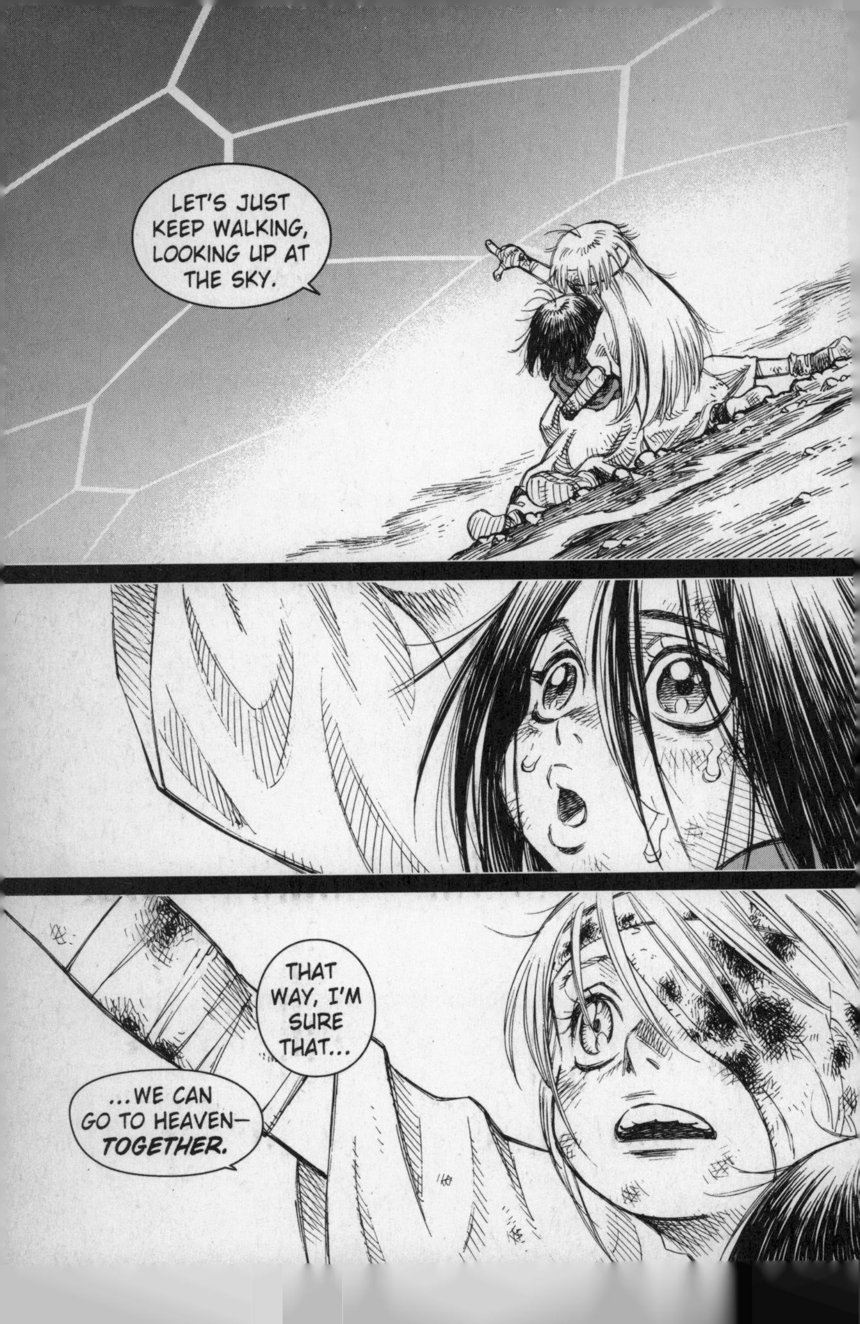
LET'S JUST KEEP WALKING, LOOKING UP AT THE SKY.
THAT WAY, I'M SURE THAT...
...WE CAN GO TO HEAVEN— TOGETHER.

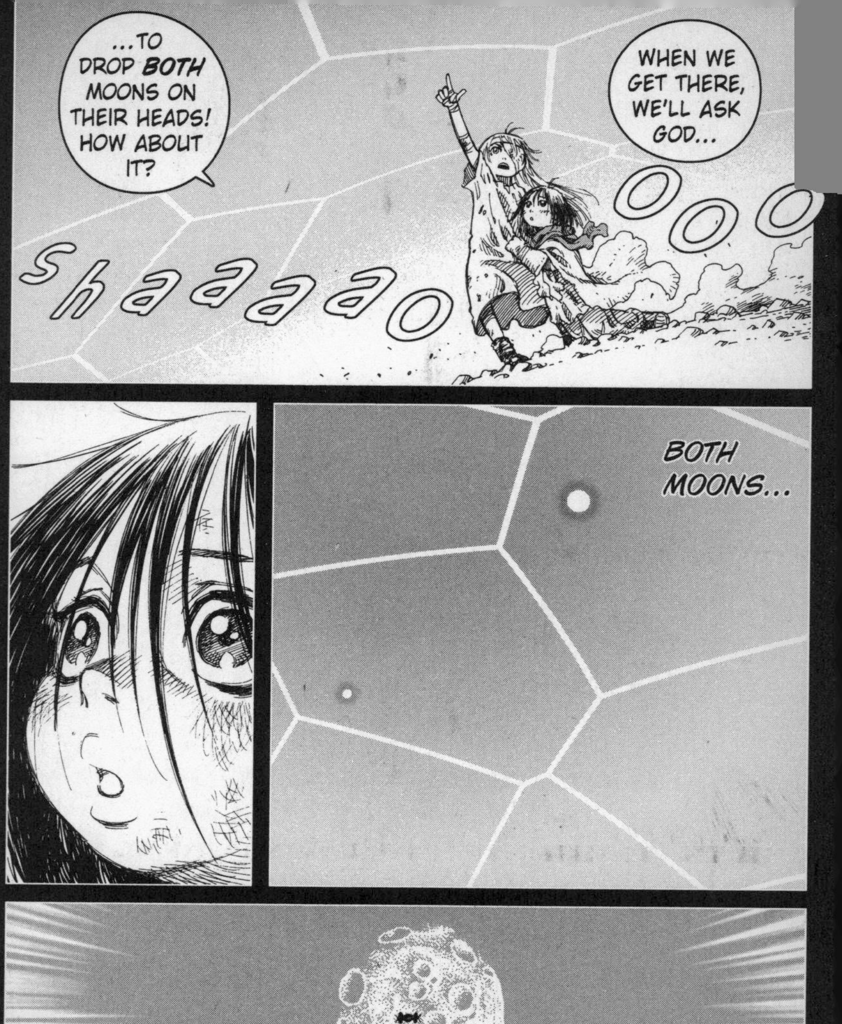
WHEN WE GET THERE, WE'LL ASK GOD...
...TO DROP BOTH MOONS ON THEIR HEADS! HOW ABOUT IT?
Shaaaaoooo
BOTH MOONS...

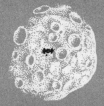

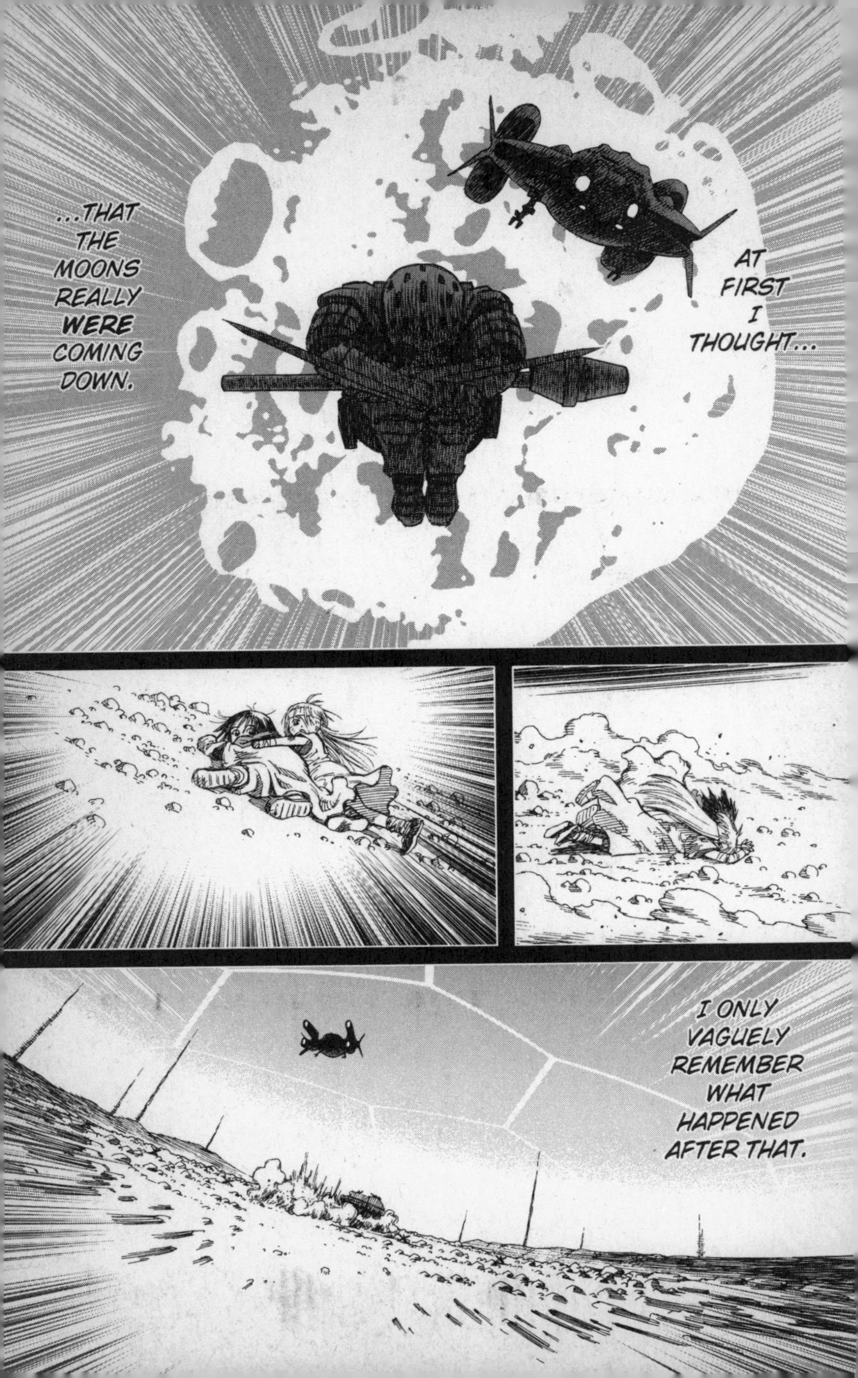
AT FIRST I THOUGHT...
...THAT THE MOONS REALLY WERE COMING DOWN.
I ONLY VAGUELY REMEMBER WHAT HAPPENED AFTER THAT.

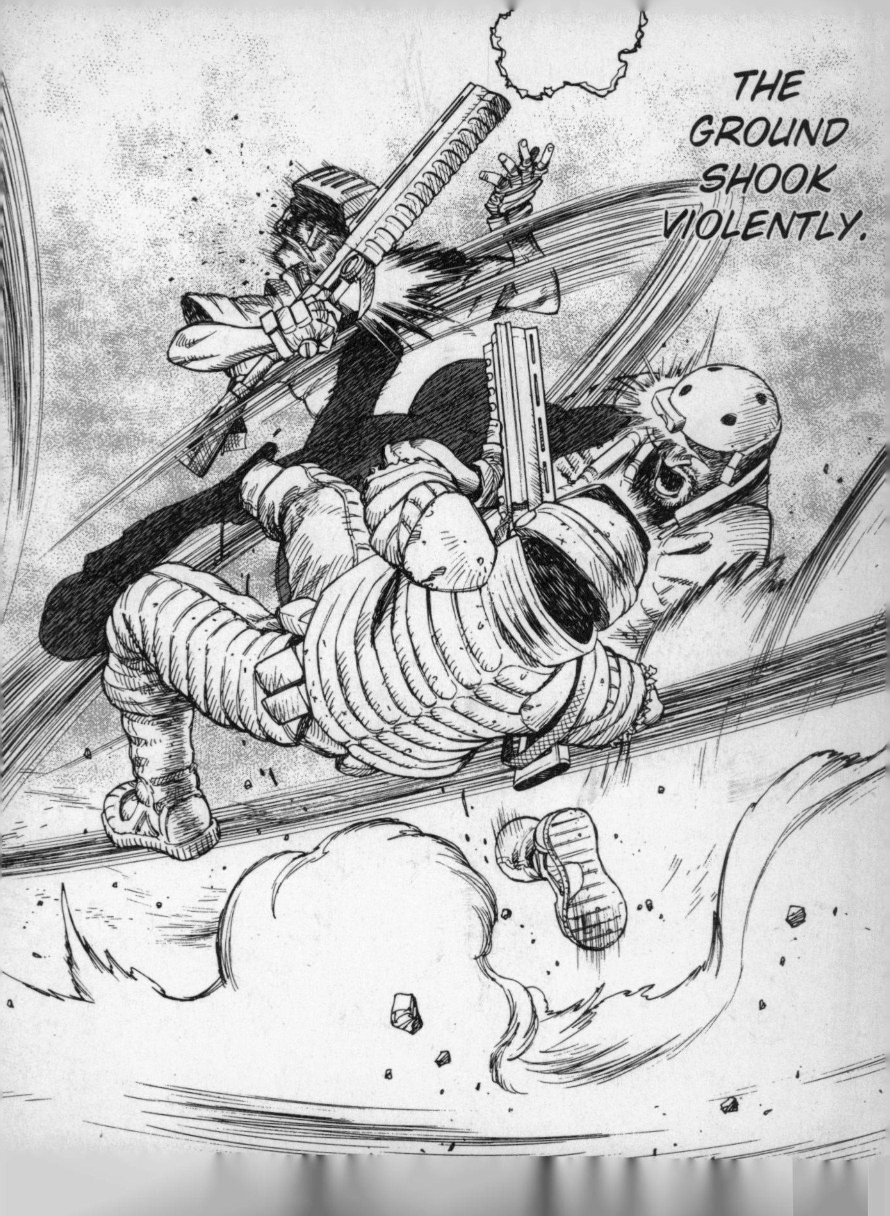
THE GROUND SHOOK VIOLENTLY.

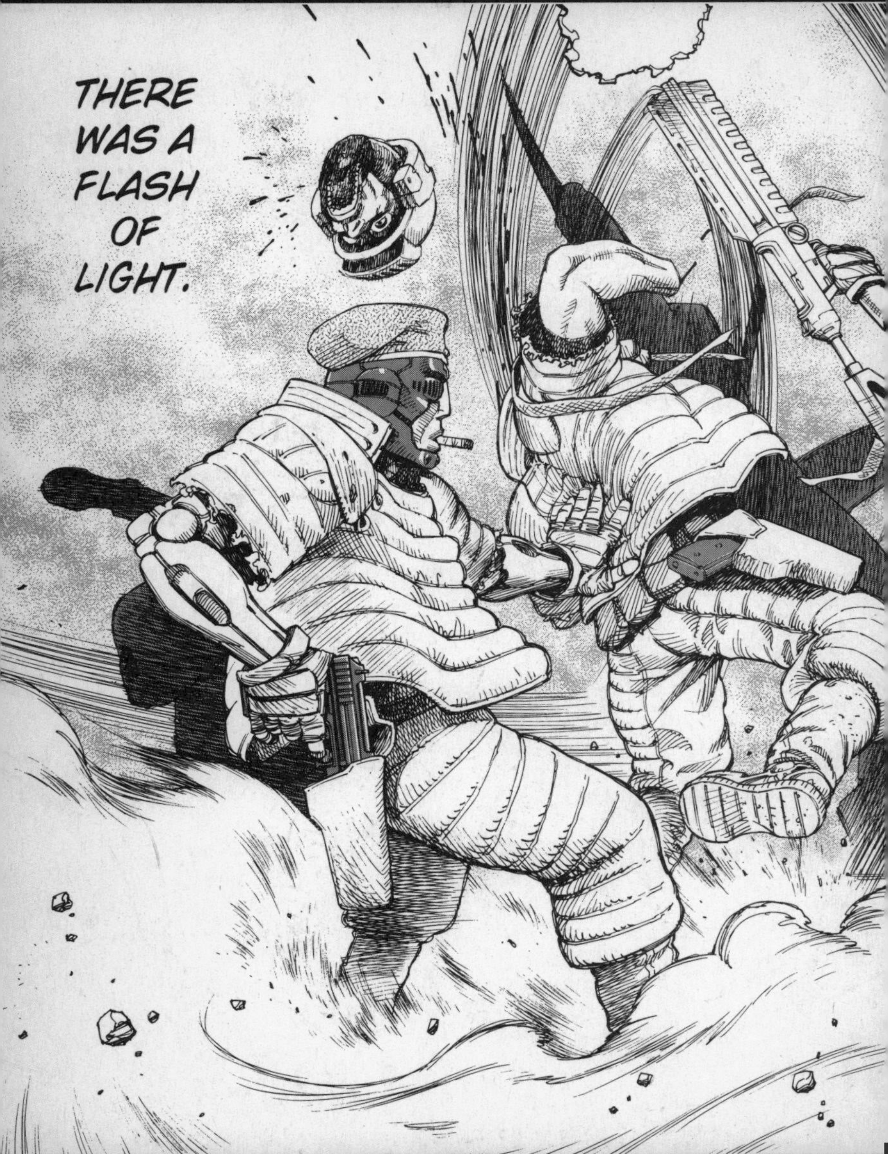
THERE WAS A FLASH OF LIGHT.

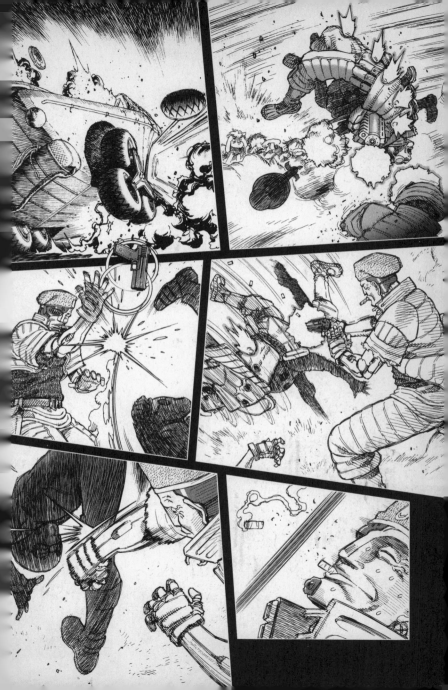

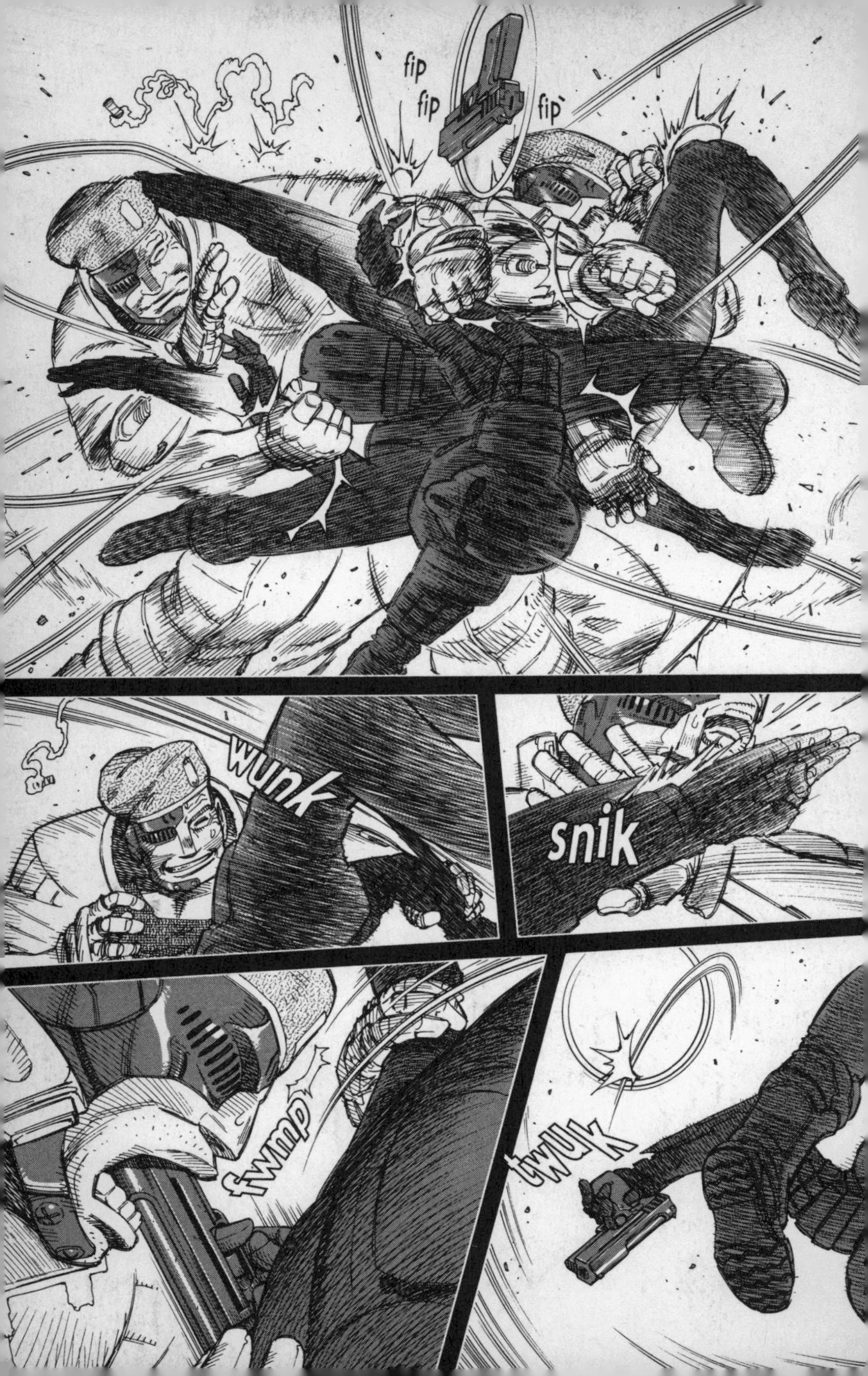
fip
fip
fip
snik
wunk
twuk
fwmp

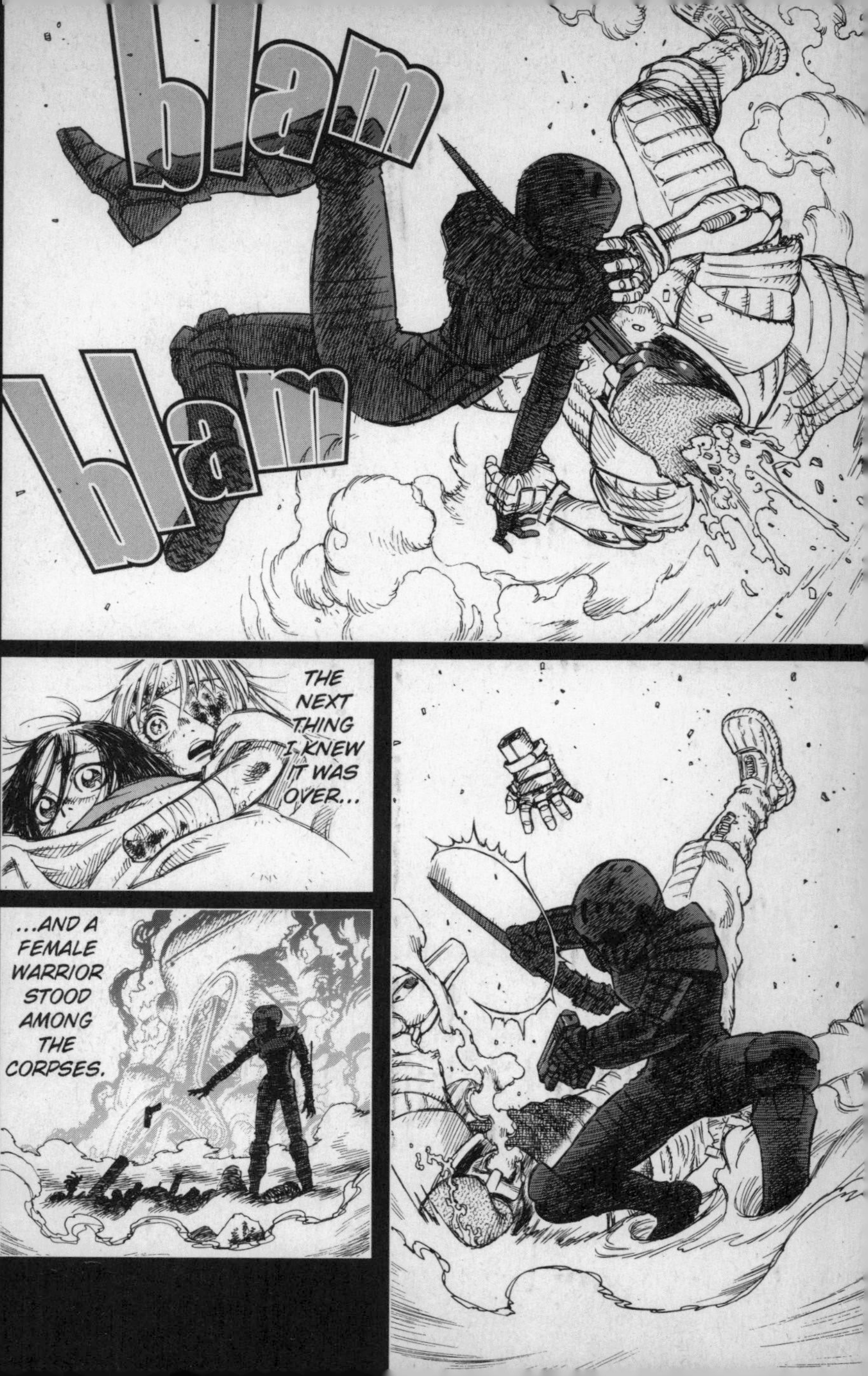
blam
blam
THE NEXT THING I KNEW IT WAS OVER...
...AND A FEMALE WARRIOR STOOD AMONG THE CORPSES.

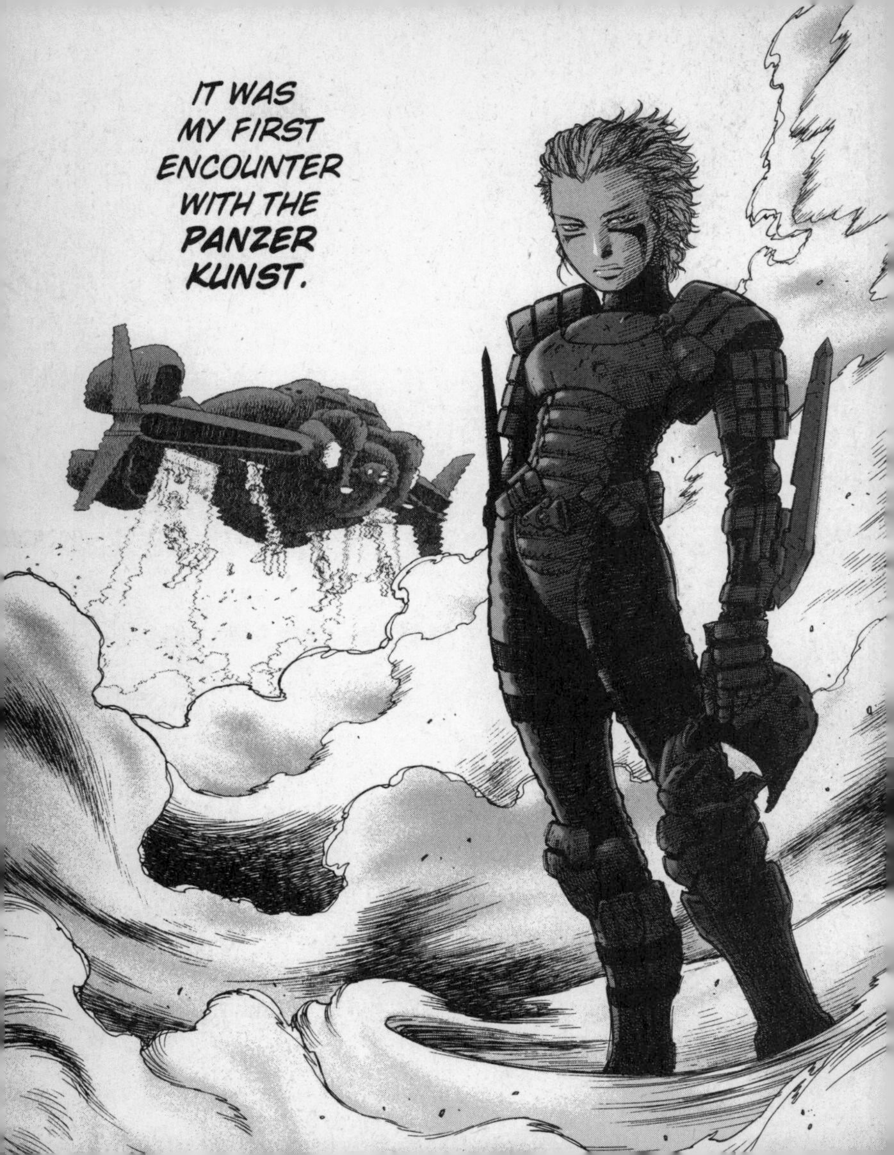
IT WAS MY FIRST ENCOUNTER WITH THE PANZER KUNST.

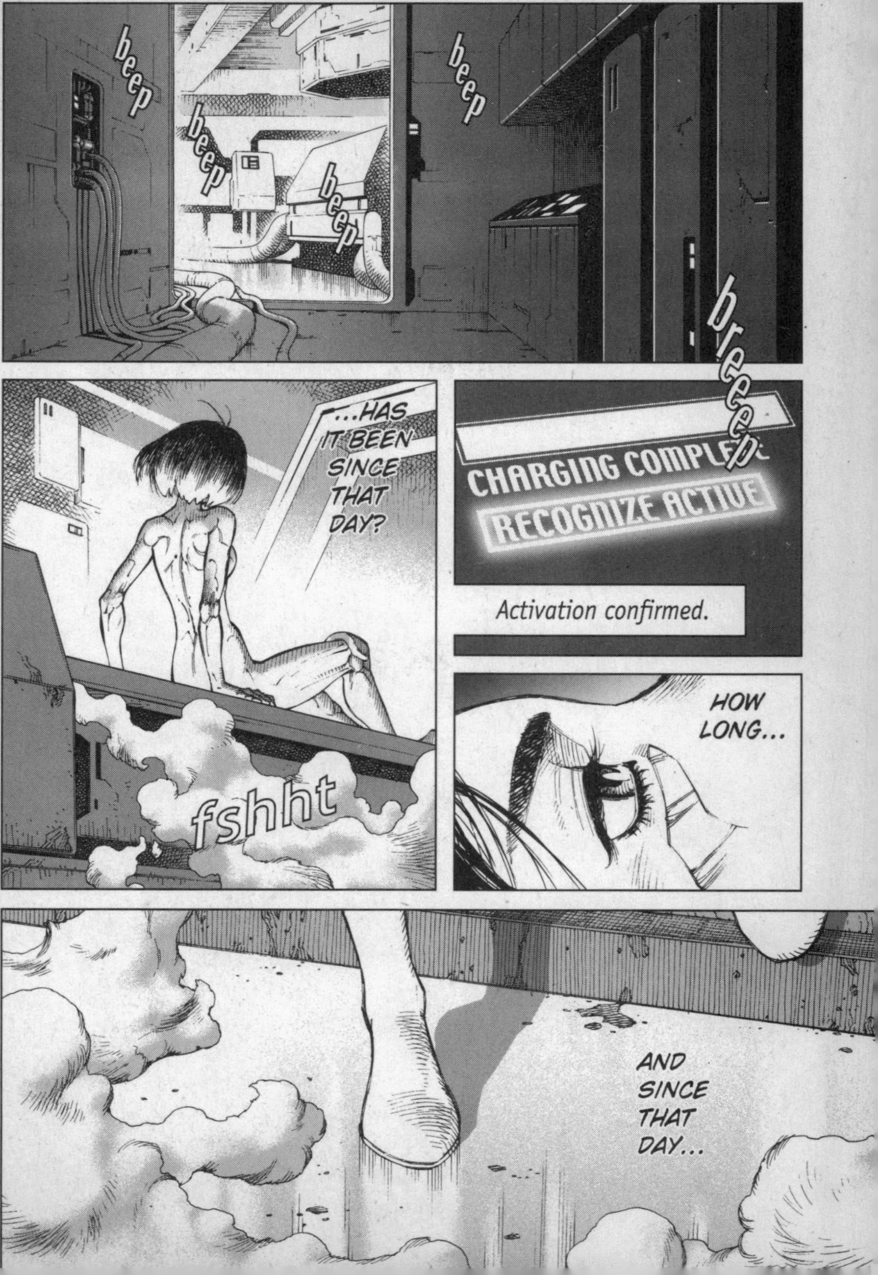
beep
beep
beep
beep
breeep
CHARGING COMPLE
RECOGNIZE ACTIVE
Activation confirmed.
HOW LONG...
...HAS IT BEEN SINCE THAT DAY?
fshht
AND SINCE THAT DAY...

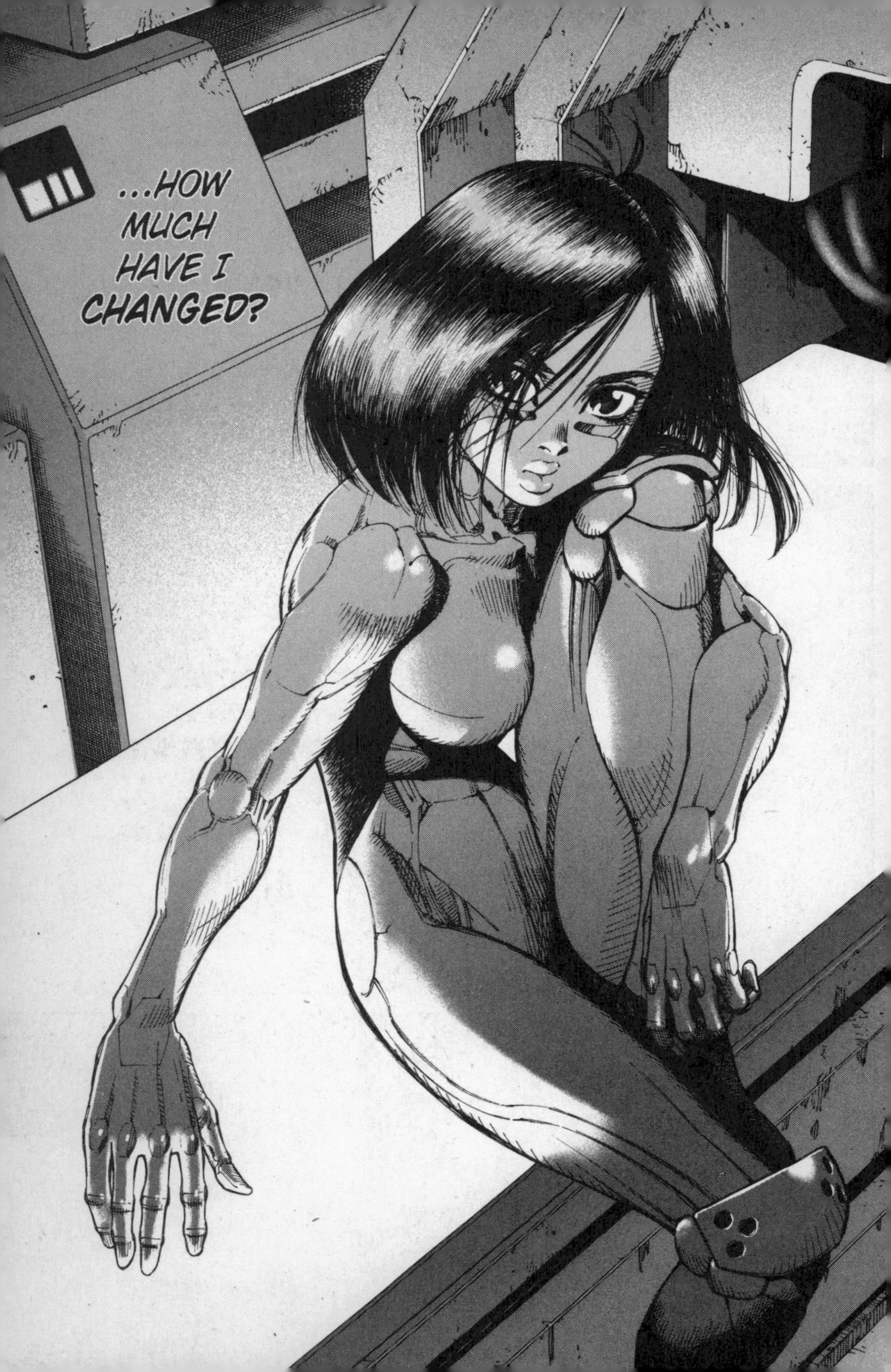
...HOW MUCH HAVE I CHANGED?

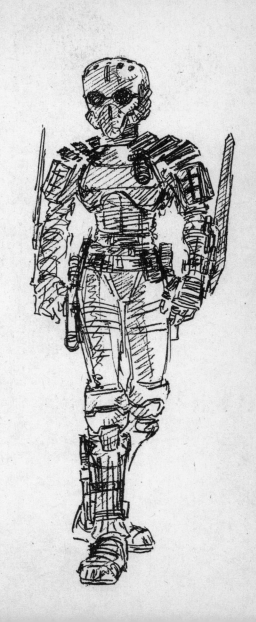

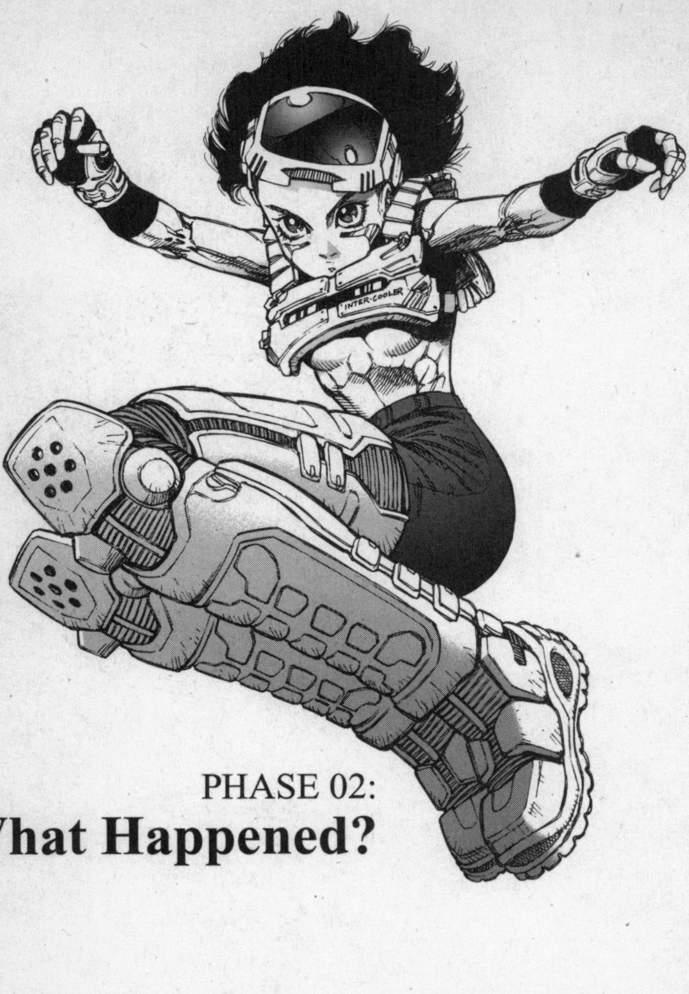
INTER-COOLER

PHASE 02:

What Happened?

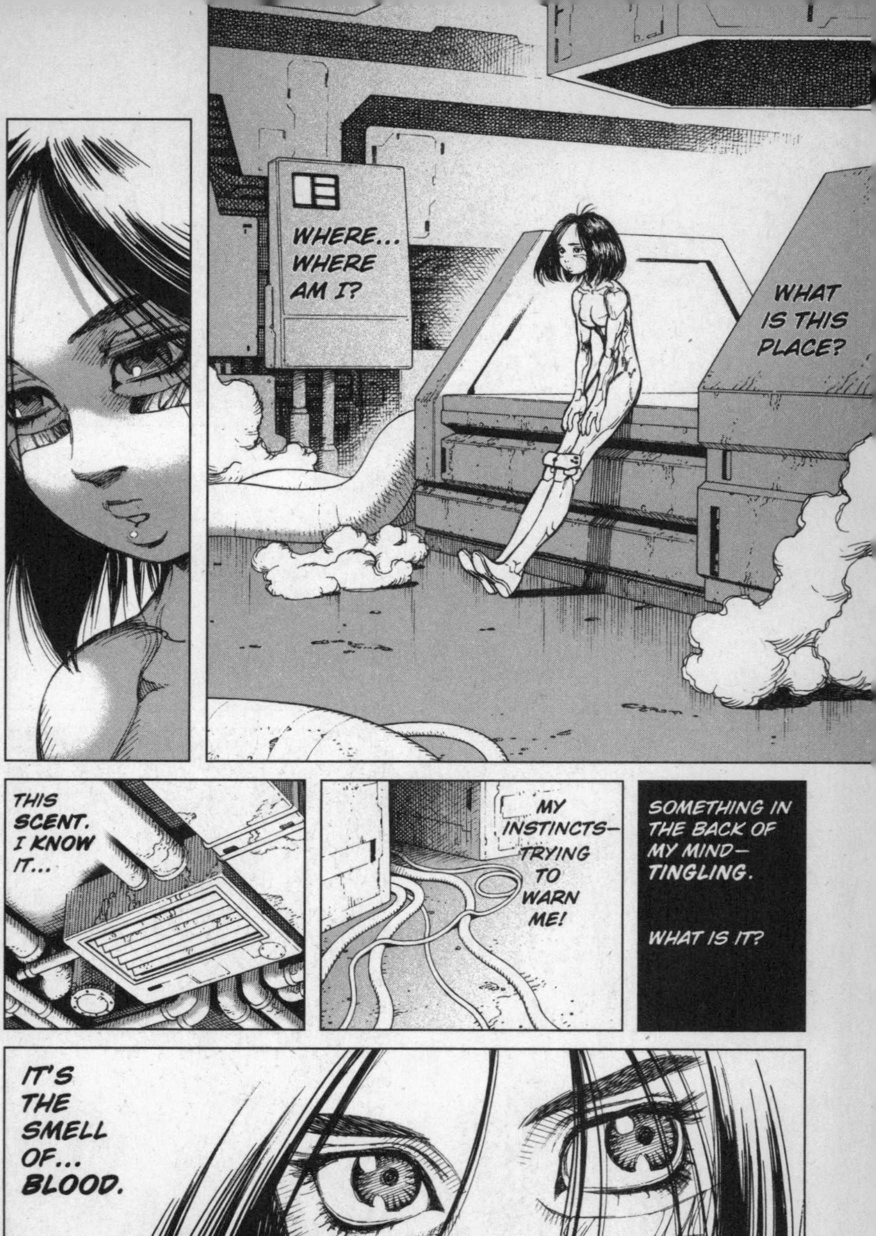
WHERE... WHERE AM I?
WHAT IS THIS PLACE?
THIS SCENT. I KNOW IT...
MY INSTINCTS-TRYING TO WARN ME!
SOMETHING IN THE BACK OF MY MIND-TINGLING.
WHAT IS IT?
IT'S THE SMELL OF... BLOOD.

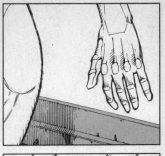
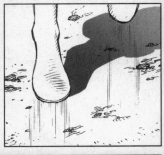

47

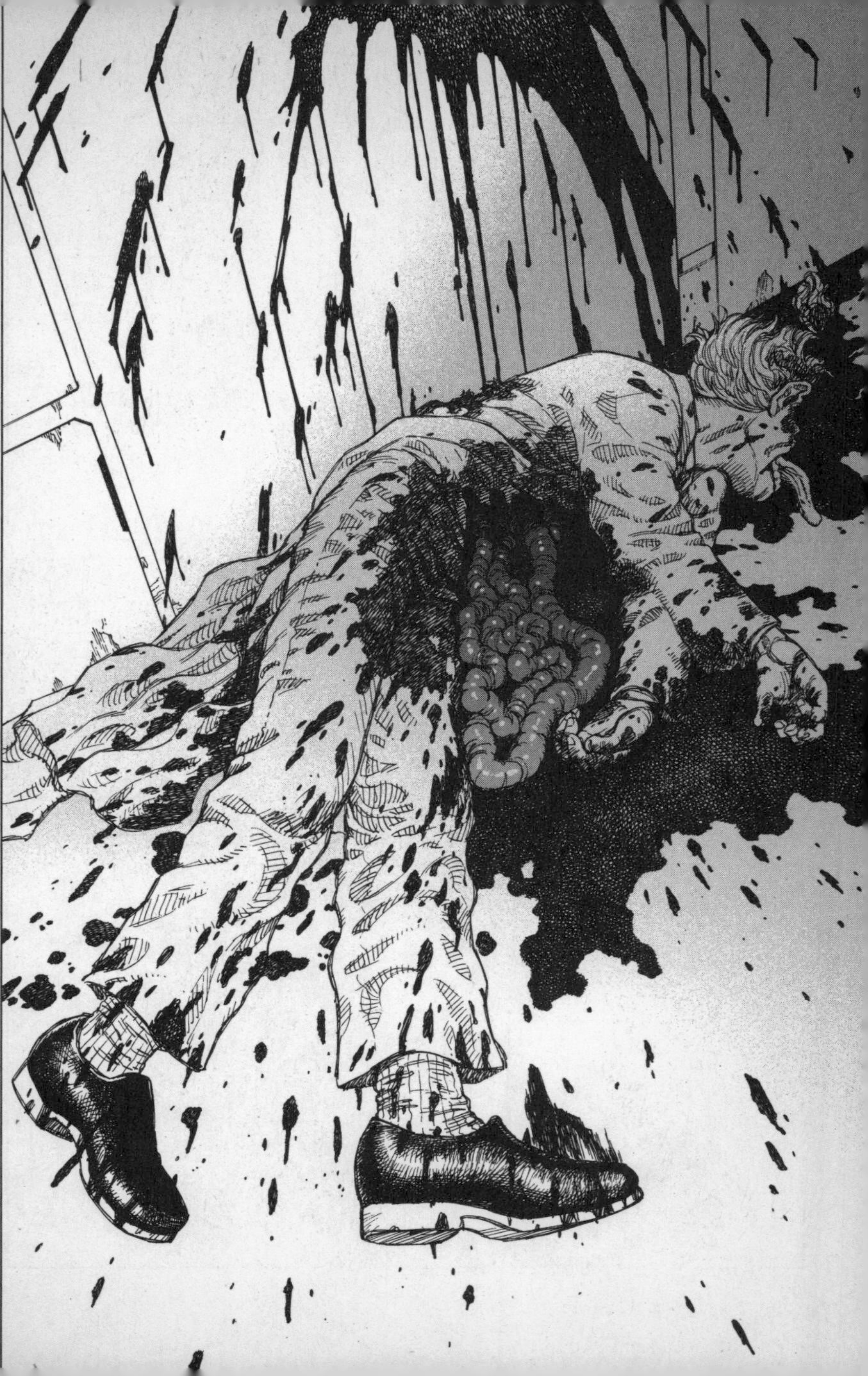

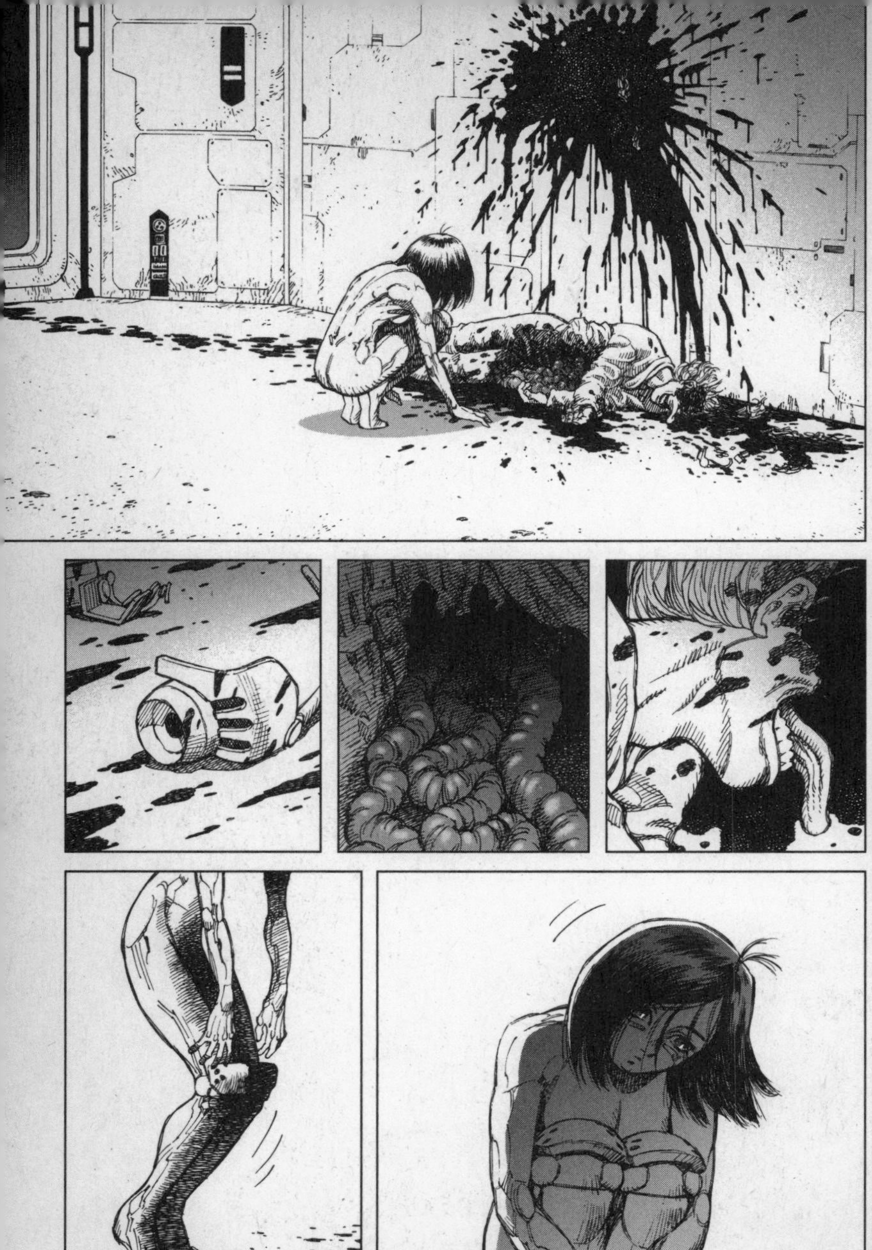

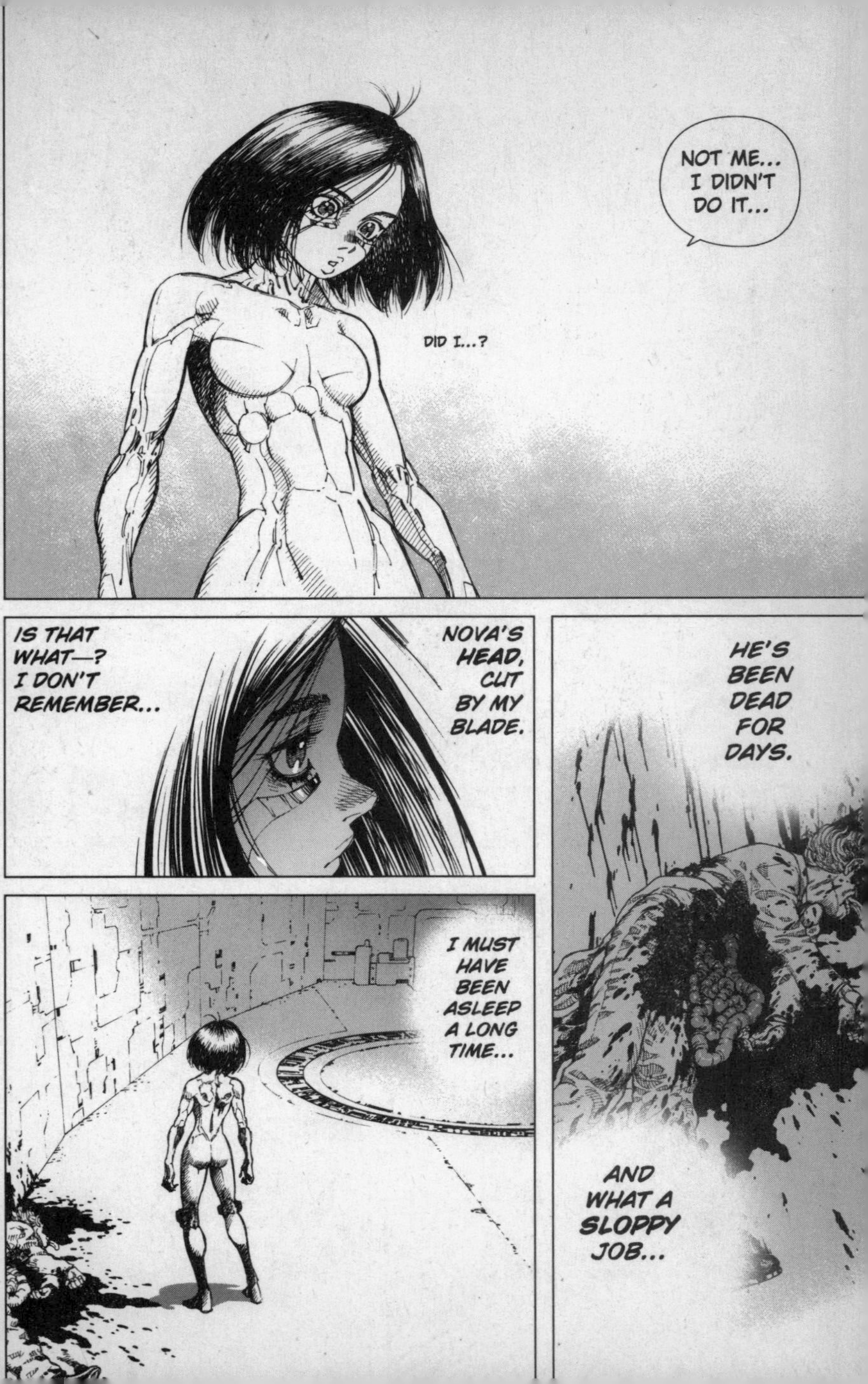
NOT ME... I DIDN'T DO IT...
DID I...?
NOVA'S HEAD, CUT BY MY BLADE.
IS THAT WHAT—? I DON'T REMEMBER...
I MUST HAVE BEEN ASLEEP A LONG TIME...
HE'S BEEN DEAD FOR DAYS.
AND WHAT A SLOPPY JOB...

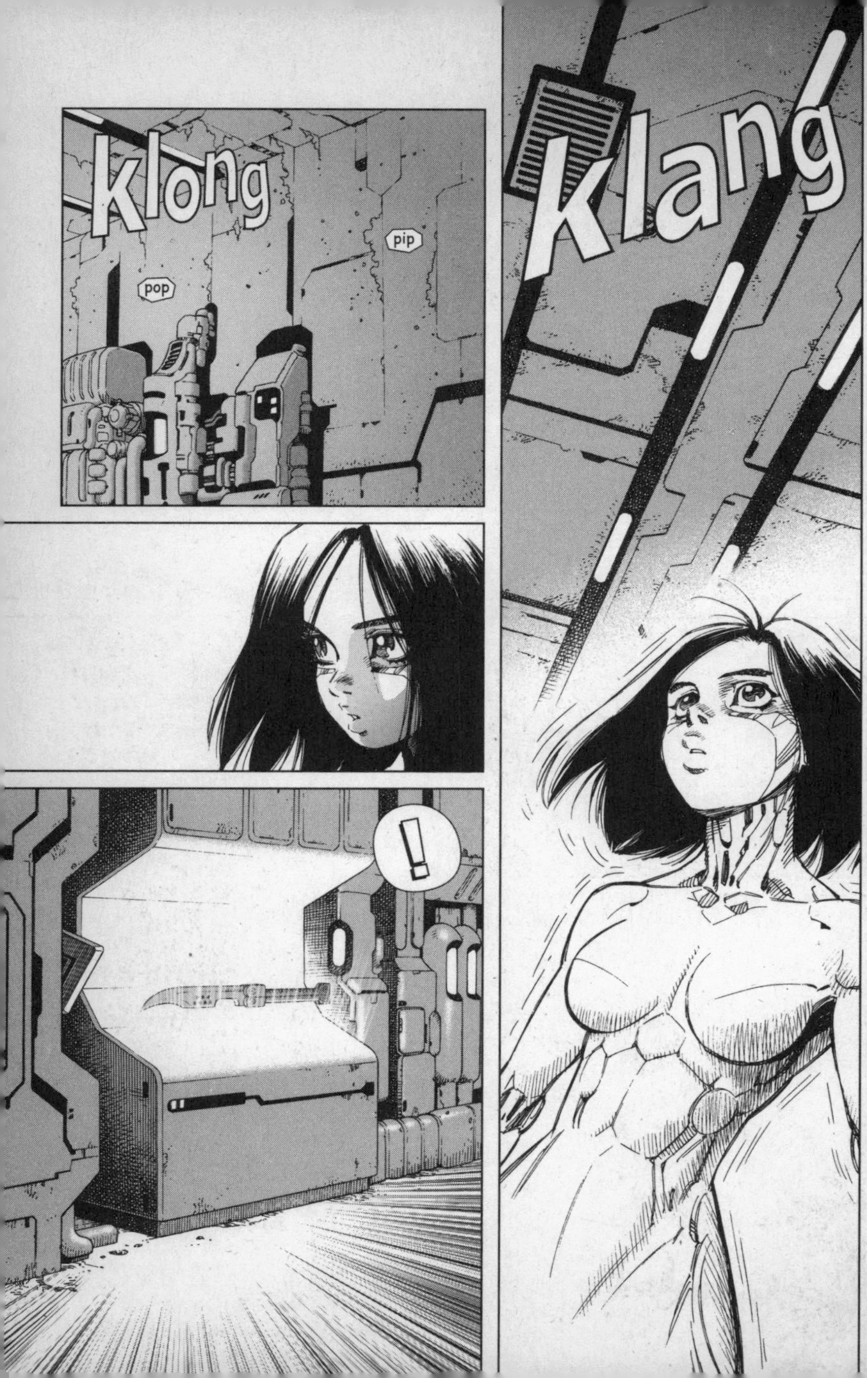
klang
klong
pip
pop
!

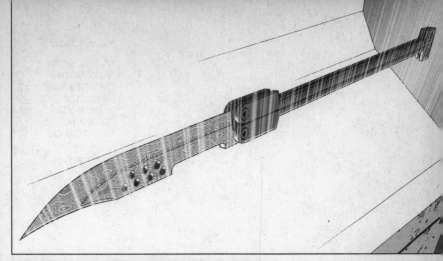

THE DAMAS-CUS BLADE!

shaa

?!

zzt

AH, ALITA! YOU'RE AWAKE.

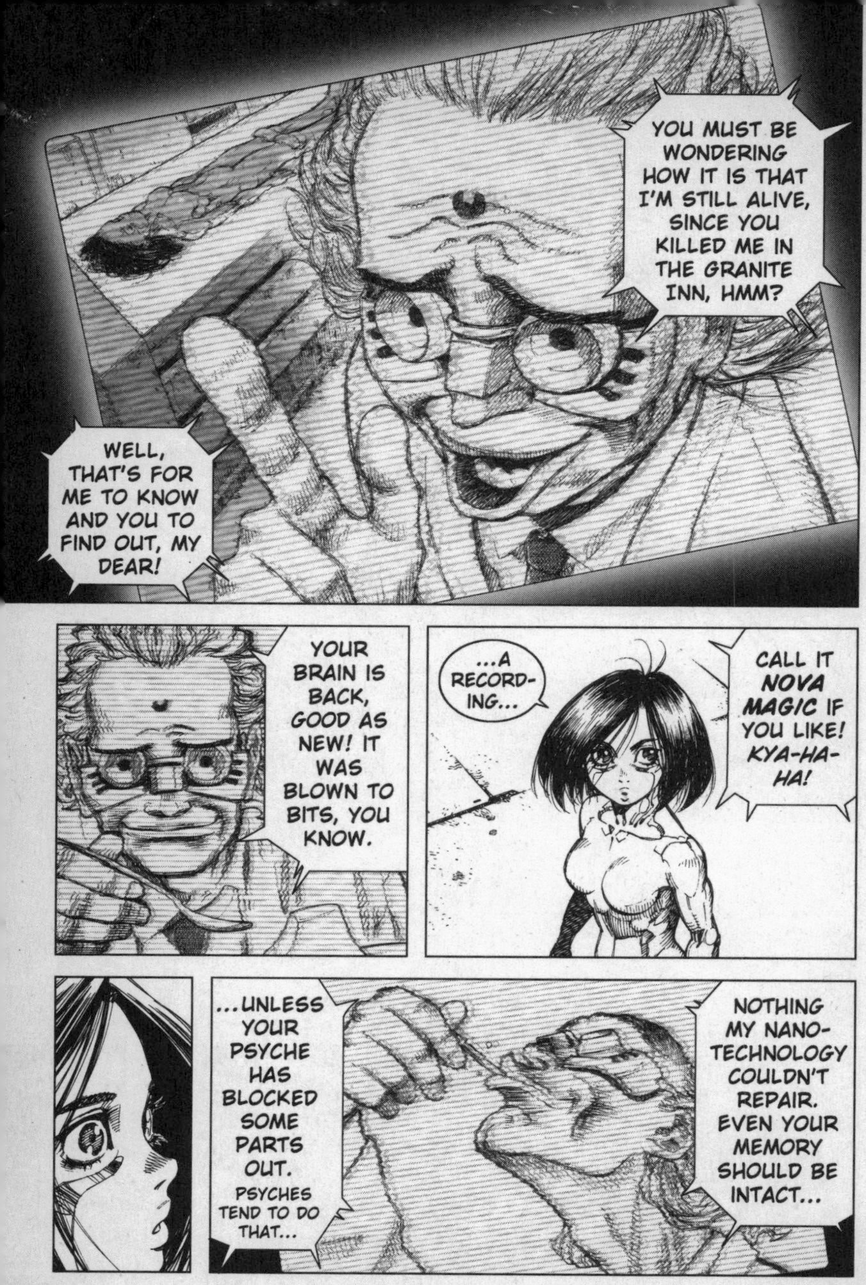
YOU MUST BE WONDERING HOW IT IS THAT I'M STILL ALIVE, SINCE YOU KILLED ME IN THE GRANITE INN, HMM?
WELL, THAT'S FOR ME TO KNOW AND YOU TO FIND OUT, MY DEAR!
CALL IT *NOVA MAGIC* IF YOU LIKE! *KYA-HA-HA!*
...A RECORDING...
YOUR BRAIN IS BACK, GOOD AS NEW! IT WAS BLOWN TO BITS, YOU KNOW.
NOTHING MY NANO-TECHNOLOGY COULDN'T REPAIR. EVEN YOUR MEMORY SHOULD BE INTACT...
...UNLESS YOUR PSYCHE HAS BLOCKED SOME PARTS OUT.
PSYCHES TEND TO DO THAT...

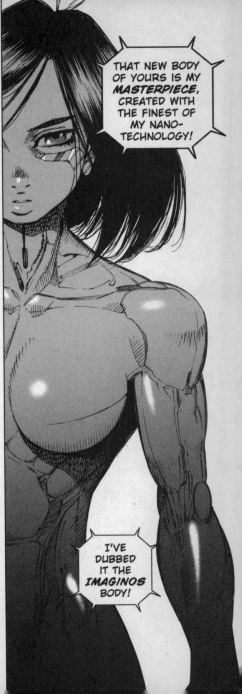

THAT NEW BODY OF YOURS IS MY MASTERPIECE, CREATED WITH THE FINEST OF MY NANO-TECHNOLOGY!
I'VE DUBBED IT THE IMAGINOS BODY!
IT CAN MATCH YOUR THOUGHTS—CHANGE ITS VERY FORM TO SUIT YOU...
SORT OF AN INFINITE ATOMIC LEVEL UPGRADE! HEH...!
LET'S DO A SIMPLE ACTION TEST.
ENVISION YOUR FAVORITE COLOR. GO ON...TRY!

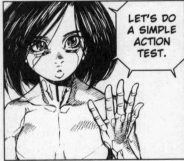

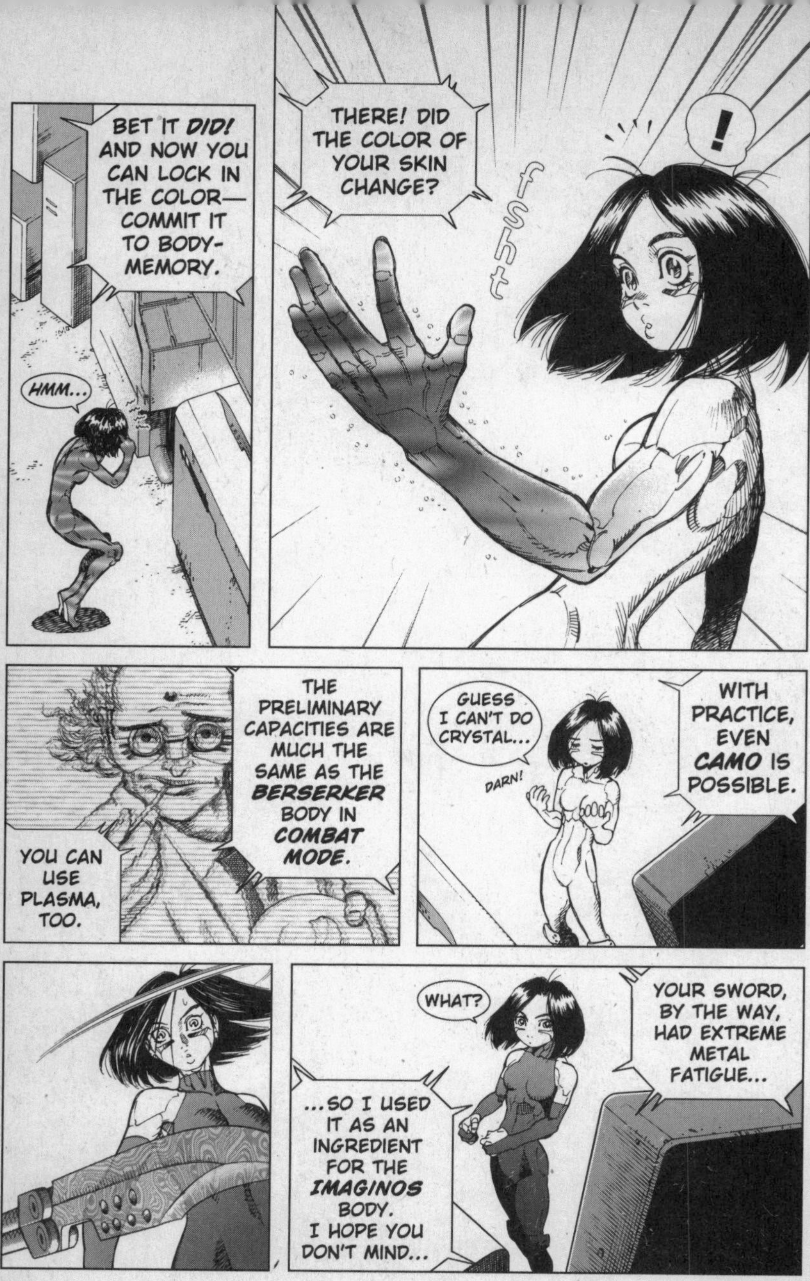
THERE! DID THE COLOR OF YOUR SKIN CHANGE?
fsht
!
BET IT *DID!* AND NOW YOU CAN LOCK IN THE COLOR—COMMIT IT TO BODY-MEMORY.
HMM...
GUESS I CAN'T DO CRYSTAL...
DARN!
WITH PRACTICE, EVEN *CAMO* IS POSSIBLE.
THE PRELIMINARY CAPACITIES ARE MUCH THE SAME AS THE *BERSERKER* BODY IN *COMBAT MODE.*
YOU CAN USE PLASMA, TOO.
YOUR SWORD, BY THE WAY, HAD EXTREME METAL FATIGUE...
WHAT?
...SO I USED IT AS AN INGREDIENT FOR THE *IMAGINOS* BODY. I HOPE YOU DON'T MIND...

WHAT GAVE YOU THE RIGHT...!?

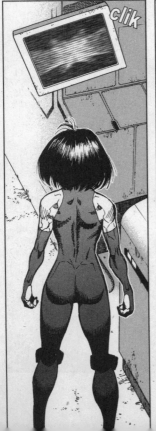

clik

YEAH, RIGHT...

I ASSURE YOU, I HAVEN'T *TINKERED* WITH YOUR FREE WILL.

EVERY DECISION IS STILL UP TO YOU...

HEH, HEH... THINGS ARE ABOUT TO GET INTERESTING NOW THAT YOU'RE AWAKE!

GOOD DAY, ALITA!

56

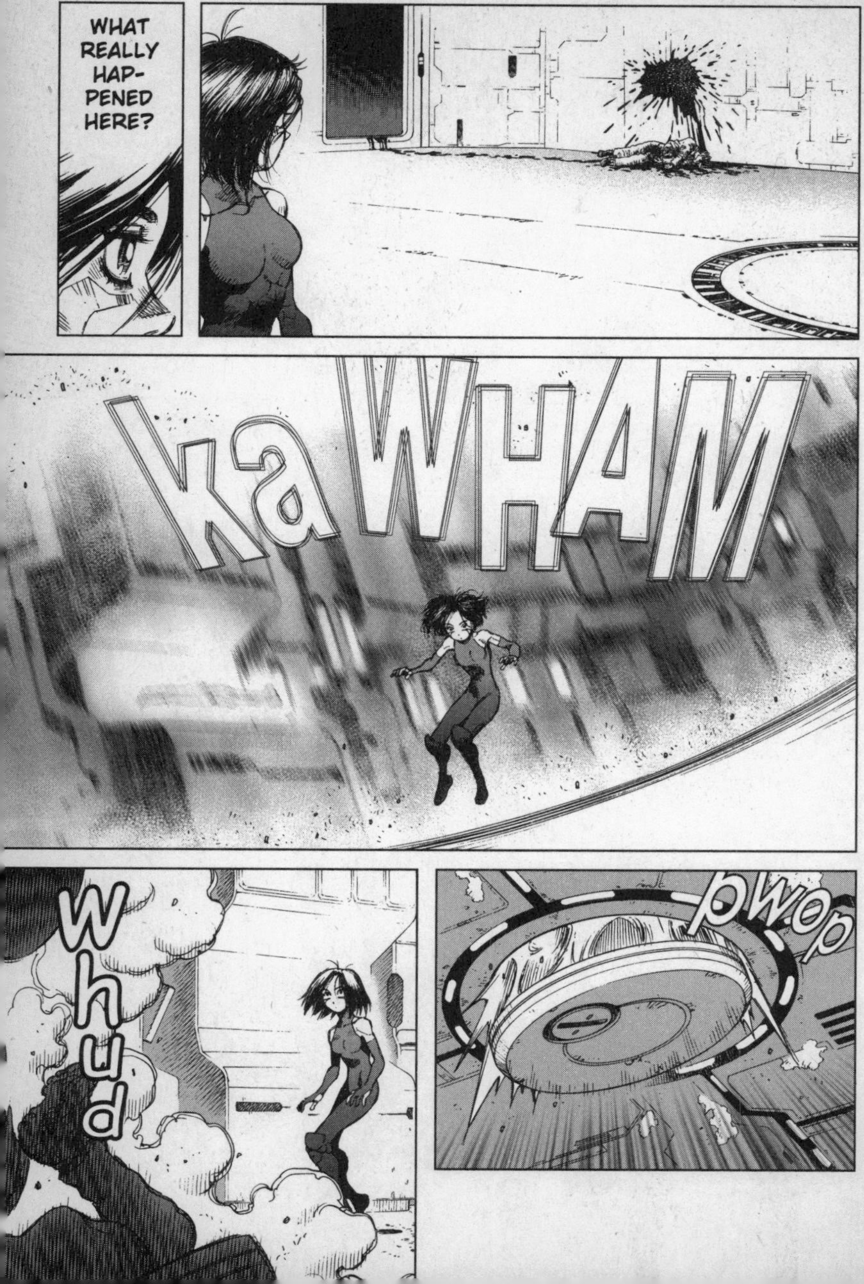
WHAT REALLY HAP-PENED HERE?
kaWHAM
pwop
whud

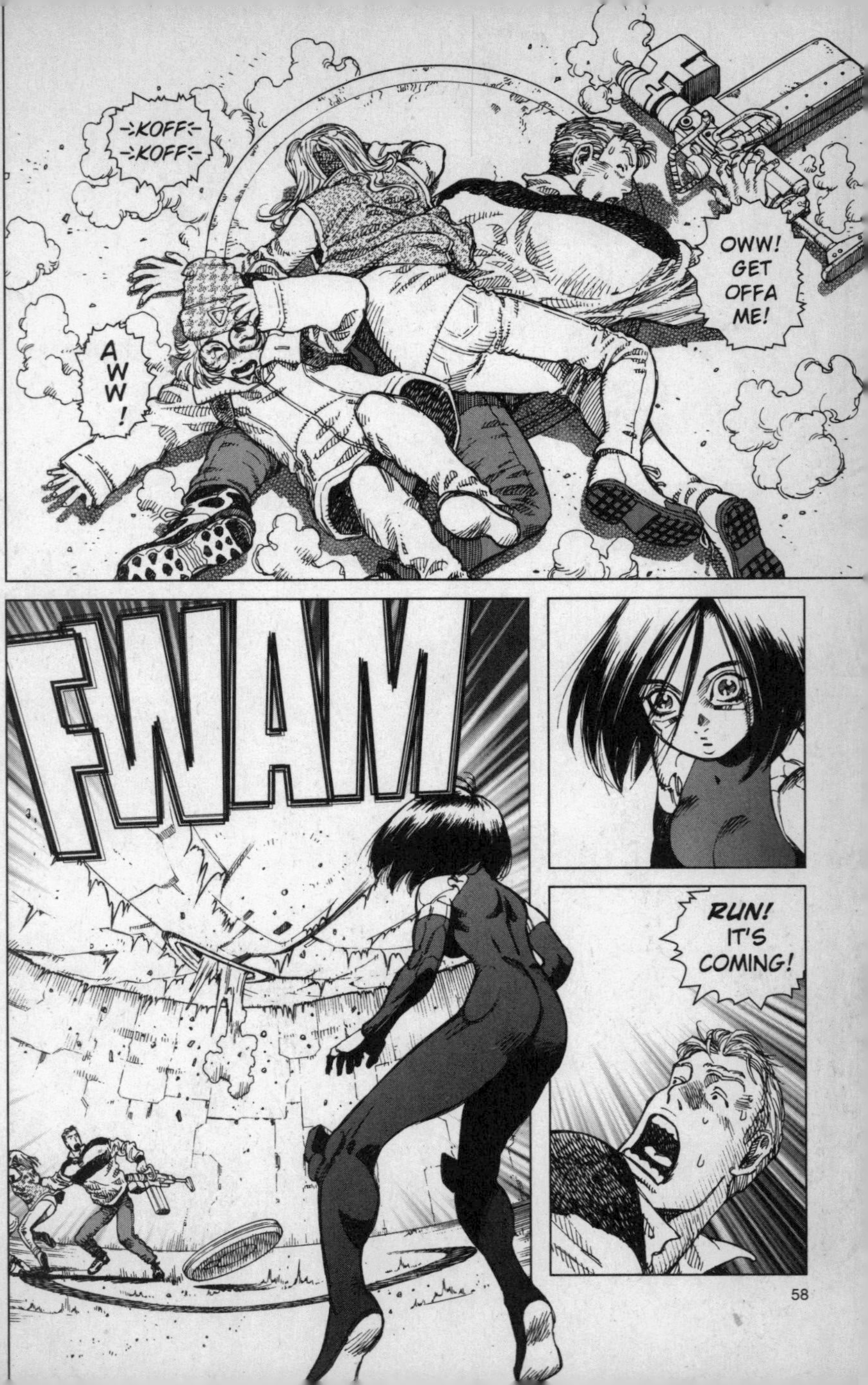
-KOFF-
-KOFF-
OWW! GET OFFA ME!
AWW!
RUN! IT'S COMING!
FWAM

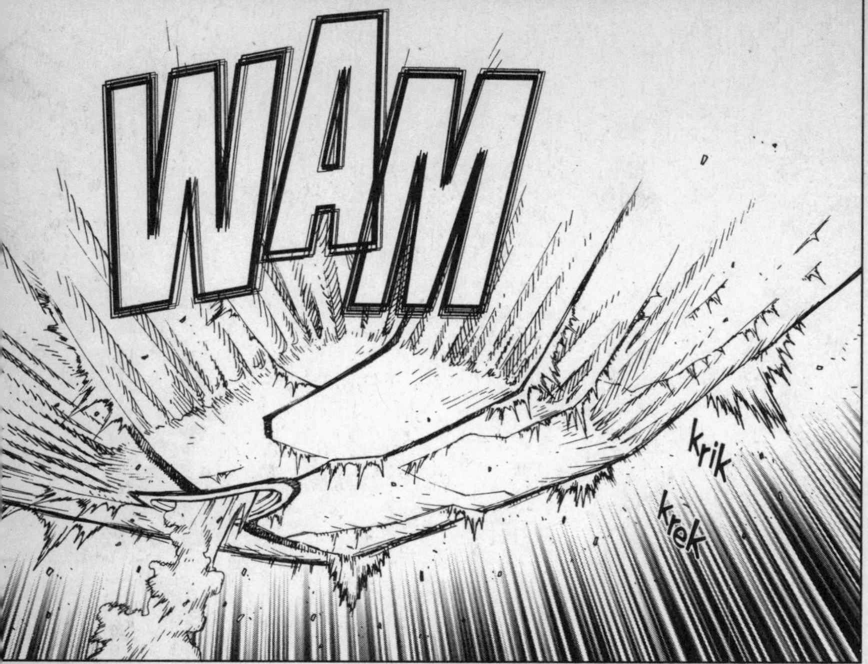
WAM
krik
krek
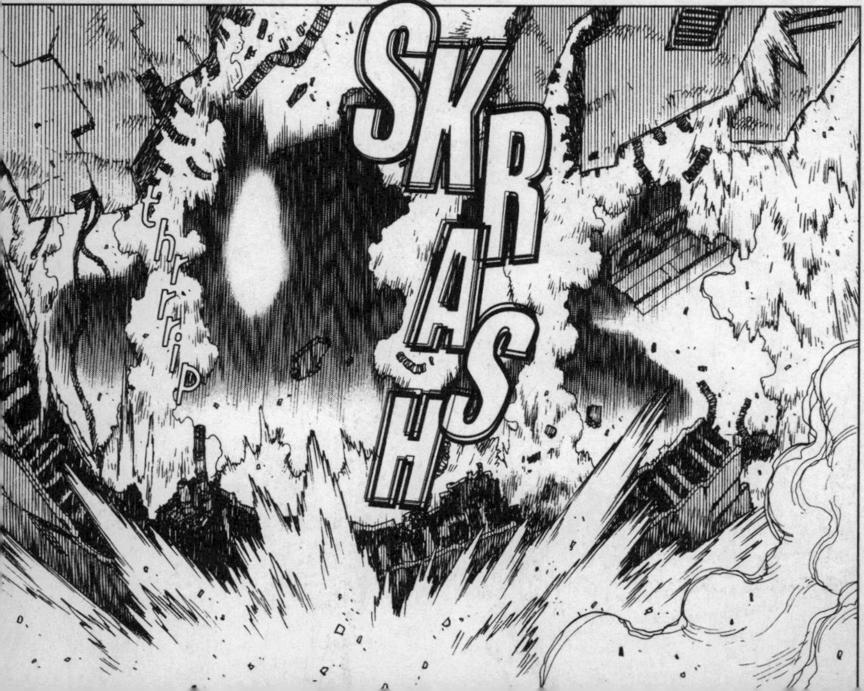
SKRASH
thrrrip

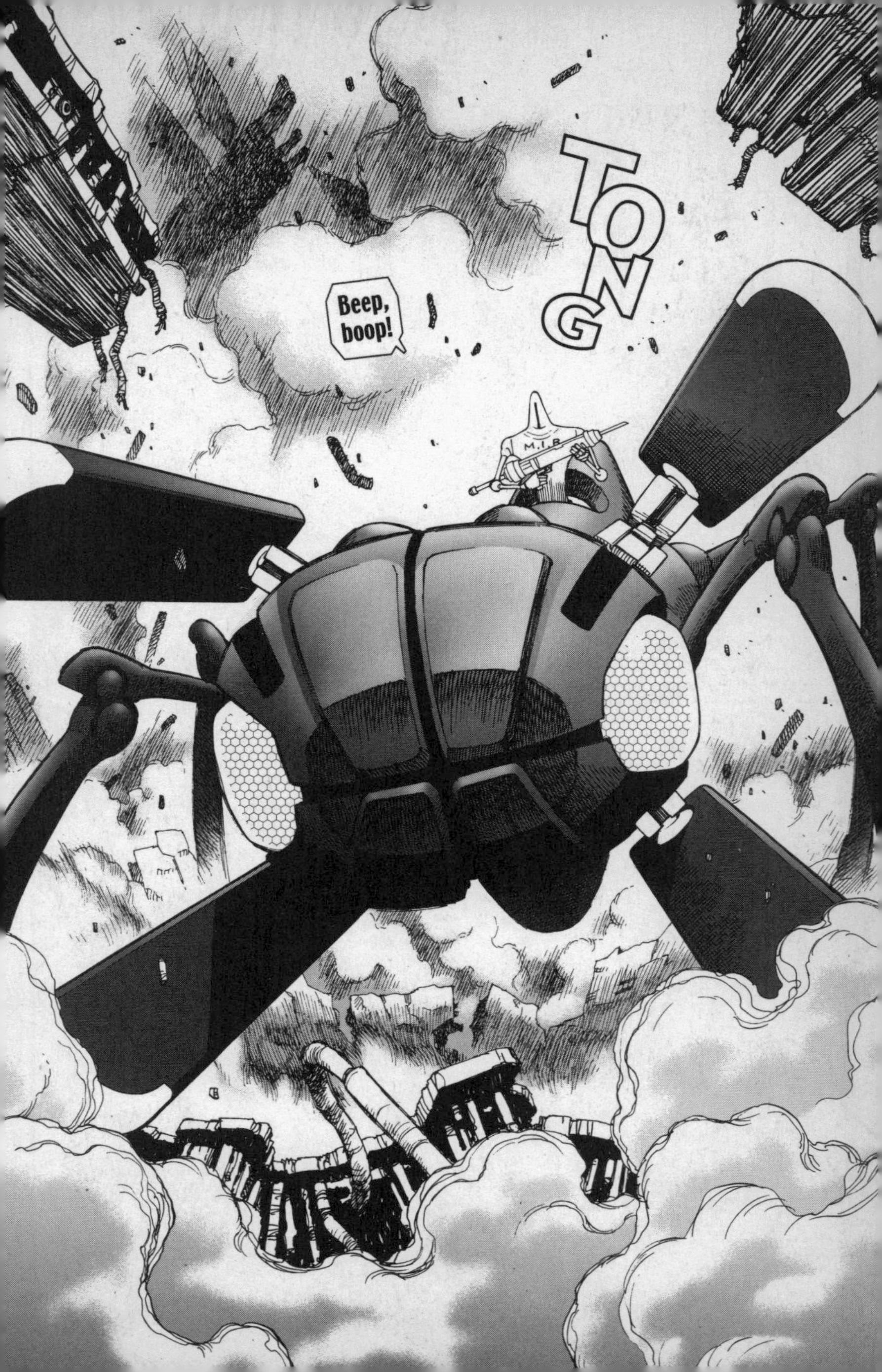
TONG
Beep, boop!
M.I.B.

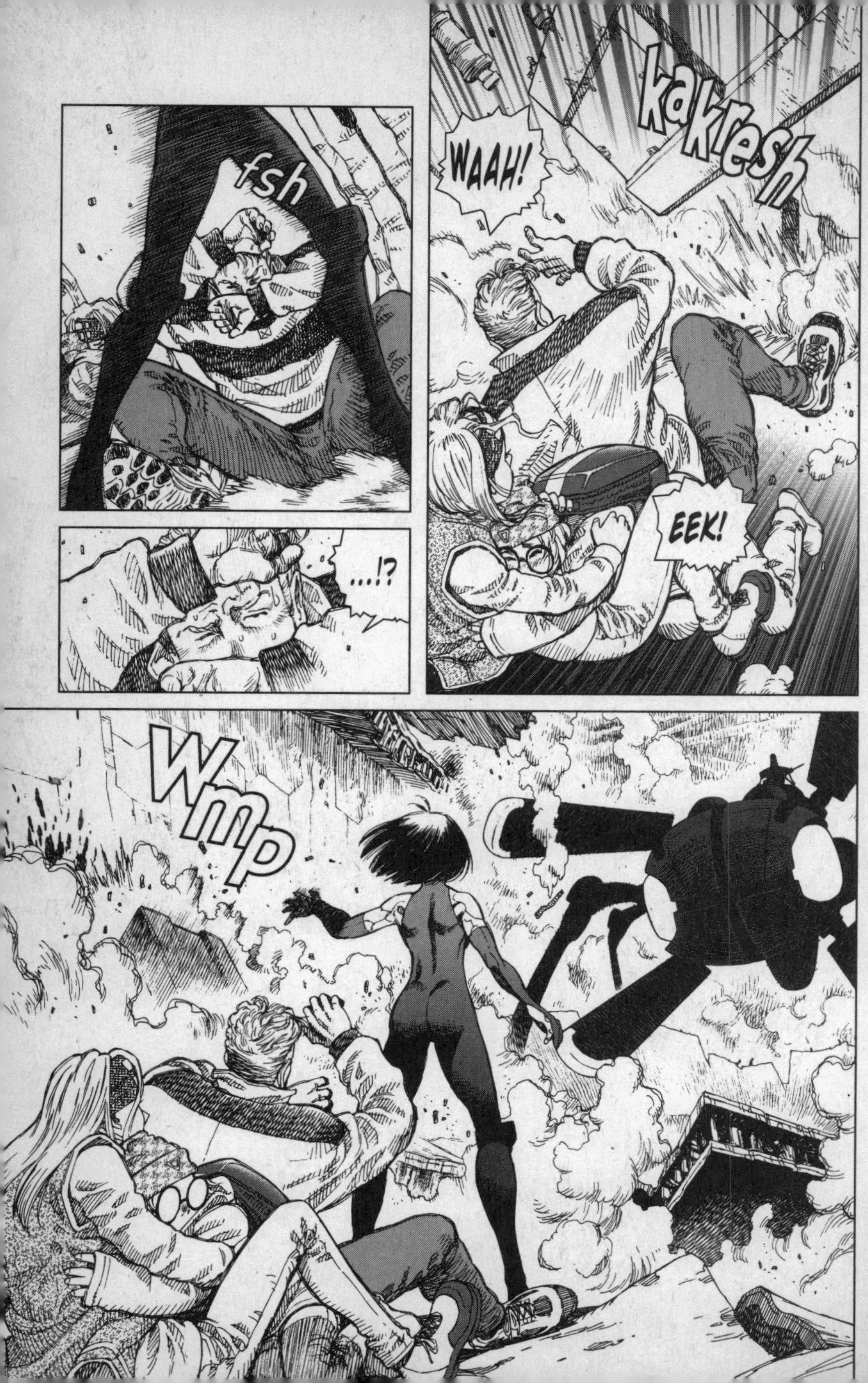
kakresh
WAAH!
EEK!
fsh
...!?
Wmp

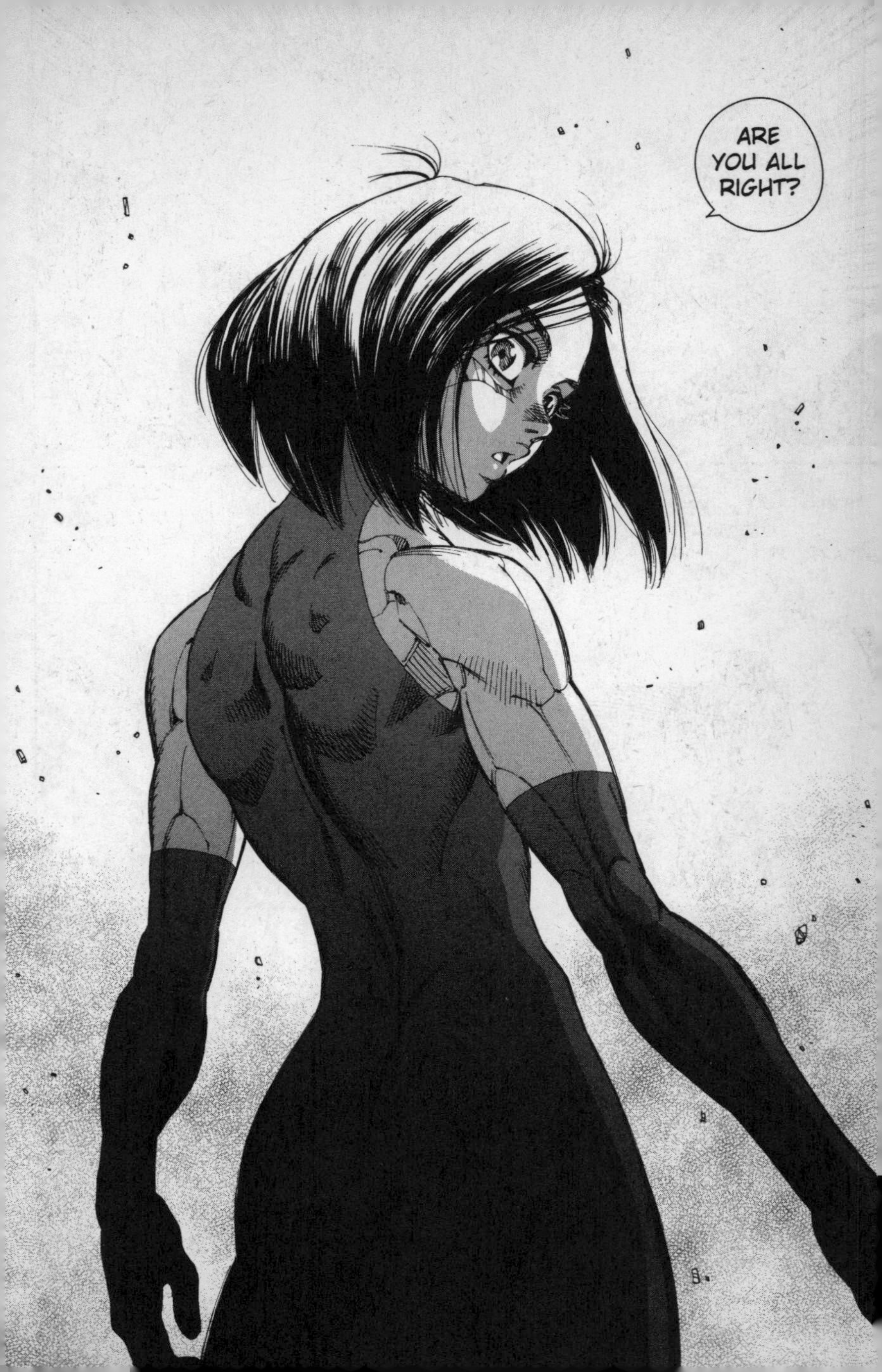
ARE YOU ALL RIGHT?

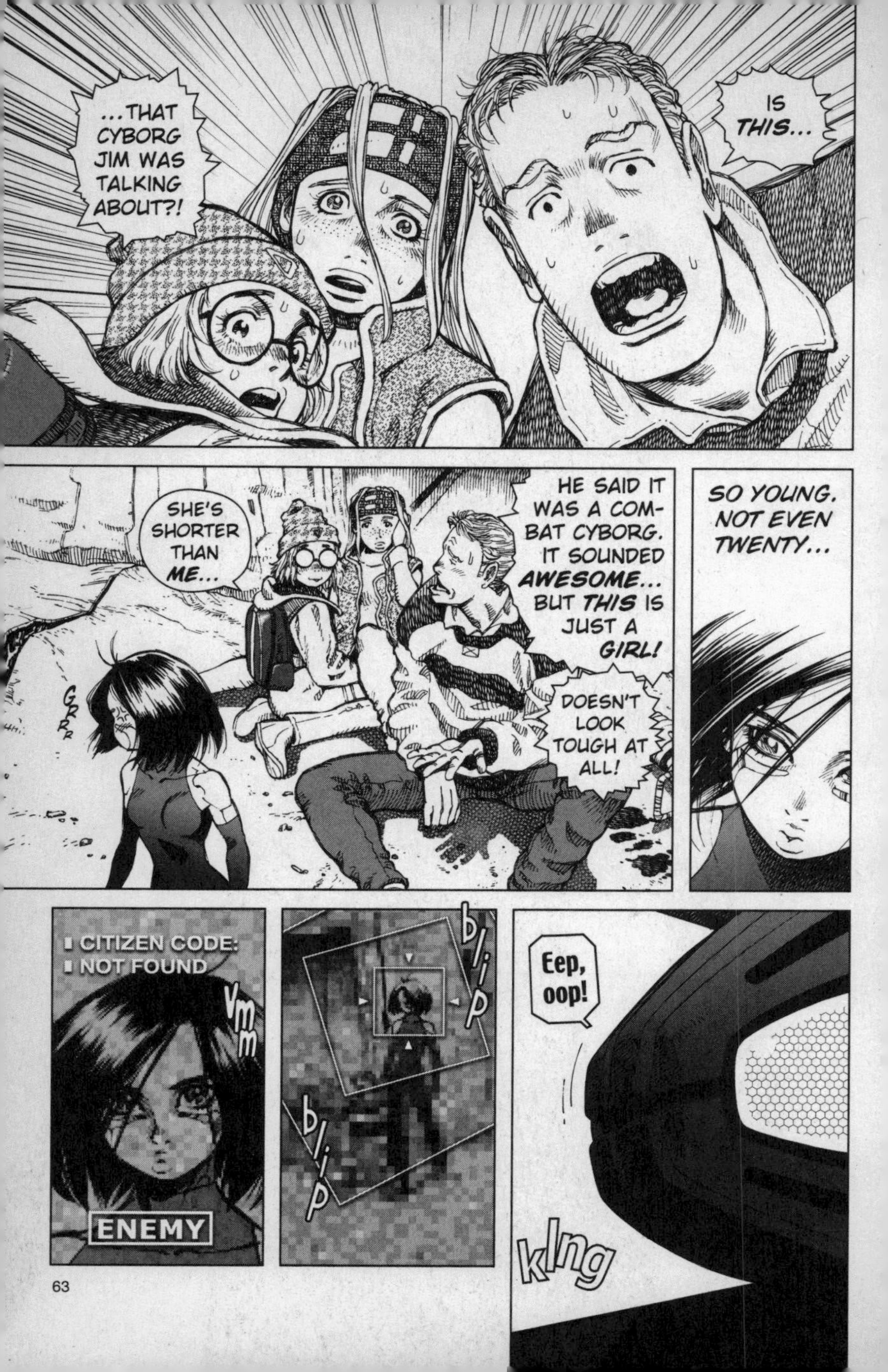
IS THIS...
...THAT CYBORG JIM WAS TALKING ABOUT?!
SO YOUNG. NOT EVEN TWENTY...
HE SAID IT WAS A COMBAT CYBORG. IT SOUNDED AWESOME... BUT THIS IS JUST A GIRL!
DOESN'T LOOK TOUGH AT ALL!
SHE'S SHORTER THAN ME...
GRRR
Eep, oop!
kIng
blip
blip
CITIZEN CODE:
NOT FOUND
vmm
ENEMY

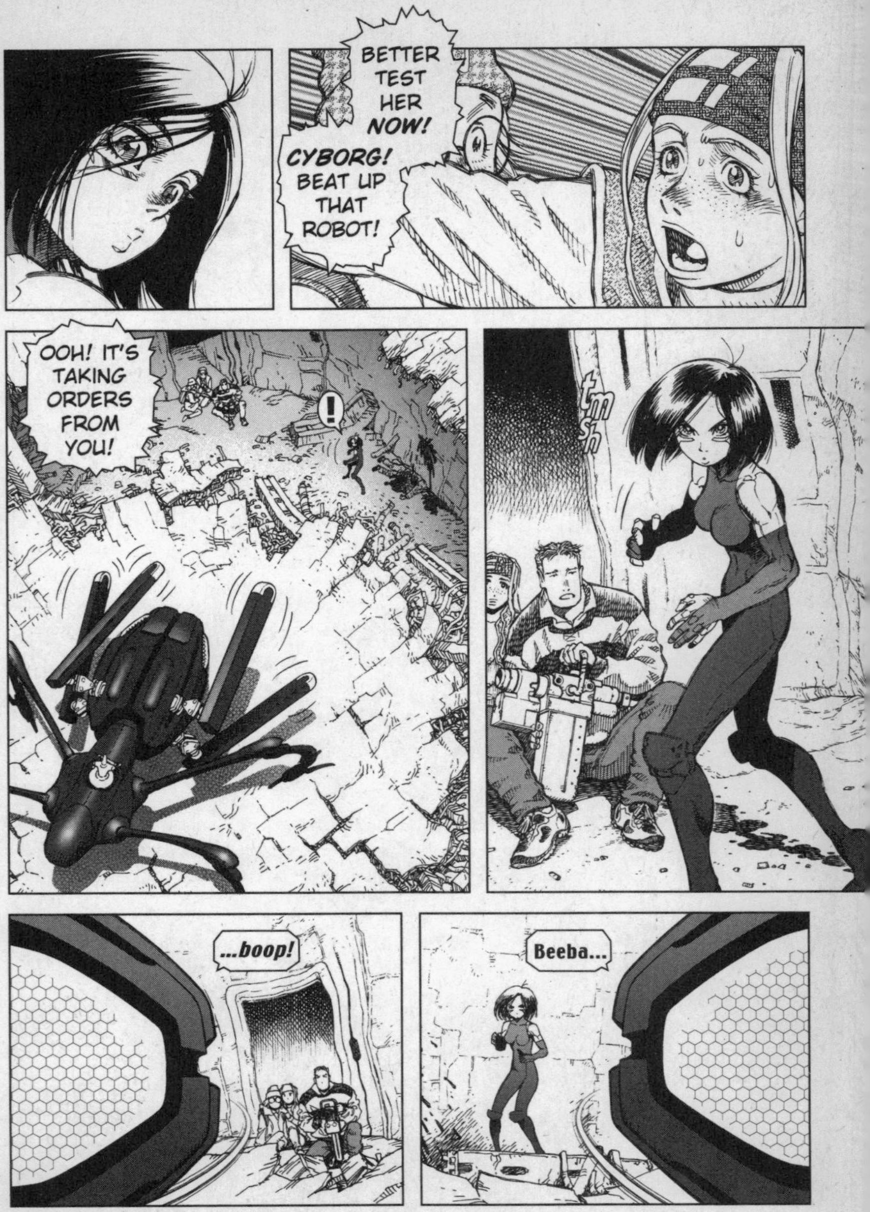
BETTER TEST HER NOW!
CYBORG! BEAT UP THAT ROBOT!
tmsh
!
OOH! IT'S TAKING ORDERS FROM YOU!
Beeba...
...boop!

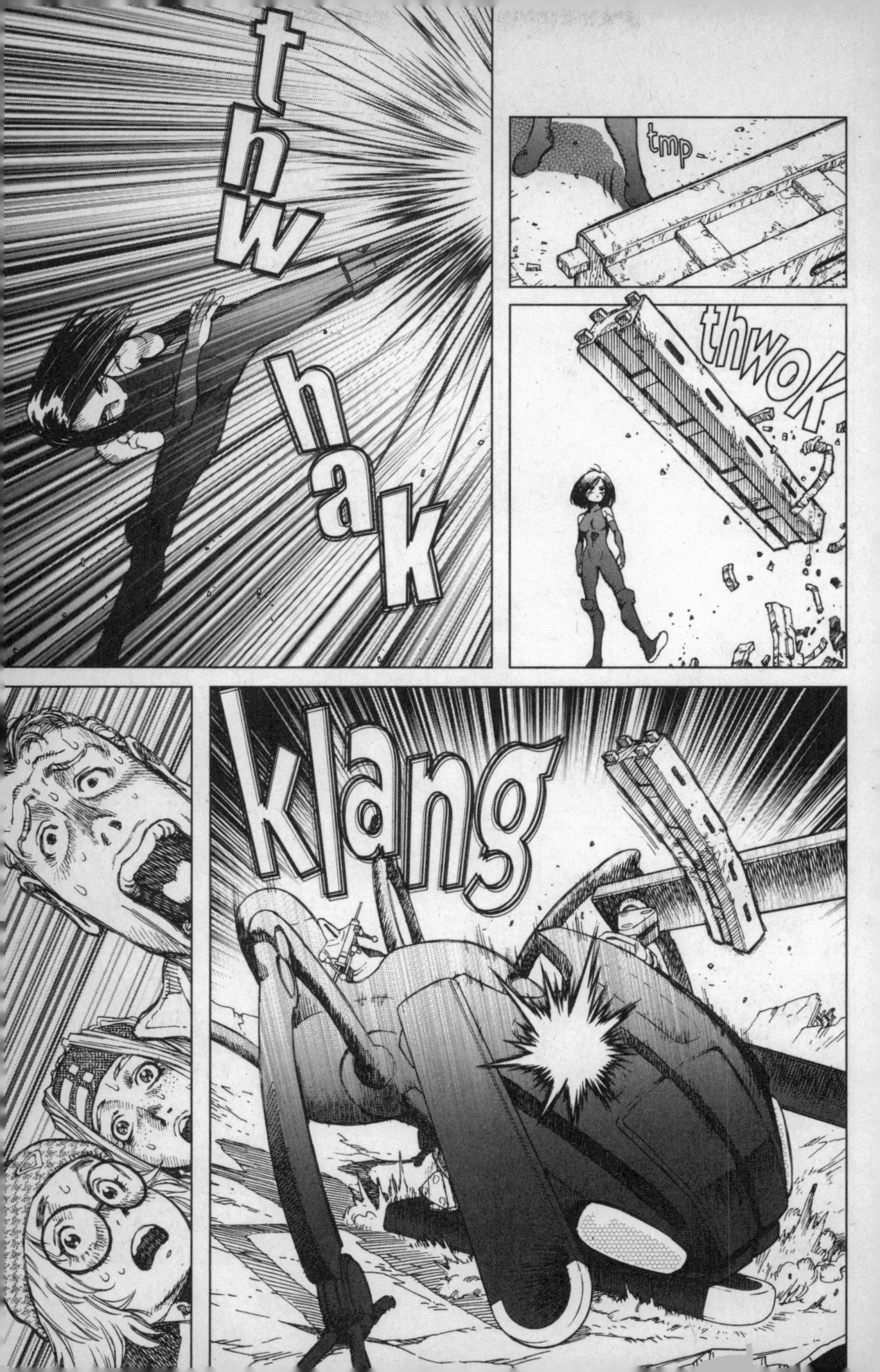
tmp
thwok
thw
hak
klang

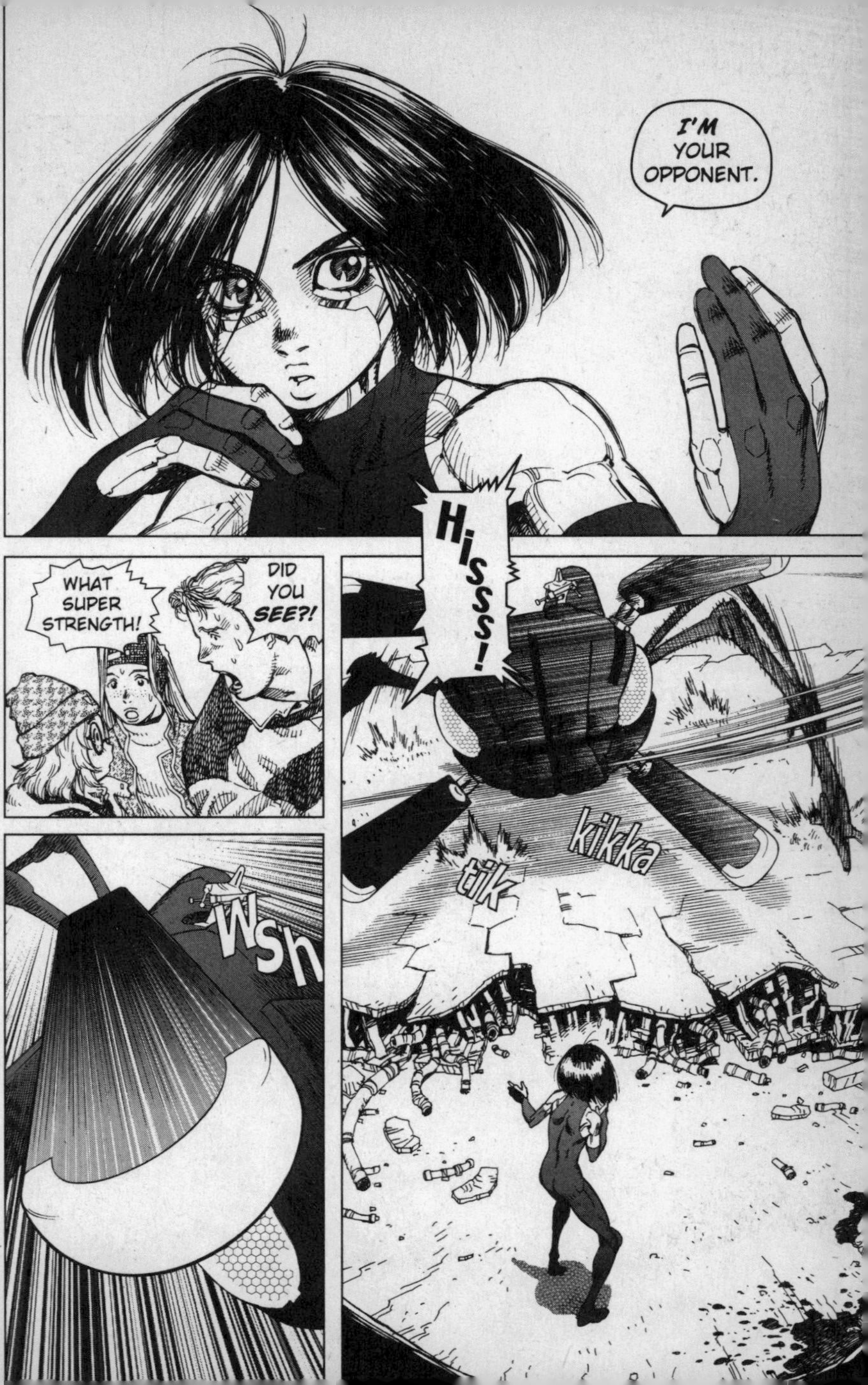
I'M YOUR OPPONENT.
HISSS!
kikka
tik
DID YOU SEE?!
WHAT SUPER STRENGTH!
Wsh

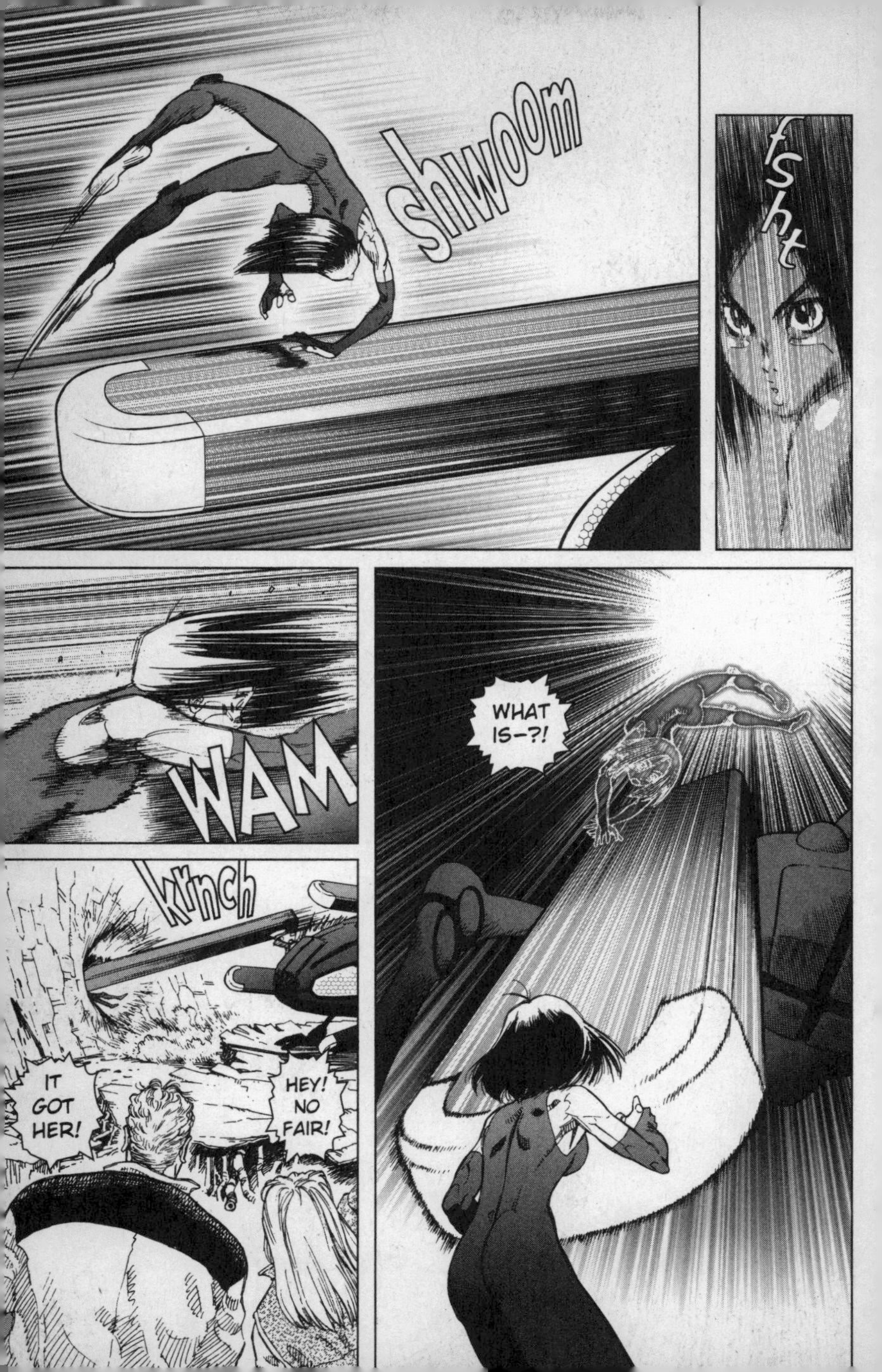
fsht
shwoom
WHAT IS-?!
WAM
krnch
HEY! NO FAIR!
IT GOT HER!

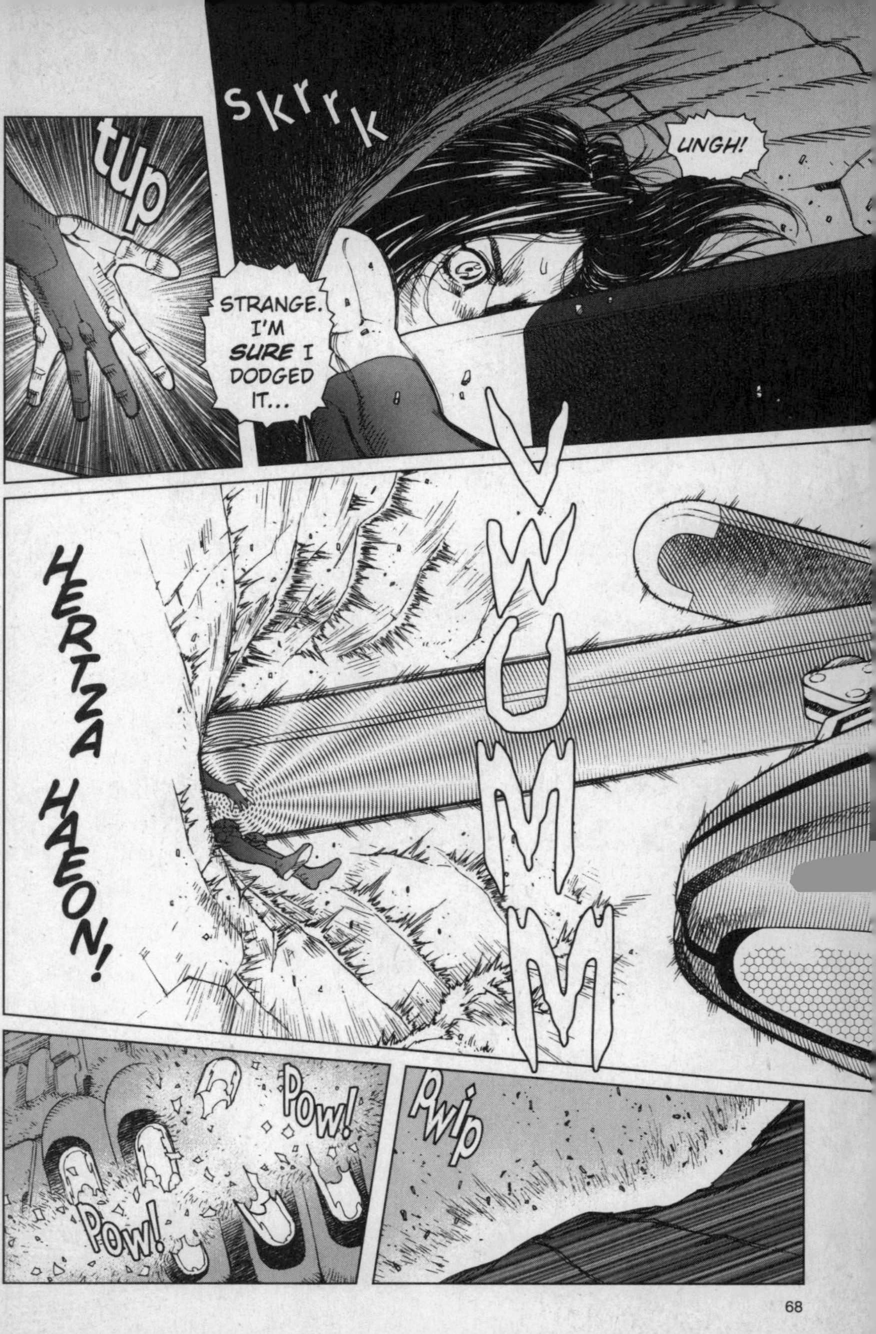
SKRRK
UNGH!
STRANGE. I'M SURE I DODGED IT...
tup
VWUMMM
HERTZA HAEON!
pwip
Pow!
Pow!

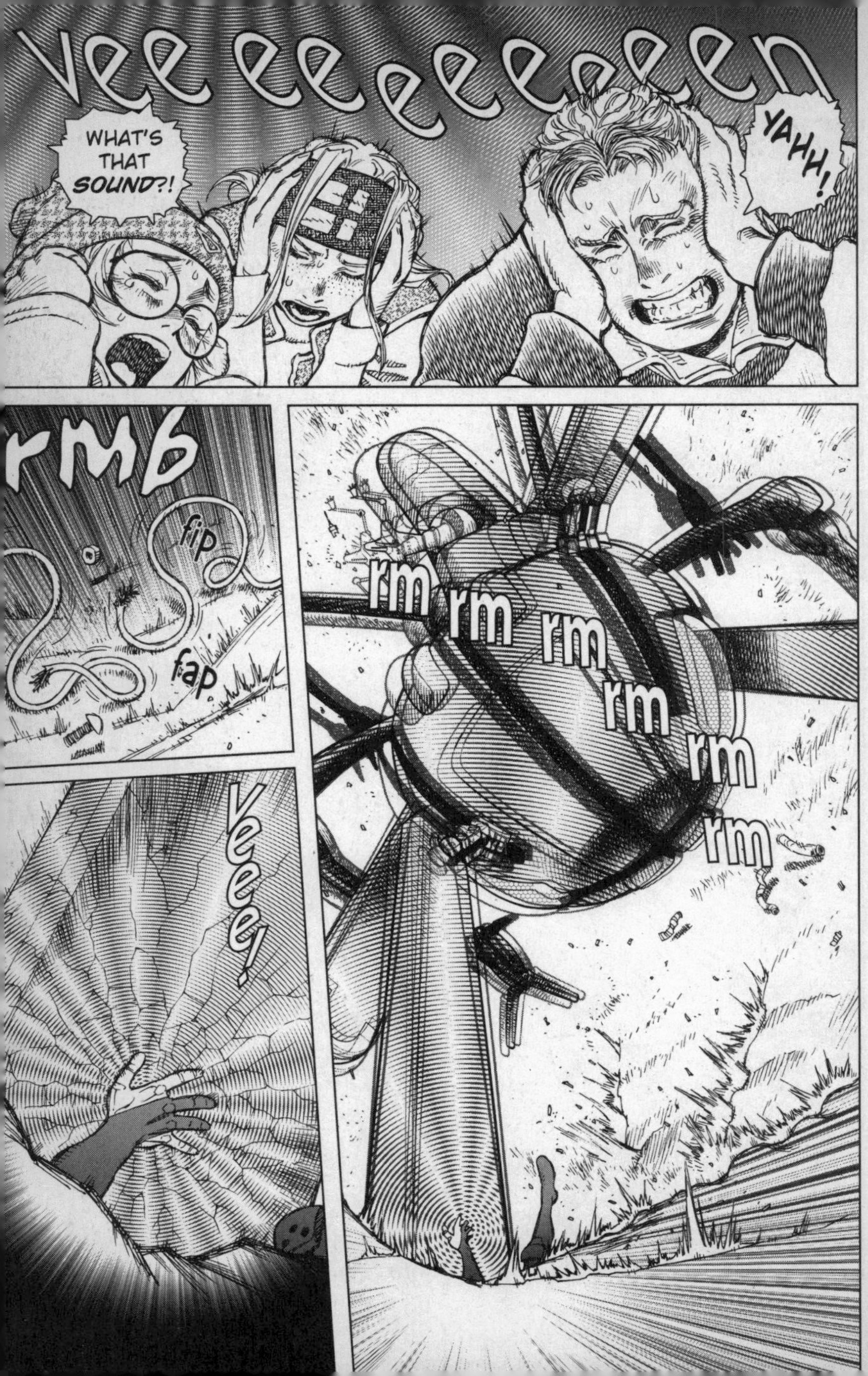
Vee eeeeeeen
YAHH!
WHAT'S THAT *SOUND*?!
rm rm rm rm rm rm
rmb
fip
fap
Veee!

bwam

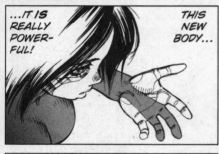

...IT IS REALLY POWER-FUL!

THIS NEW BODY...

Bwap!

Ha!

WHOA!

THE WALL DISPERSED MUCH OF THAT SOUND WAVE.

STILL...

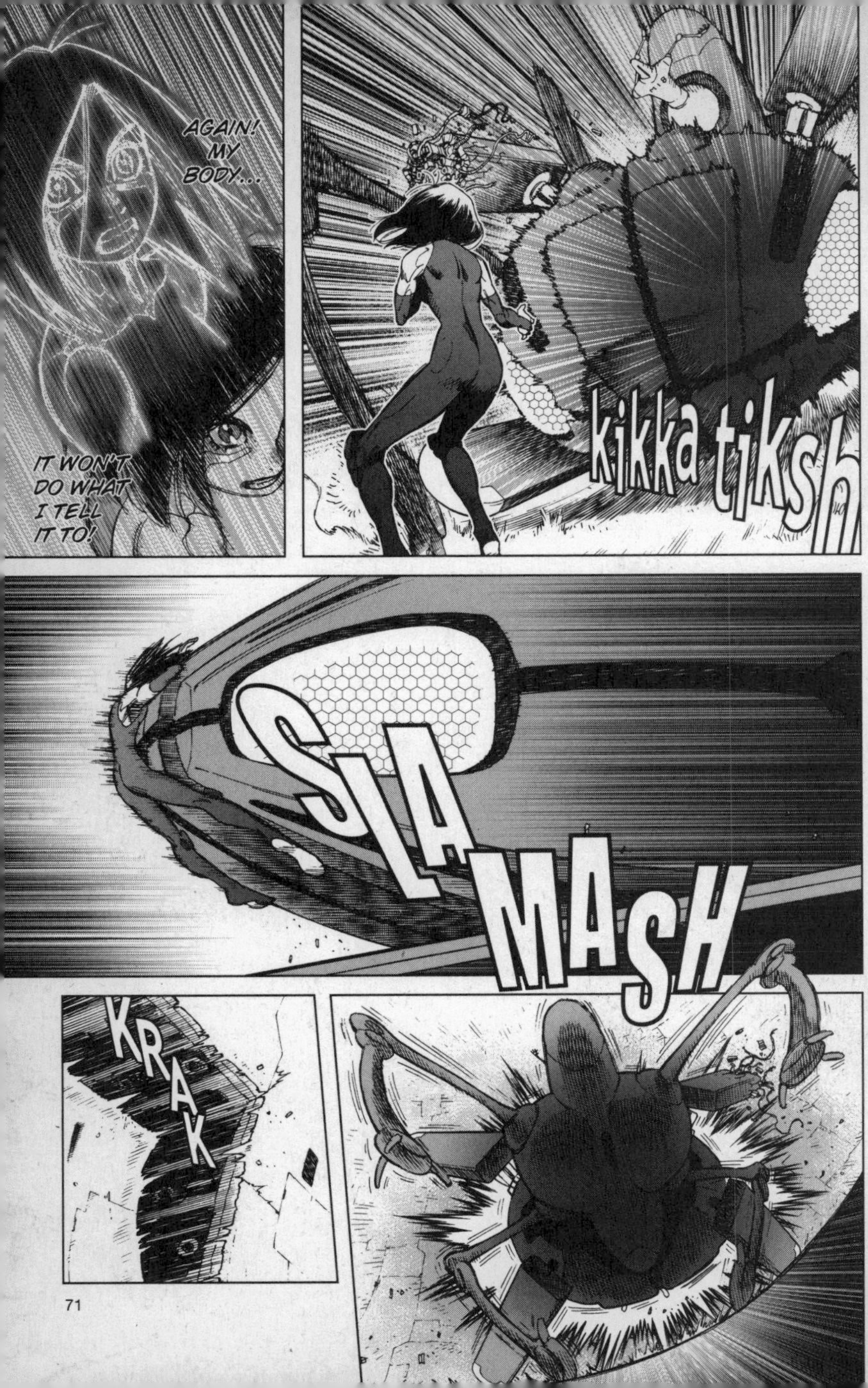
kikka tiksh
AGAIN! MY BODY...
IT WON'T DO WHAT I TELL IT TO!
SLAMASH
KRAK

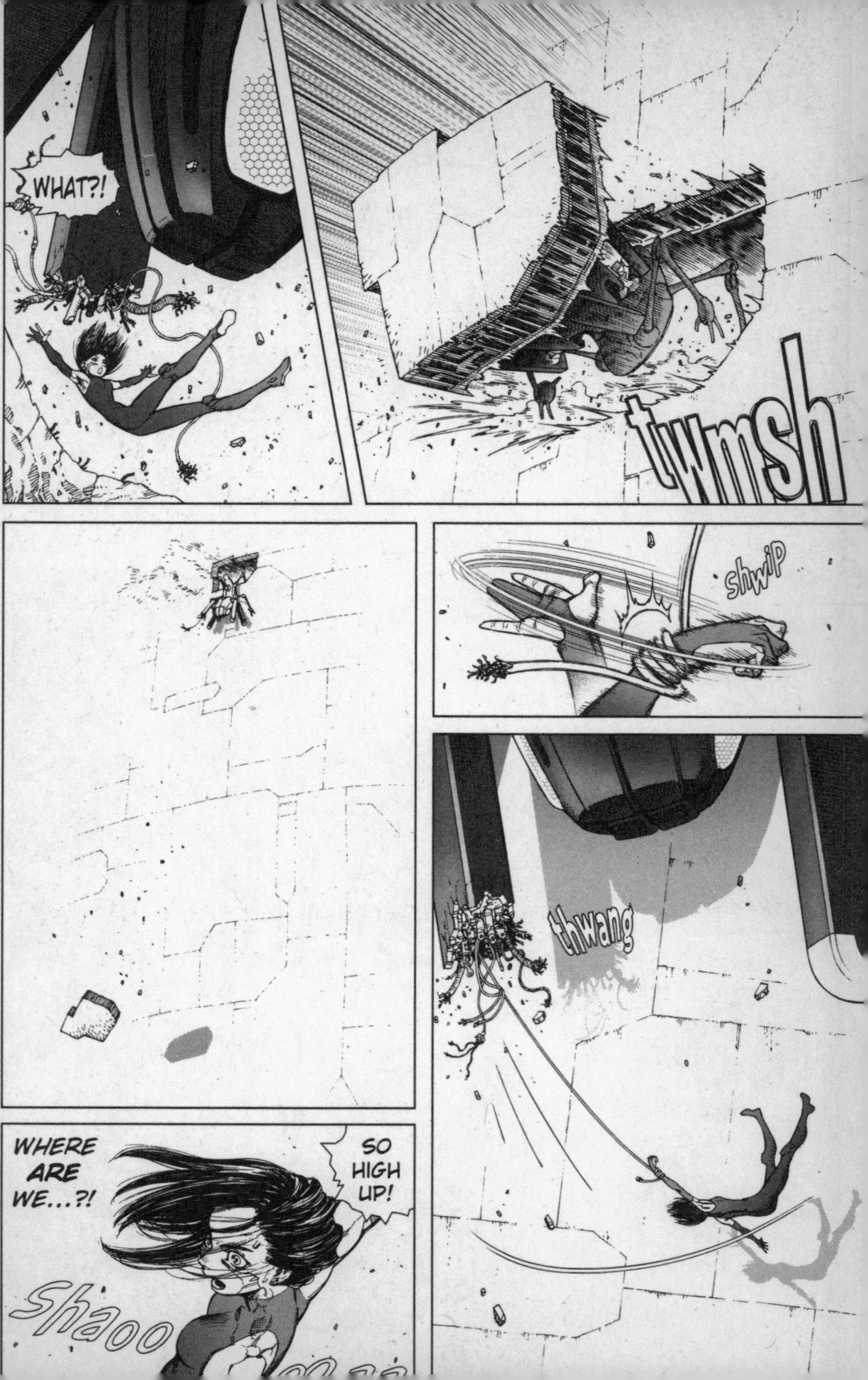
twmsh
WHAT?!
shwip
thwang
SO HIGH UP!
WHERE ARE WE...?!
Shaoo

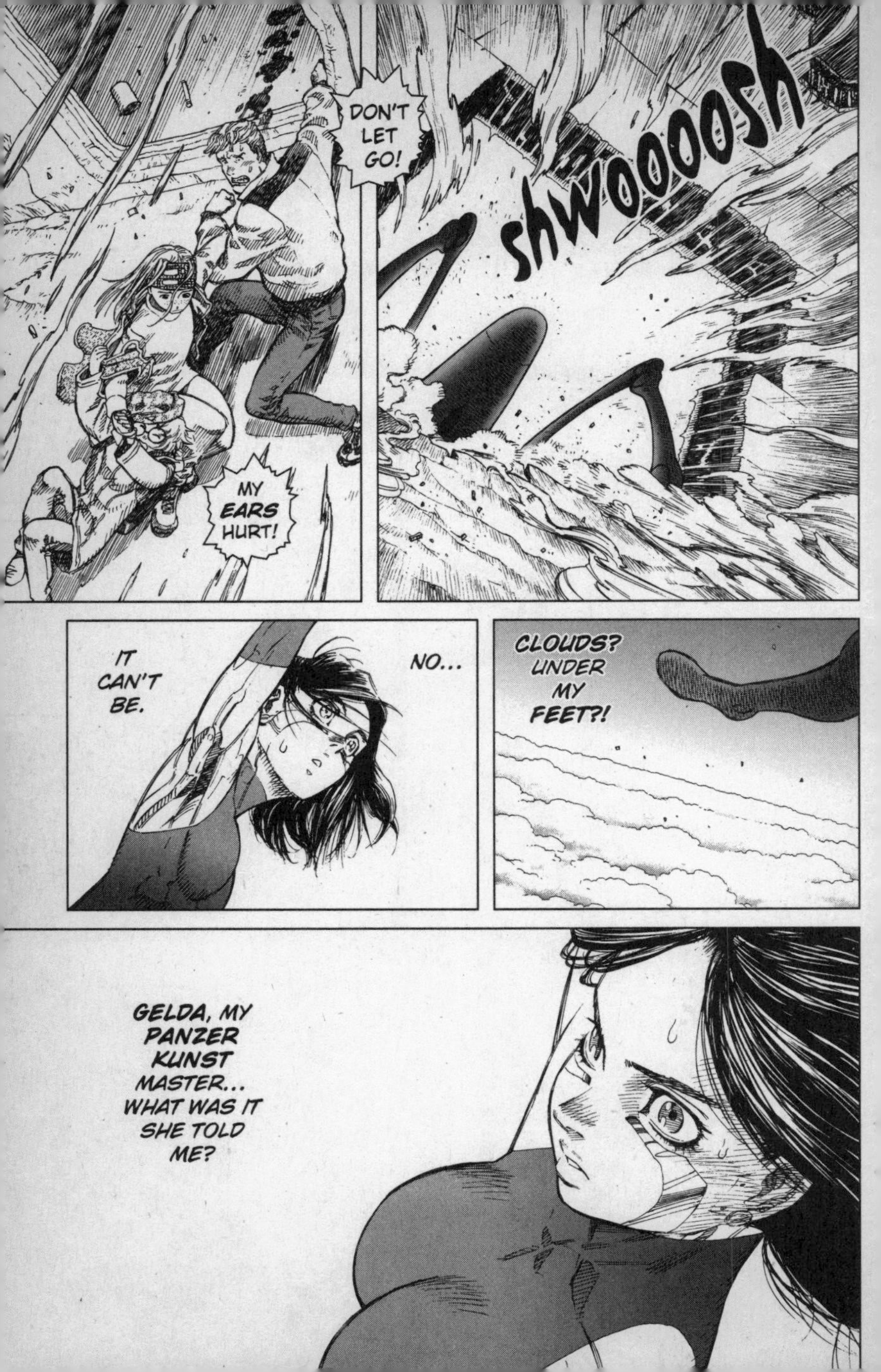
shwoooosh
DON'T LET GO!
MY EARS HURT!
CLOUDS? UNDER MY FEET?!
NO...
IT CAN'T BE.
GELDA, MY PANZER KUNST MASTER... WHAT WAS IT SHE TOLD ME?

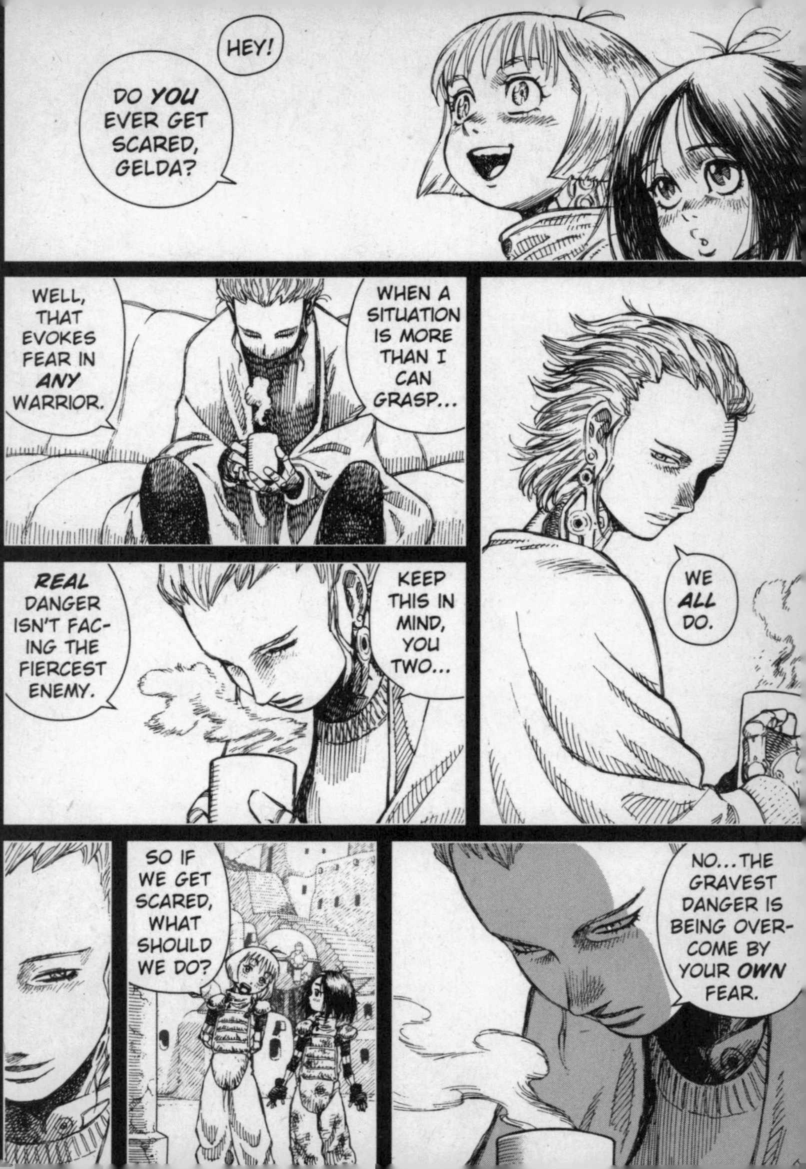
HEY!
DO YOU EVER GET SCARED, GELDA?
WE ALL DO.
WHEN A SITUATION IS MORE THAN I CAN GRASP...
WELL, THAT EVOKES FEAR IN ANY WARRIOR.
KEEP THIS IN MIND, YOU TWO...
REAL DANGER ISN'T FAC-ING THE FIERCEST ENEMY.
NO...THE GRAVEST DANGER IS BEING OVER-COME BY YOUR OWN FEAR.
SO IF WE GET SCARED, WHAT SHOULD WE DO?

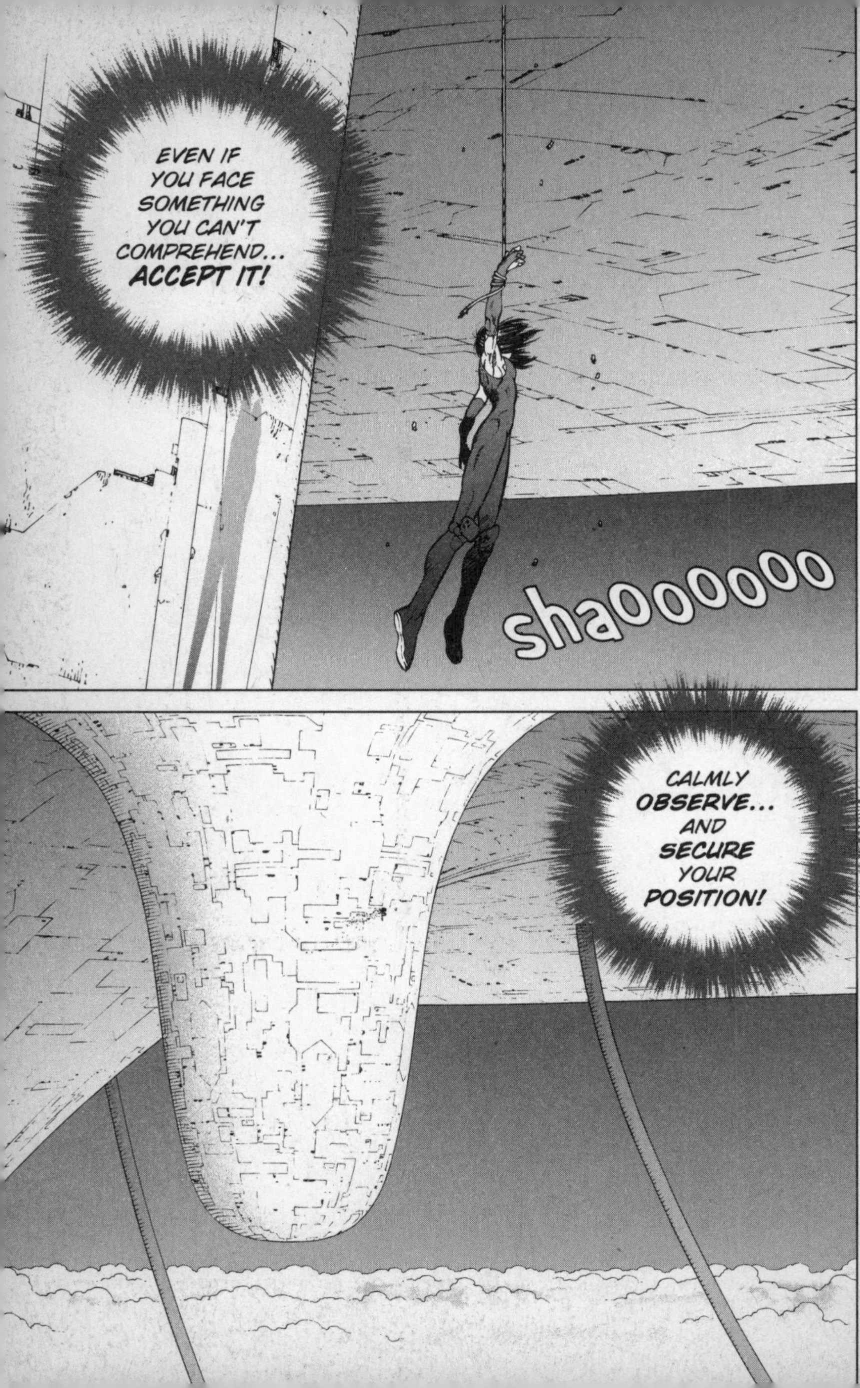
EVEN IF YOU FACE SOMETHING YOU CAN'T COMPREHEND... ACCEPT IT!
shaoooooo
CALMLY OBSERVE... AND SECURE YOUR POSITION!

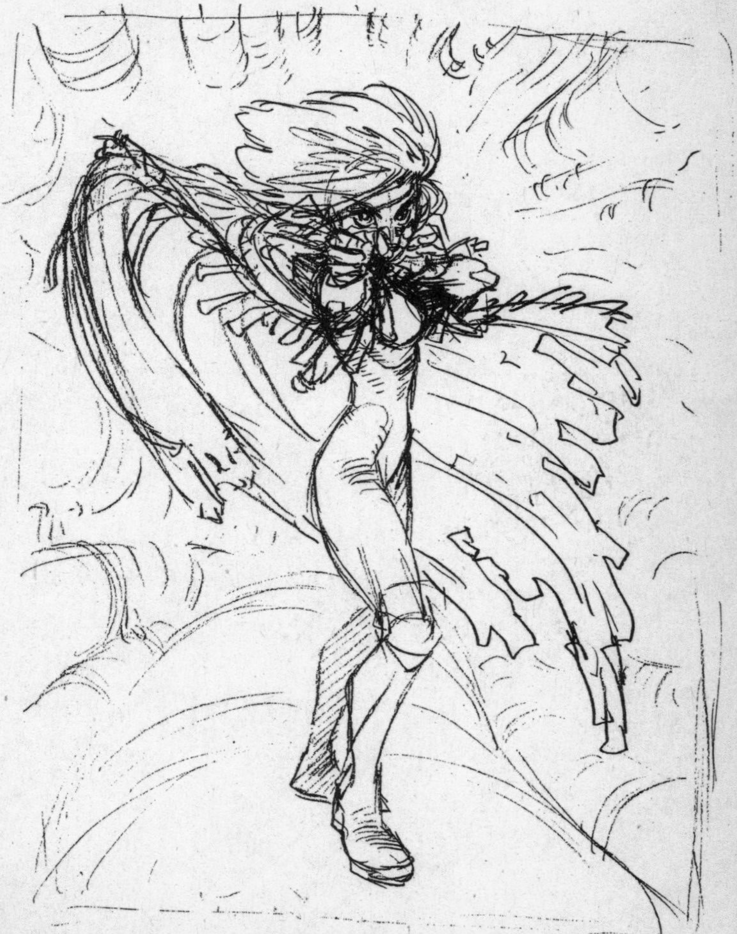

PHASE 03:
I Am Not a Robot

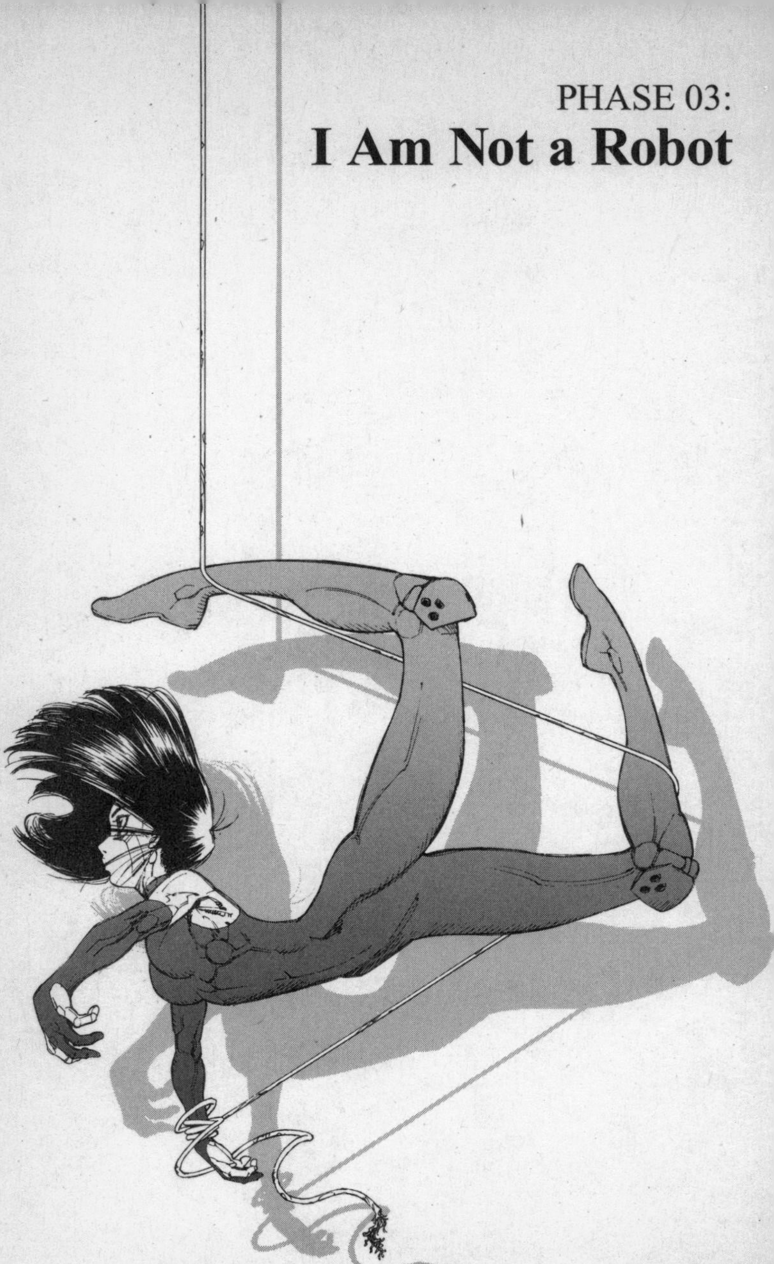

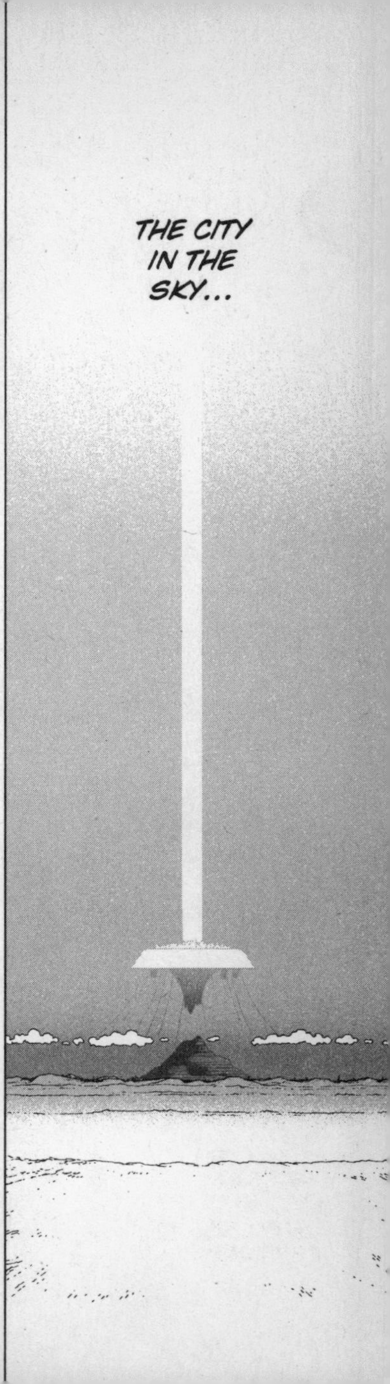
THE CITY IN THE SKY...
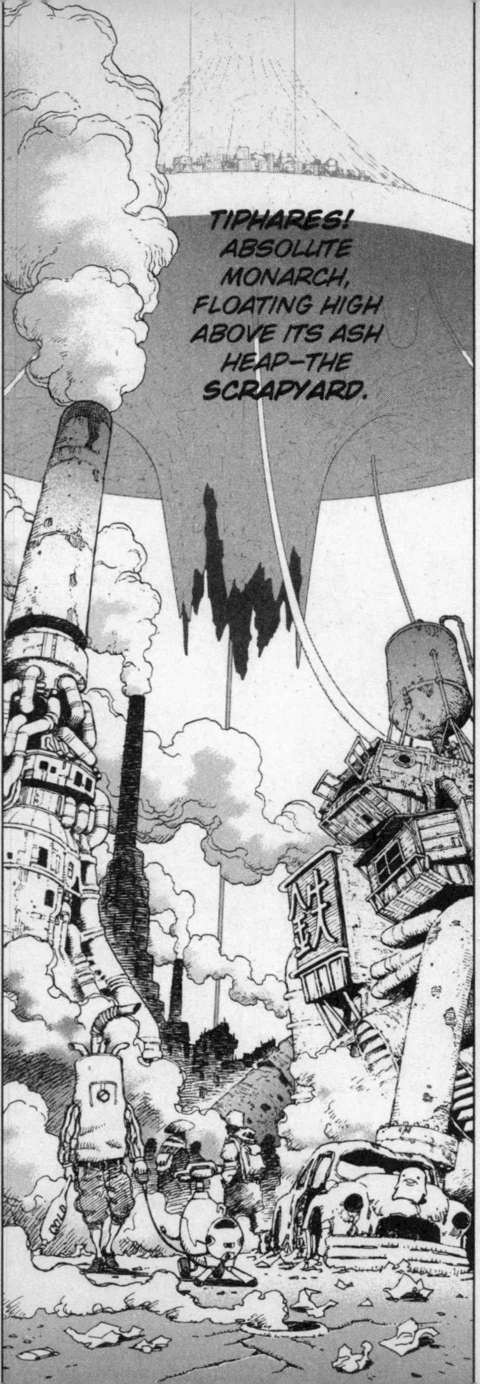
TIPHARES! ABSOLUTE MONARCH, FLOATING HIGH ABOVE ITS ASH HEAP—THE SCRAPYARD.
鉄

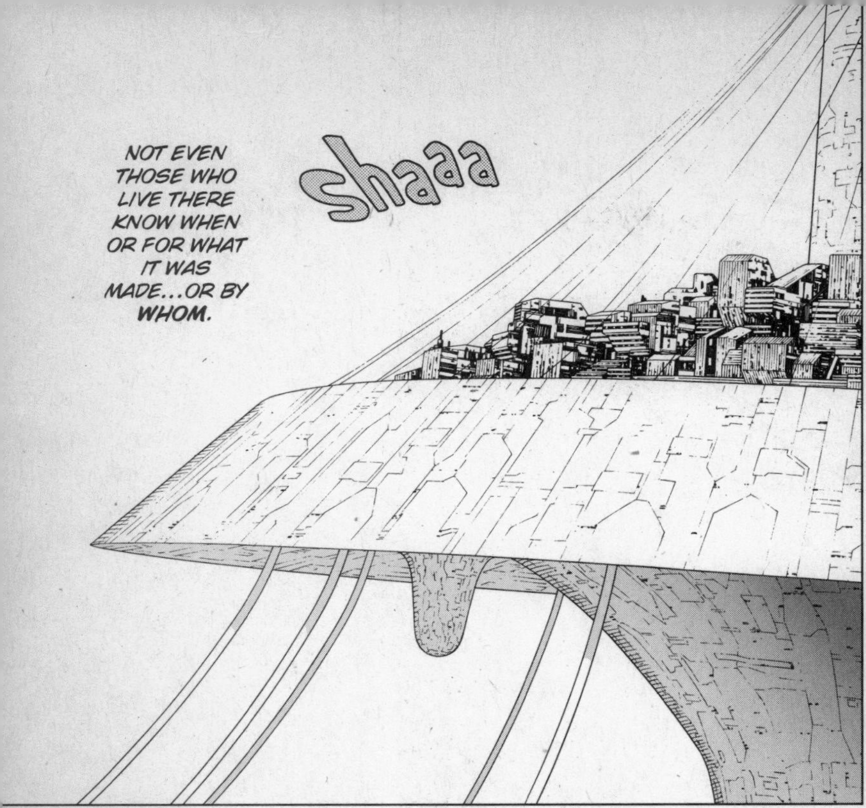
NOT EVEN THOSE WHO LIVE THERE KNOW WHEN OR FOR WHAT IT WAS MADE...OR BY WHOM.
Shaaa
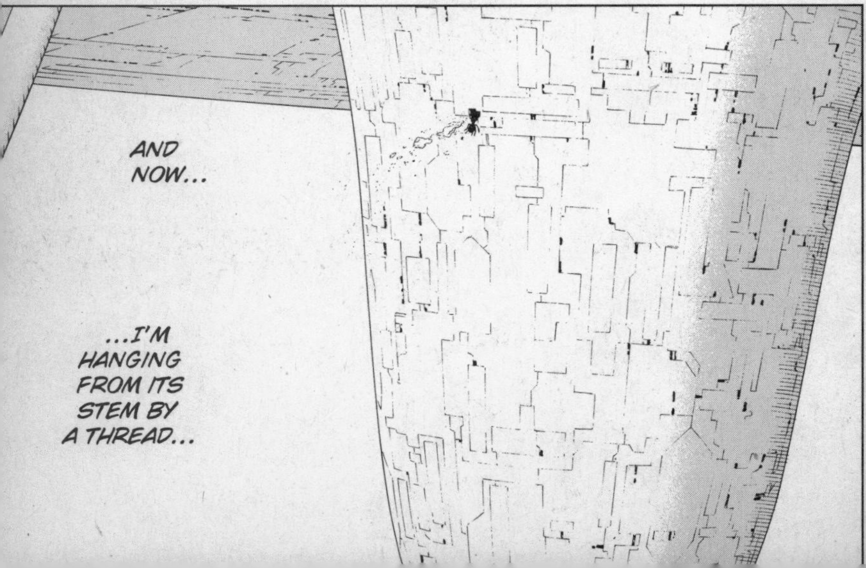
AND NOW...
...I'M HANGING FROM ITS STEM BY A THREAD...

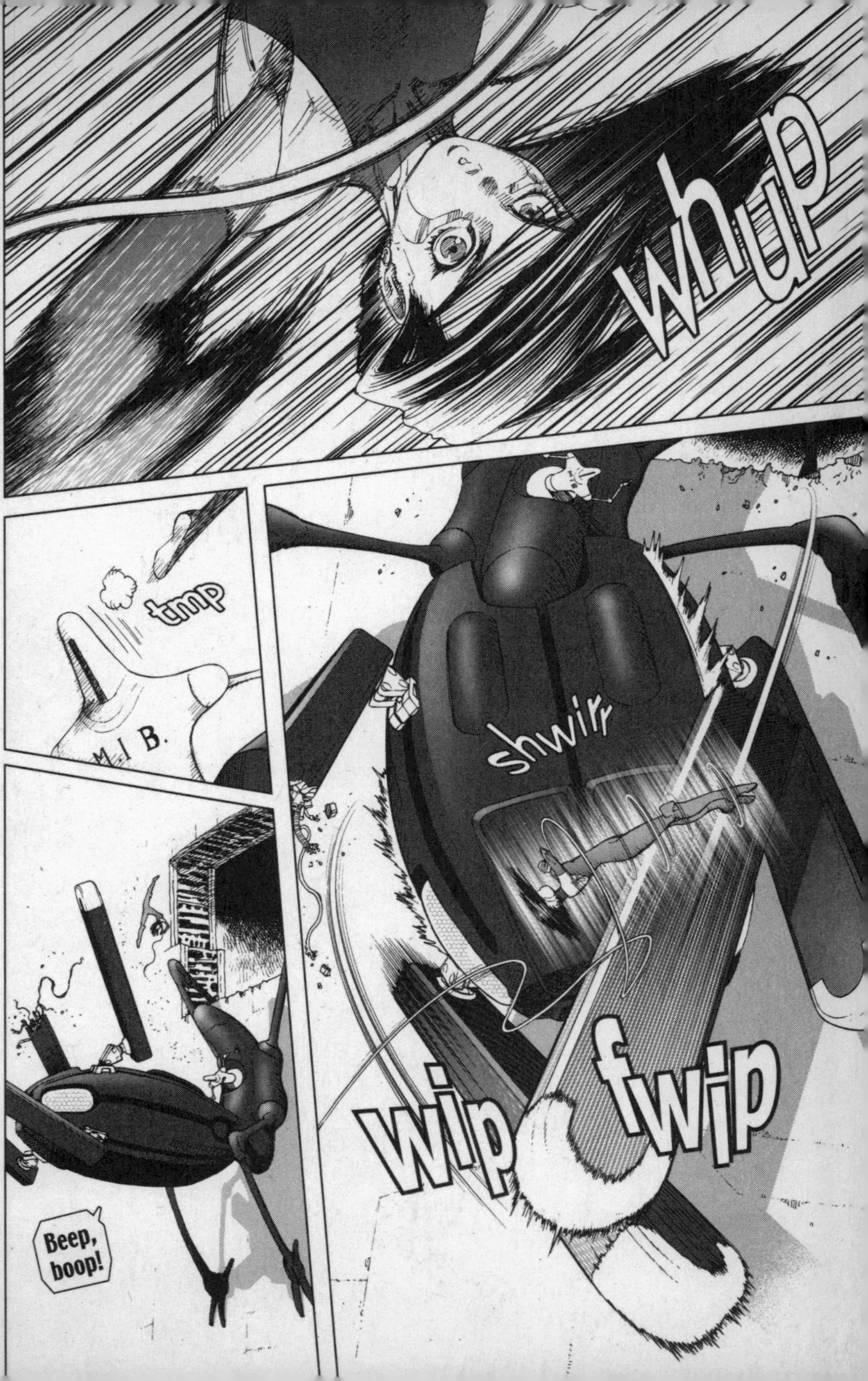
whup
shwirr
fwip
wip
tmp
M.I.B.
Beep, boop!

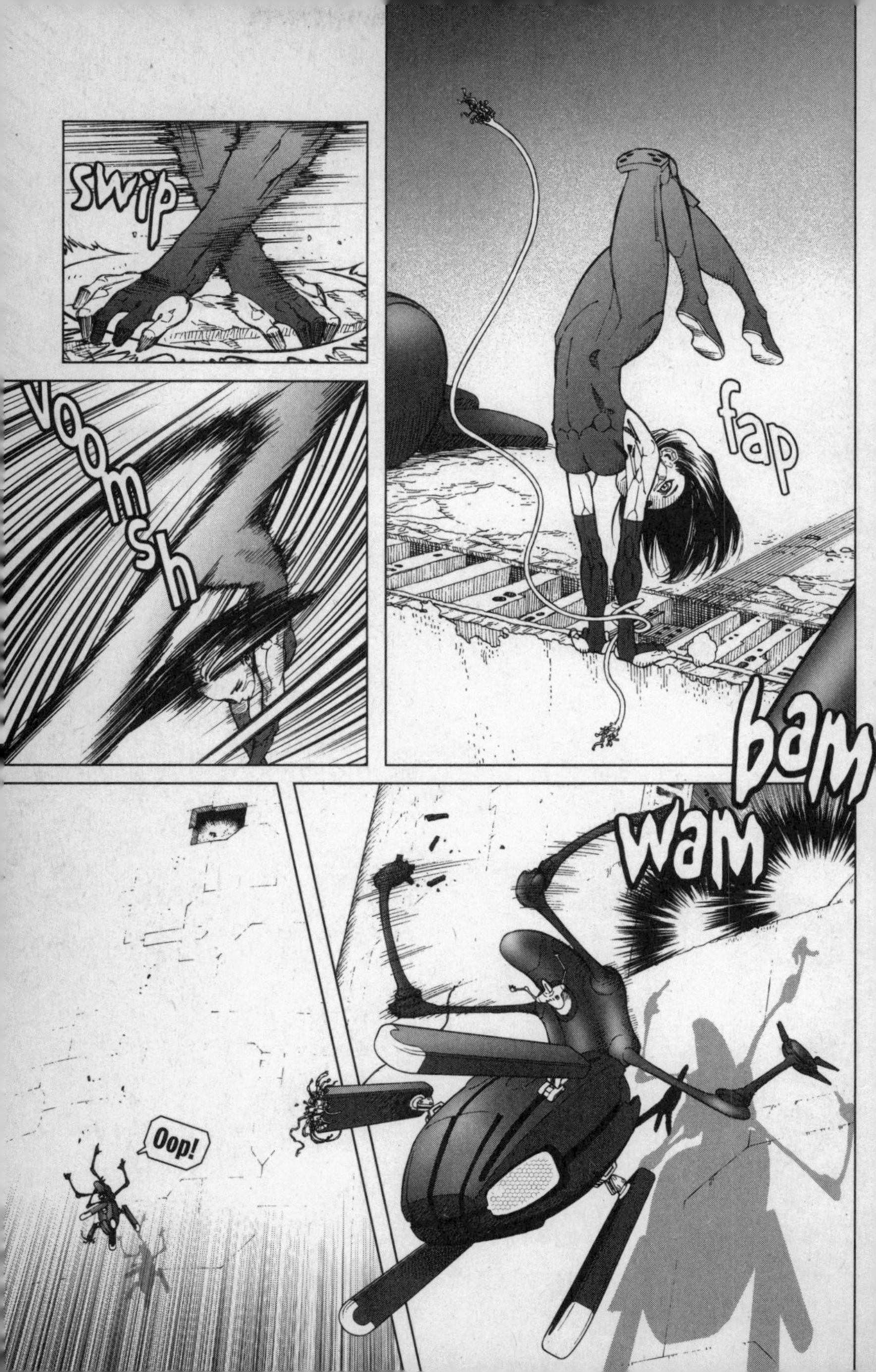
fap
swip
voomsh
bam
wam
Oop!

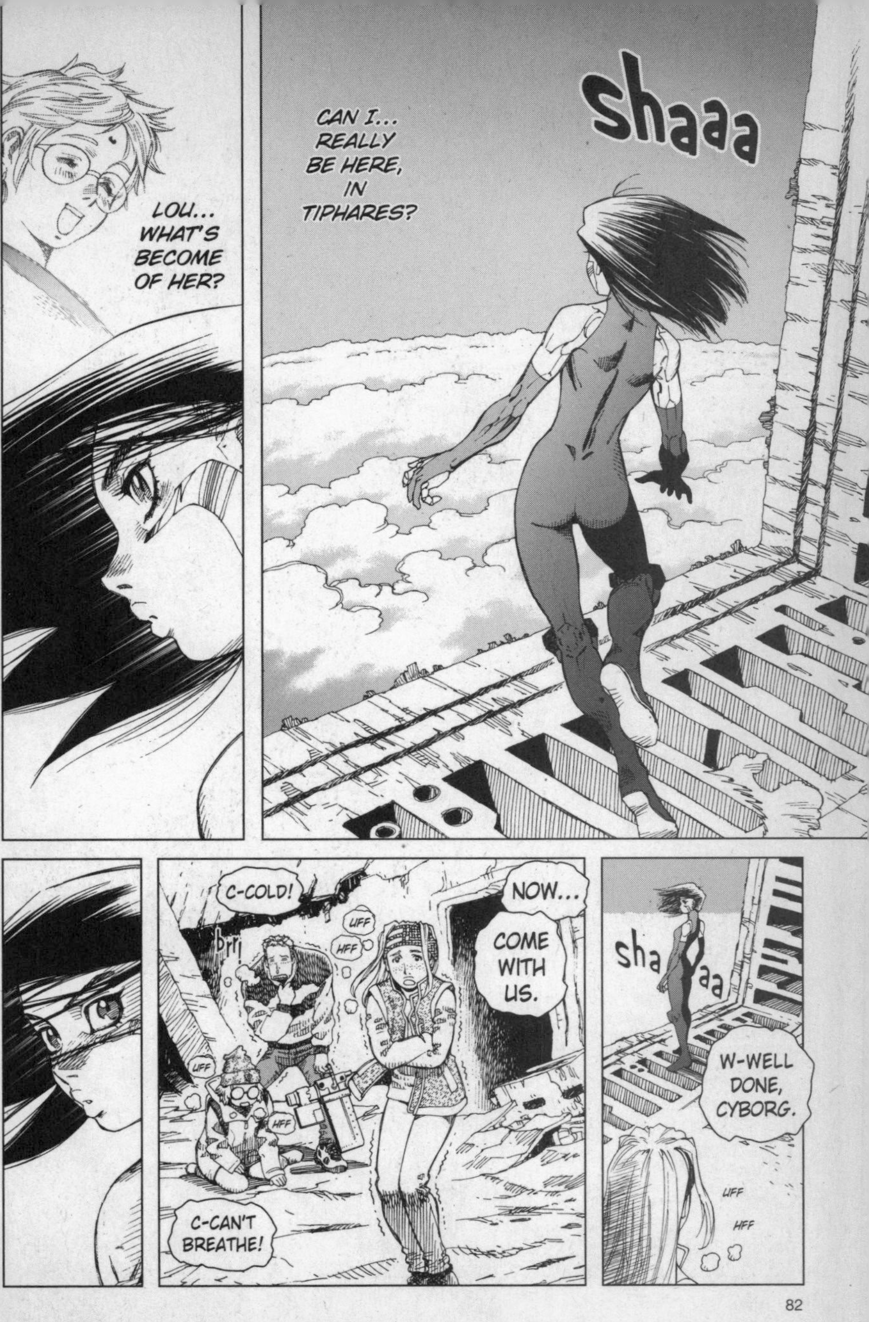
shaaa
CAN I... REALLY BE HERE, IN TIPHARES?
LOU... WHAT'S BECOME OF HER?
shaaa
W-WELL DONE, CYBORG.
UFF
HFF
NOW...
COME WITH US.
C-COLD!
brr
UFF
HFF
UFF
HFF
C-CAN'T BREATHE!

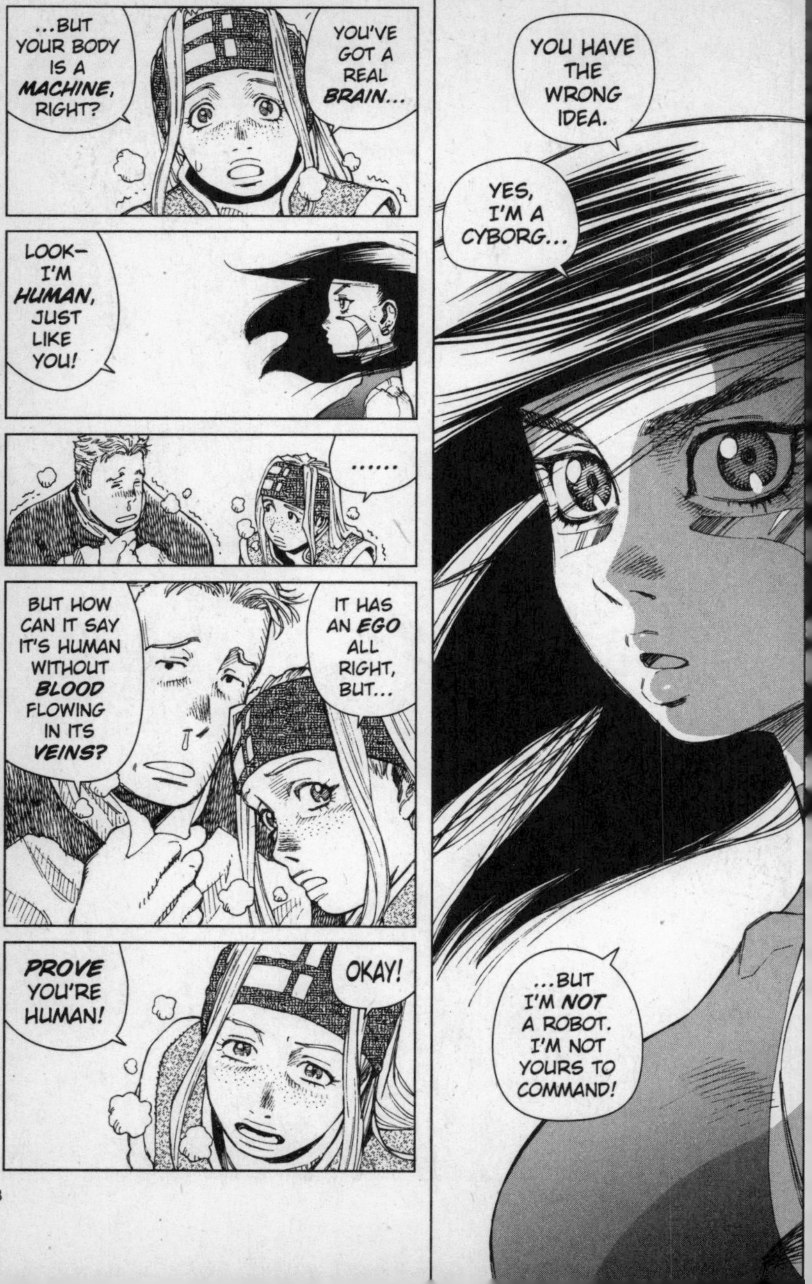
YOU'VE GOT A REAL BRAIN...
...BUT YOUR BODY IS A MACHINE, RIGHT?
LOOK— I'M HUMAN, JUST LIKE YOU!
......
IT HAS AN EGO ALL RIGHT, BUT...
BUT HOW CAN IT SAY IT'S HUMAN WITHOUT BLOOD FLOWING IN ITS VEINS?
OKAY!
PROVE YOU'RE HUMAN!
YOU HAVE THE WRONG IDEA.
YES, I'M A CYBORG...
...BUT I'M NOT A ROBOT. I'M NOT YOURS TO COMMAND!

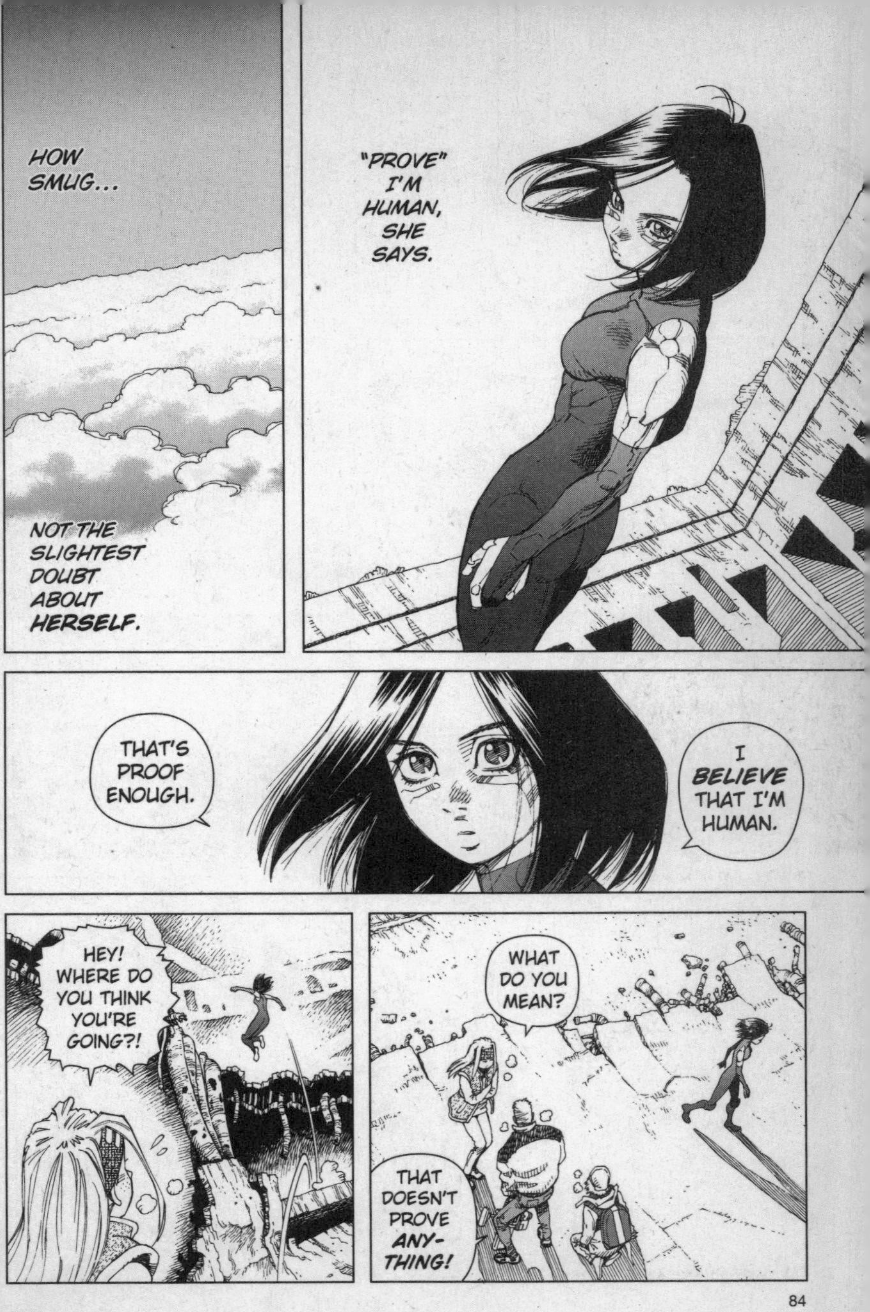
"PROVE" I'M HUMAN, SHE SAYS.
HOW SMUG...
NOT THE SLIGHTEST DOUBT ABOUT HERSELF.
I BELIEVE THAT I'M HUMAN.
THAT'S PROOF ENOUGH.
WHAT DO YOU MEAN?
THAT DOESN'T PROVE ANY-THING!
HEY! WHERE DO YOU THINK YOU'RE GOING?!

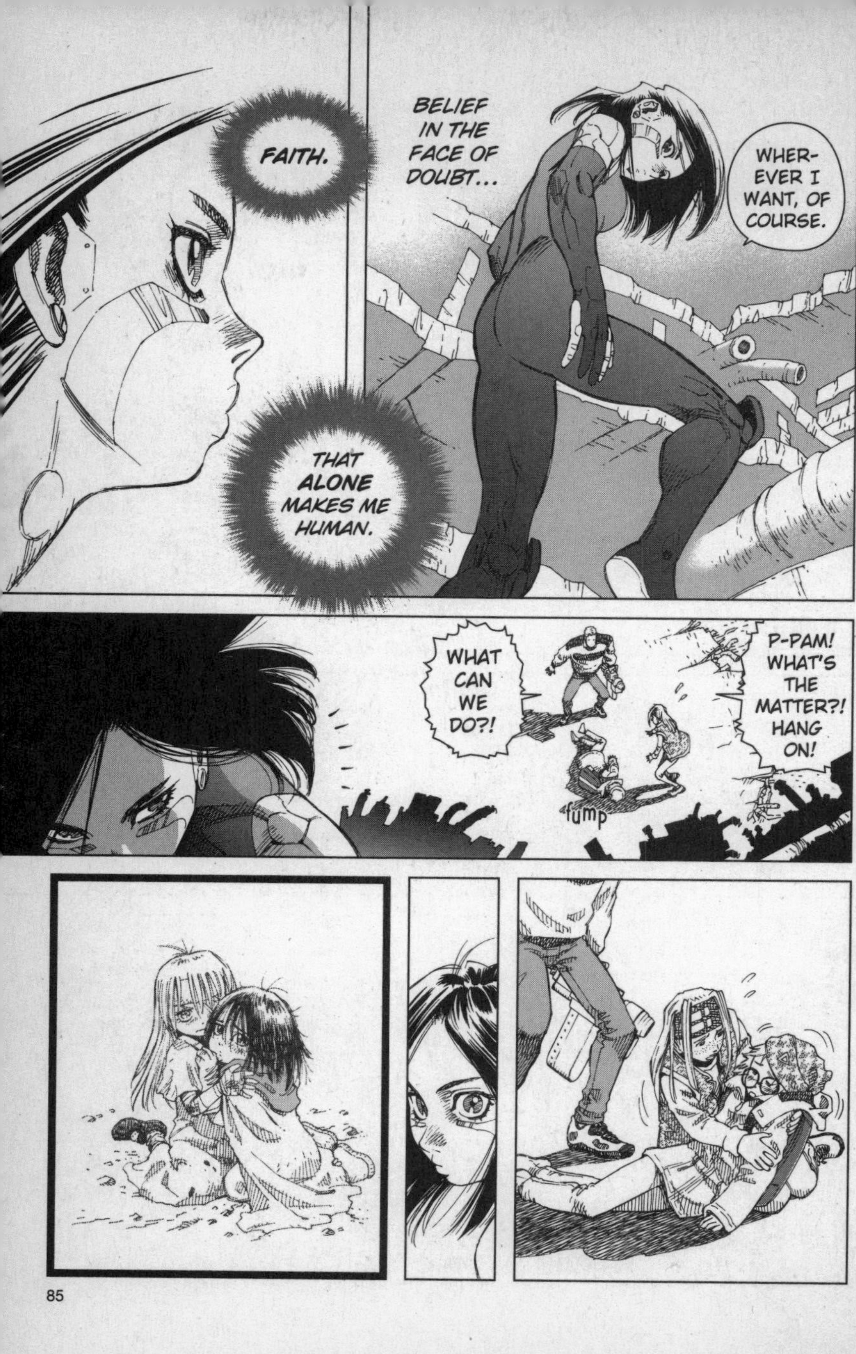
FAITH.
BELIEF IN THE FACE OF DOUBT...
THAT ALONE MAKES ME HUMAN.
WHER-EVER I WANT, OF COURSE.
WHAT CAN WE DO?!
P-PAM! WHAT'S THE MATTER?! HANG ON!
fump

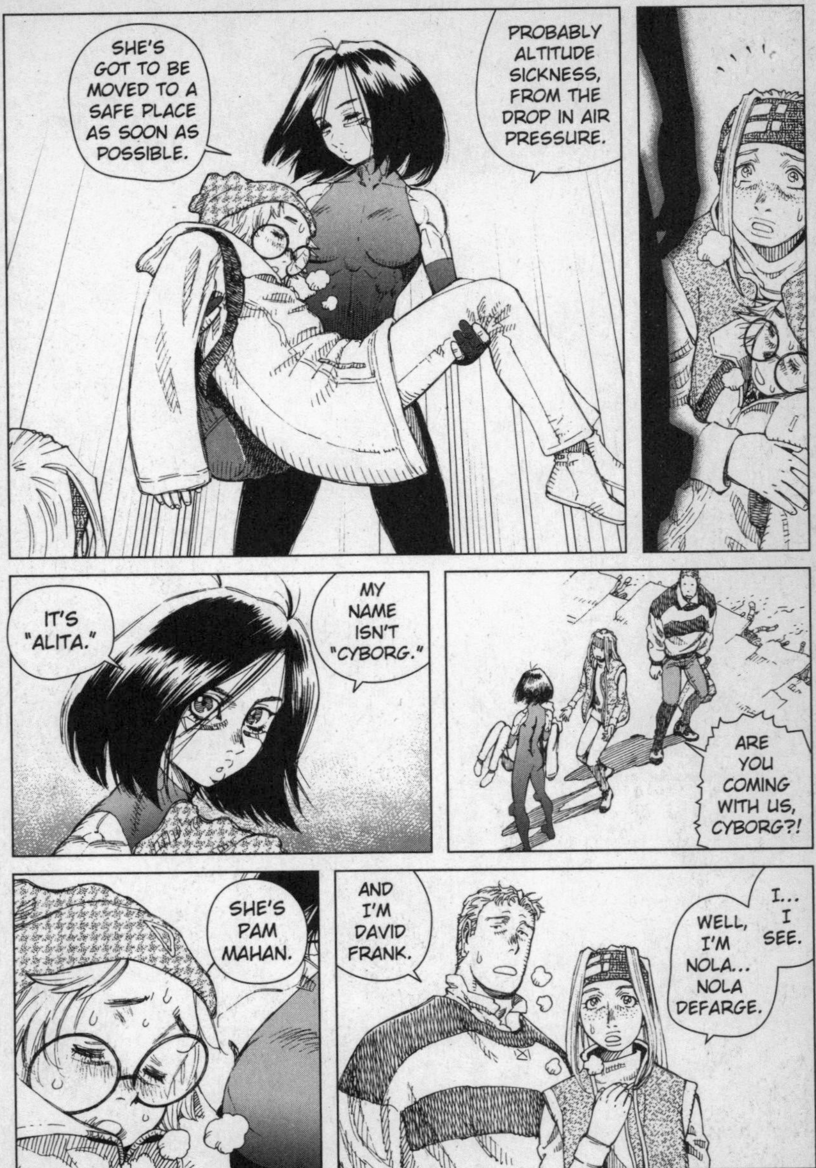
PROBABLY ALTITUDE SICKNESS, FROM THE DROP IN AIR PRESSURE.
SHE'S GOT TO BE MOVED TO A SAFE PLACE AS SOON AS POSSIBLE.
ARE YOU COMING WITH US, CYBORG?!
MY NAME ISN'T "CYBORG."
IT'S "ALITA."
I... I SEE.
WELL, I'M NOLA... NOLA DEFARGE.
AND I'M DAVID FRANK.
SHE'S PAM MAHAN.

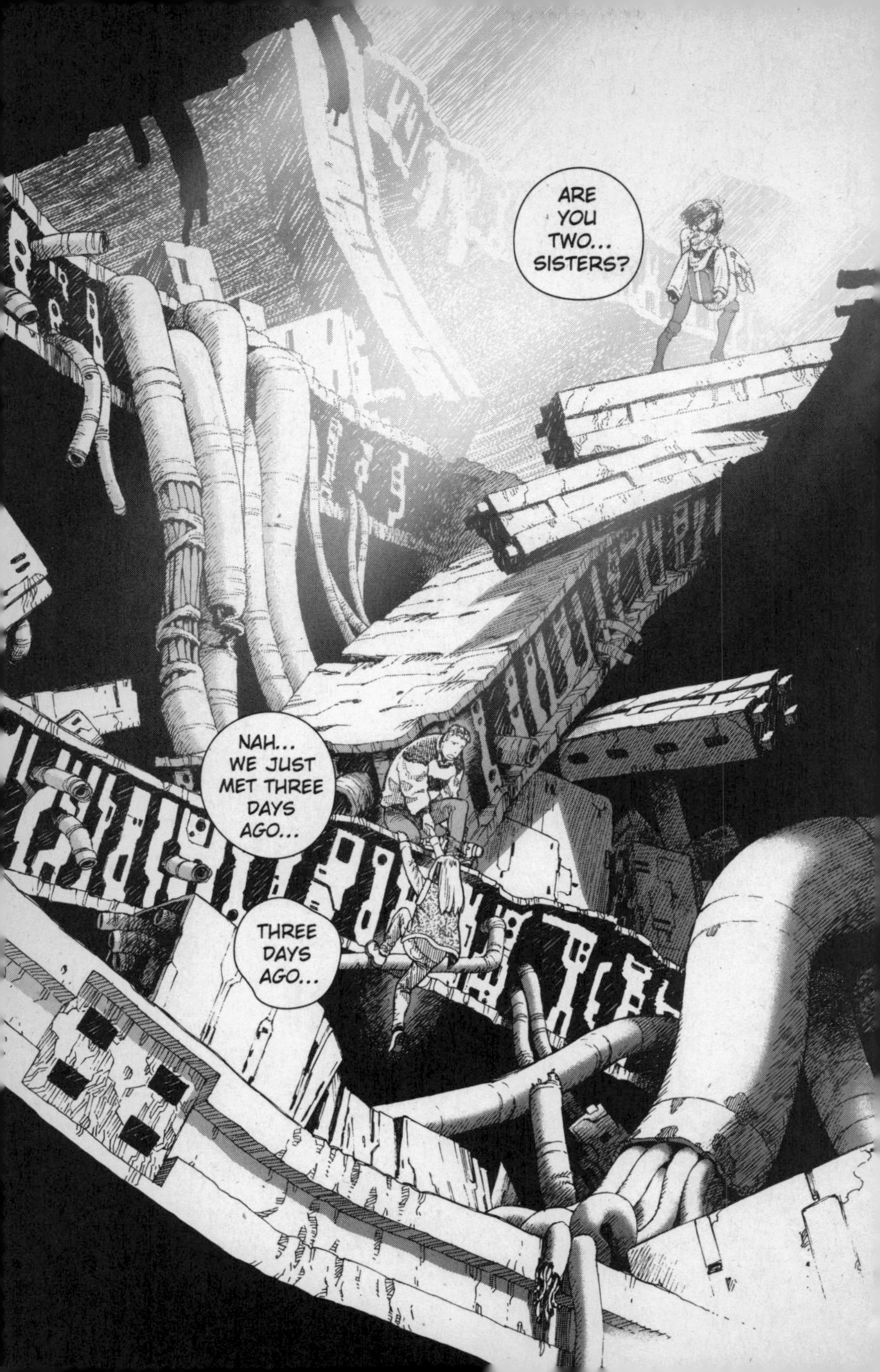
ARE YOU TWO... SISTERS?
NAH... WE JUST MET THREE DAYS AGO...
THREE DAYS AGO...

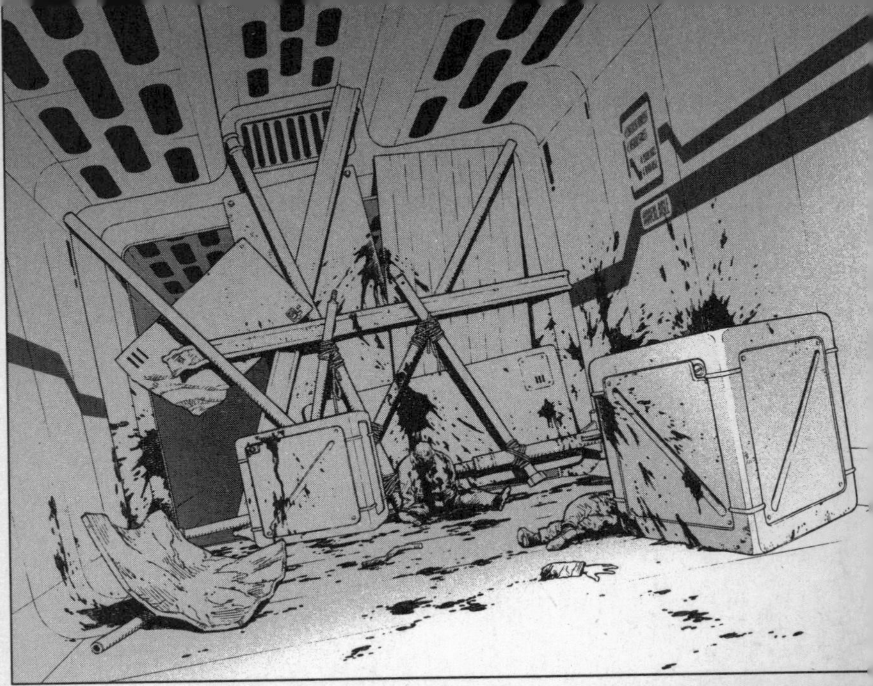
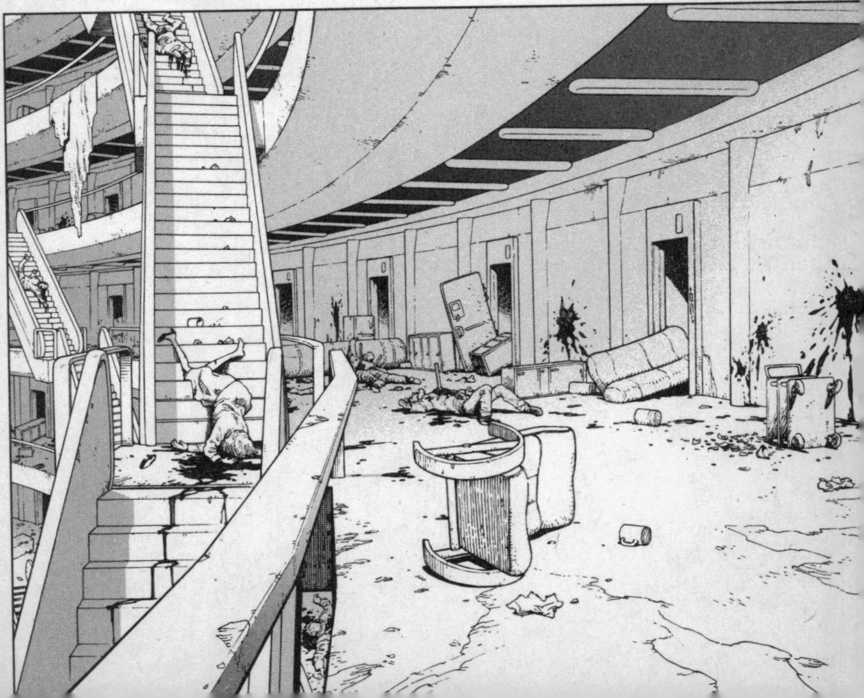

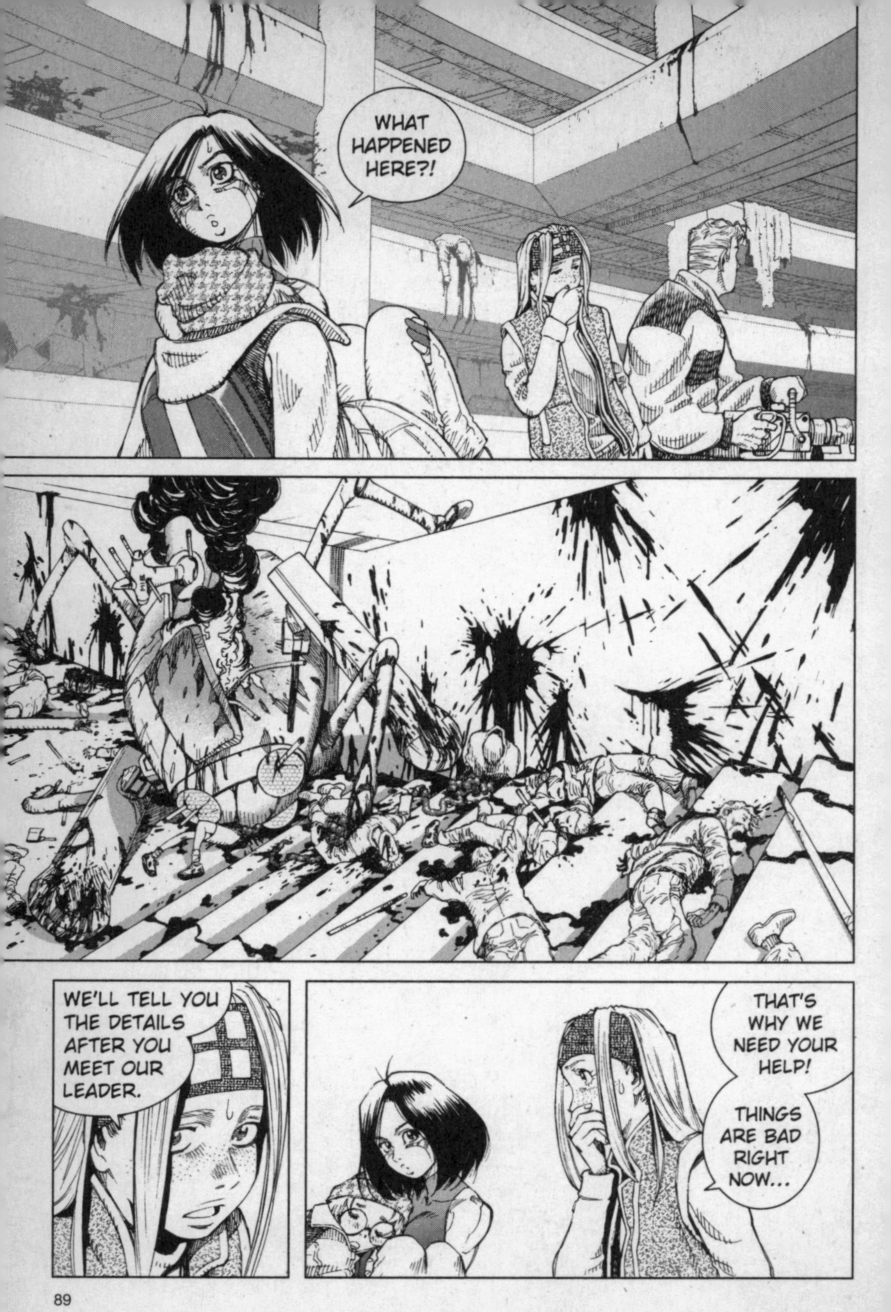
WHAT HAPPENED HERE?!
WE'LL TELL YOU THE DETAILS AFTER YOU MEET OUR LEADER.
THAT'S WHY WE NEED YOUR HELP!
THINGS ARE BAD RIGHT NOW...

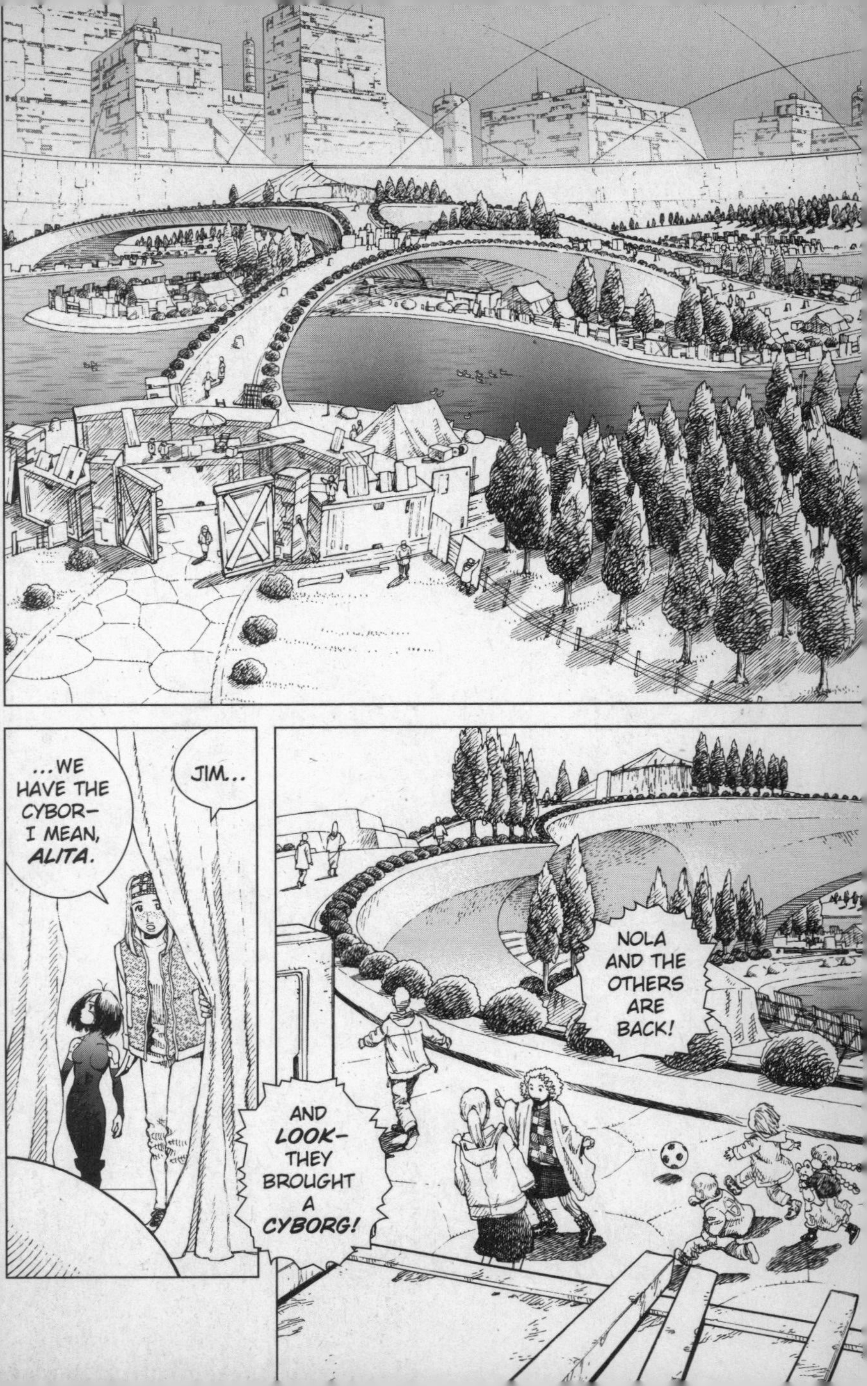
NOLA AND THE OTHERS ARE BACK!
AND LOOK—THEY BROUGHT A CYBORG!
JIM...
...WE HAVE THE CYBOR—I MEAN, ALITA.

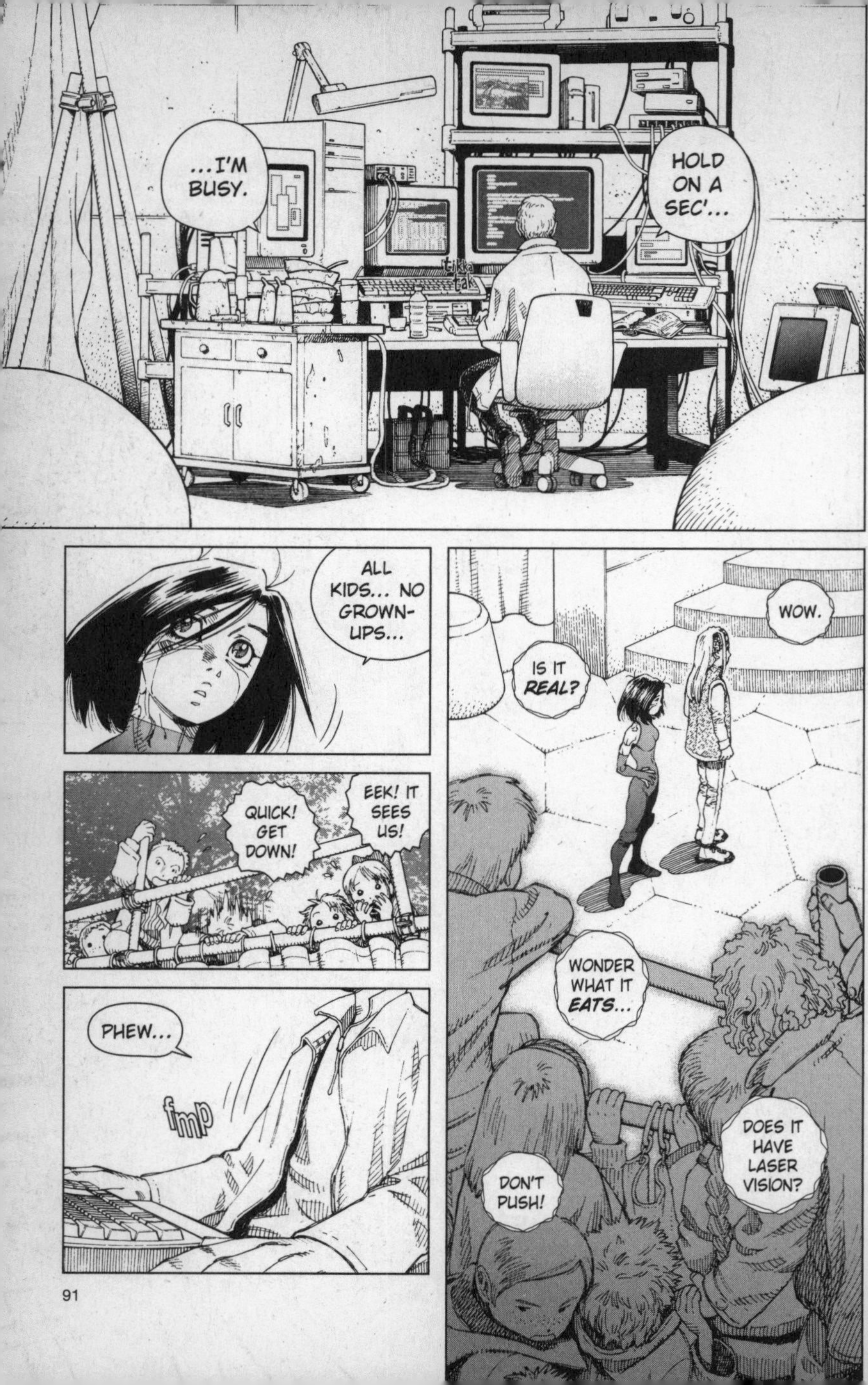
...I'M BUSY.
HOLD ON A SEC'...
tikka tak
ALL KIDS... NO GROWN-UPS...
QUICK! GET DOWN!
EEK! IT SEES US!
PHEW...
fmp
WOW.
IS IT *REAL?*
WONDER WHAT IT *EATS...*
DOES IT HAVE LASER VISION?
DON'T PUSH!

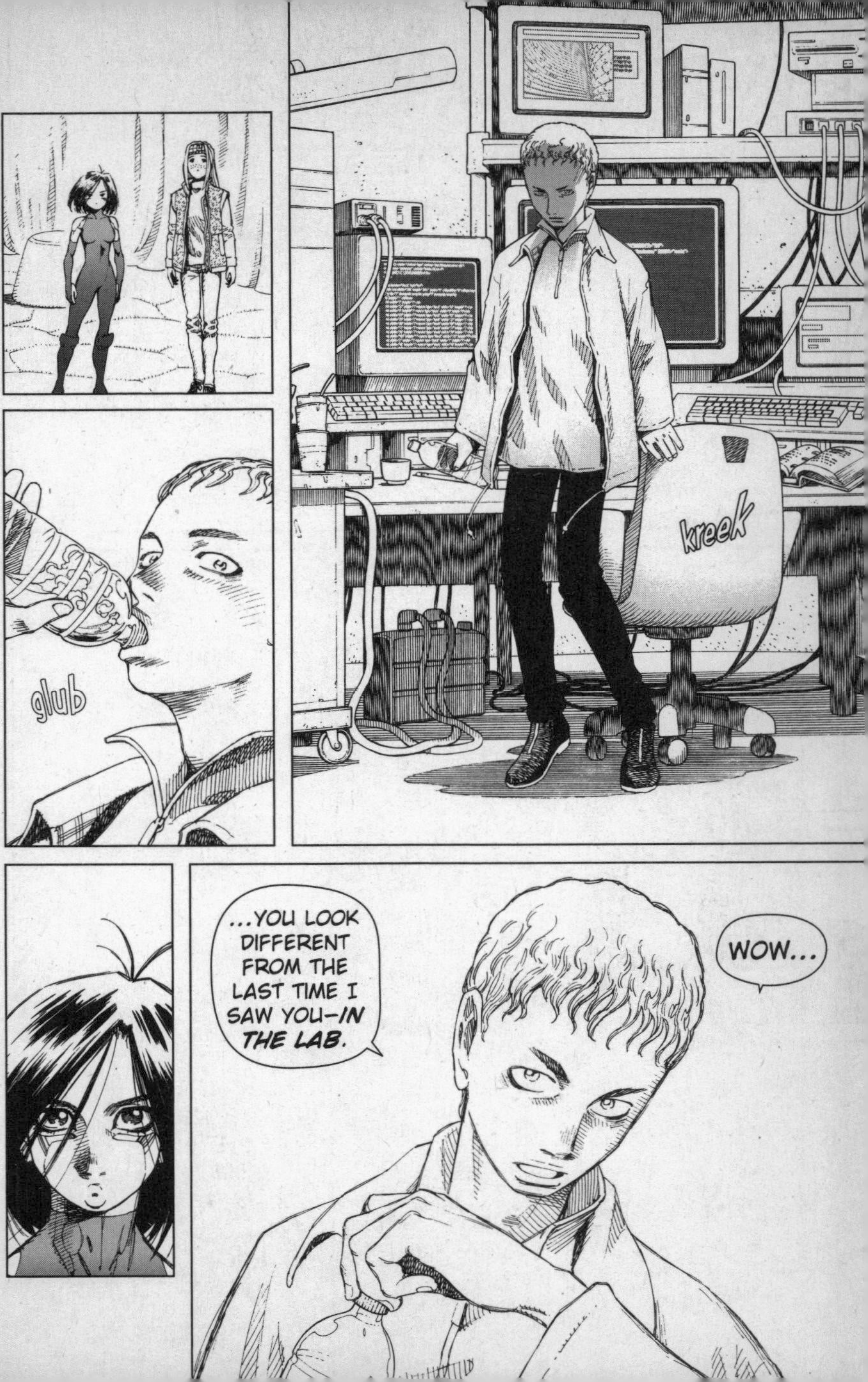
kreek
glub
WOW...
...YOU LOOK DIFFERENT FROM THE LAST TIME I SAW YOU—*IN THE LAB.*

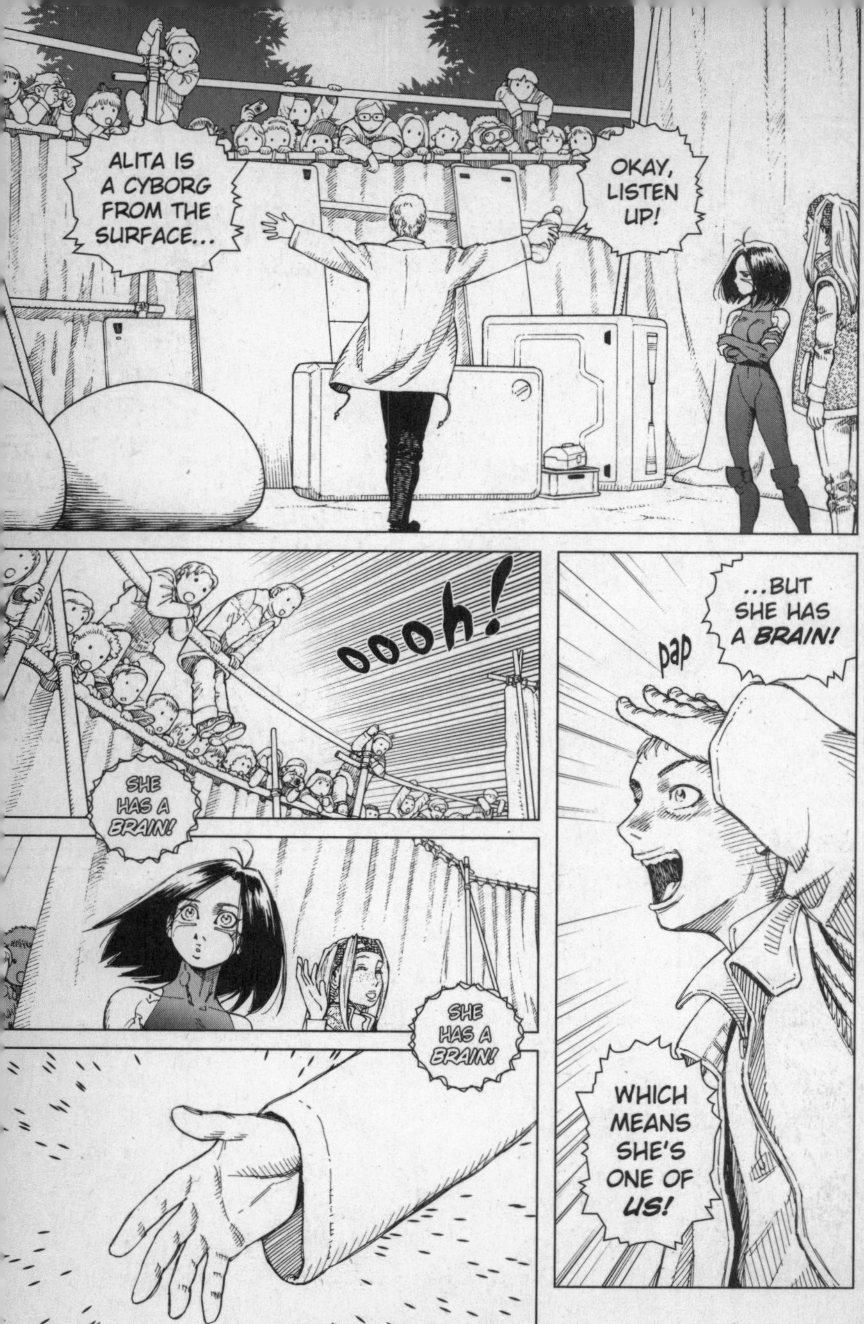
OKAY, LISTEN UP!
ALITA IS A CYBORG FROM THE SURFACE...
...BUT SHE HAS A BRAIN!
pap
WHICH MEANS SHE'S ONE OF US!
oooh!
SHE HAS A BRAIN!
SHE HAS A BRAIN!

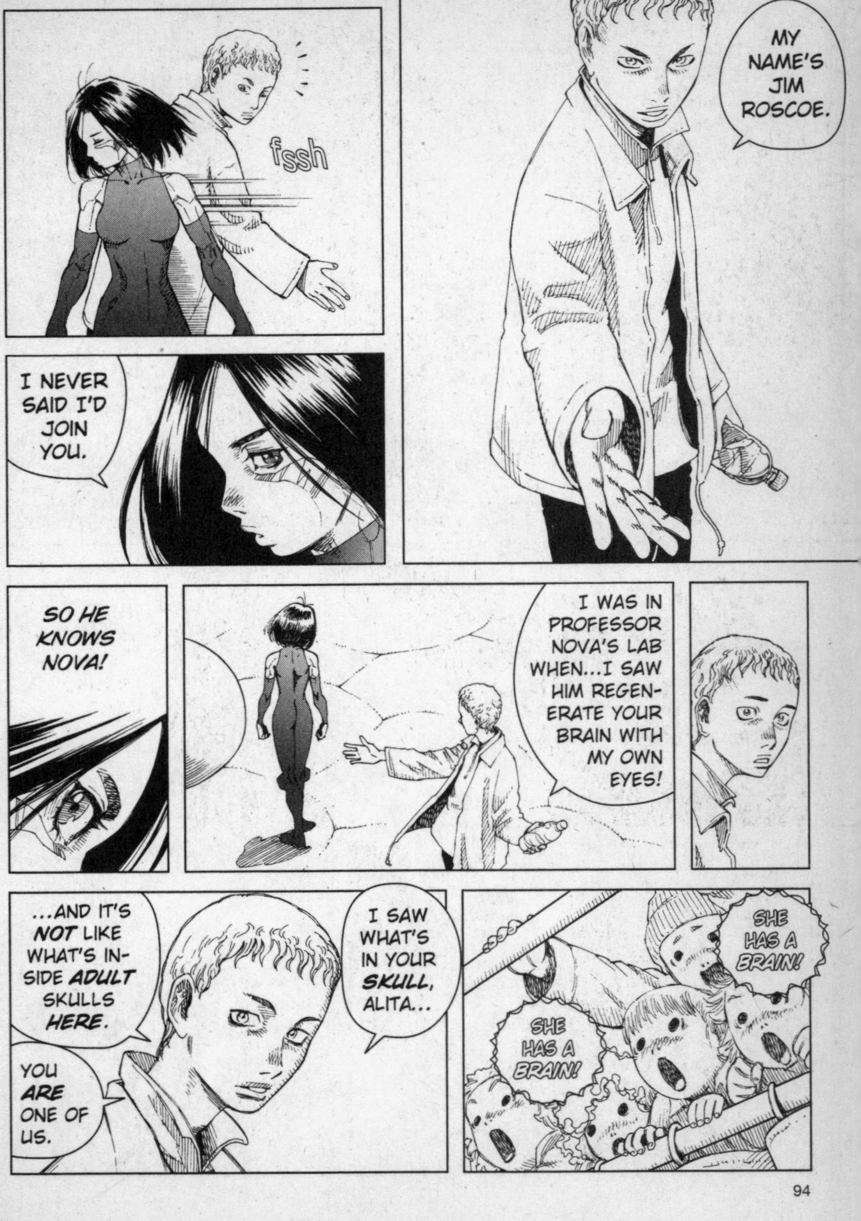
MY NAME'S JIM ROSCOE.
fssh
I NEVER SAID I'D JOIN YOU.
I WAS IN PROFESSOR NOVA'S LAB WHEN...I SAW HIM REGENERATE YOUR BRAIN WITH MY OWN EYES!
SO HE KNOWS NOVA!
SHE HAS A BRAIN!
SHE HAS A BRAIN!
I SAW WHAT'S IN YOUR SKULL, ALITA...
...AND IT'S NOT LIKE WHAT'S INSIDE ADULT SKULLS HERE.
YOU ARE ONE OF US.

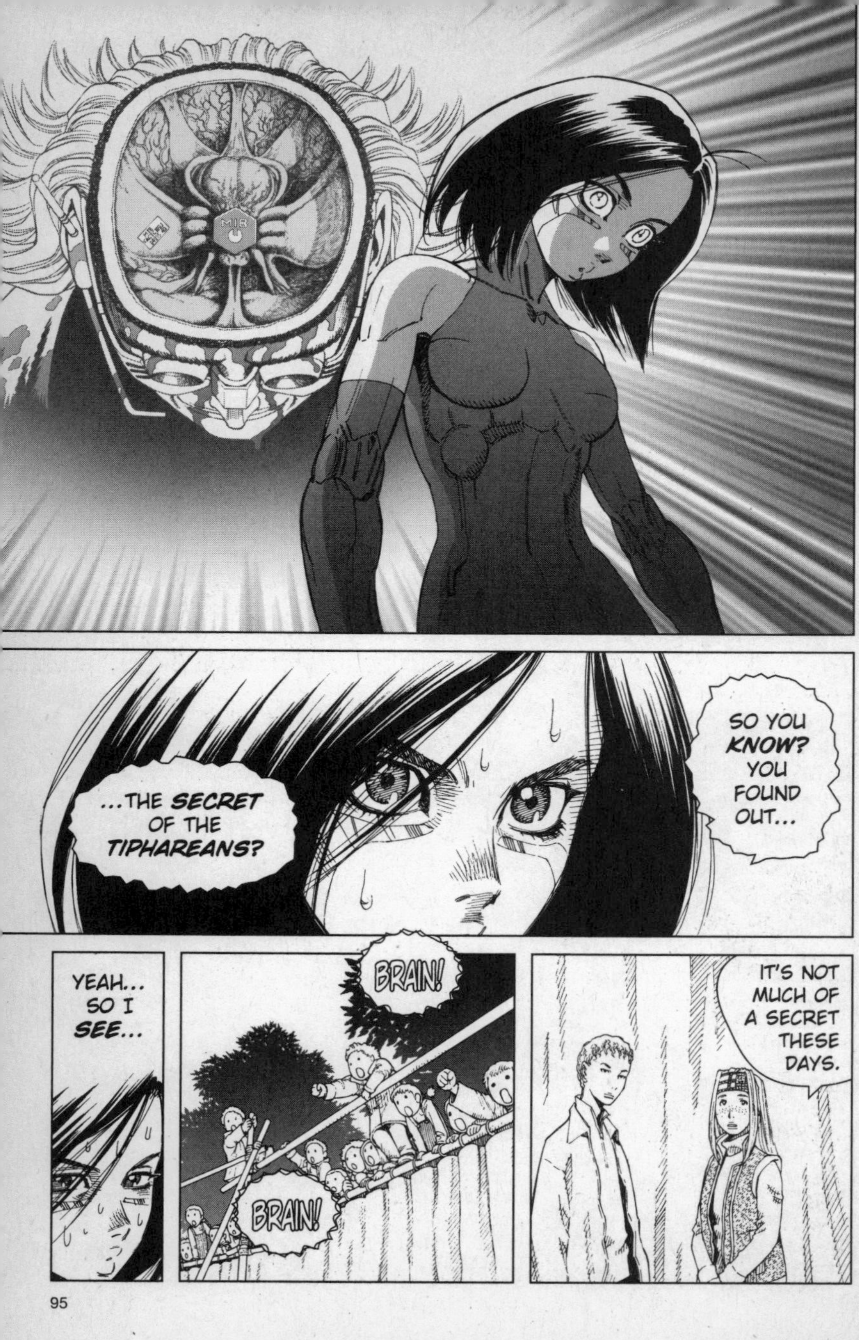
SO YOU KNOW? YOU FOUND OUT...
...THE SECRET OF THE TIPHAREANS?
IT'S NOT MUCH OF A SECRET THESE DAYS.
BRAIN!
BRAIN!
YEAH... SO I SEE...

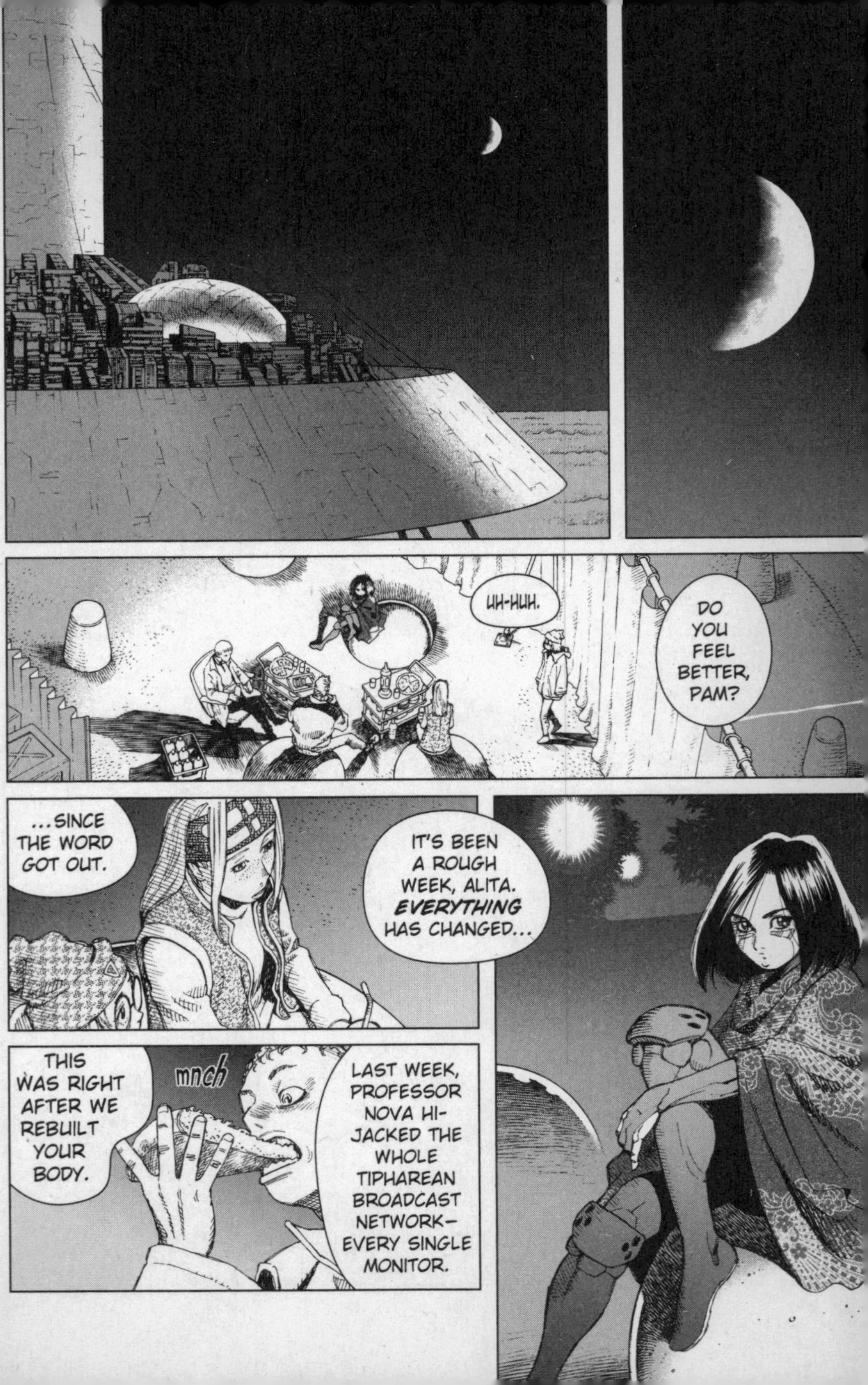
DO YOU FEEL BETTER, PAM?
UH-HUH.
IT'S BEEN A ROUGH WEEK, ALITA. EVERYTHING HAS CHANGED...
...SINCE THE WORD GOT OUT.
LAST WEEK, PROFESSOR NOVA HI-JACKED THE WHOLE TIPHAREAN BROADCAST NETWORK– EVERY SINGLE MONITOR.
mnch
THIS WAS RIGHT AFTER WE REBUILT YOUR BODY.

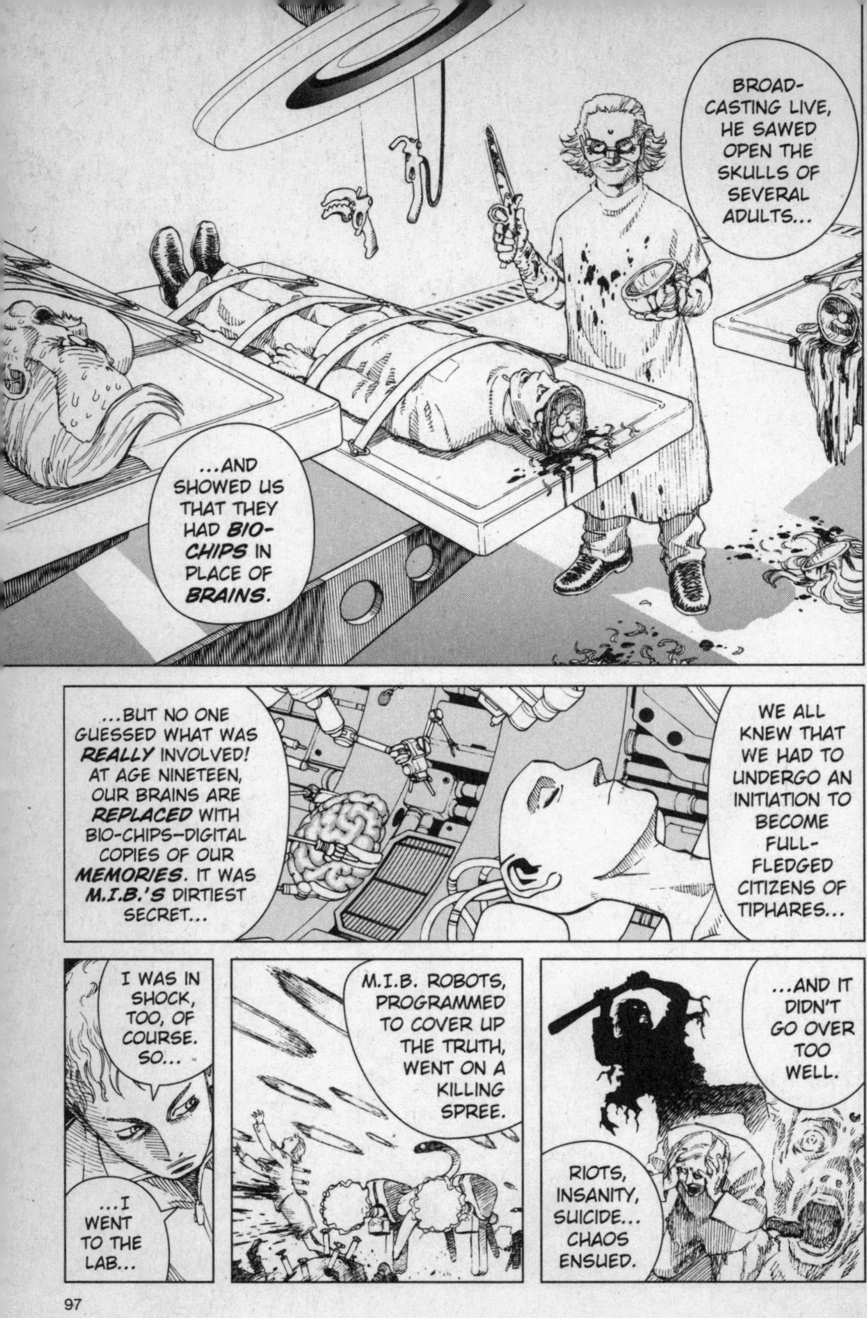
BROAD-CASTING LIVE, HE SAWED OPEN THE SKULLS OF SEVERAL ADULTS...
...AND SHOWED US THAT THEY HAD *BIO-CHIPS* IN PLACE OF *BRAINS*.
WE ALL KNEW THAT WE HAD TO UNDERGO AN INITIATION TO BECOME FULL-FLEDGED CITIZENS OF TIPHARES...
...BUT NO ONE GUESSED WHAT WAS *REALLY* INVOLVED! AT AGE NINETEEN, OUR BRAINS ARE *REPLACED* WITH BIO-CHIPS—DIGITAL COPIES OF OUR *MEMORIES*. IT WAS *M.I.B.'S* DIRTIEST SECRET...
...AND IT DIDN'T GO OVER TOO WELL.
RIOTS, INSANITY, SUICIDE... CHAOS ENSUED.
M.I.B. ROBOTS, PROGRAMMED TO COVER UP THE TRUTH, WENT ON A KILLING SPREE.
I WAS IN SHOCK, TOO, OF COURSE. SO...
...I WENT TO THE LAB...

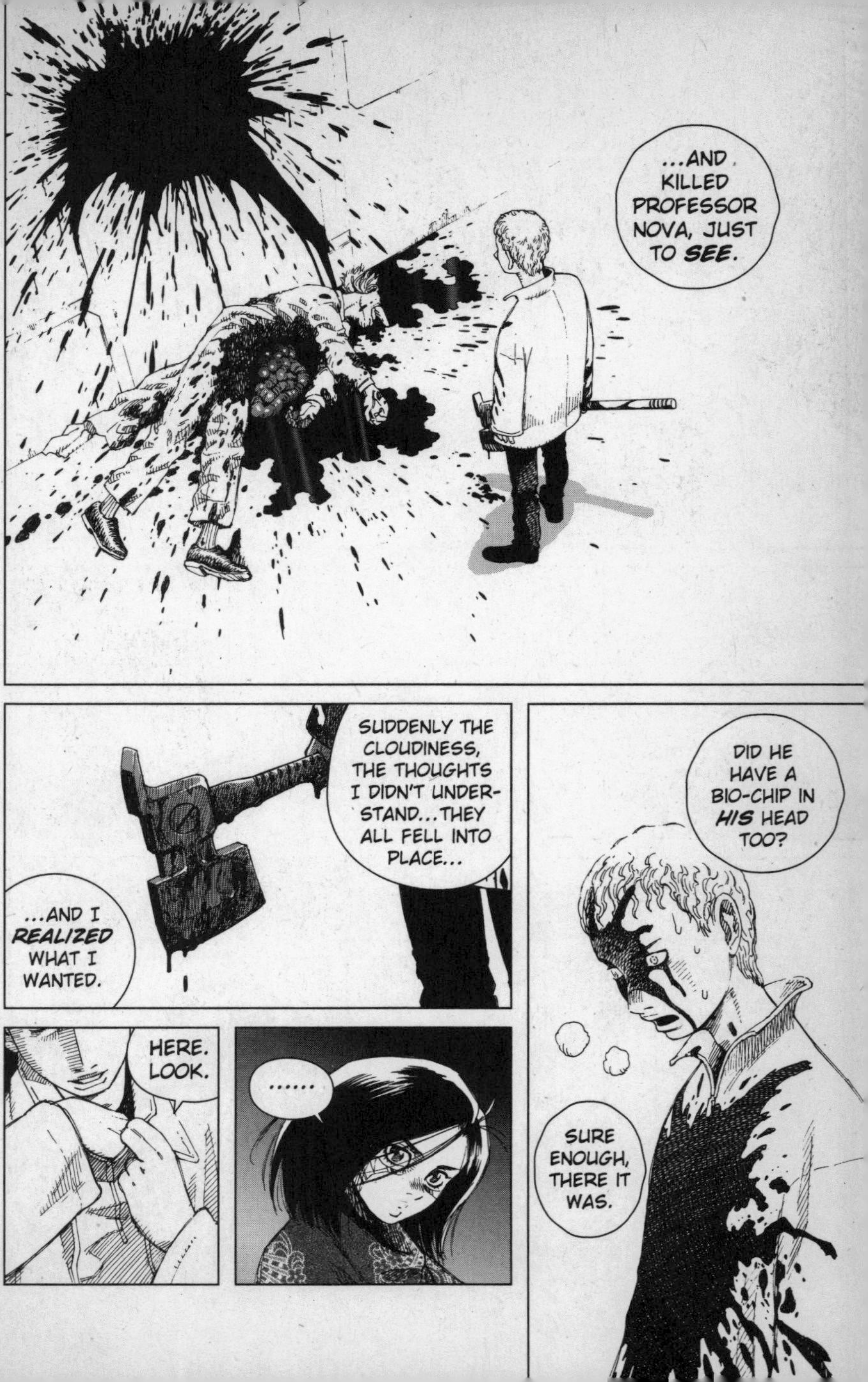
...AND KILLED PROFESSOR NOVA, JUST TO SEE.
SUDDENLY THE CLOUDINESS, THE THOUGHTS I DIDN'T UNDER-STAND...THEY ALL FELL INTO PLACE...
...AND I REALIZED WHAT I WANTED.
HERE. LOOK.
......
DID HE HAVE A BIO-CHIP IN HIS HEAD TOO?
SURE ENOUGH, THERE IT WAS.

THE PROFESSOR'S BIO-CHIPS. THEY'RE MINE NOW.

THE SECOND ONE IS THE BACKUP FROM HIS STOMACH...

MIB

Wink

WE HAVE 235 CHILDREN IN THIS STRONG-HOLD...

NO. GIMME ONE.

EIGHTY PERCENT OF ALL TIPHARES LOST IN *ONE WEEK*...

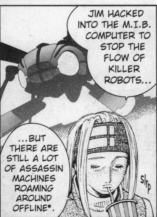

JIM HACKED INTO THE M.I.B. COMPUTER TO STOP THE FLOW OF KILLER ROBOTS...

...BUT THERE ARE STILL A LOT OF ASSASSIN MACHINES ROAMING AROUND OFFLINE*.

slrp

OUR SCOUTS SAY 4000 SANE ADULTS SURVIVE ON THE OTHER SIDE OF TIPHARES.

*Offline: cut off from central systems but functioning independently.

99

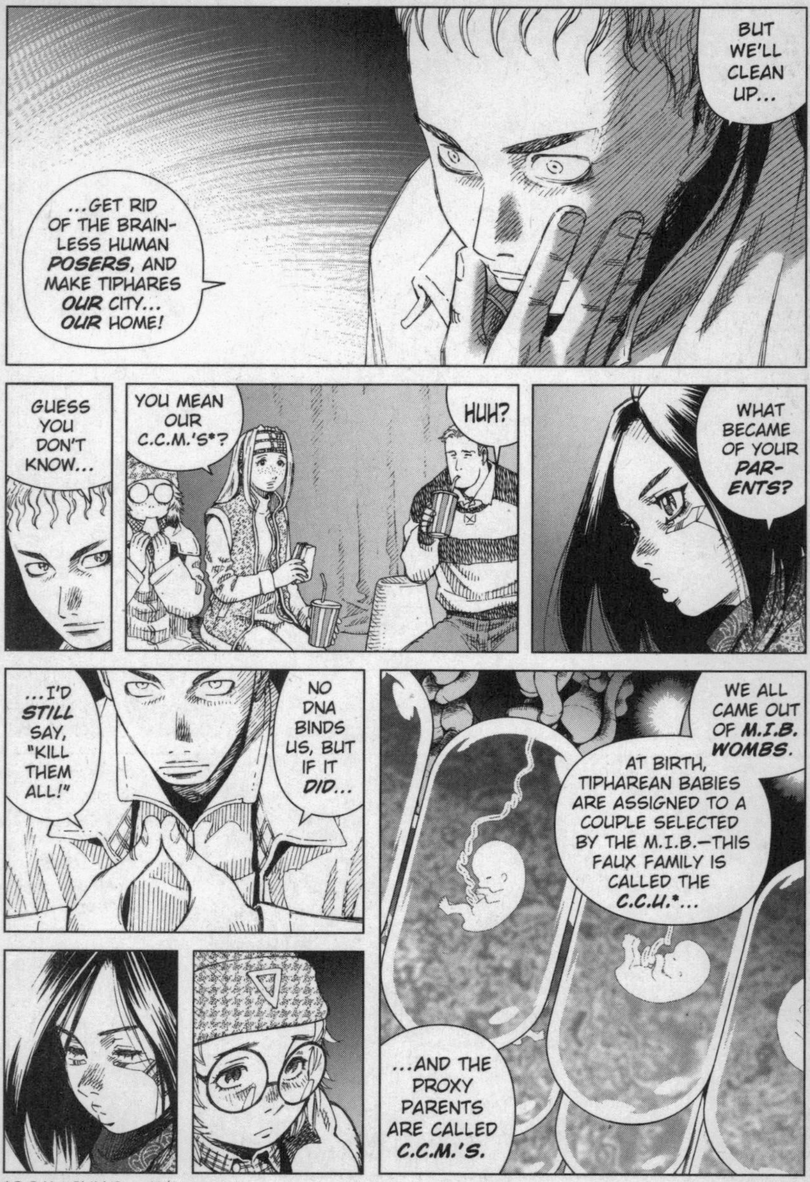
BUT WE'LL CLEAN UP...
...GET RID OF THE BRAIN-LESS HUMAN POSERS, AND MAKE TIPHARES OUR CITY... OUR HOME!
WHAT BECAME OF YOUR PAR-ENTS?
HUH?
YOU MEAN OUR C.C.M.'S*?
GUESS YOU DON'T KNOW...
WE ALL CAME OUT OF M.I.B. WOMBS.
AT BIRTH, TIPHAREAN BABIES ARE ASSIGNED TO A COUPLE SELECTED BY THE M.I.B.—THIS FAUX FAMILY IS CALLED THE C.C.U.*...
...AND THE PROXY PARENTS ARE CALLED C.C.M.'S.
NO DNA BINDS US, BUT IF IT DID...
...I'D STILL SAY, "KILL THEM ALL!"

*C.C.M.: Child Care Manager
*C.C.U.: Child Care Unit

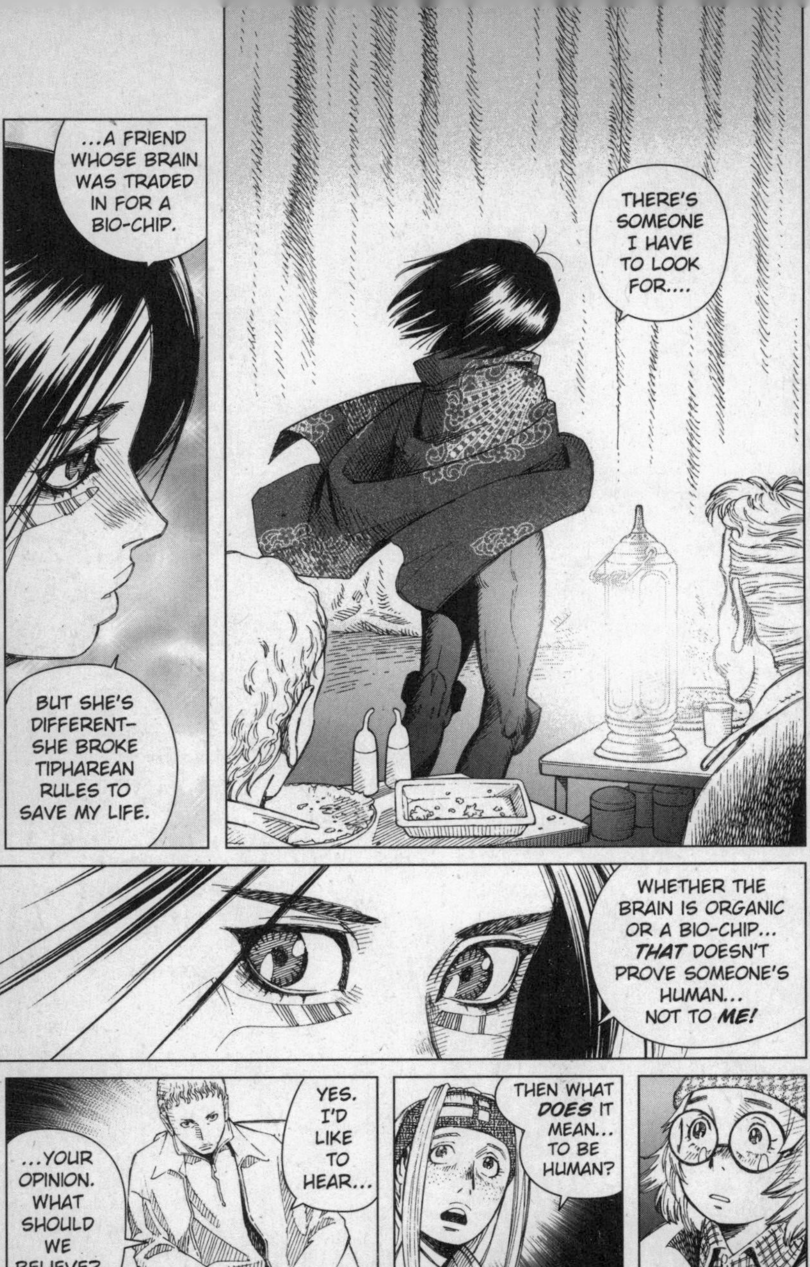
THERE'S SOMEONE I HAVE TO LOOK FOR....
...A FRIEND WHOSE BRAIN WAS TRADED IN FOR A BIO-CHIP.
BUT SHE'S DIFFERENT- SHE BROKE TIPHAREAN RULES TO SAVE MY LIFE.
WHETHER THE BRAIN IS ORGANIC OR A BIO-CHIP... *THAT* DOESN'T PROVE SOMEONE'S HUMAN... NOT TO ***ME!***
THEN WHAT ***DOES*** IT MEAN... TO BE HUMAN?
YES. I'D LIKE TO HEAR...
...YOUR OPINION. WHAT SHOULD WE BELIEVE?

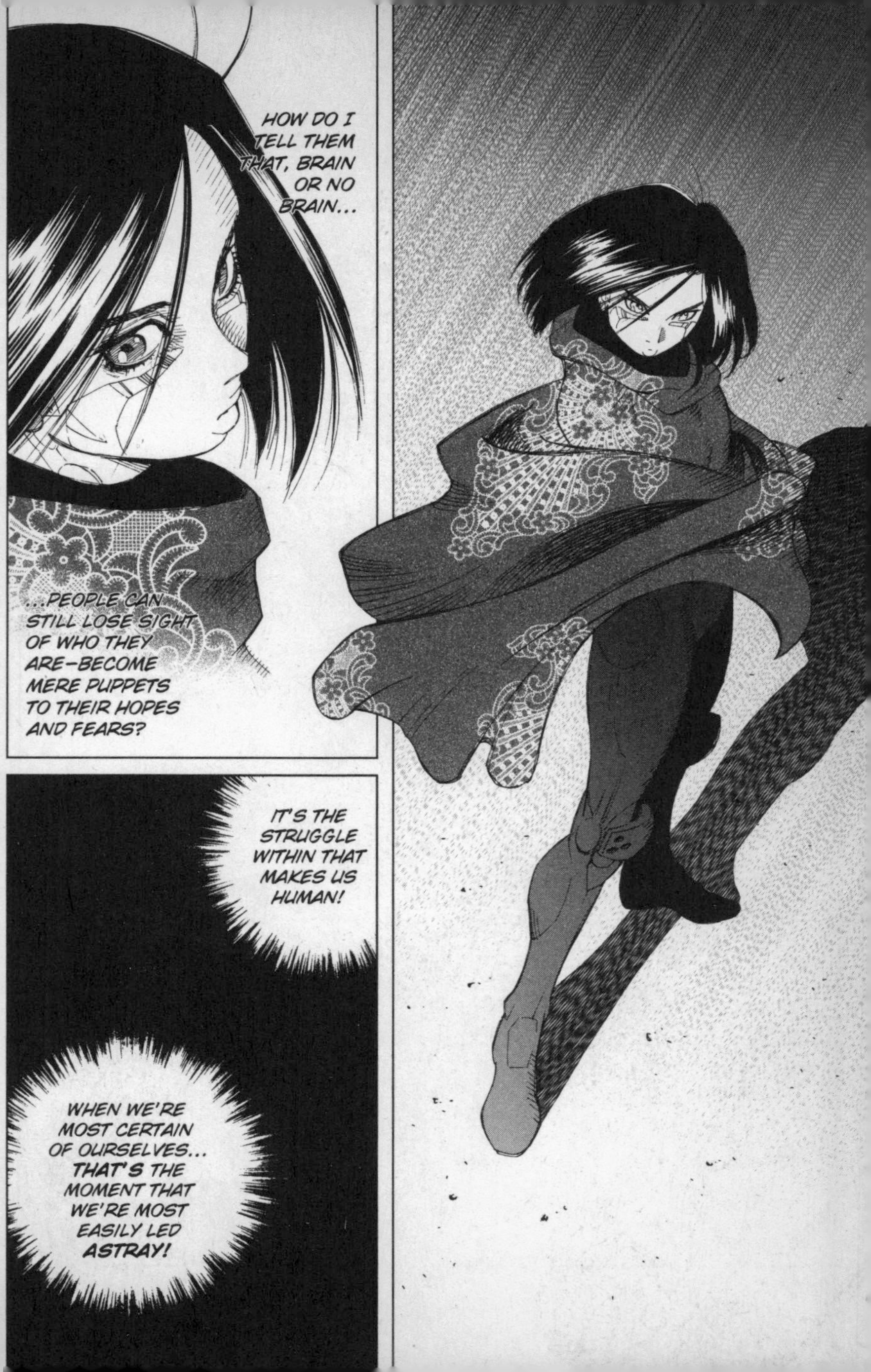
HOW DO I TELL THEM THAT, BRAIN OR NO BRAIN...
...PEOPLE CAN STILL LOSE SIGHT OF WHO THEY ARE—BECOME MERE PUPPETS TO THEIR HOPES AND FEARS?
IT'S THE STRUGGLE WITHIN THAT MAKES US HUMAN!
WHEN WE'RE MOST CERTAIN OF OURSELVES... THAT'S THE MOMENT THAT WE'RE MOST EASILY LED ASTRAY!

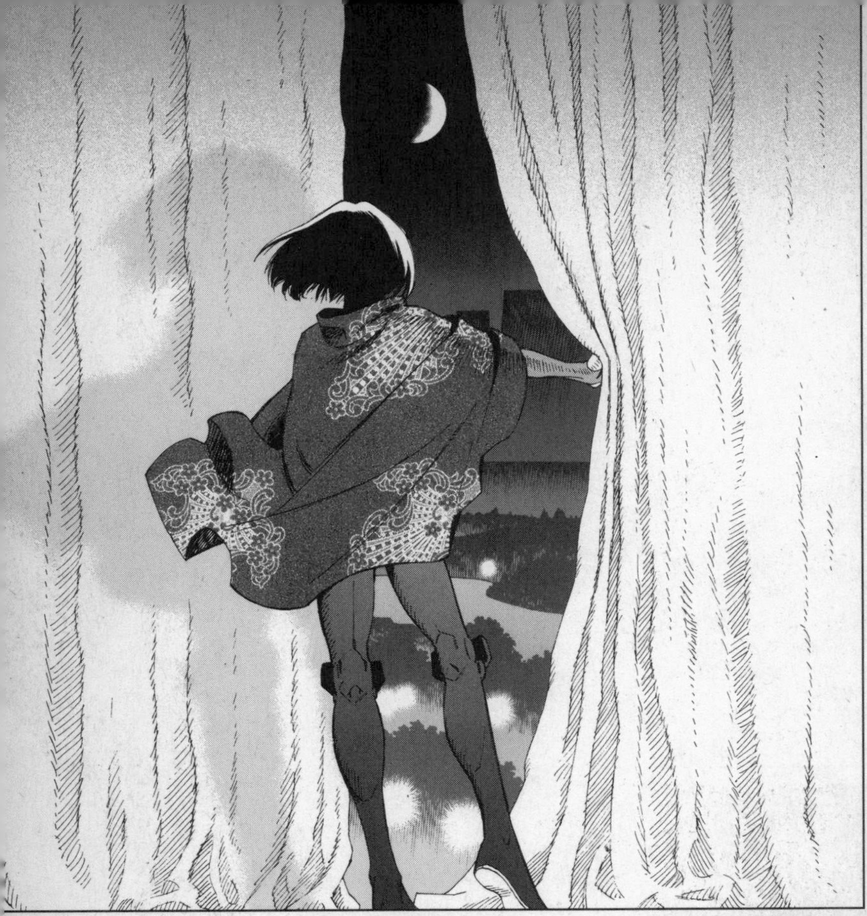
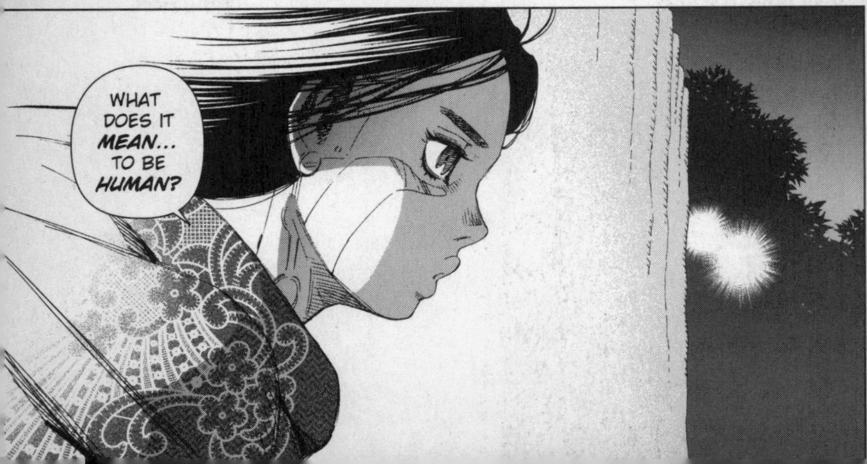
WHAT DOES IT *MEAN*... TO BE *HUMAN?*

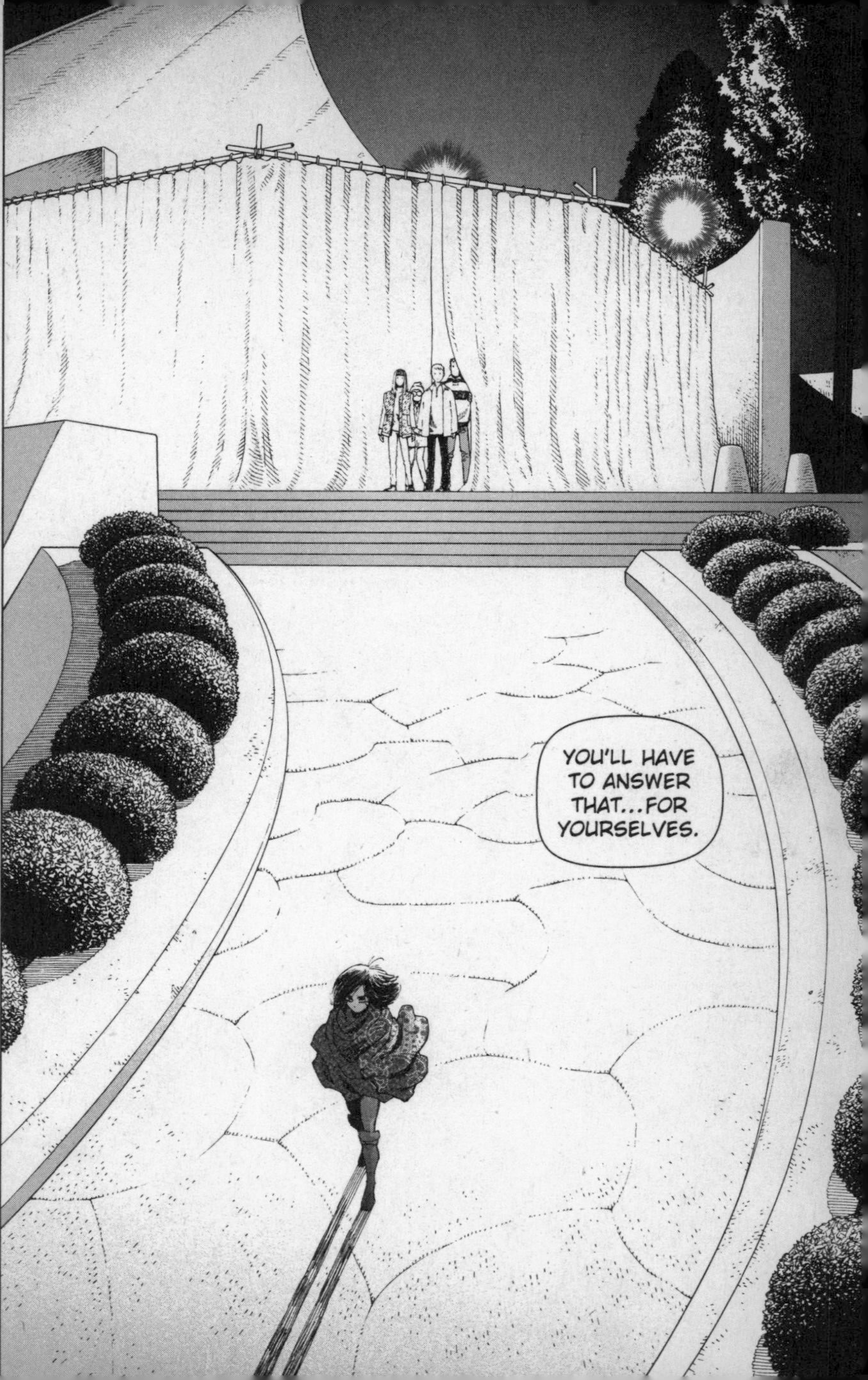
YOU'LL HAVE TO ANSWER THAT...FOR YOURSELVES.

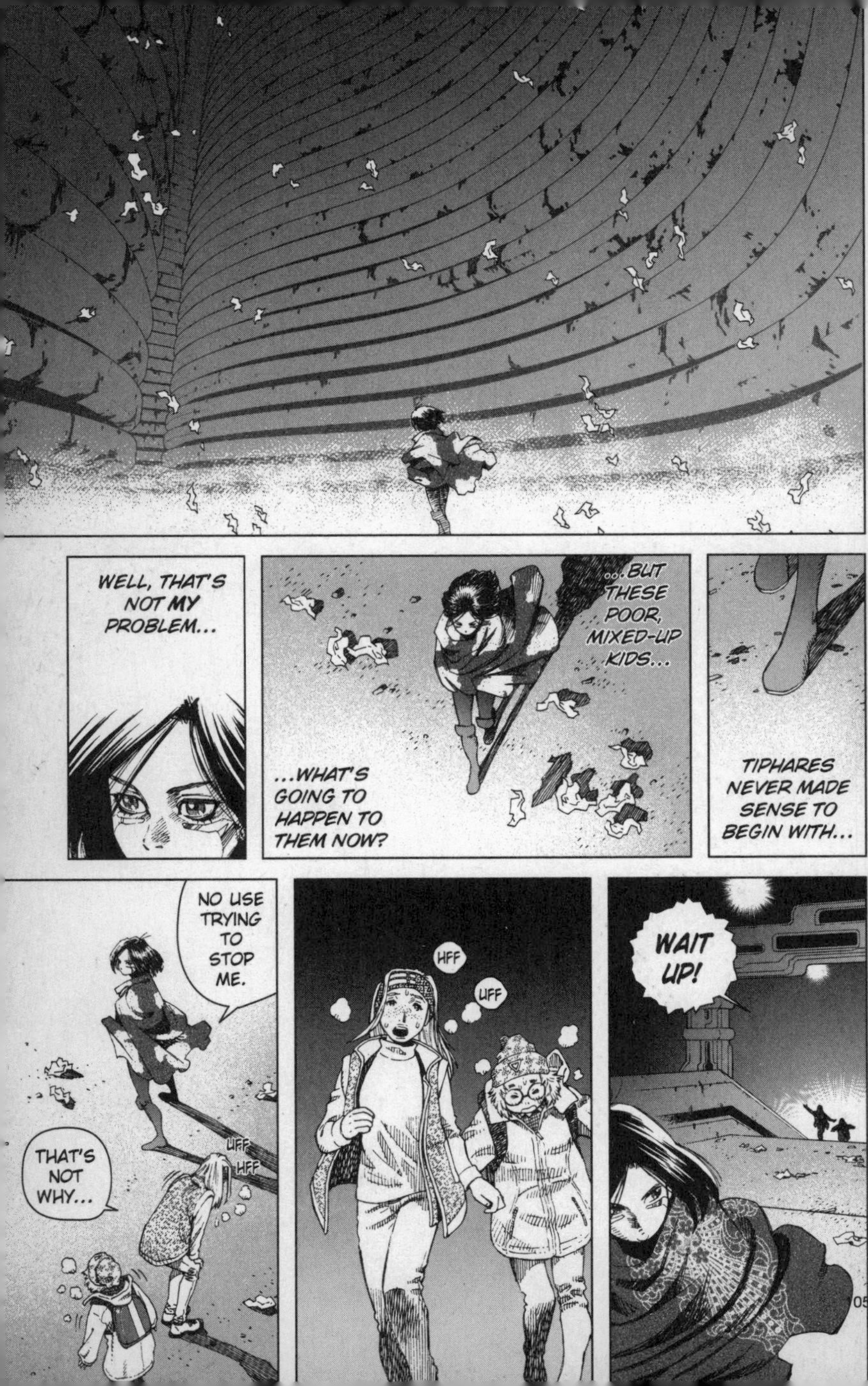
TIPHARES NEVER MADE SENSE TO BEGIN WITH...
...BUT THESE POOR, MIXED-UP KIDS...
...WHAT'S GOING TO HAPPEN TO THEM NOW?
WELL, THAT'S NOT MY PROBLEM...
WAIT UP!
HFF
UFF
NO USE TRYING TO STOP ME.
UFF
HFF
THAT'S NOT WHY...

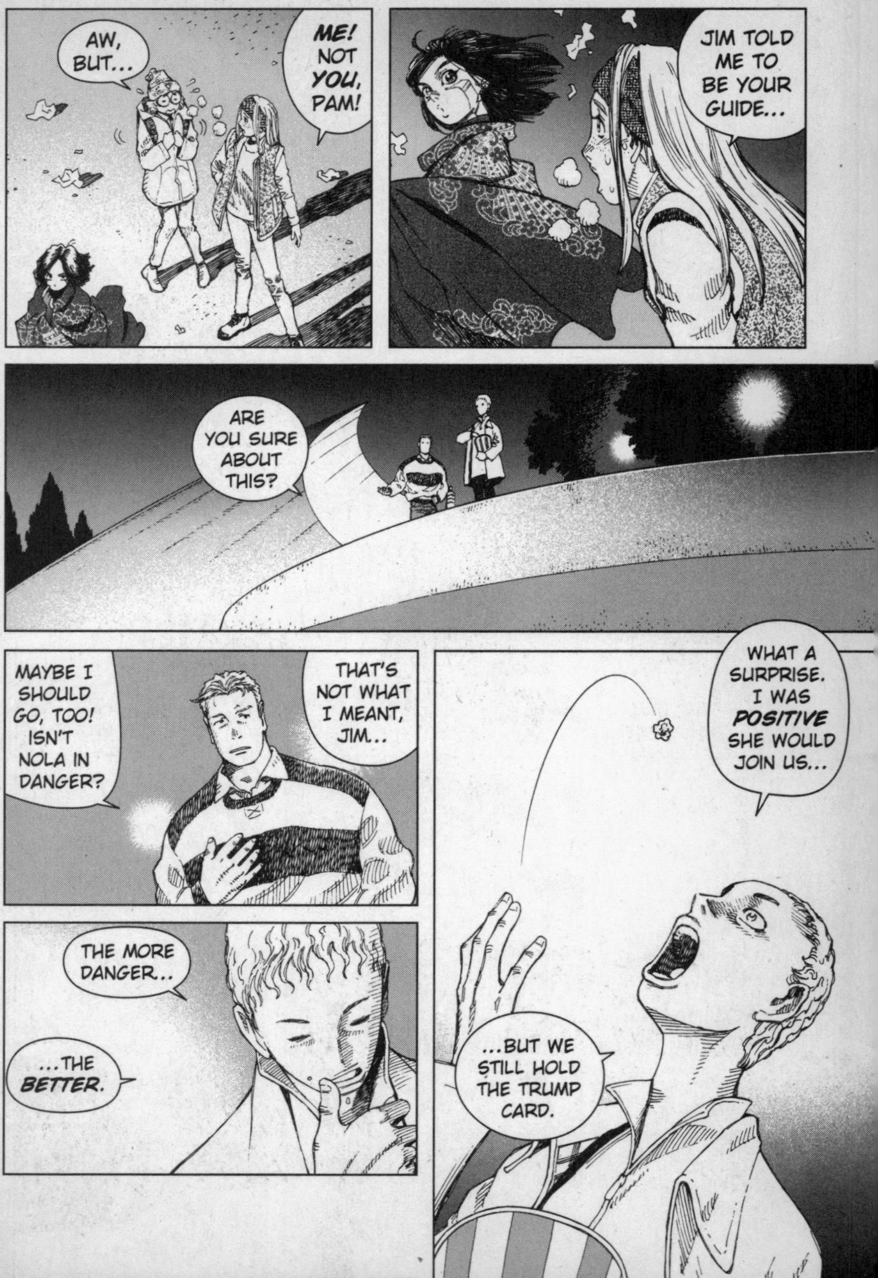
AW, BUT...
ME! NOT YOU, PAM!
JIM TOLD ME TO BE YOUR GUIDE...
ARE YOU SURE ABOUT THIS?
MAYBE I SHOULD GO, TOO! ISN'T NOLA IN DANGER?
THAT'S NOT WHAT I MEANT, JIM...
THE MORE DANGER...
...THE BETTER.
WHAT A SURPRISE. I WAS POSITIVE SHE WOULD JOIN US...
...BUT WE STILL HOLD THE TRUMP CARD.

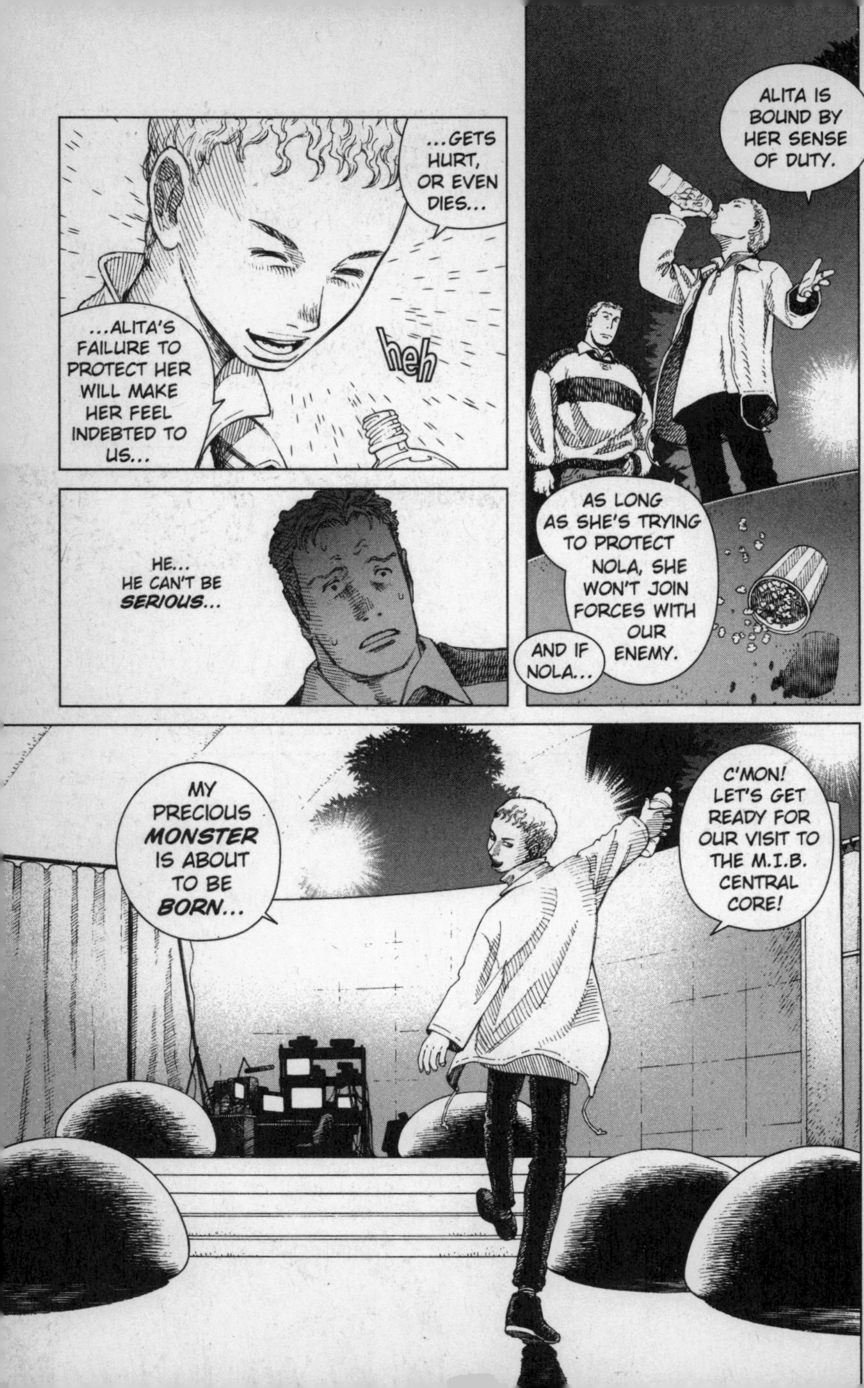
ALITA IS BOUND BY HER SENSE OF DUTY.
AS LONG AS SHE'S TRYING TO PROTECT NOLA, SHE WON'T JOIN FORCES WITH OUR ENEMY.
AND IF NOLA...
...GETS HURT, OR EVEN DIES...
heh
...ALITA'S FAILURE TO PROTECT HER WILL MAKE HER FEEL INDEBTED TO US...
HE... HE CAN'T BE *SERIOUS*...
C'MON! LET'S GET READY FOR OUR VISIT TO THE M.I.B. CENTRAL CORE!
MY PRECIOUS *MONSTER* IS ABOUT TO BE *BORN*...

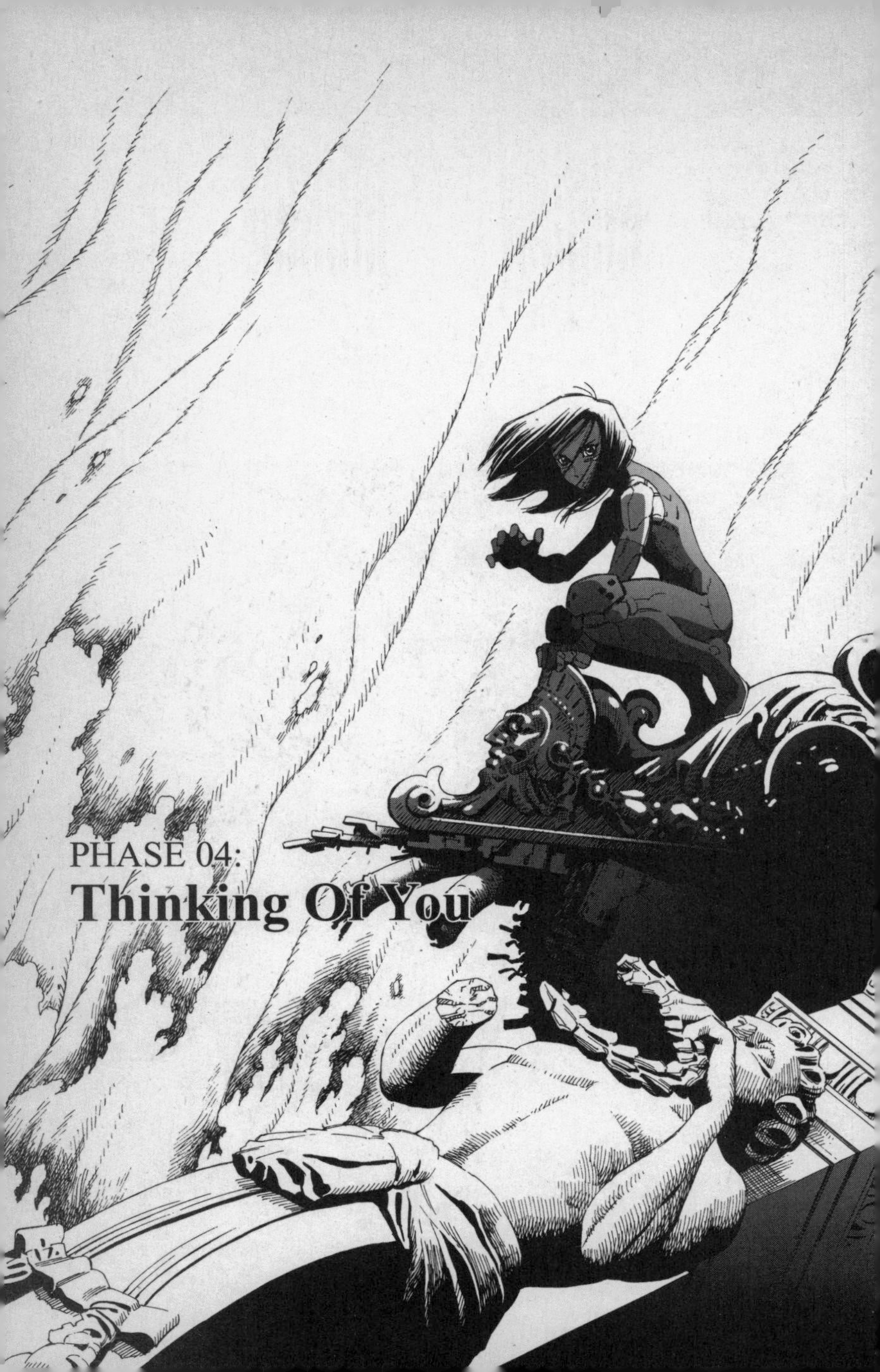
PHASE 04:
Thinking Of You

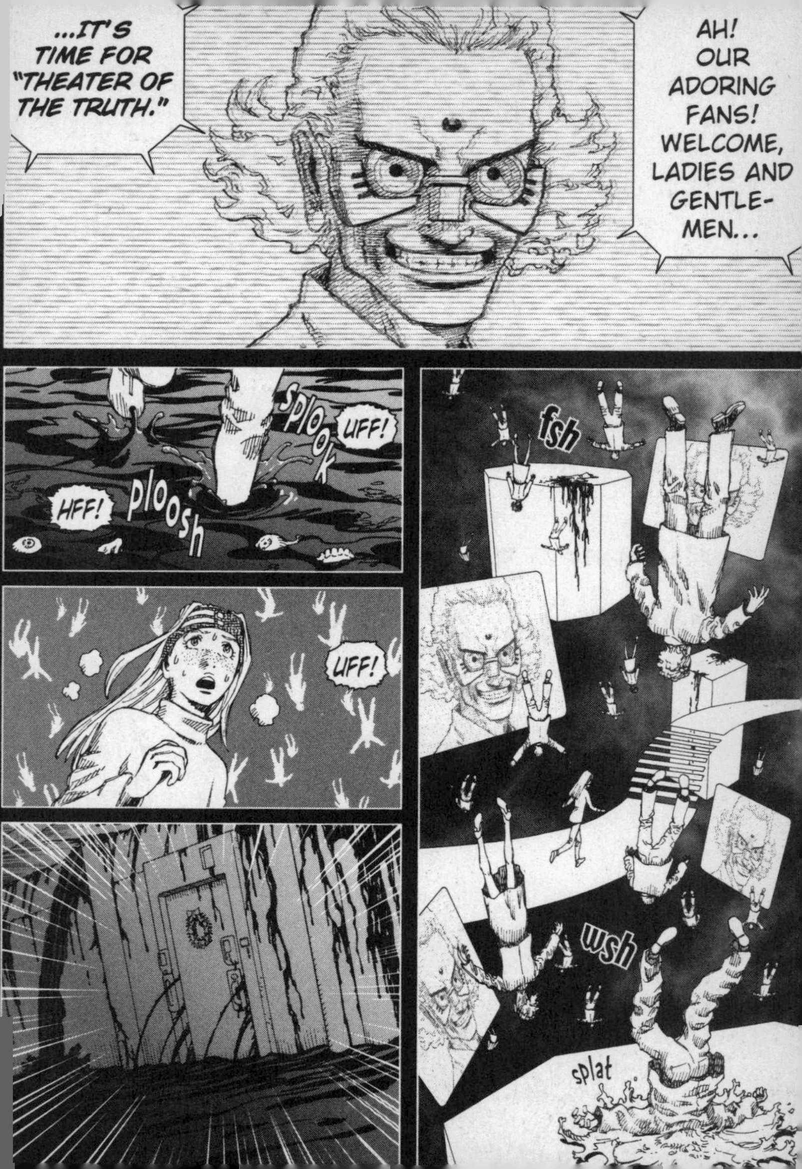
AH! OUR ADORING FANS! WELCOME, LADIES AND GENTLE-MEN...
...IT'S TIME FOR "THEATER OF THE TRUTH."
fsh
wsh
splat
splook
UFF!
HFF!
ploosh
UFF!

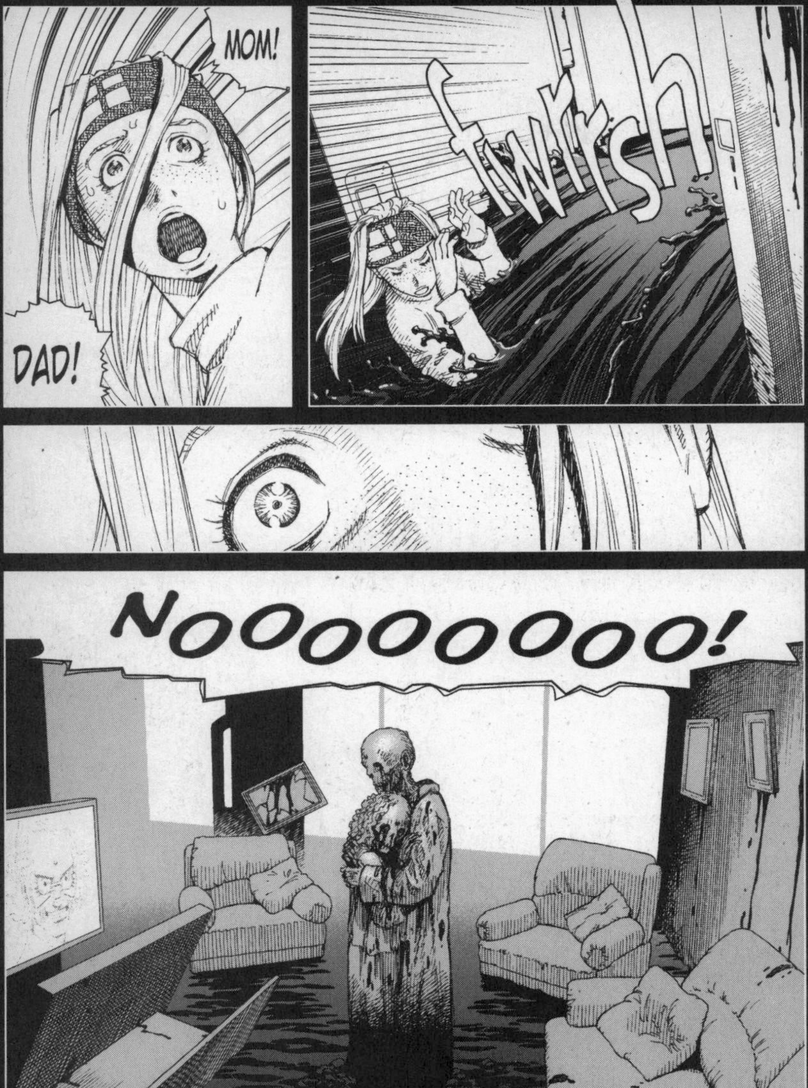
fwrrsh
MOM!
DAD!
NOOOOOOOO!

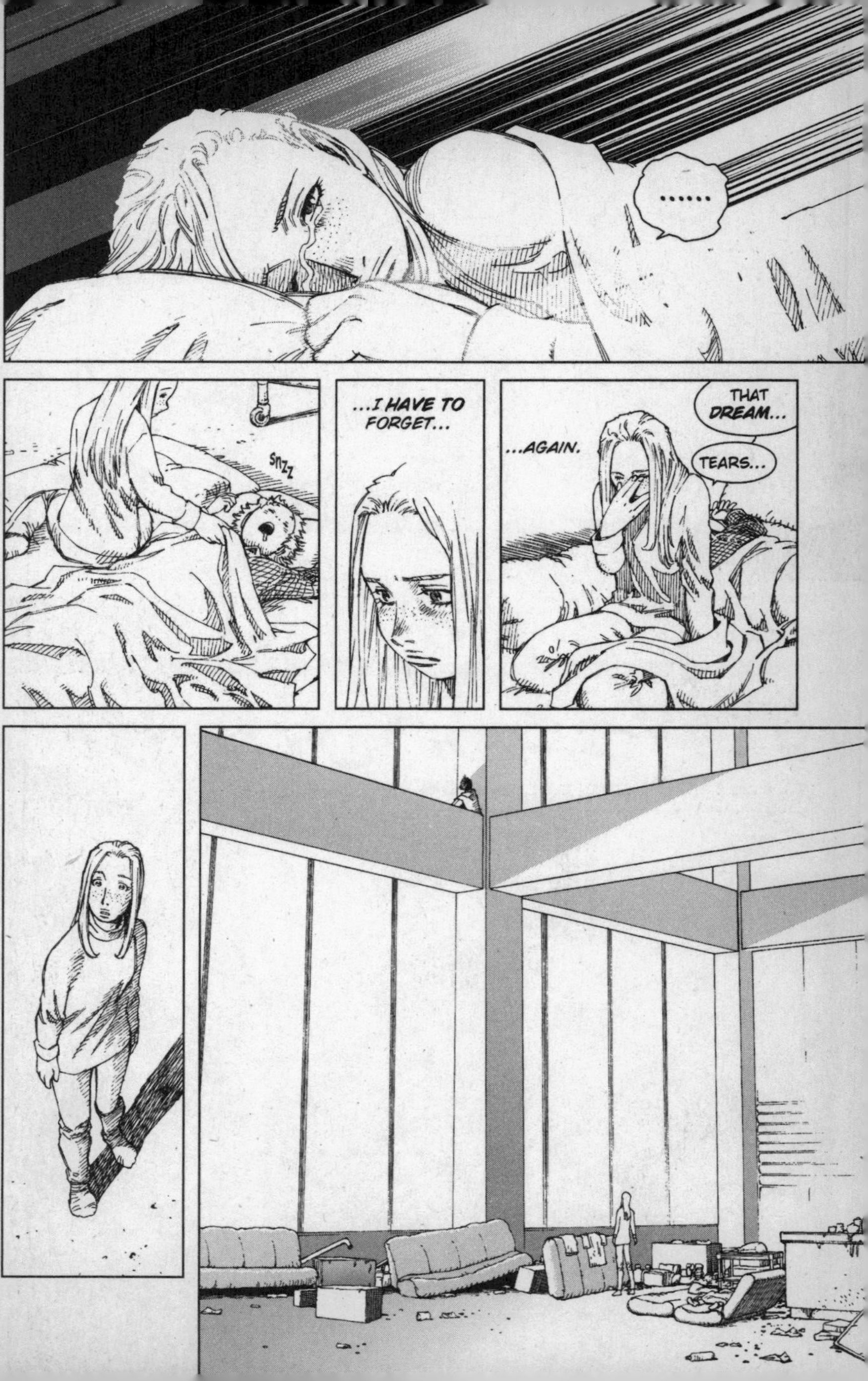
......
THAT DREAM...
TEARS...
...AGAIN.
...I HAVE TO FORGET...
SNZZ

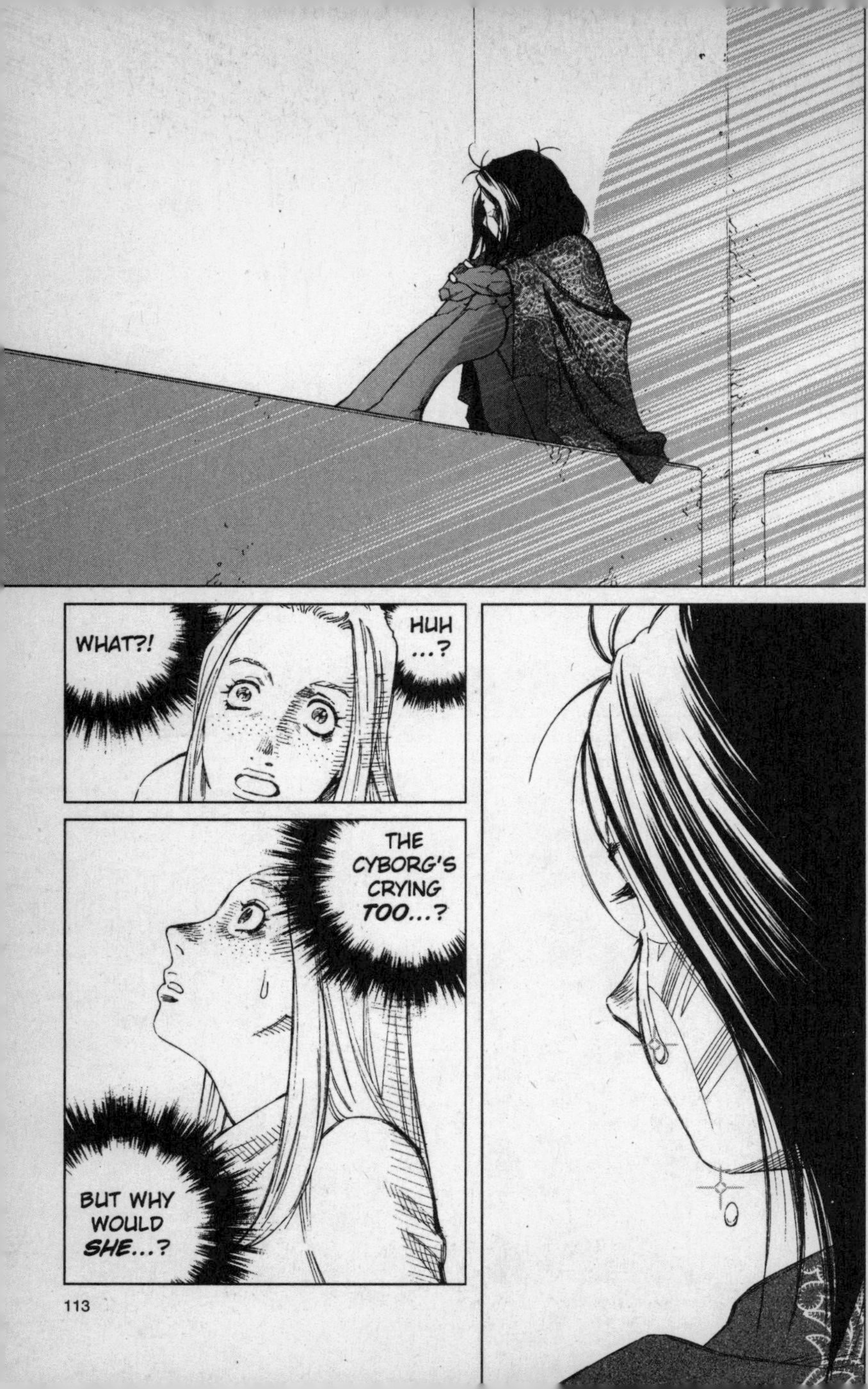
HUH ...?
WHAT?!
THE CYBORG'S CRYING *TOO*...?
BUT WHY WOULD *SHE*...?

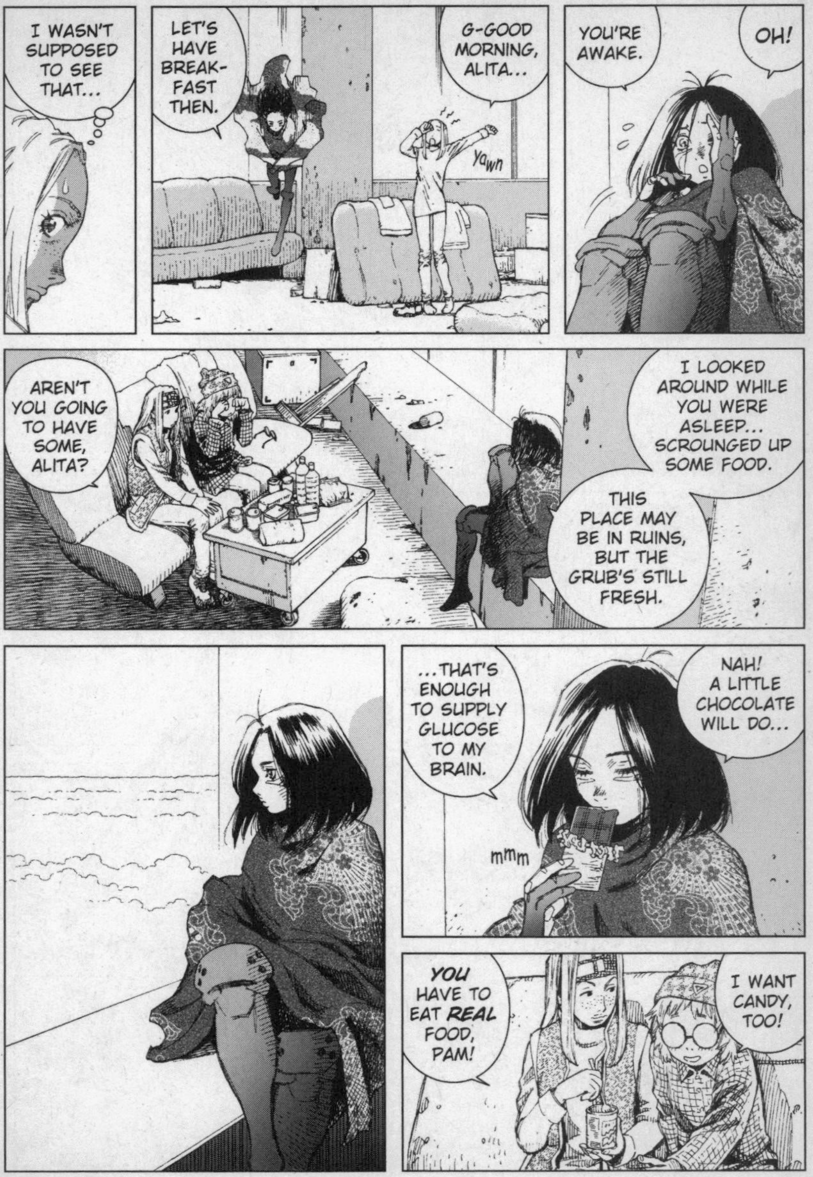
OH!
YOU'RE AWAKE.
G-GOOD MORNING, ALITA...
yawn
LET'S HAVE BREAK-FAST THEN.
I WASN'T SUPPOSED TO SEE THAT...
I LOOKED AROUND WHILE YOU WERE ASLEEP... SCROUNGED UP SOME FOOD.
THIS PLACE MAY BE IN RUINS, BUT THE GRUB'S STILL FRESH.
AREN'T YOU GOING TO HAVE SOME, ALITA?
NAH! A LITTLE CHOCOLATE WILL DO...
mmm
...THAT'S ENOUGH TO SUPPLY GLUCOSE TO MY BRAIN.
I WANT CANDY, TOO!
YOU HAVE TO EAT *REAL* FOOD, PAM!

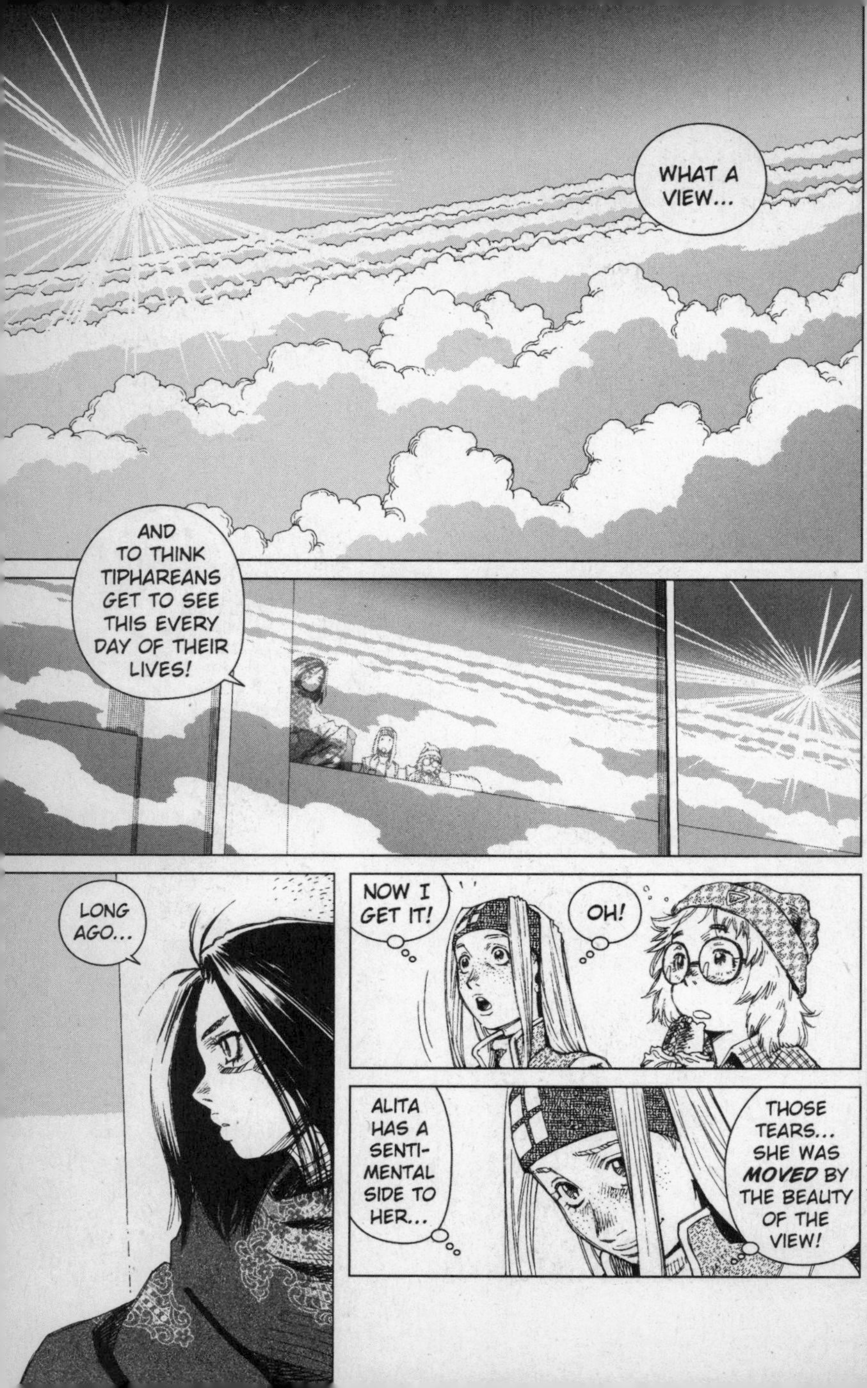
WHAT A VIEW...
AND TO THINK TIPHAREANS GET TO SEE THIS EVERY DAY OF THEIR LIVES!
OH!
NOW I GET IT!
THOSE TEARS... SHE WAS *MOVED* BY THE BEAUTY OF THE VIEW!
ALITA HAS A SENTI-MENTAL SIDE TO HER...
LONG AGO...

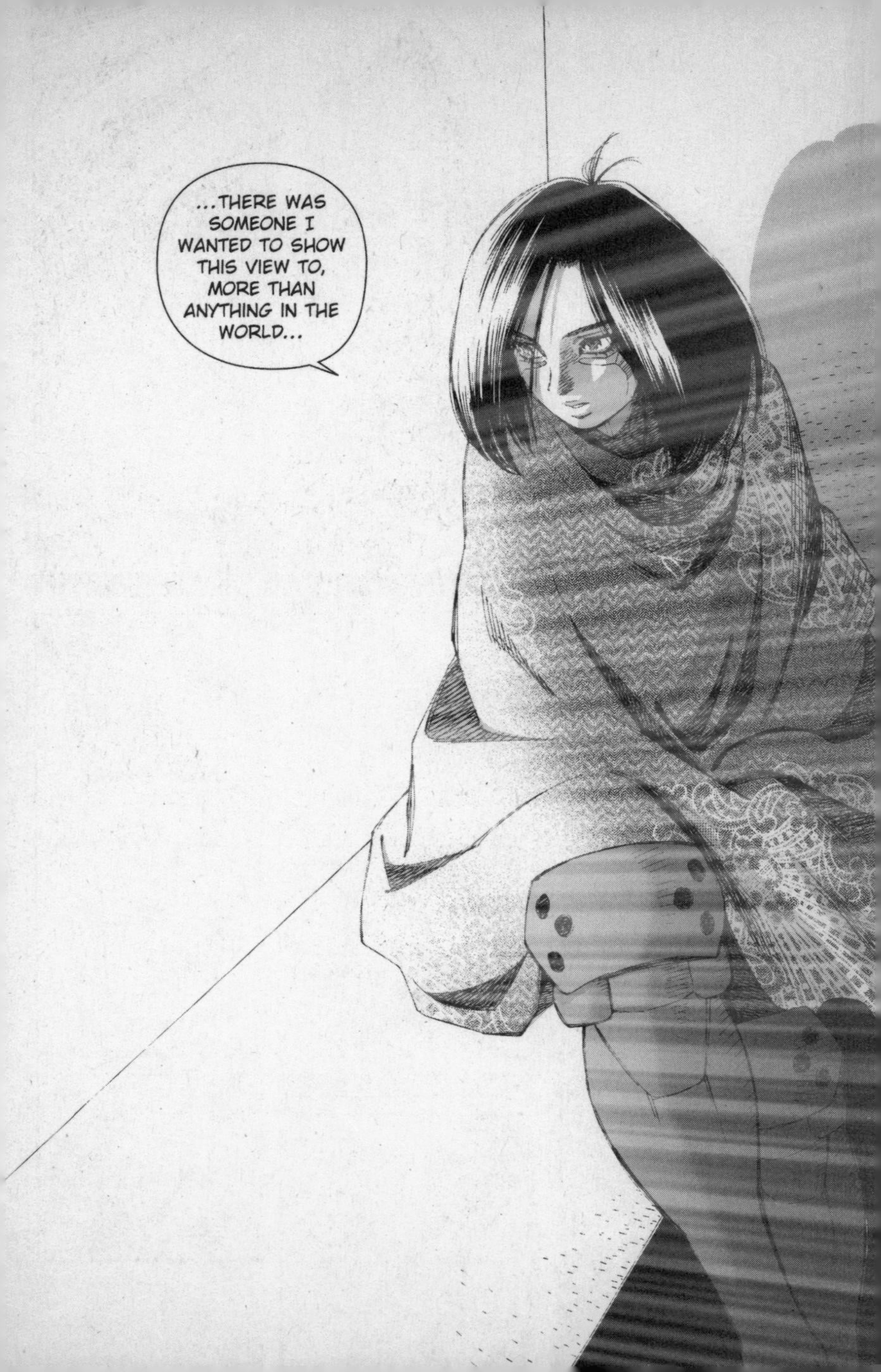
...THERE WAS SOMEONE I WANTED TO SHOW THIS VIEW TO, MORE THAN ANYTHING IN THE WORLD...

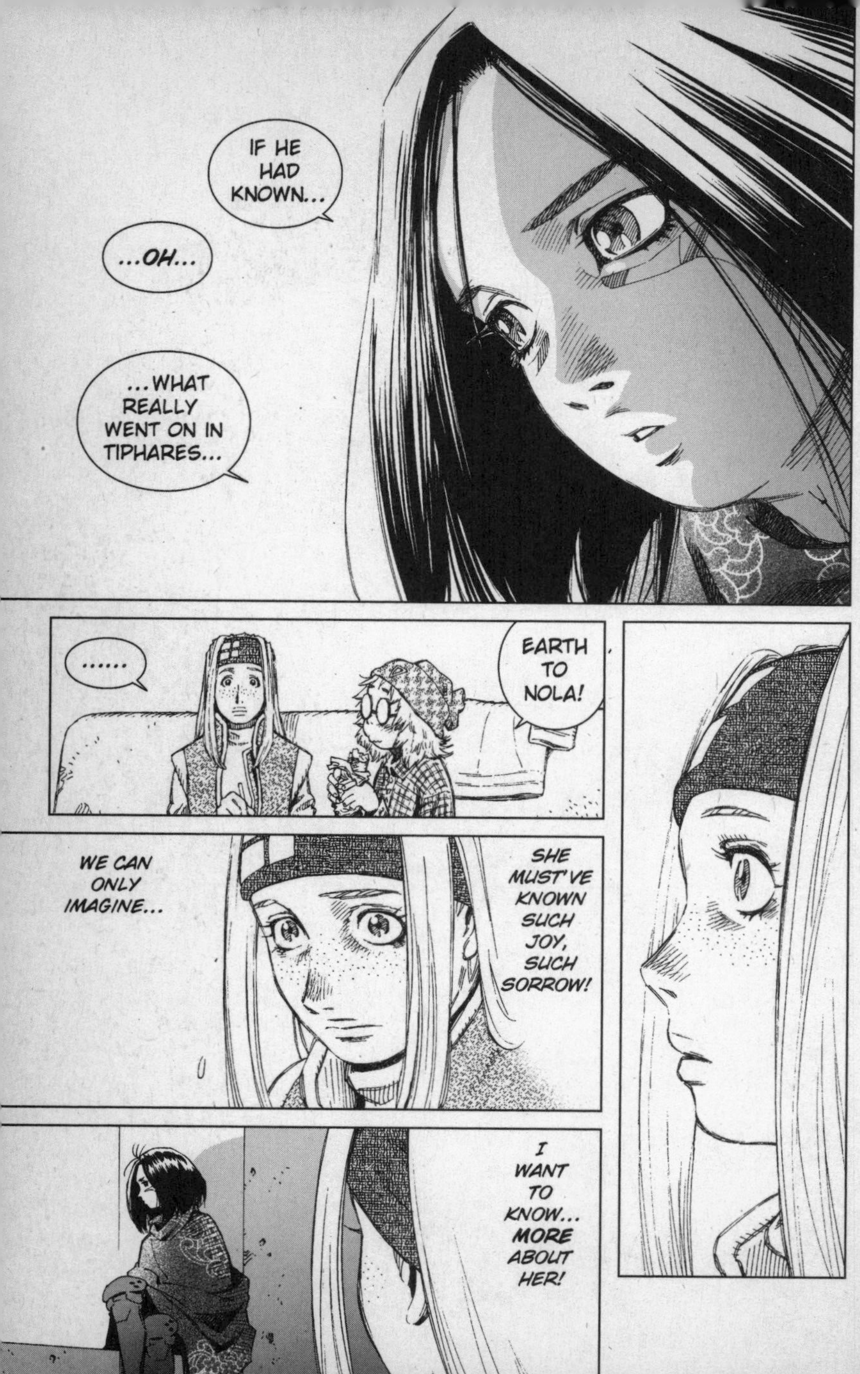
IF HE HAD KNOWN...
...OH...
...WHAT REALLY WENT ON IN TIPHARES...
EARTH TO NOLA!
......
SHE MUST'VE KNOWN SUCH JOY, SUCH SORROW!
WE CAN ONLY IMAGINE...
I WANT TO KNOW... MORE ABOUT HER!

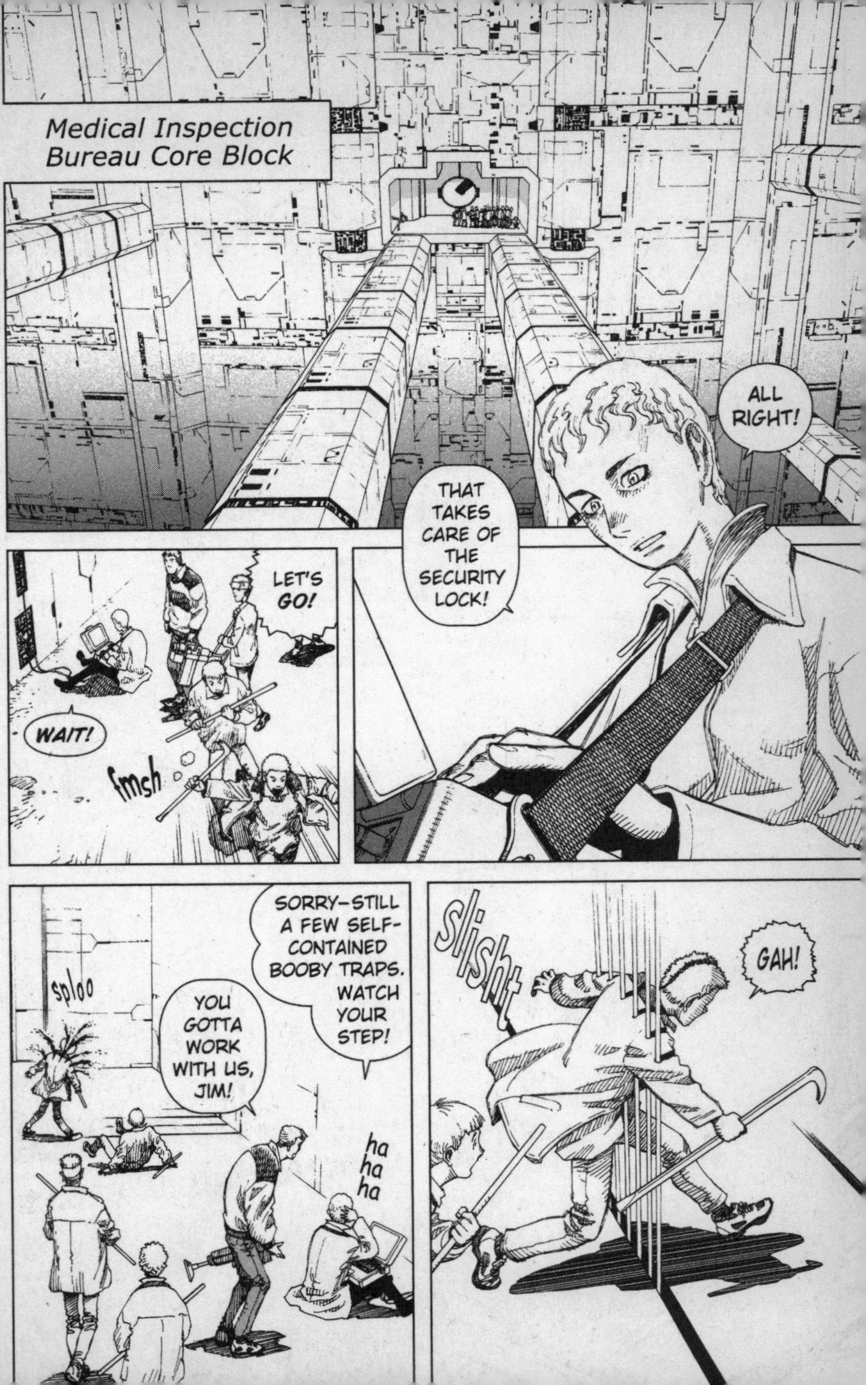

Medical Inspection Bureau Core Block
ALL RIGHT!
THAT TAKES CARE OF THE SECURITY LOCK!
LET'S GO!
WAIT!
fmsh
slisht
GAH!
SORRY—STILL A FEW SELF-CONTAINED BOOBY TRAPS. WATCH YOUR STEP!
YOU GOTTA WORK WITH US, JIM!
sploo
ha ha ha

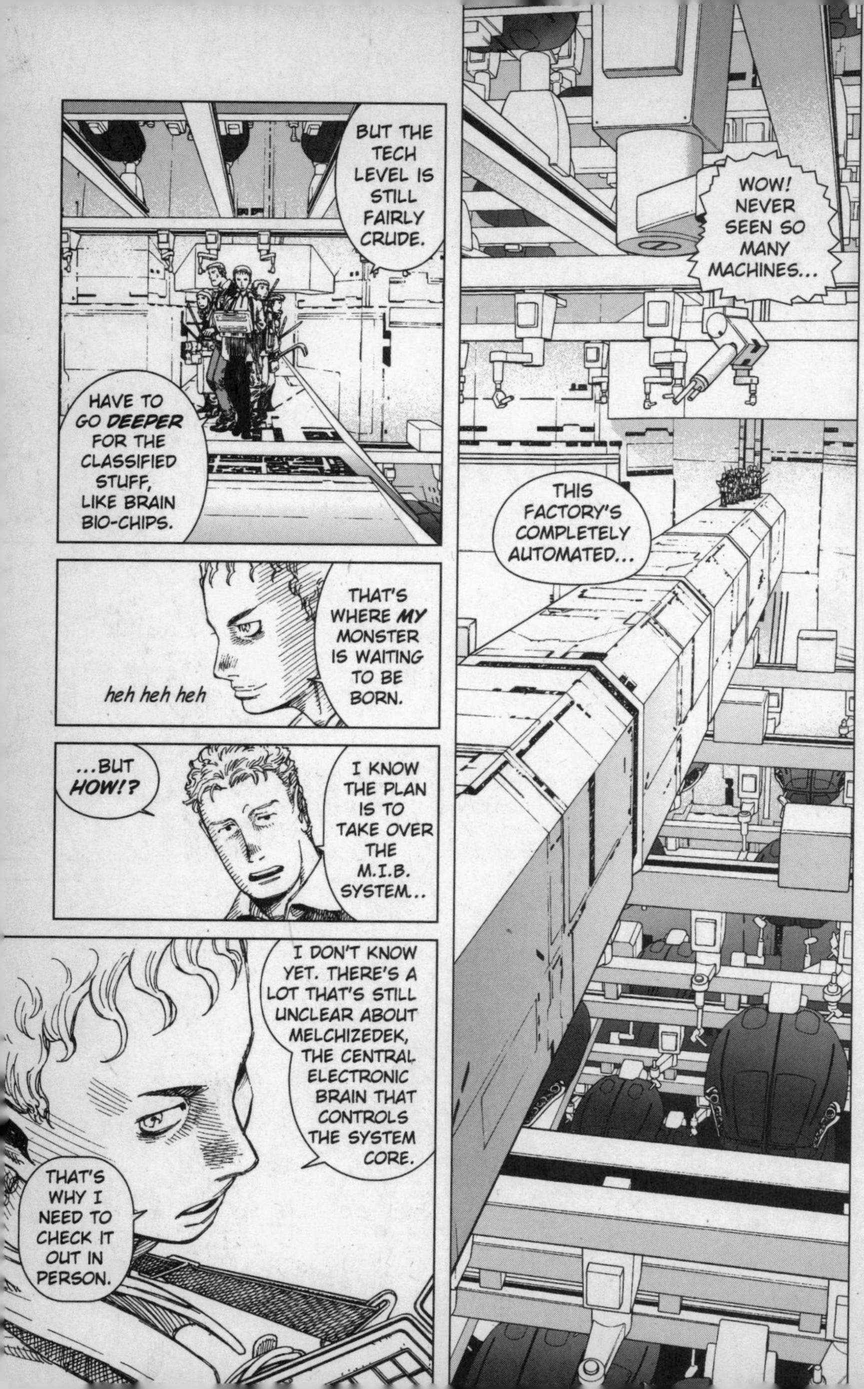
WOW! NEVER SEEN SO MANY MACHINES...
THIS FACTORY'S COMPLETELY AUTOMATED...
BUT THE TECH LEVEL IS STILL FAIRLY CRUDE.
HAVE TO GO *DEEPER* FOR THE CLASSIFIED STUFF, LIKE BRAIN BIO-CHIPS.
THAT'S WHERE *MY* MONSTER IS WAITING TO BE BORN.
heh heh heh
I KNOW THE PLAN IS TO TAKE OVER THE M.I.B. SYSTEM...
...BUT ***HOW!?***
I DON'T KNOW YET. THERE'S A LOT THAT'S STILL UNCLEAR ABOUT MELCHIZEDEK, THE CENTRAL ELECTRONIC BRAIN THAT CONTROLS THE SYSTEM CORE.
THAT'S WHY I NEED TO CHECK IT OUT IN PERSON.

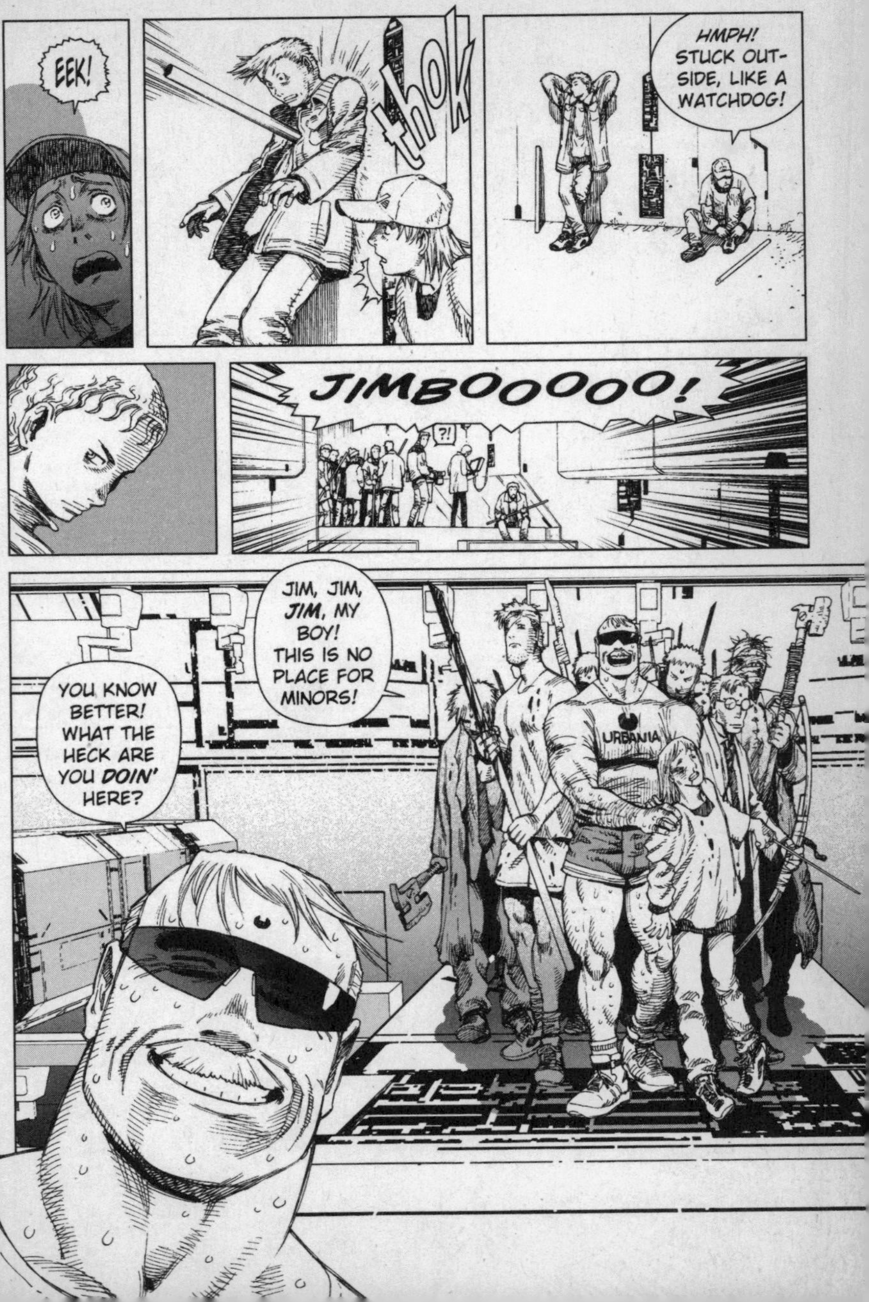
EEK!
thok
HMPH! STUCK OUT-SIDE, LIKE A WATCHDOG!
JIMBOOOOOO!
?!
JIM, JIM, JIM, MY BOY! THIS IS NO PLACE FOR MINORS!
YOU KNOW BETTER! WHAT THE HECK ARE YOU DOIN' HERE?
URBANIA

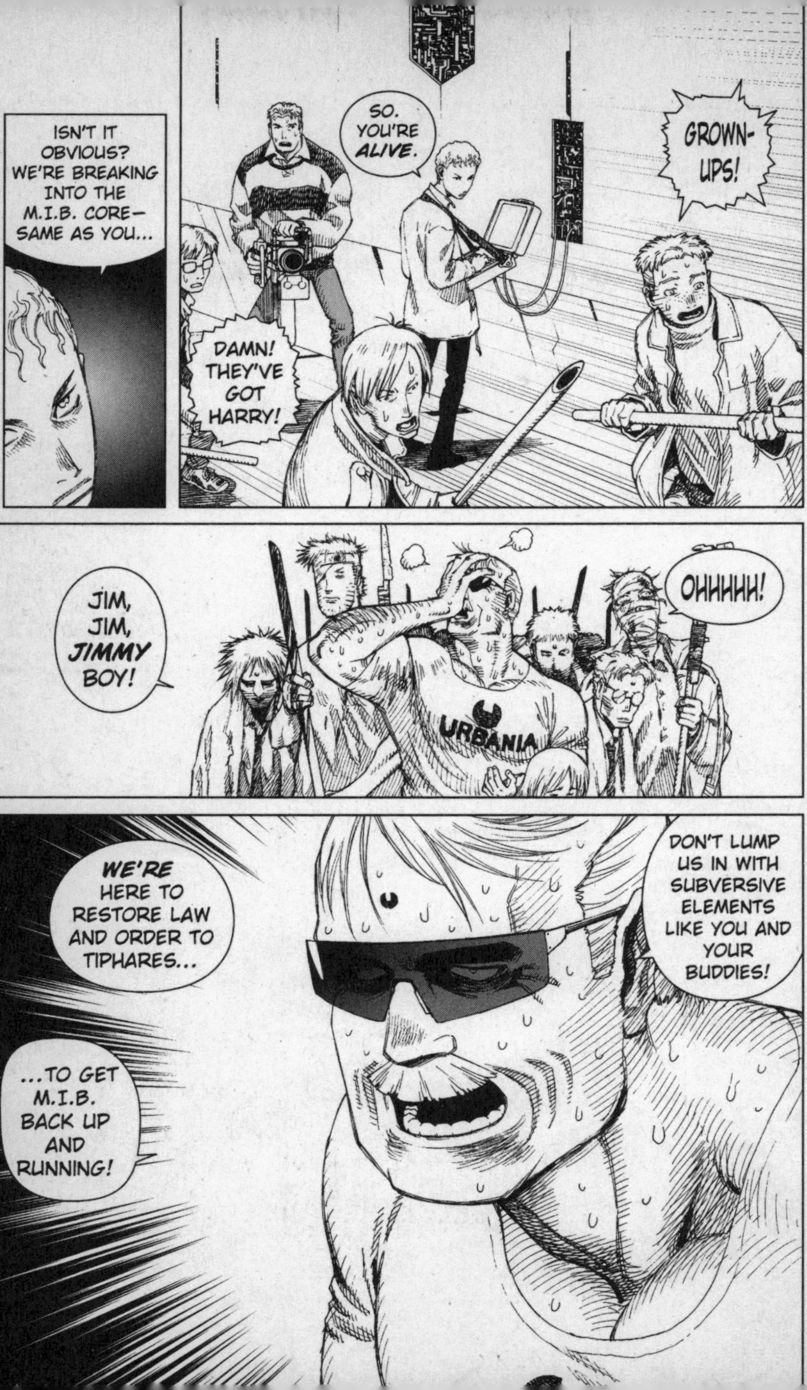
GROWN-UPS!
SO. YOU'RE ALIVE.
DAMN! THEY'VE GOT HARRY!
ISN'T IT OBVIOUS? WE'RE BREAKING INTO THE M.I.B. CORE—SAME AS YOU...
OHHHHH!
JIM, JIM, JIMMY BOY!
URBANIA
DON'T LUMP US IN WITH SUBVERSIVE ELEMENTS LIKE YOU AND YOUR BUDDIES!
WE'RE HERE TO RESTORE LAW AND ORDER TO TIPHARES...
...TO GET M.I.B. BACK UP AND RUNNING!

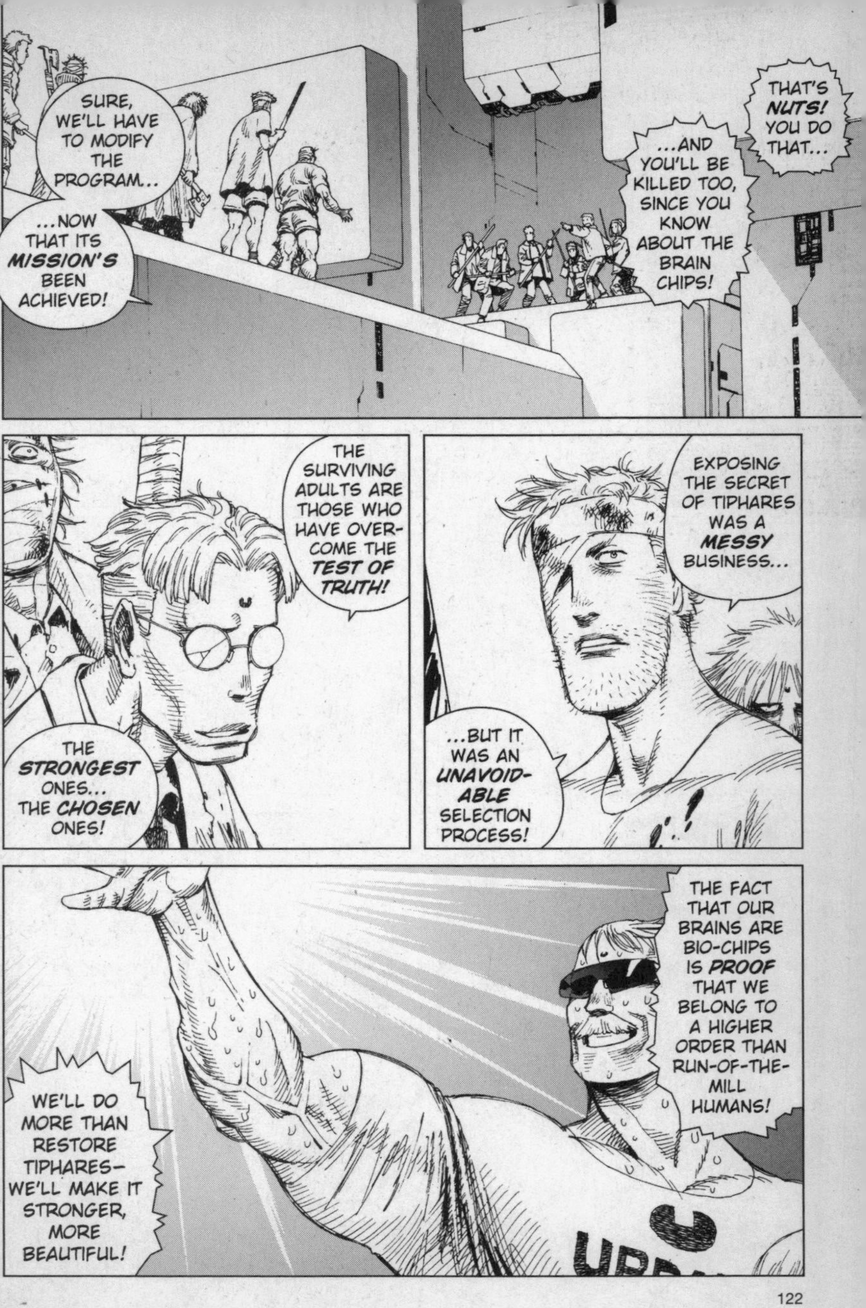
THAT'S NUTS! YOU DO THAT...
...AND YOU'LL BE KILLED TOO, SINCE YOU KNOW ABOUT THE BRAIN CHIPS!
SURE, WE'LL HAVE TO MODIFY THE PROGRAM...
...NOW THAT ITS MISSION'S BEEN ACHIEVED!
EXPOSING THE SECRET OF TIPHARES WAS A MESSY BUSINESS...
...BUT IT WAS AN UNAVOID-ABLE SELECTION PROCESS!
THE SURVIVING ADULTS ARE THOSE WHO HAVE OVER-COME THE TEST OF TRUTH!
THE STRONGEST ONES... THE CHOSEN ONES!
THE FACT THAT OUR BRAINS ARE BIO-CHIPS IS PROOF THAT WE BELONG TO A HIGHER ORDER THAN RUN-OF-THE-MILL HUMANS!
WE'LL DO MORE THAN RESTORE TIPHARES— WE'LL MAKE IT STRONGER, MORE BEAUTIFUL!

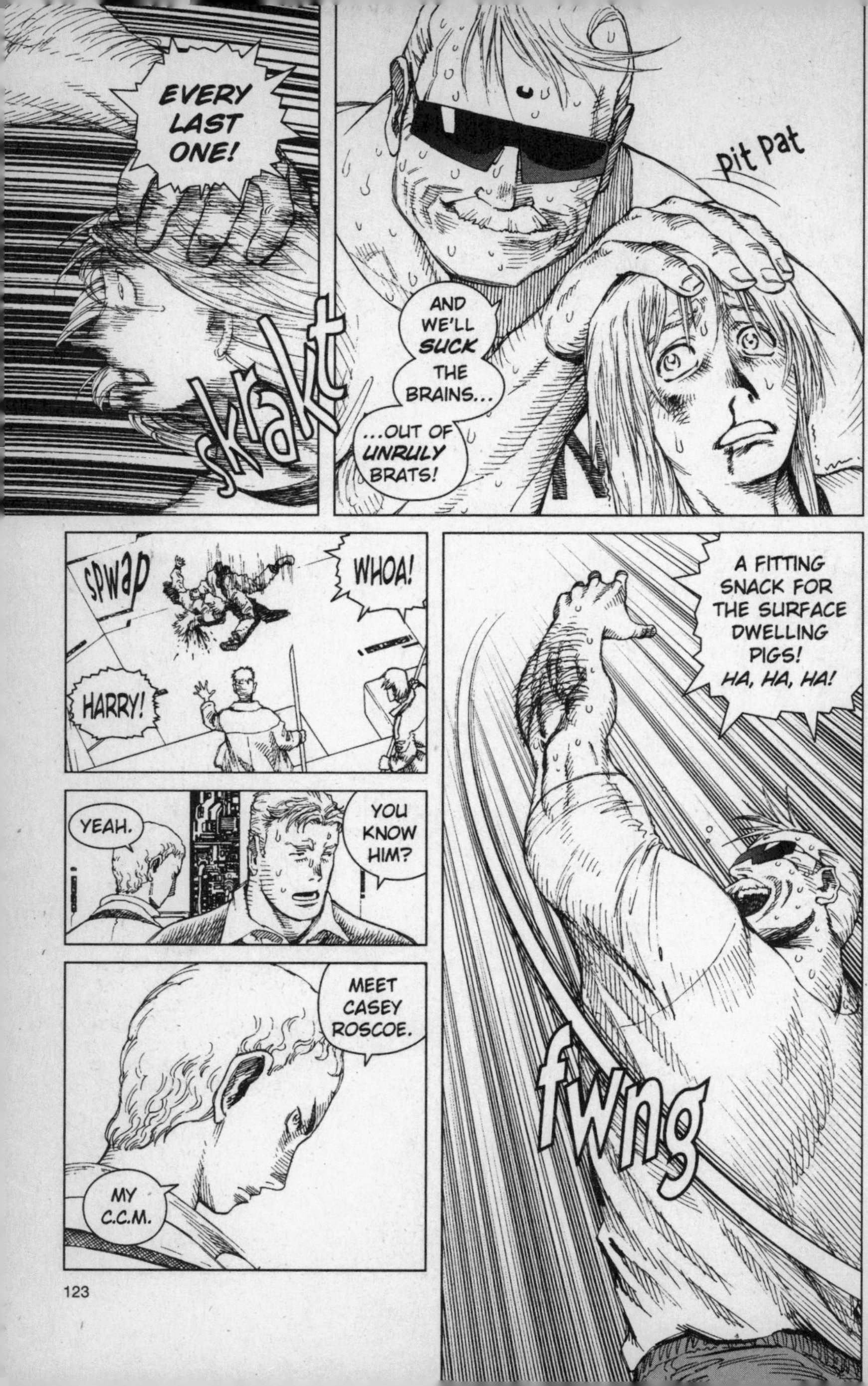
pit pat
AND WE'LL SUCK THE BRAINS...
...OUT OF UNRULY BRATS!
EVERY LAST ONE!
skrakt
A FITTING SNACK FOR THE SURFACE DWELLING PIGS! HA, HA, HA!
fwng
WHOA!
spwap
HARRY!
YOU KNOW HIM?
YEAH.
MEET CASEY ROSCOE.
MY C.C.M.

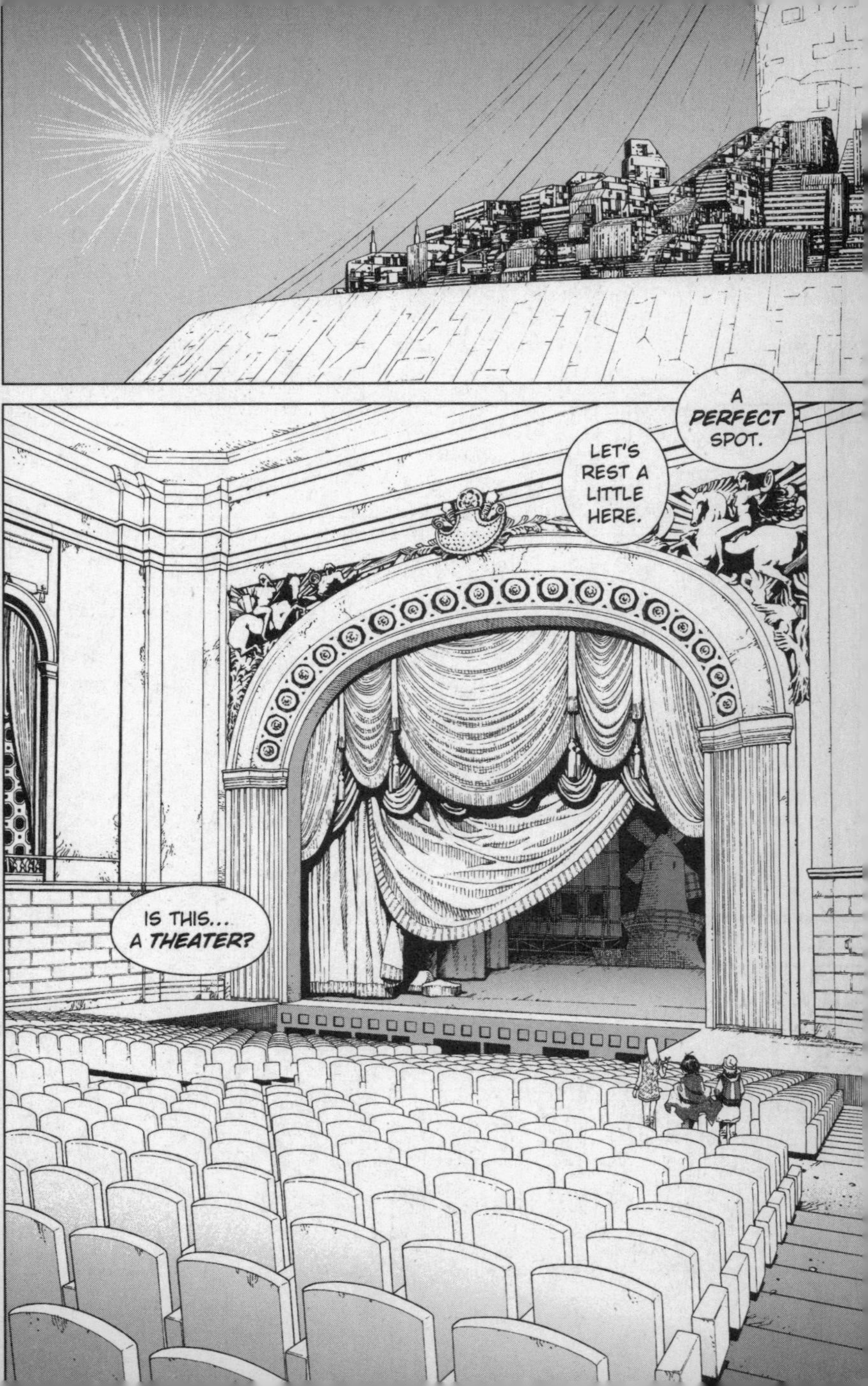
A *PERFECT* SPOT.
LET'S REST A LITTLE HERE.
IS THIS... A *THEATER?*

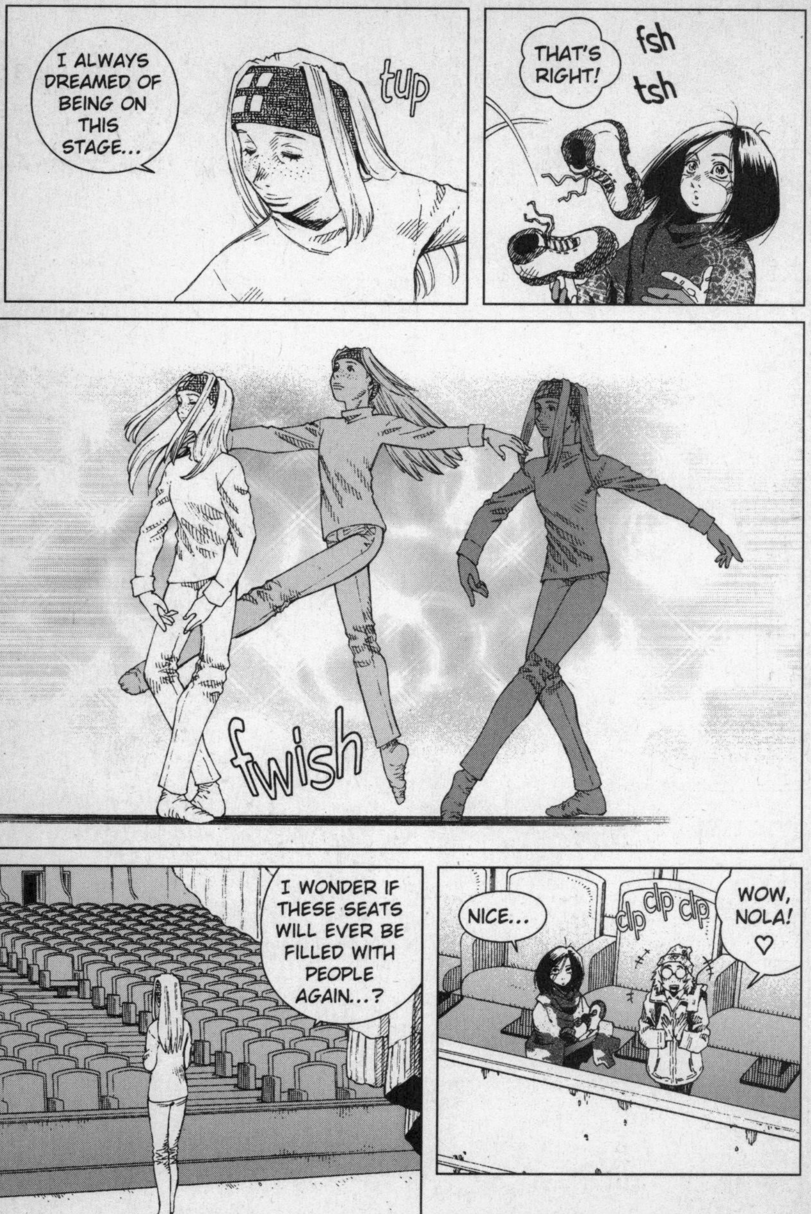
I ALWAYS DREAMED OF BEING ON THIS STAGE...
tup
THAT'S RIGHT!
fsh
tsh
fwish
I WONDER IF THESE SEATS WILL EVER BE FILLED WITH PEOPLE AGAIN...?
NICE...
clp clp clp
WOW, NOLA! ♡

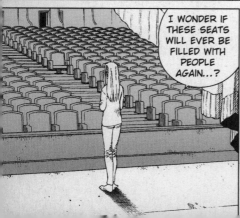

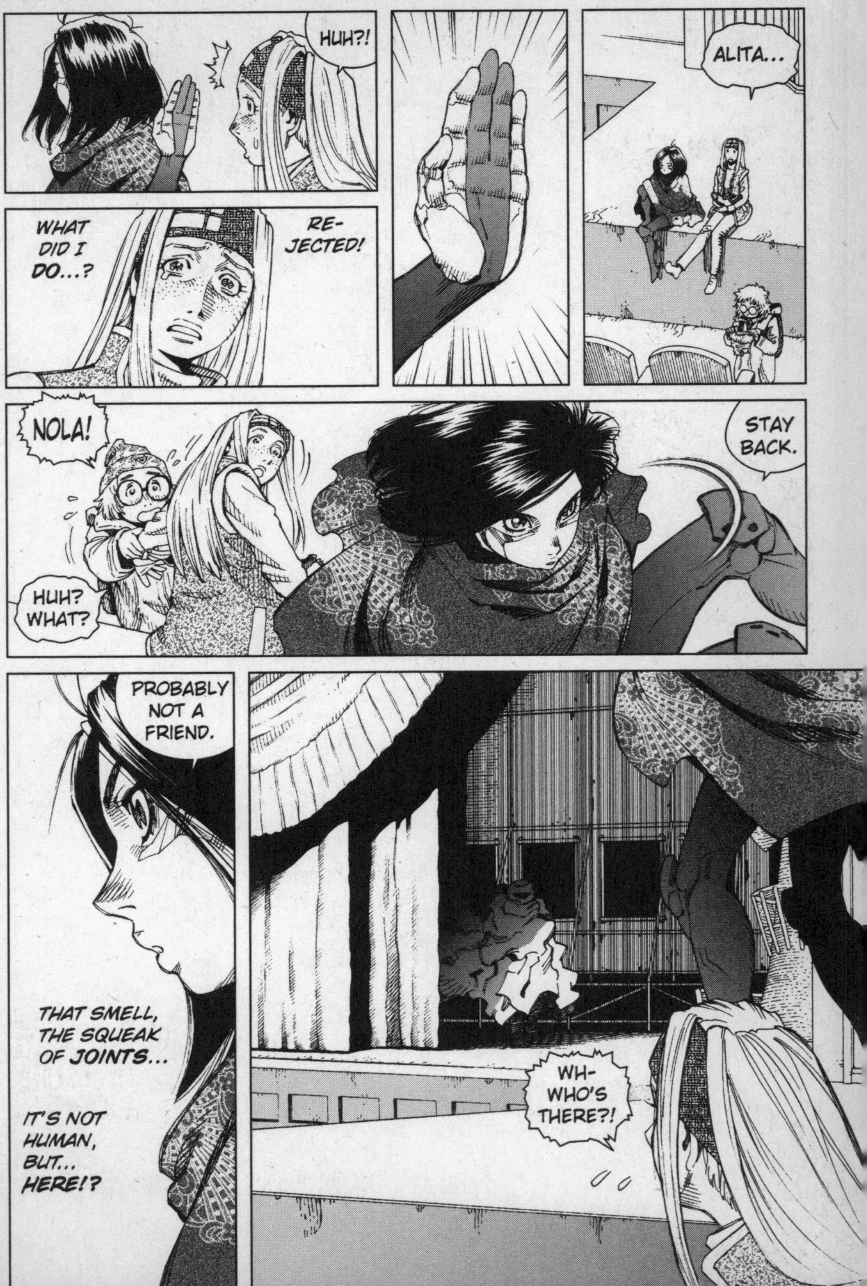
HUH?!
WHAT DID I DO...?
RE-JECTED!
ALITA...
NOLA!
HUH? WHAT?
STAY BACK.
PROBABLY NOT A FRIEND.
THAT SMELL, THE SQUEAK OF JOINTS...
IT'S NOT HUMAN, BUT... HERE!?
WH-WHO'S THERE?!

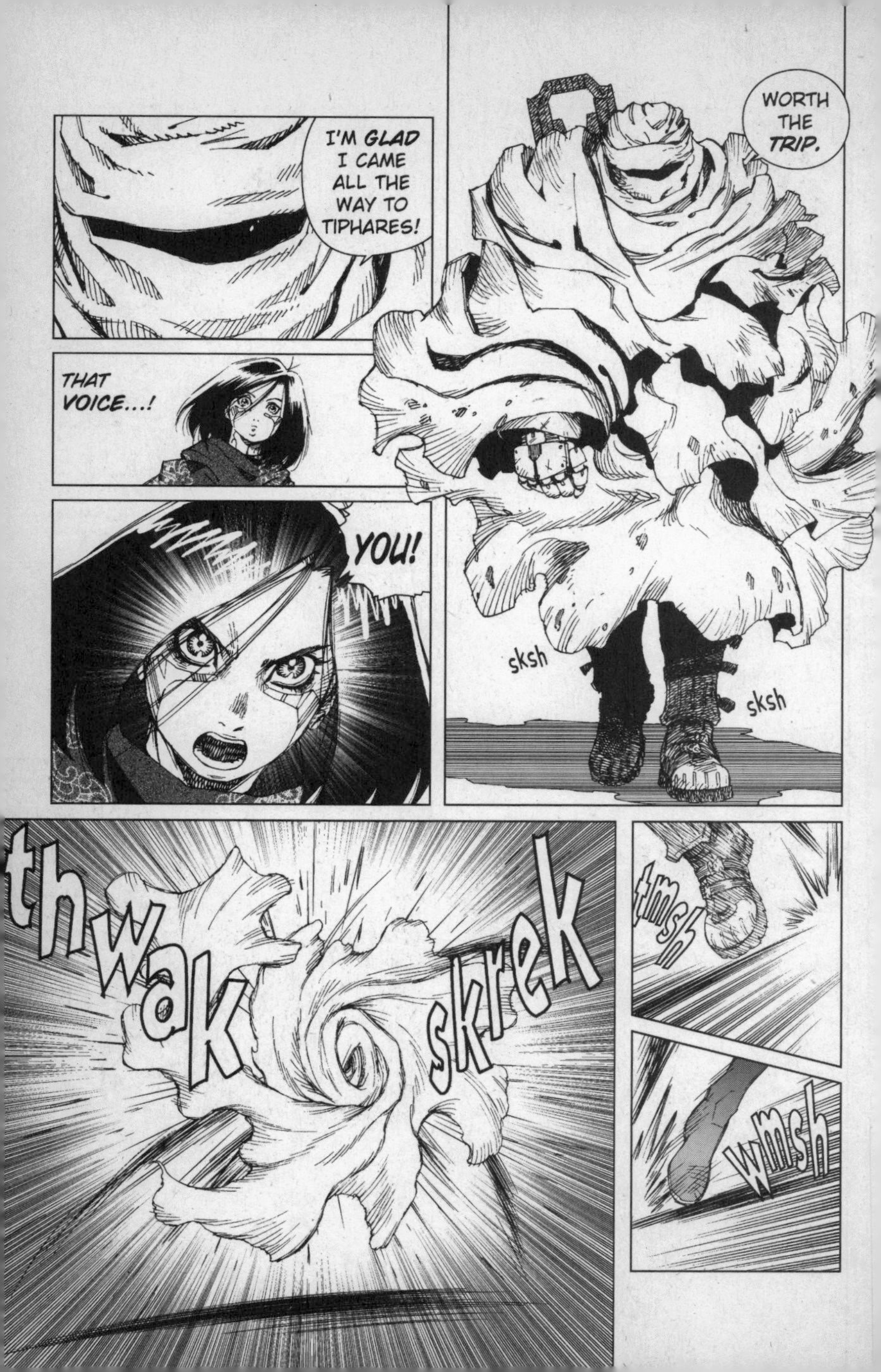

WORTH THE TRIP.
sksh
sksh
I'M GLAD I CAME ALL THE WAY TO TIPHARES!
THAT VOICE...!
YOU!
tmsh
wmsh
skrek
thwak

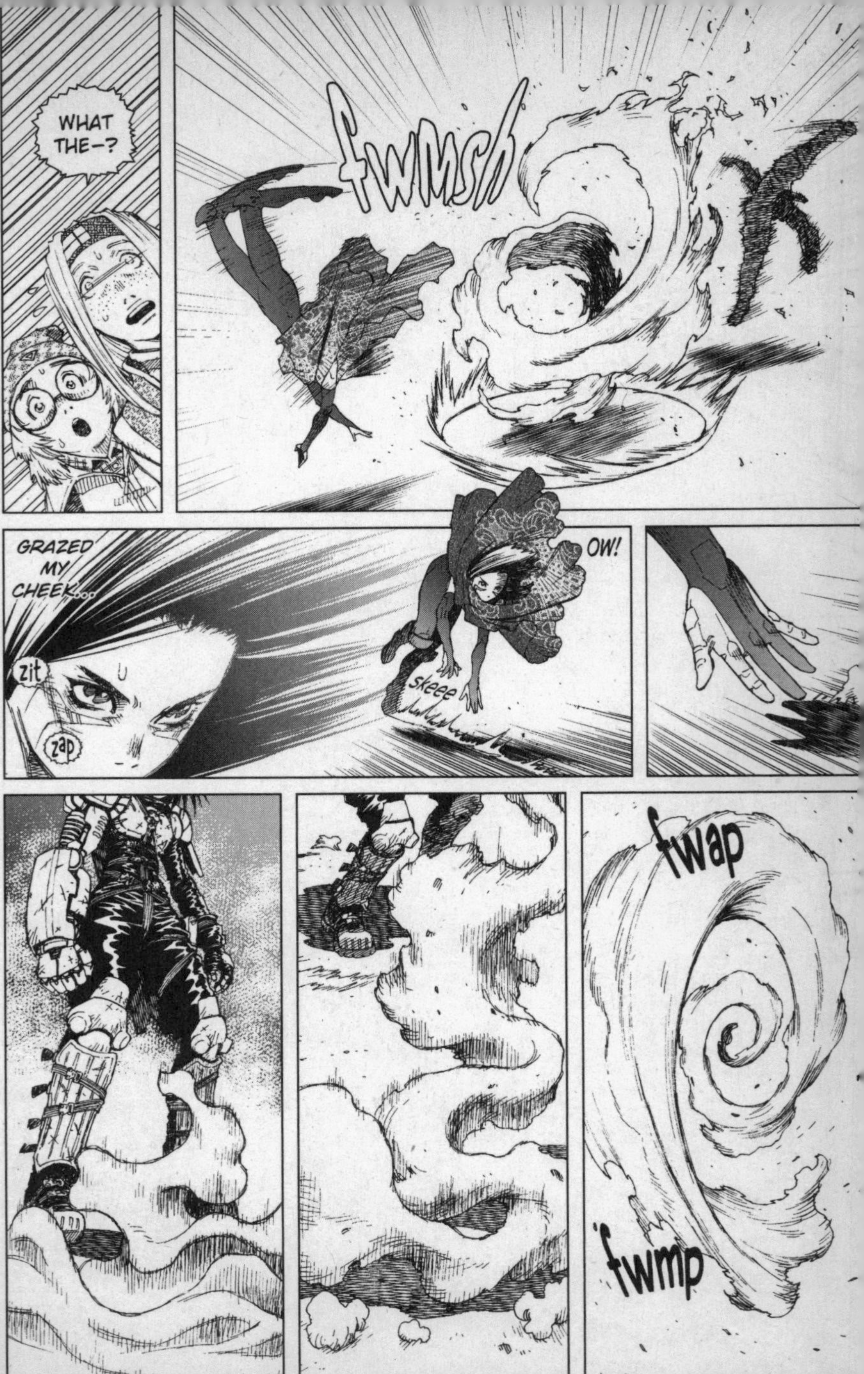
fwmsh
WHAT THE–?
OW!
skeee
GRAZED MY CHEEK...
zit
zap
fwap
fwmp

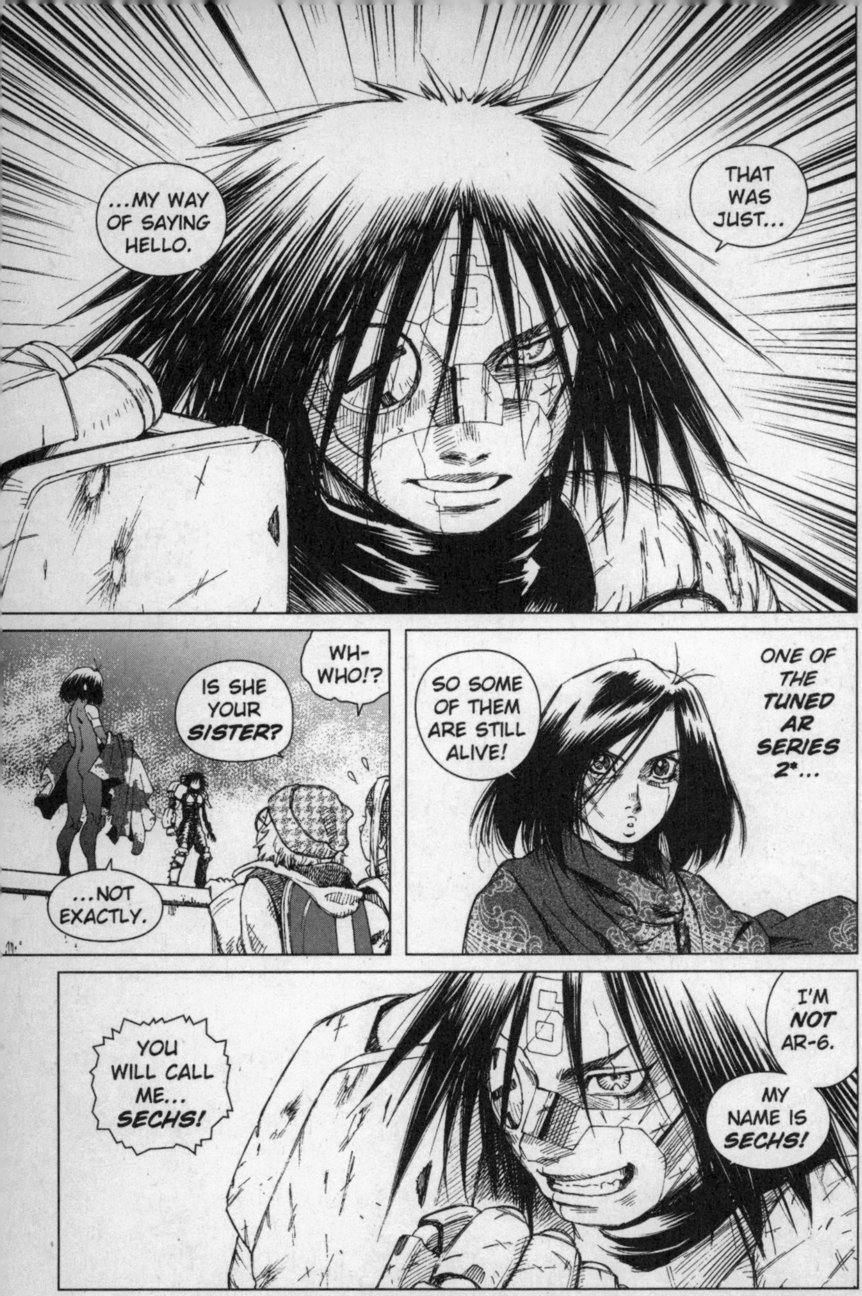
THAT WAS JUST...
...MY WAY OF SAYING HELLO.
ONE OF THE TUNED AR SERIES 2*...
SO SOME OF THEM ARE STILL ALIVE!
WH-WHO!?
IS SHE YOUR SISTER?
...NOT EXACTLY.
I'M NOT AR-6.
MY NAME IS SECHS!
YOU WILL CALL ME... SECHS!

__Tuned AR Series 2__: Twelve androids created by G.I.B. from Alita's battle data while she was a ÒTUNEDÓ.

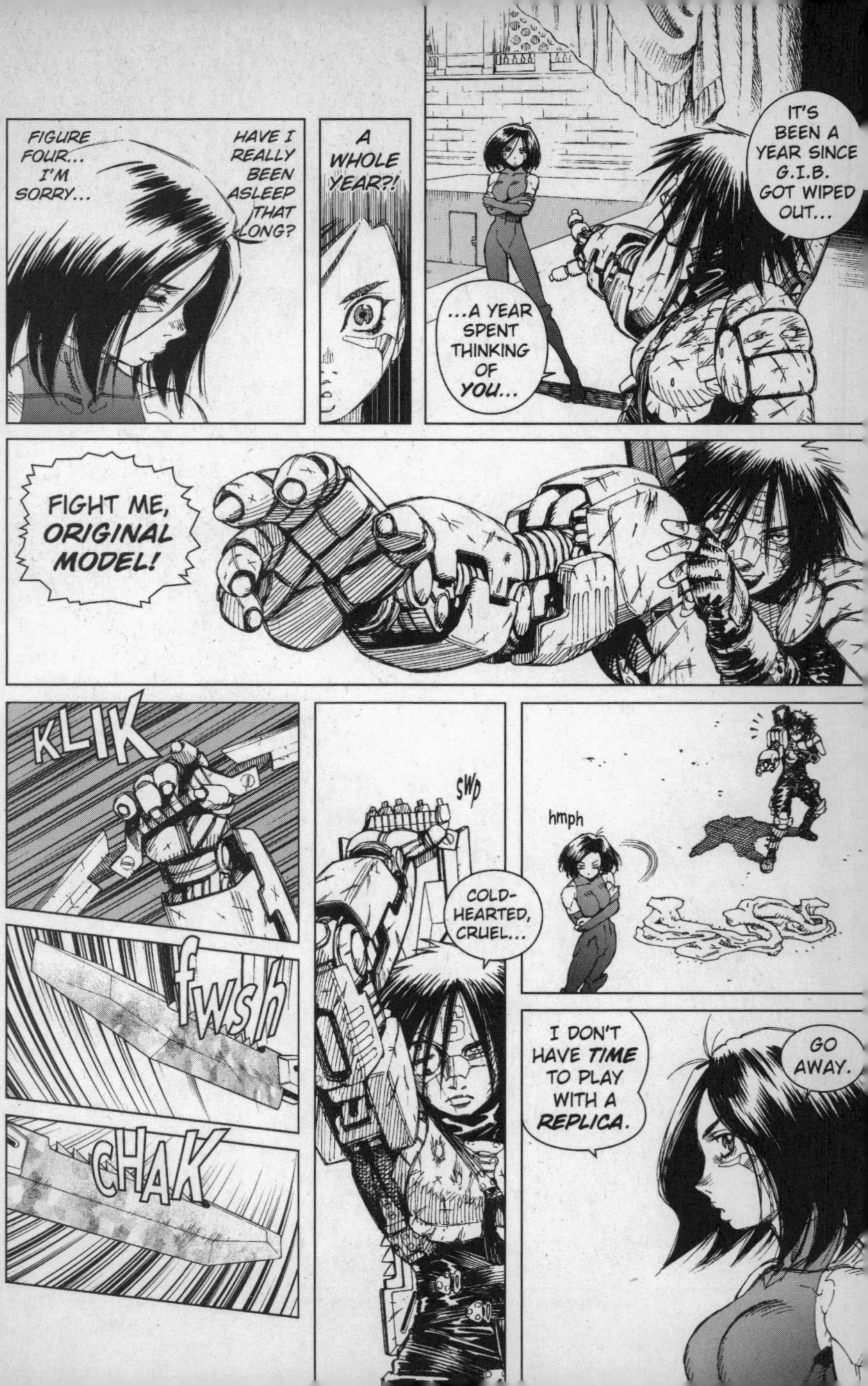
IT'S BEEN A YEAR SINCE G.I.B. GOT WIPED OUT...
...A YEAR SPENT THINKING OF YOU...
A WHOLE YEAR?!
HAVE I REALLY BEEN ASLEEP THAT LONG?
FIGURE FOUR... I'M SORRY...
FIGHT ME, ORIGINAL MODEL!
hmph
I DON'T HAVE TIME TO PLAY WITH A REPLICA.
GO AWAY.
SWP
COLD-HEARTED, CRUEL...
KLIK
fwsh
CHAK

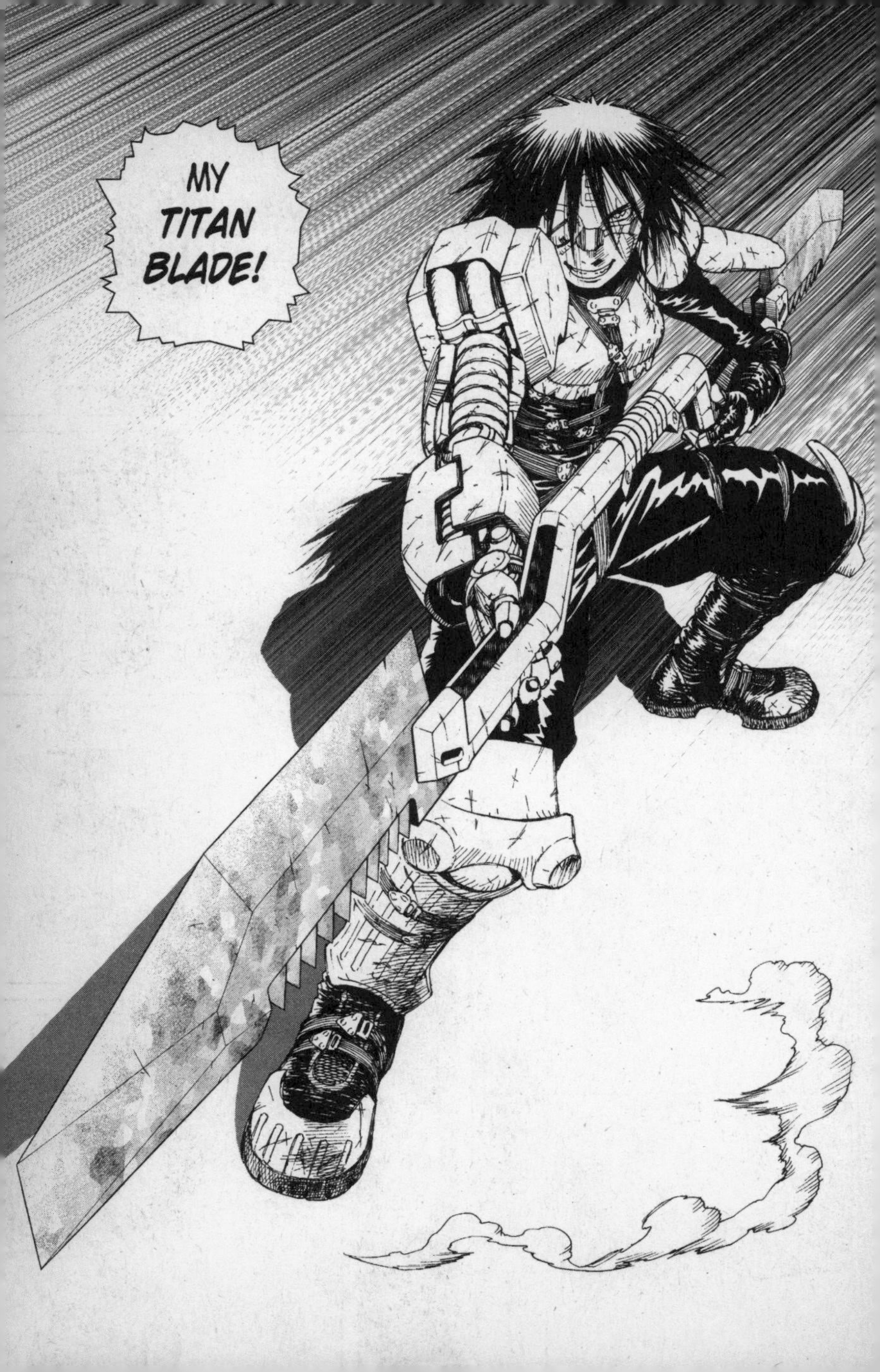
MY TITAN BLADE!

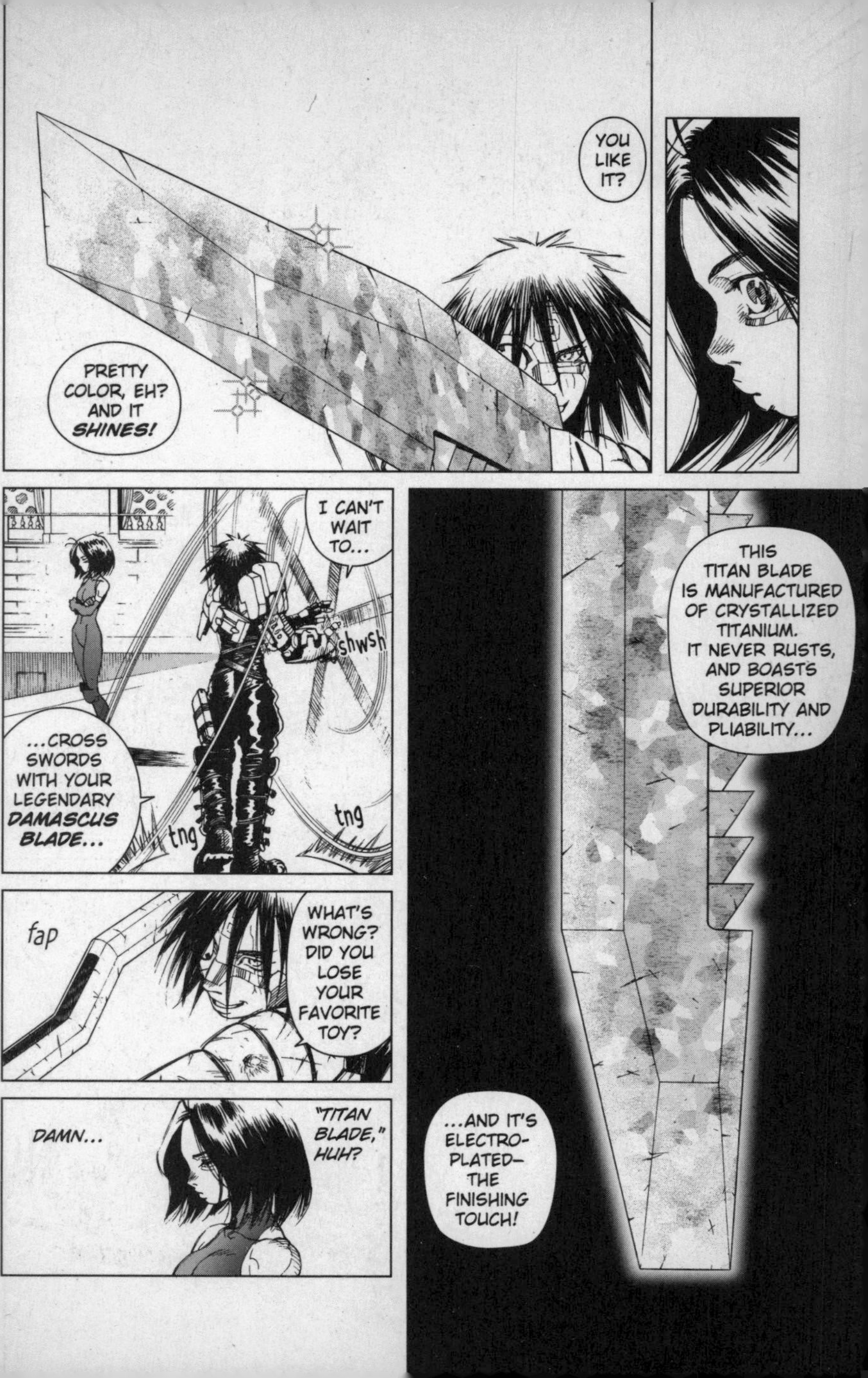
YOU LIKE IT?
PRETTY COLOR, EH? AND IT *SHINES!*
THIS TITAN BLADE IS MANUFACTURED OF CRYSTALLIZED TITANIUM. IT NEVER RUSTS, AND BOASTS SUPERIOR DURABILITY AND PLIABILITY...
...AND IT'S ELECTRO-PLATED— THE FINISHING TOUCH!
I CAN'T WAIT TO...
shwsh
...CROSS SWORDS WITH YOUR LEGENDARY *DAMASCUS BLADE...*
tng
tng
fap
WHAT'S WRONG? DID YOU LOSE YOUR FAVORITE TOY?
"TITAN BLADE," HUH?
DAMN...

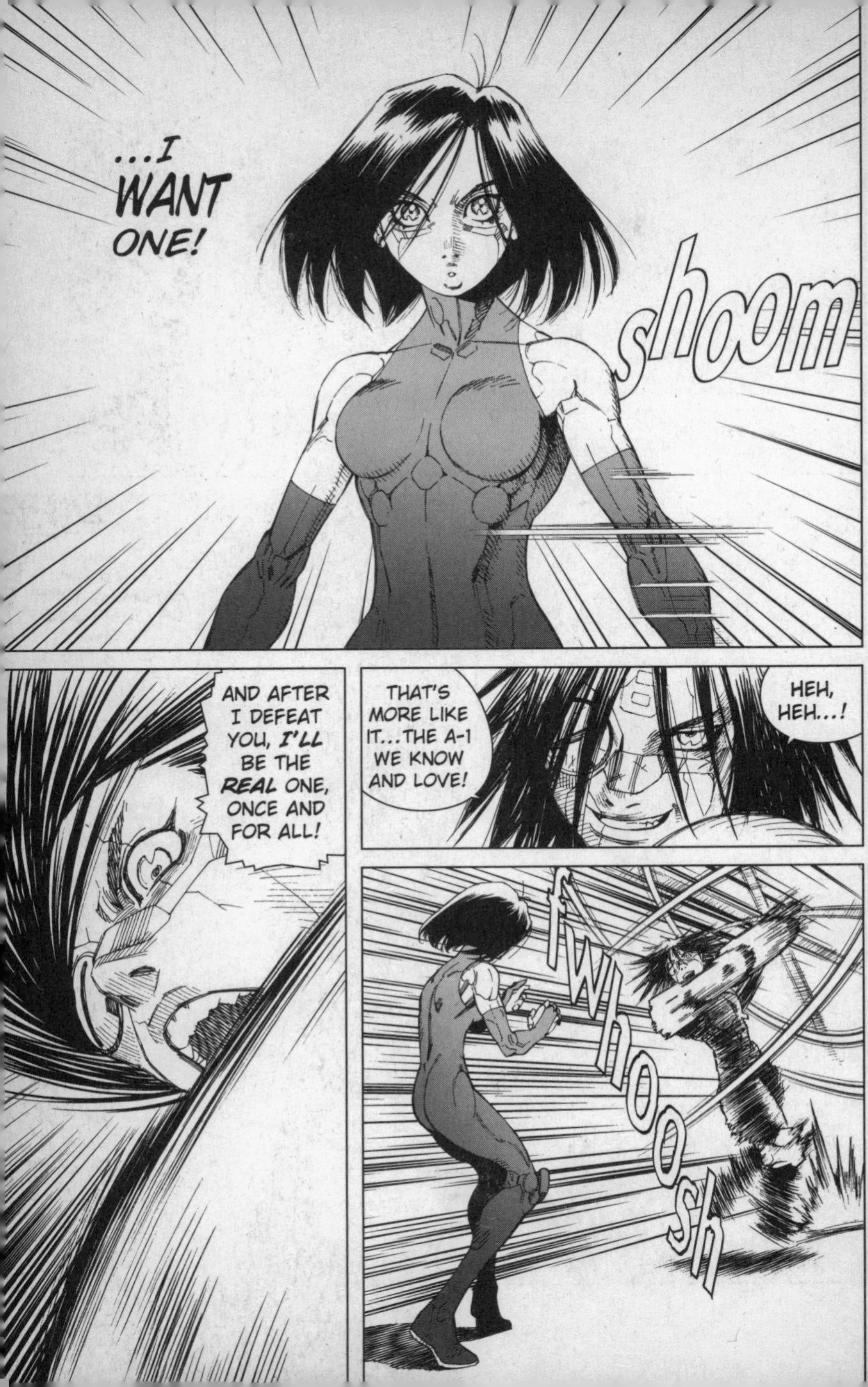
...I WANT ONE!
shoom
AND AFTER I DEFEAT YOU, I'LL BE THE REAL ONE, ONCE AND FOR ALL!
THAT'S MORE LIKE IT...THE A-1 WE KNOW AND LOVE!
HEH, HEH...!
fwhoosh

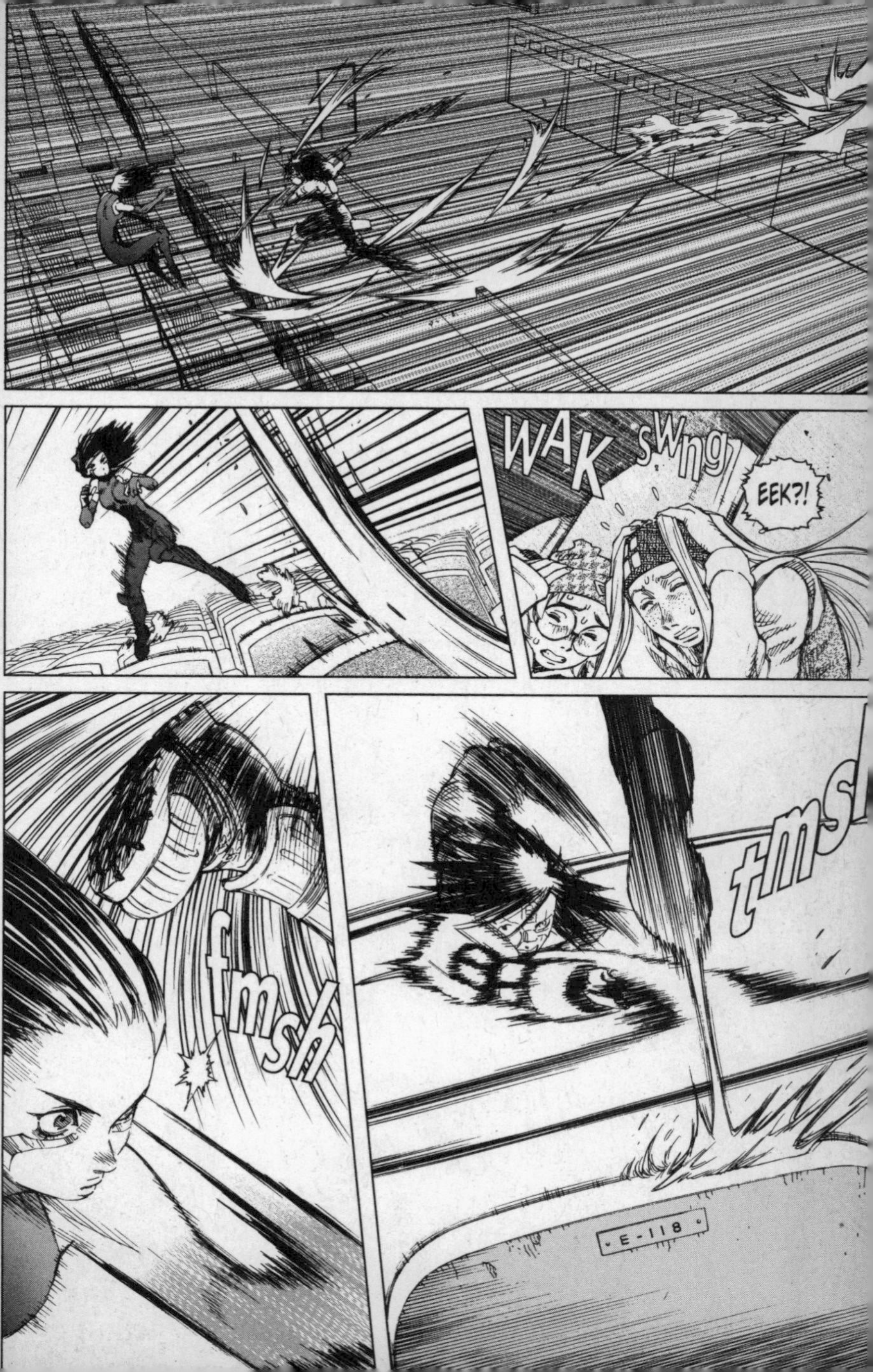
WAK
swng
EEK?!
tmsh
E-118
fmsh

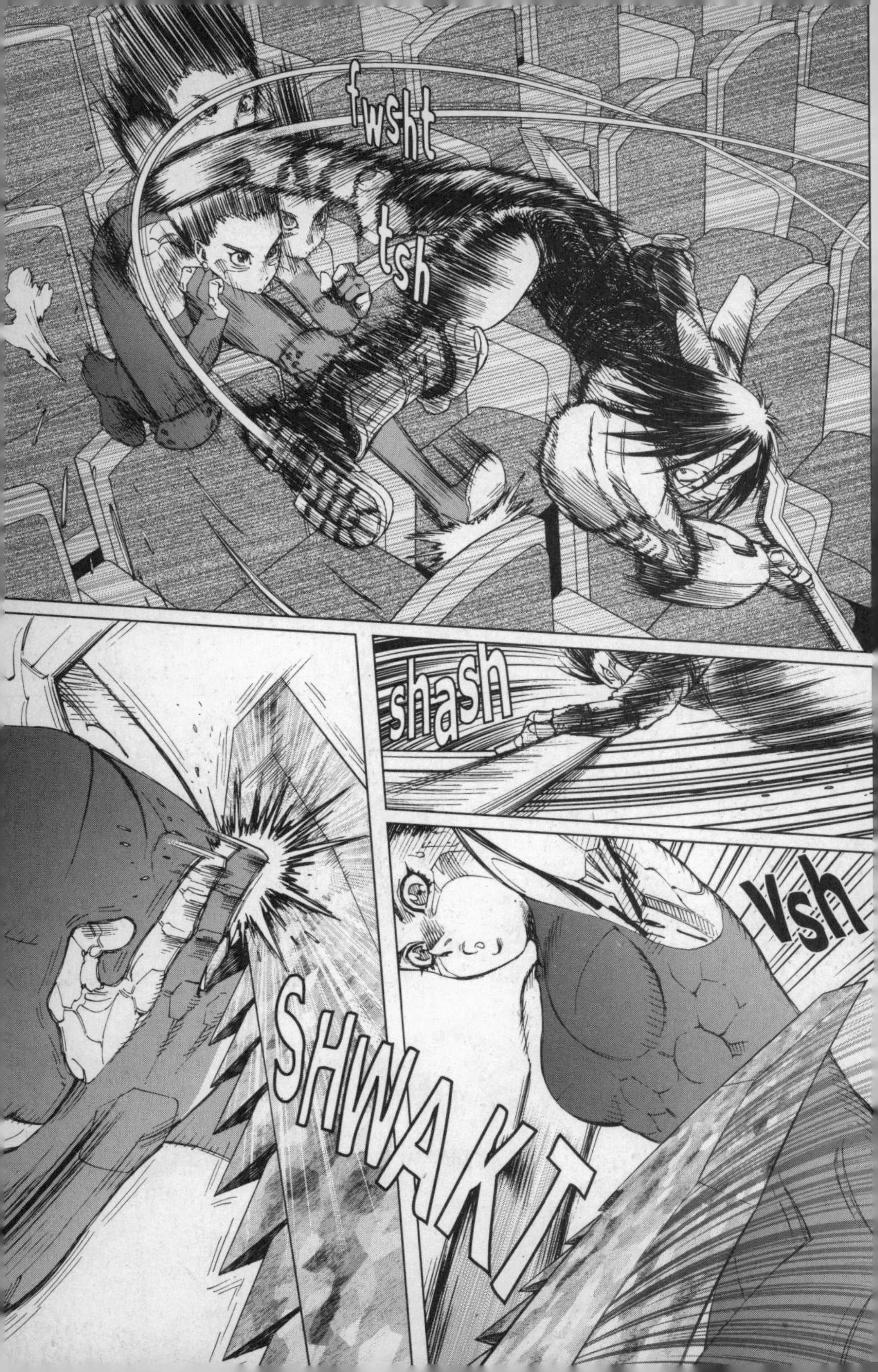
fwsht
tsh
shash
Vsh
SHWAKT

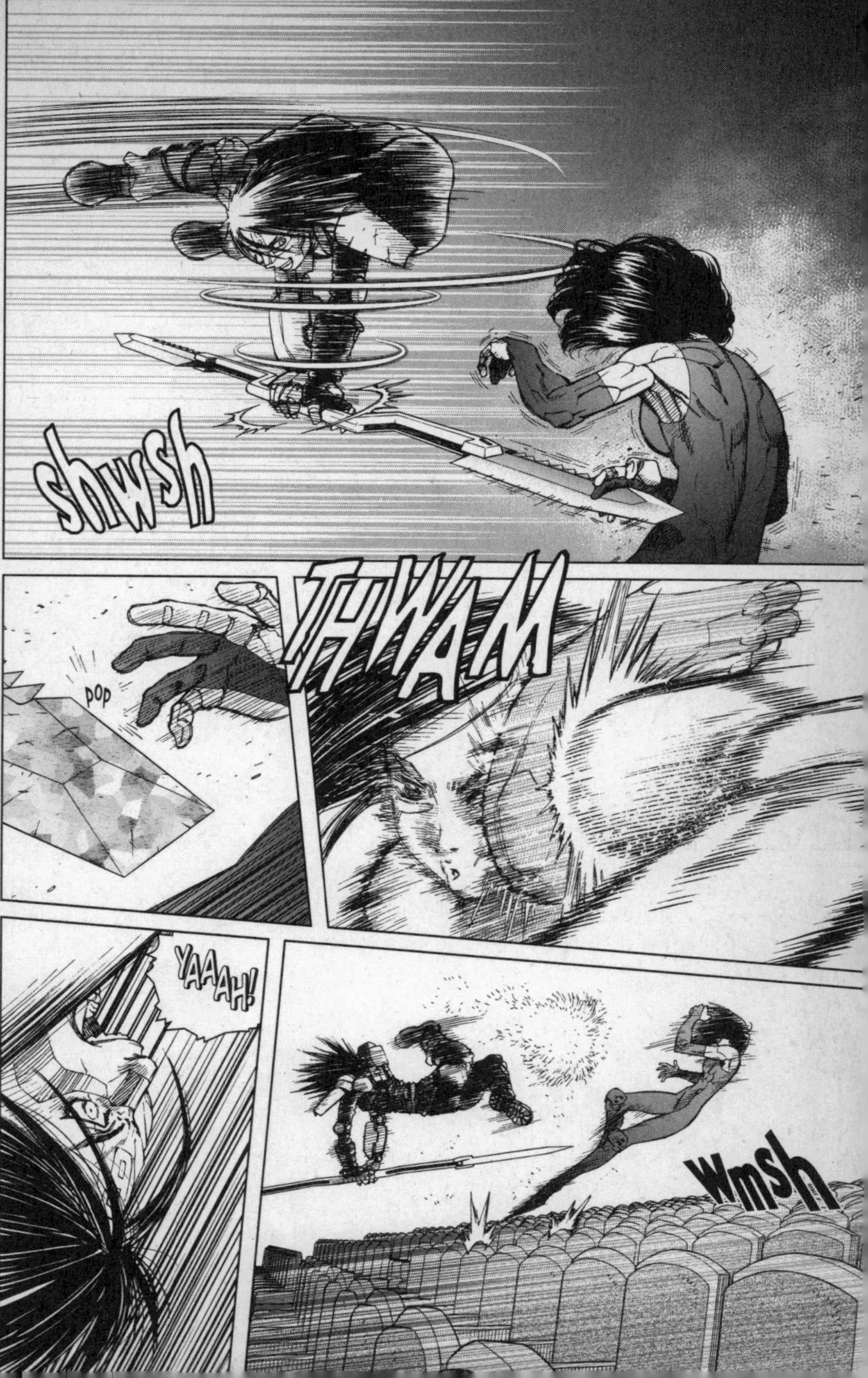
shiwsh
THWAM
pop
Wmsh
YAAAH!

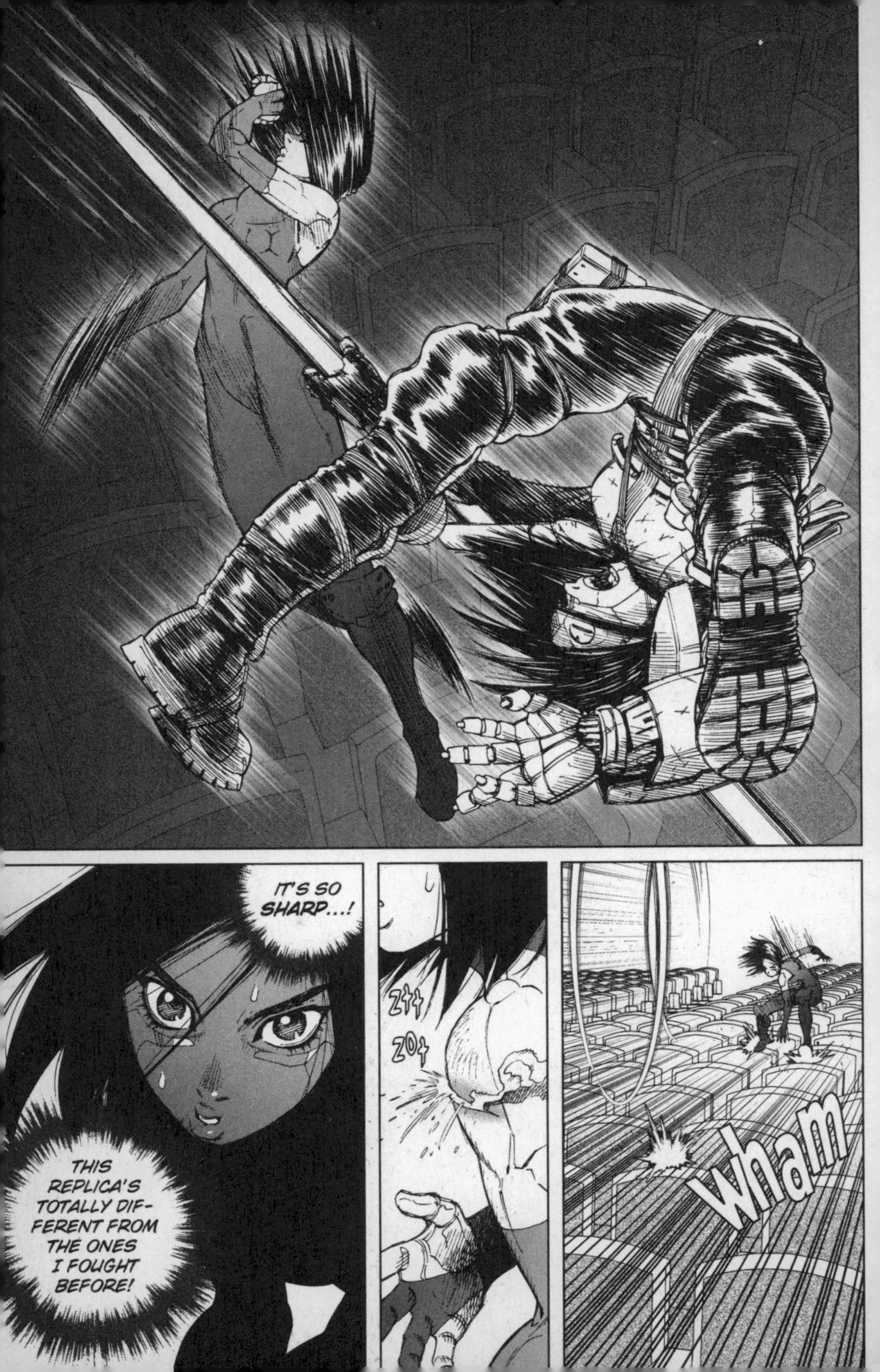
wham
IT'S SO SHARP...!
THIS REPLICA'S TOTALLY DIF-FERENT FROM THE ONES I FOUGHT BEFORE!

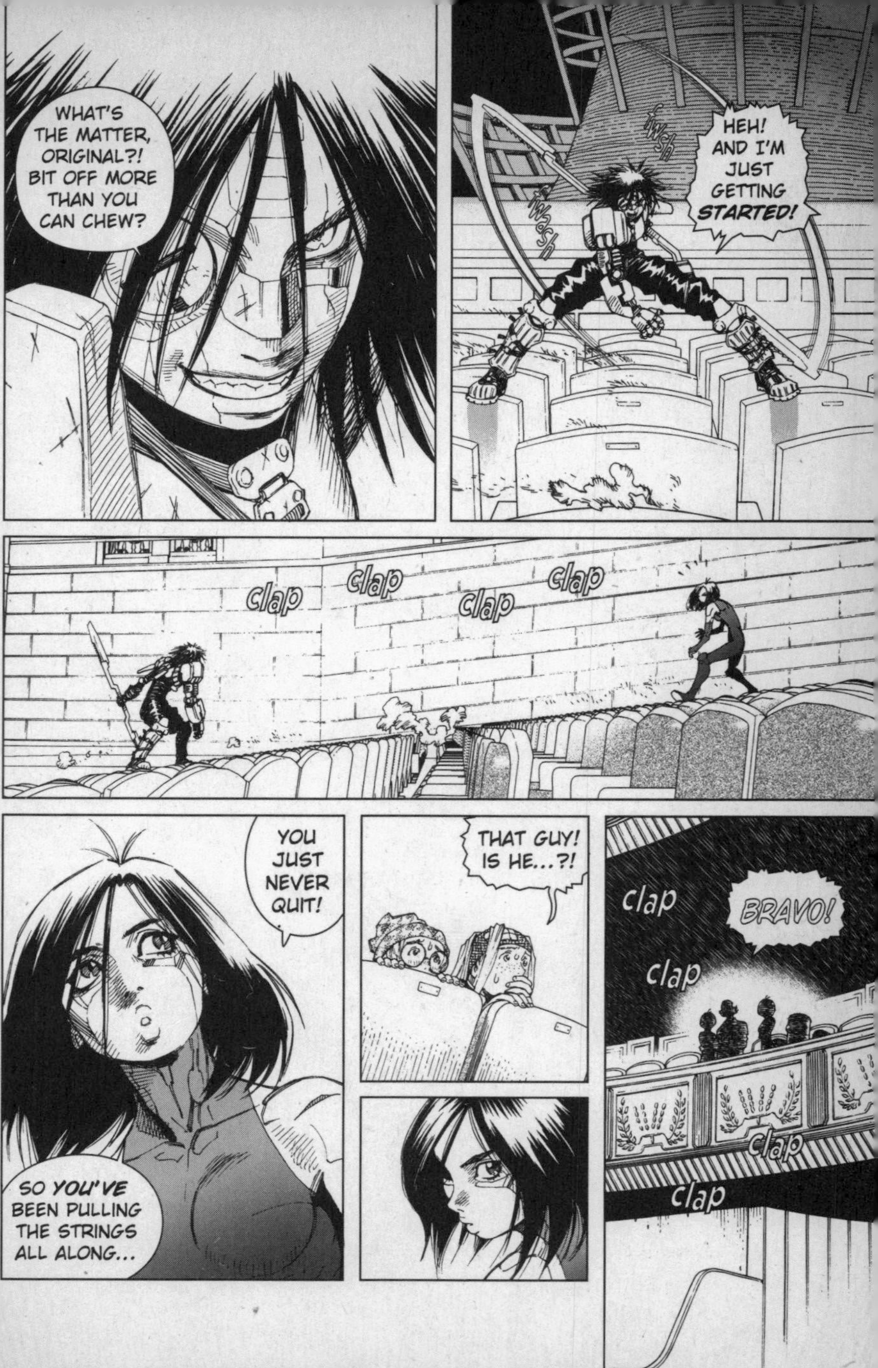
WHAT'S THE MATTER, ORIGINAL?! BIT OFF MORE THAN YOU CAN CHEW?
fwsh
fwash
HEH! AND I'M JUST GETTING STARTED!
clap
clap
clap
clap
YOU JUST NEVER QUIT!
SO YOU'VE BEEN PULLING THE STRINGS ALL ALONG...
THAT GUY! IS HE...?!
clap
BRAVO!
clap
clap
clap

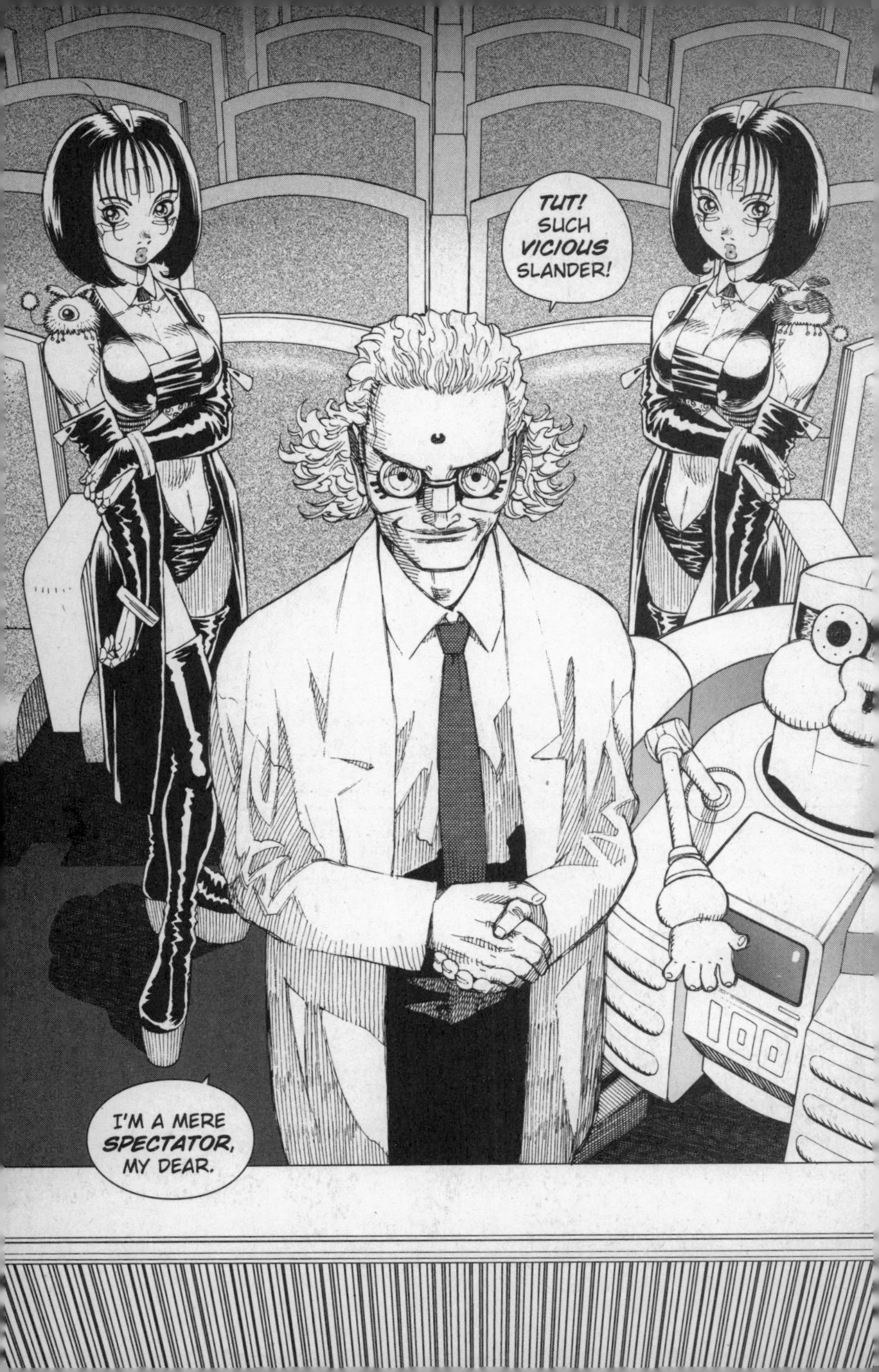
TUT! SUCH VICIOUS SLANDER!
I'M A MERE SPECTATOR, MY DEAR.

PHASE 05: No Way!

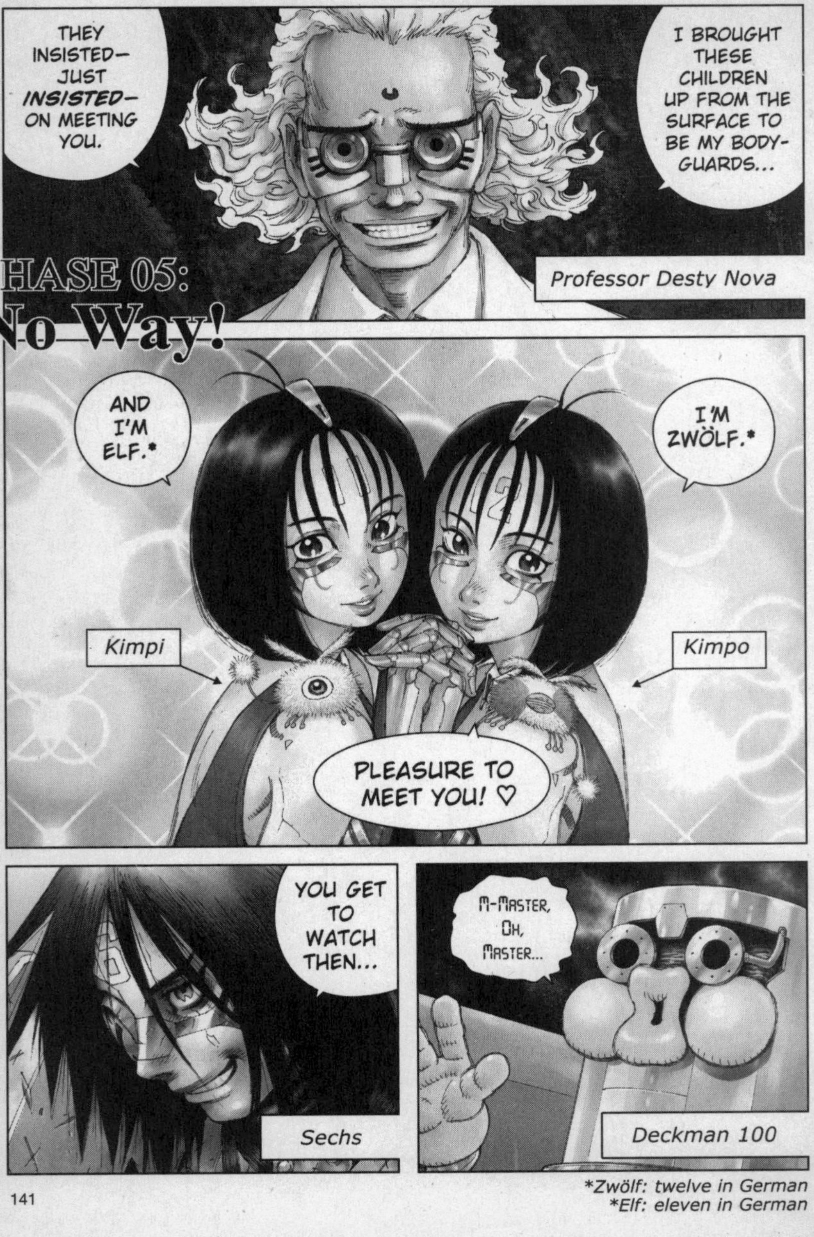
I BROUGHT THESE CHILDREN UP FROM THE SURFACE TO BE MY BODY-GUARDS...
THEY INSISTED—JUST *INSISTED*—ON MEETING YOU.
Professor Desty Nova
I'M ZWÖLF.*
AND I'M ELF.*
Kimpo
Kimpi
PLEASURE TO MEET YOU! ♡
M-MASTER, OH, MASTER...
Deckman 100
YOU GET TO WATCH THEN...
Sechs

*Zwölf: twelve in German
*Elf: eleven in German

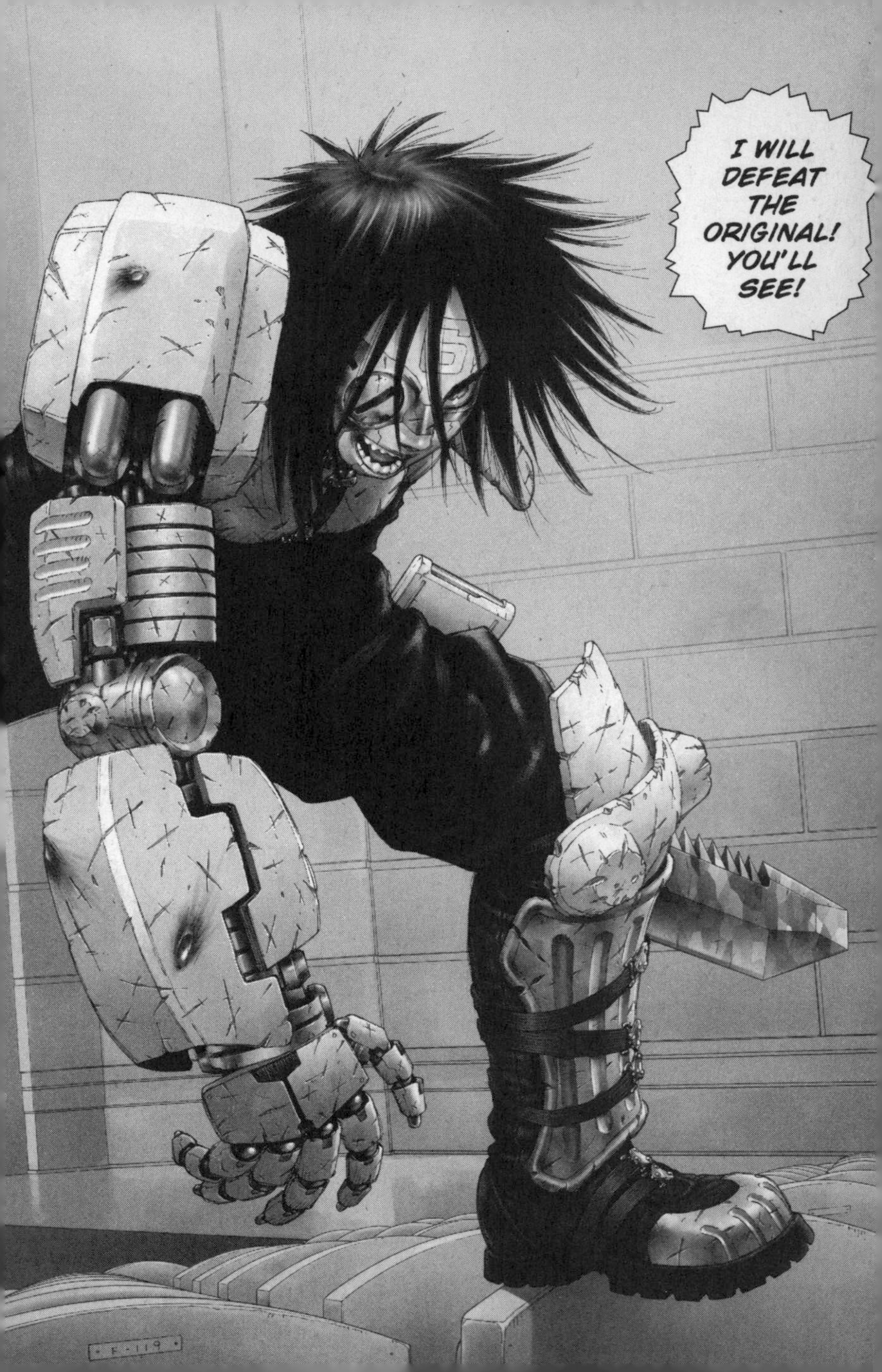
I WILL DEFEAT THE ORIGINAL! YOU'LL SEE!
F-119

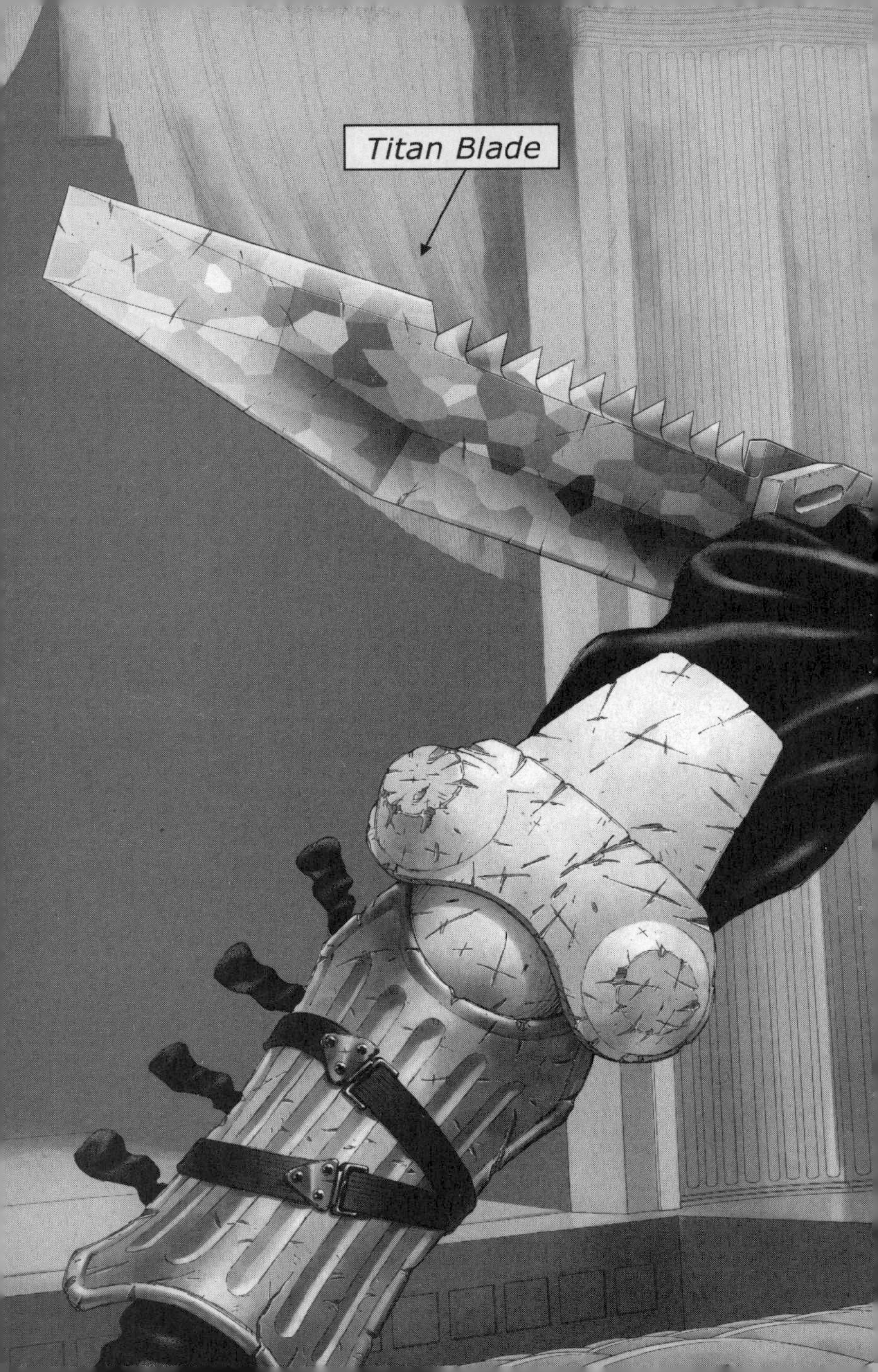
Titan Blade

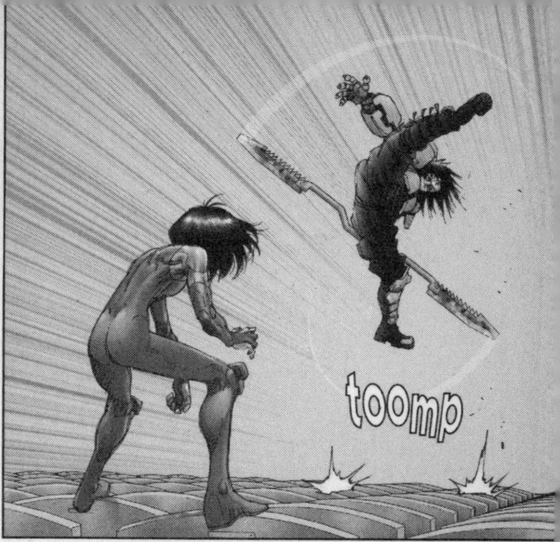
toomp

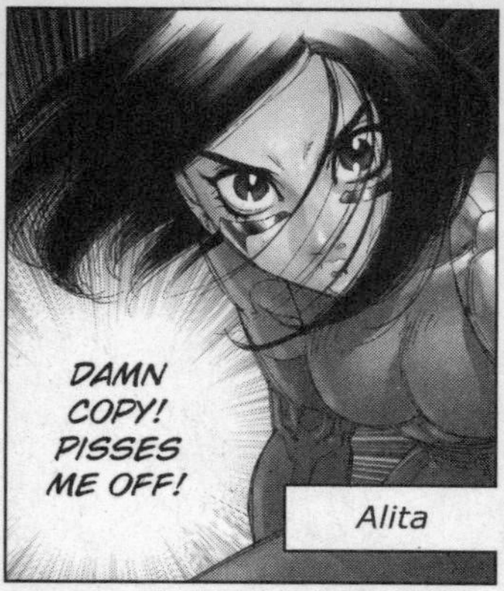
DAMN COPY! PISSES ME OFF!
Alita

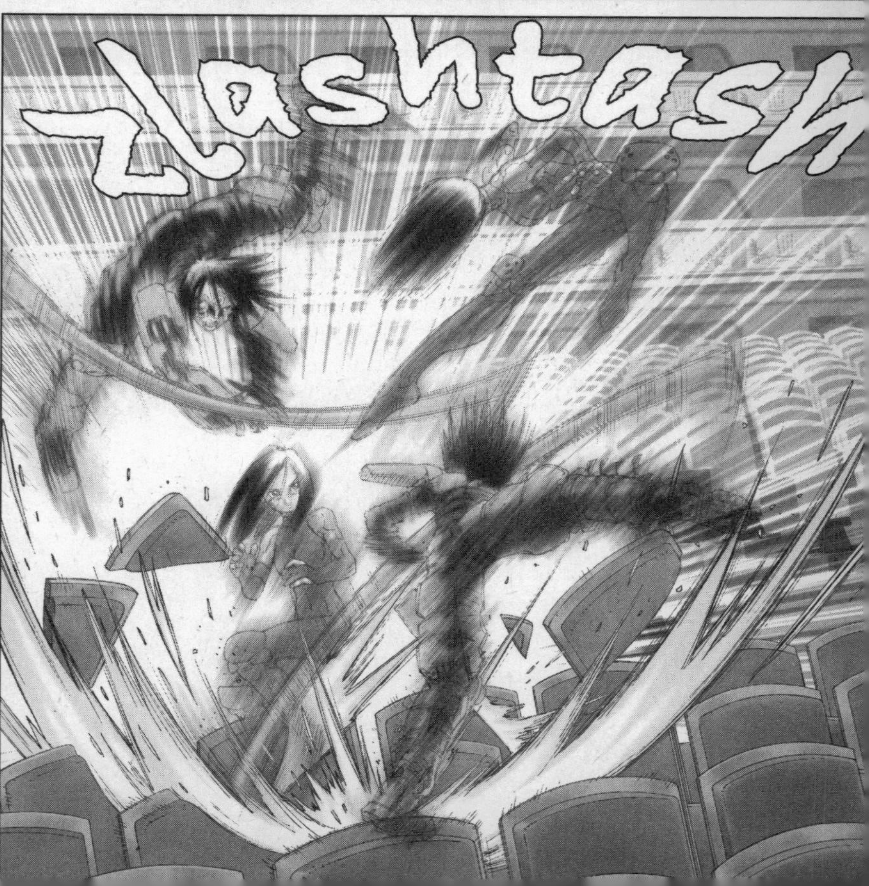
Zlashtash

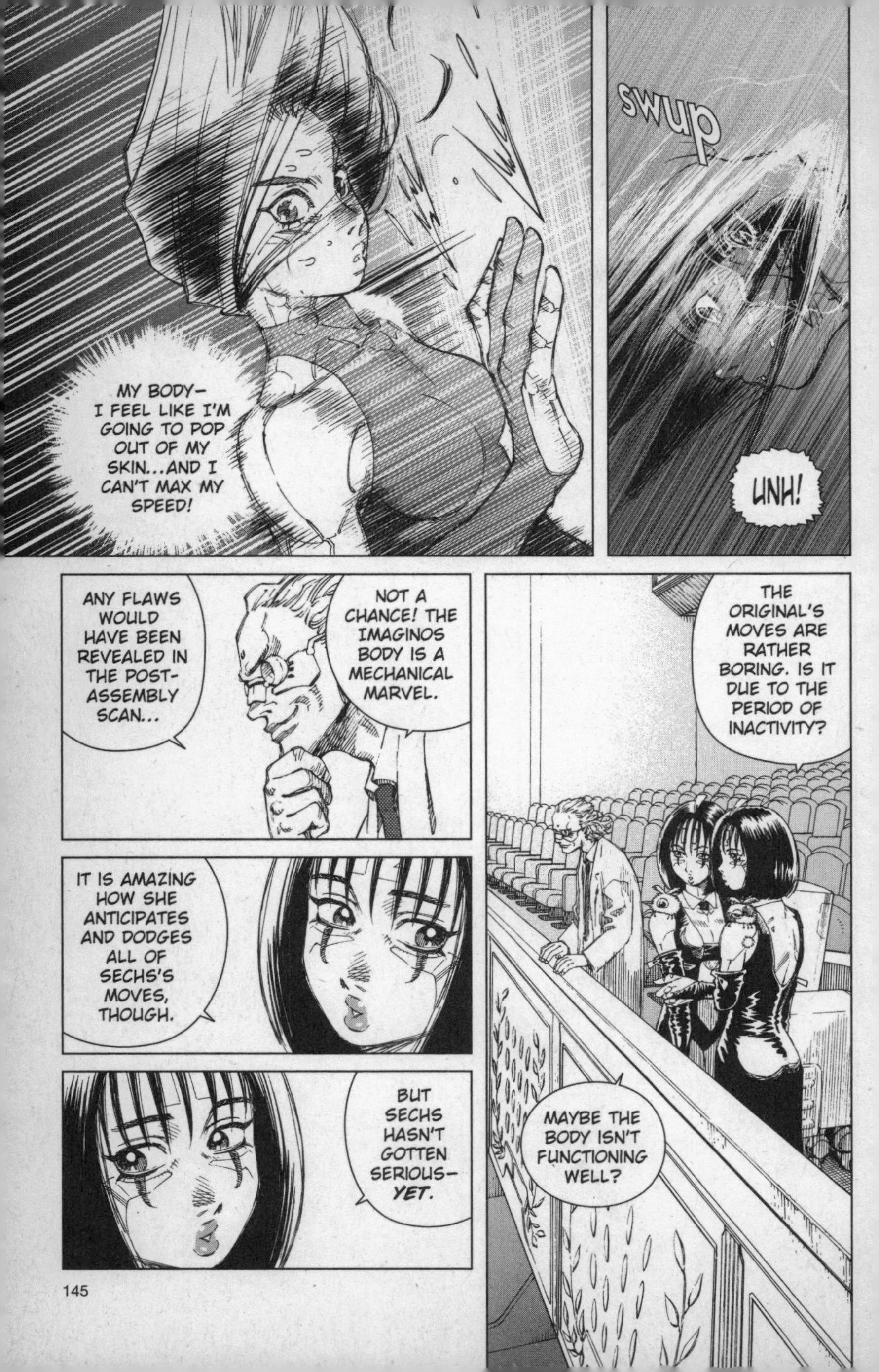
swup
UNH!
MY BODY— I FEEL LIKE I'M GOING TO POP OUT OF MY SKIN...AND I CAN'T MAX MY SPEED!
THE ORIGINAL'S MOVES ARE RATHER BORING. IS IT DUE TO THE PERIOD OF INACTIVITY?
MAYBE THE BODY ISN'T FUNCTIONING WELL?
NOT A CHANCE! THE IMAGINOS BODY IS A MECHANICAL MARVEL.
ANY FLAWS WOULD HAVE BEEN REVEALED IN THE POST-ASSEMBLY SCAN...
IT IS AMAZING HOW SHE ANTICIPATES AND DODGES ALL OF SECHS'S MOVES, THOUGH.
BUT SECHS HASN'T GOTTEN SERIOUS—*YET*.

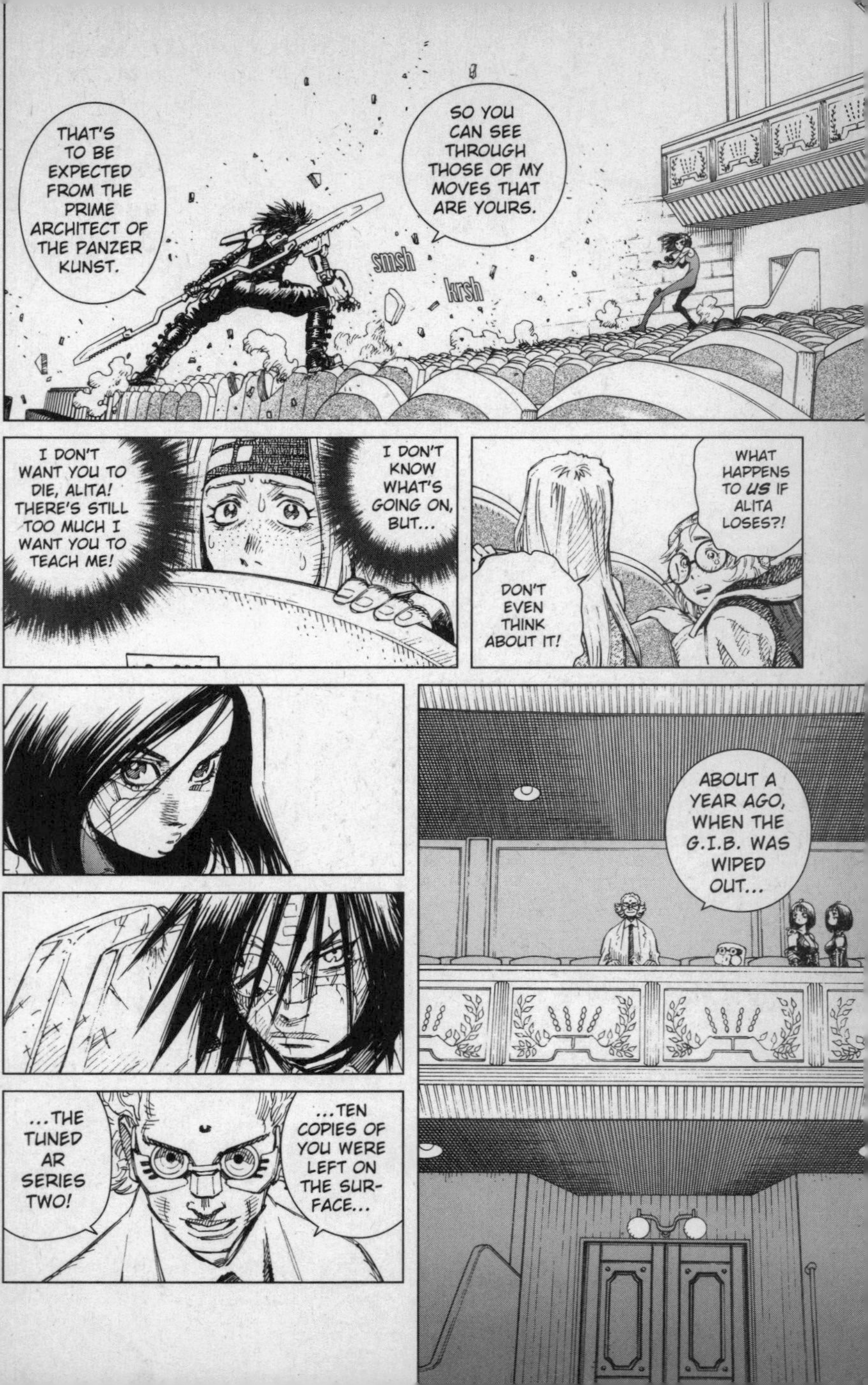
SO YOU CAN SEE THROUGH THOSE OF MY MOVES THAT ARE YOURS.
THAT'S TO BE EXPECTED FROM THE PRIME ARCHITECT OF THE PANZER KUNST.
krsh
smsh
WHAT HAPPENS TO US IF ALITA LOSES?!
DON'T EVEN THINK ABOUT IT!
I DON'T KNOW WHAT'S GOING ON, BUT...
I DON'T WANT YOU TO DIE, ALITA! THERE'S STILL TOO MUCH I WANT YOU TO TEACH ME!
ABOUT A YEAR AGO, WHEN THE G.I.B. WAS WIPED OUT...
...TEN COPIES OF YOU WERE LEFT ON THE SURFACE...
...THE TUNED AR SERIES TWO!

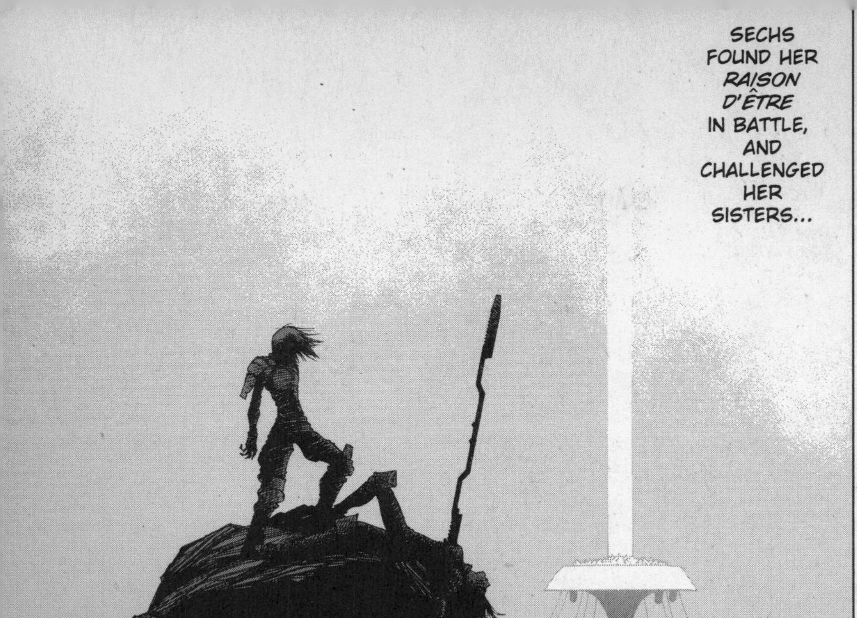
SECHS FOUND HER *RAISON D'ÊTRE* IN BATTLE, AND CHALLENGED HER SISTERS...
...DEFEATING THEM ***ALL***, EXCEPT FOR AR-11 AND AR-12 HERE.
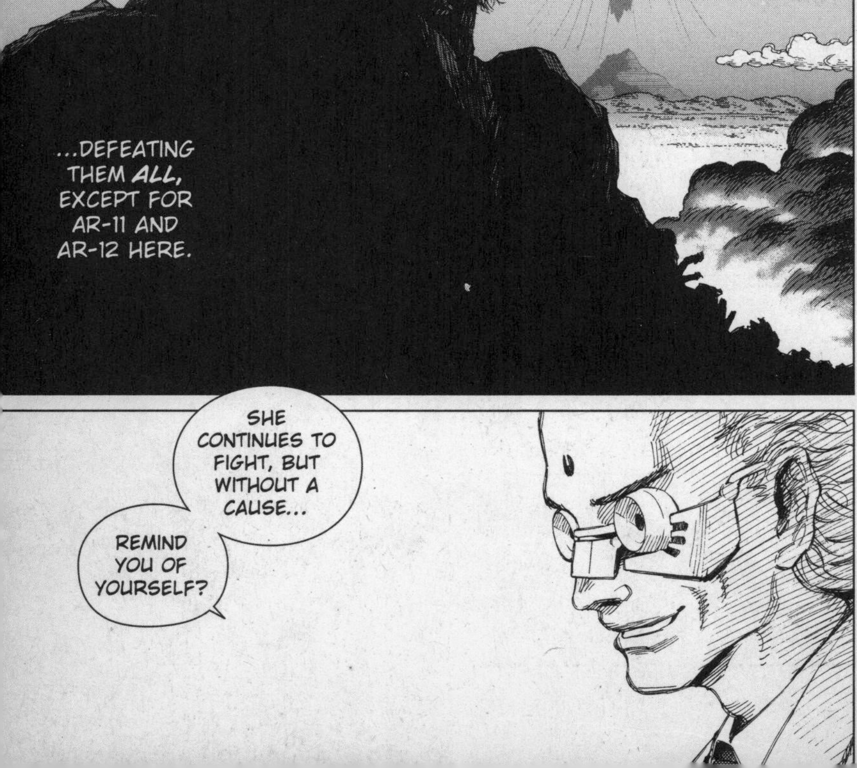
SHE CONTINUES TO FIGHT, BUT WITHOUT A CAUSE...
REMIND YOU OF YOURSELF?

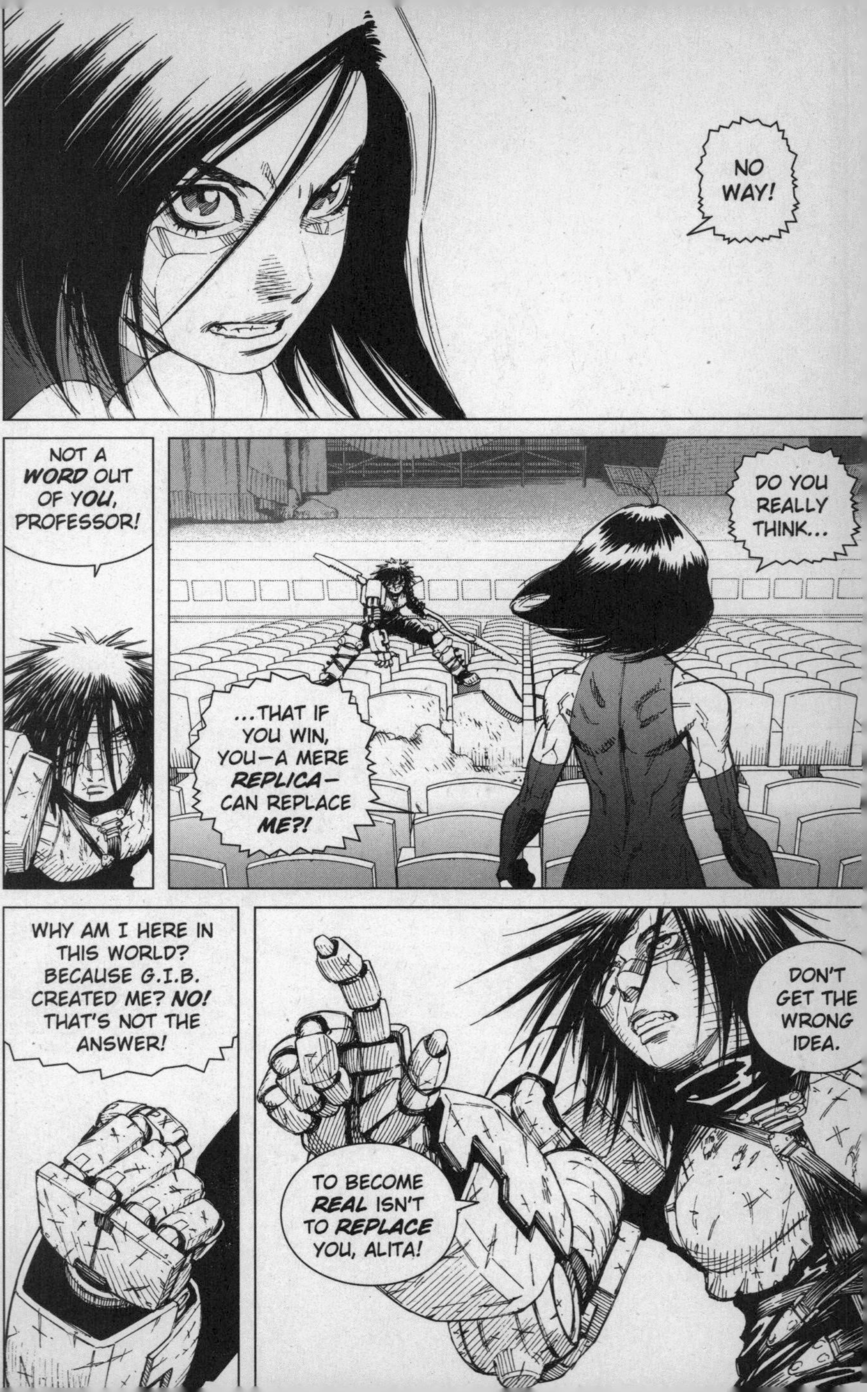
NO WAY!
DO YOU REALLY THINK...
...THAT IF YOU WIN, YOU—A MERE REPLICA—CAN REPLACE ME?!
NOT A WORD OUT OF YOU, PROFESSOR!
DON'T GET THE WRONG IDEA.
TO BECOME REAL ISN'T TO REPLACE YOU, ALITA!
WHY AM I HERE IN THIS WORLD? BECAUSE G.I.B. CREATED ME? NO! THAT'S NOT THE ANSWER!

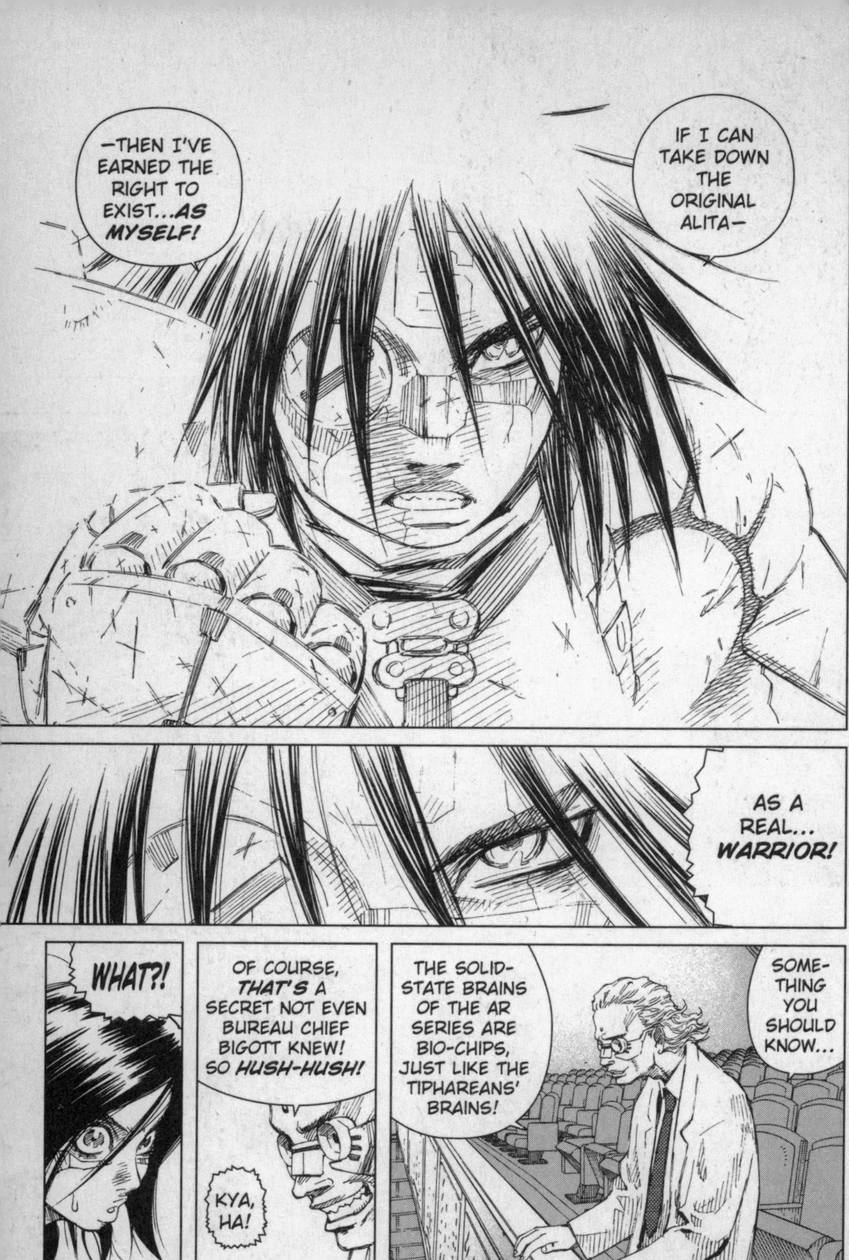
IF I CAN TAKE DOWN THE ORIGINAL ALITA—
—THEN I'VE EARNED THE RIGHT TO EXIST...AS MYSELF!
AS A REAL... WARRIOR!
SOME-THING YOU SHOULD KNOW...
THE SOLID-STATE BRAINS OF THE AR SERIES ARE BIO-CHIPS, JUST LIKE THE TIPHAREANS' BRAINS!
OF COURSE, THAT'S A SECRET NOT EVEN BUREAU CHIEF BIGOTT KNEW! SO HUSH-HUSH!
KYA, HA!
WHAT?!

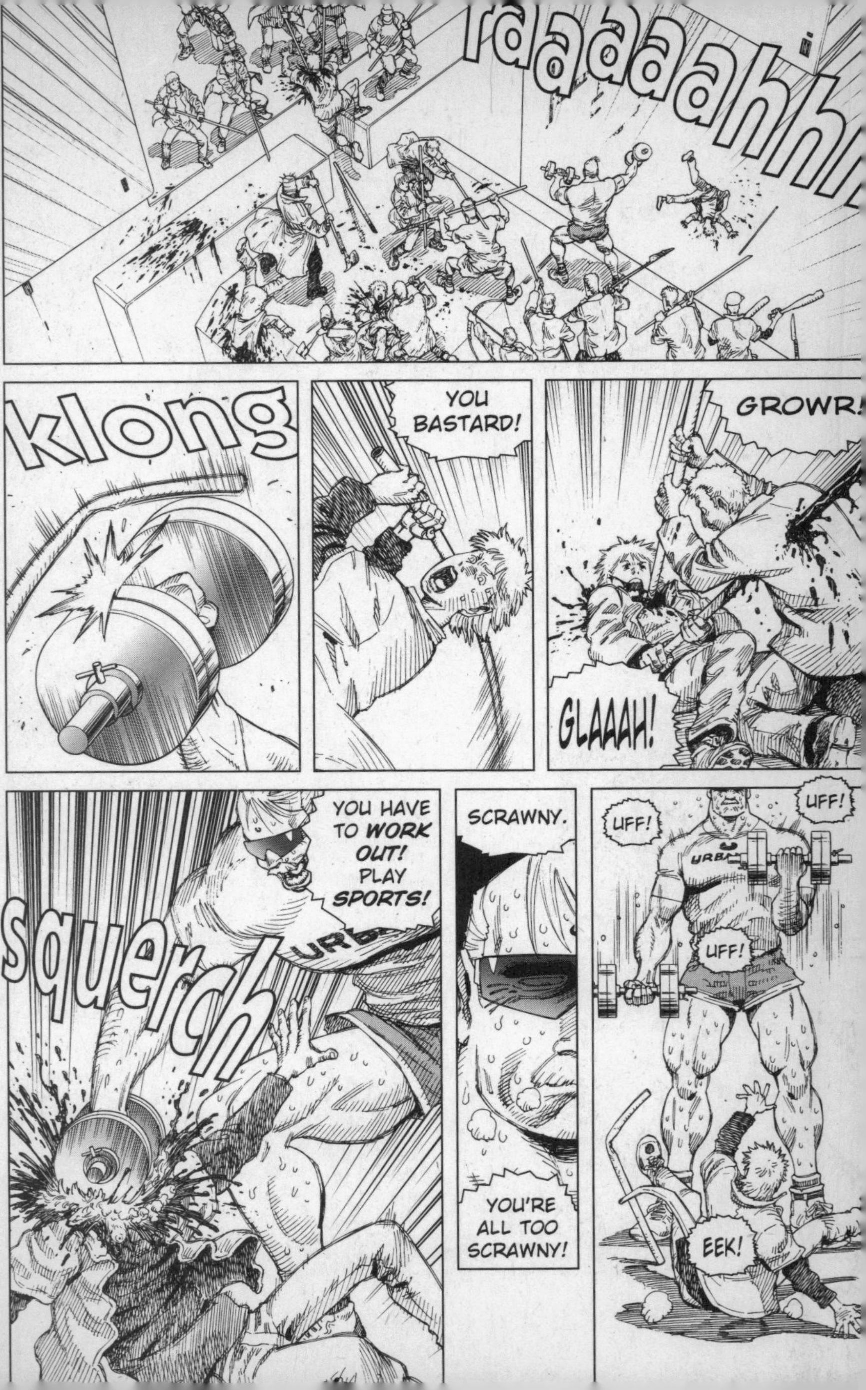
raaaaahhh
GROWR!
GLAAAH!
YOU BASTARD!
klong
UFF!
UFF!
UFF!
EEK!
SCRAWNY.
YOU'RE ALL TOO SCRAWNY!
YOU HAVE TO *WORK OUT!* PLAY *SPORTS!*
squerch

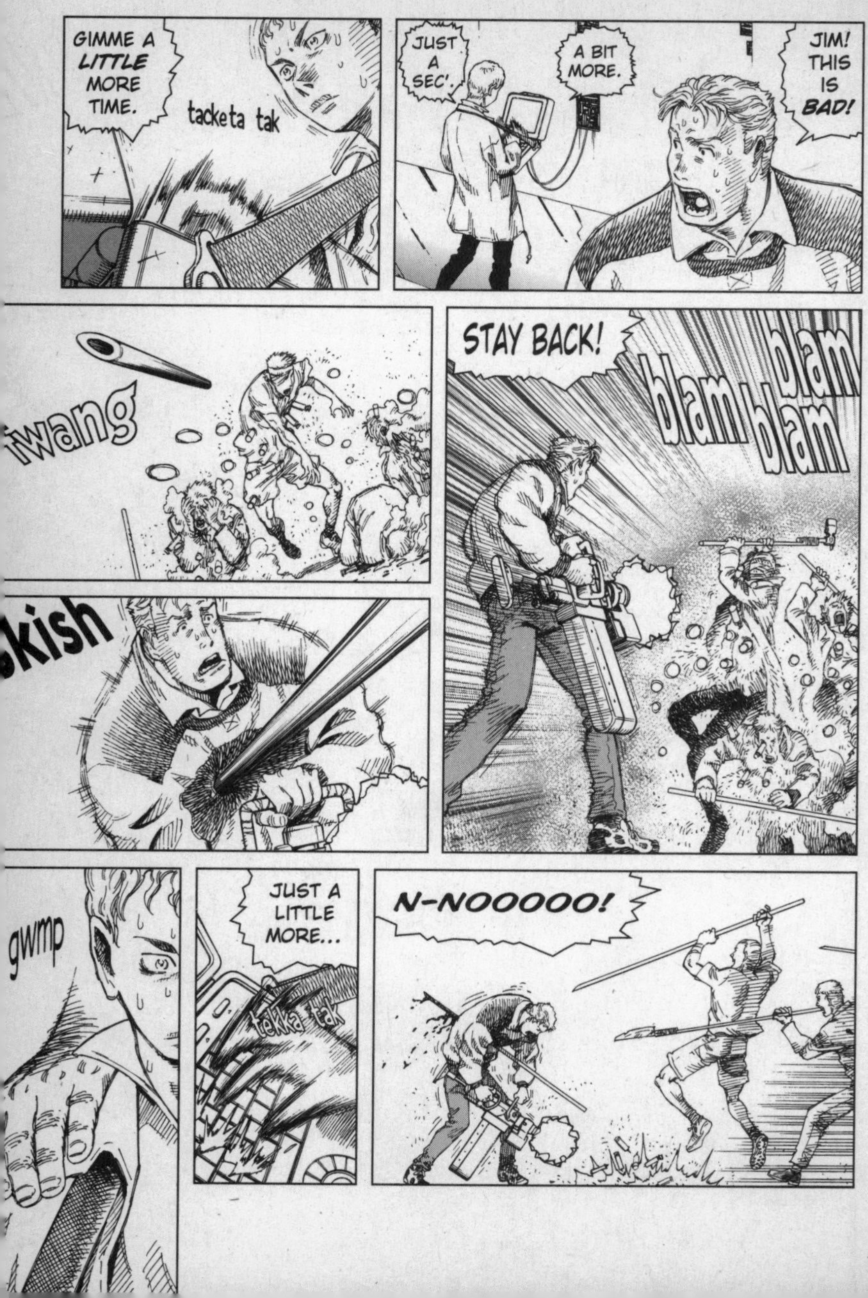

GIMME A LITTLE MORE TIME.
tacketa tak
JUST A SEC'.
A BIT MORE.
JIM! THIS IS BAD!
twang
skish
STAY BACK!
blam blam
blam blam
gwmp
JUST A LITTLE MORE...
tekka tak
N-NOOOOO!

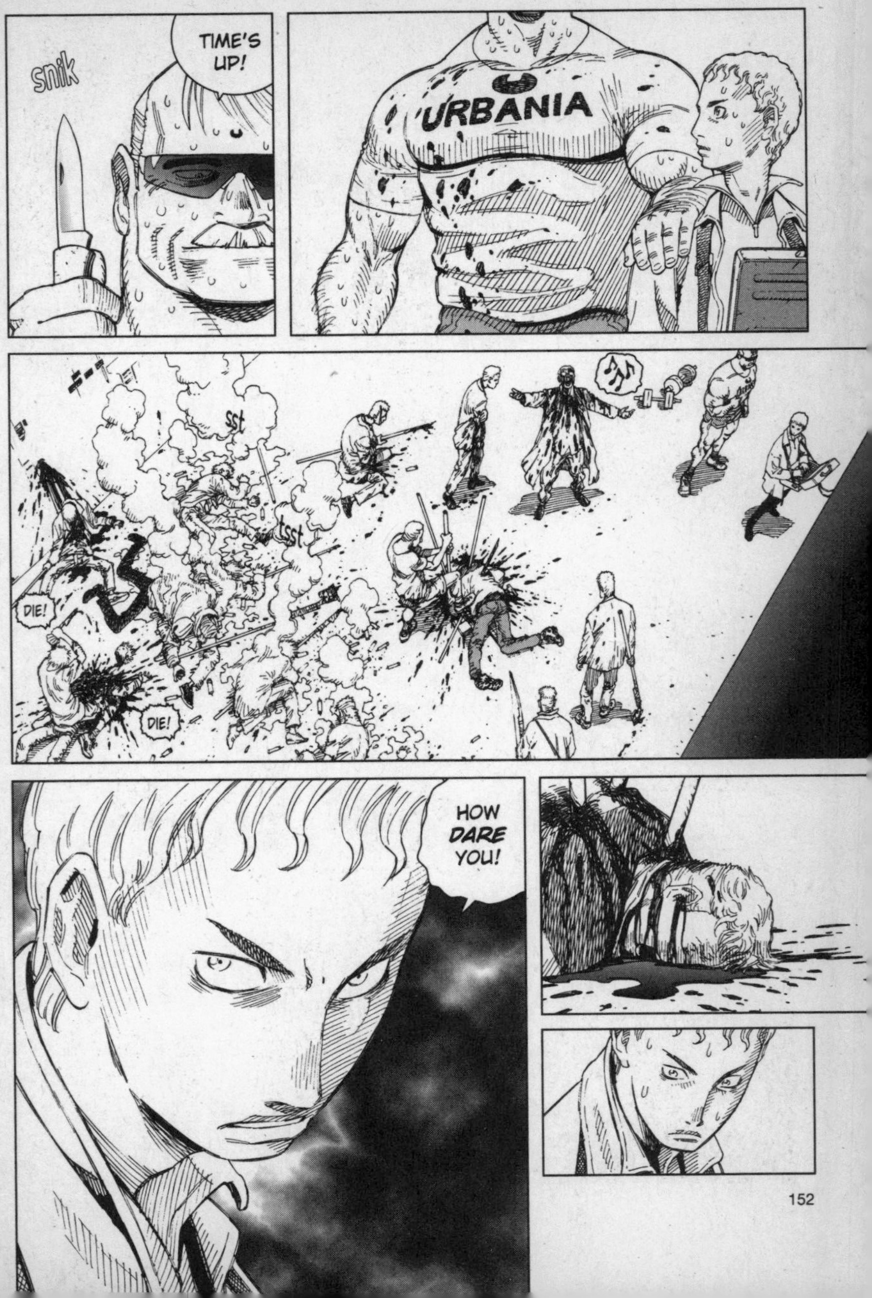
URBANIA
TIME'S UP!
snik
sst
tsst
DIE!
DIE!
HOW DARE YOU!

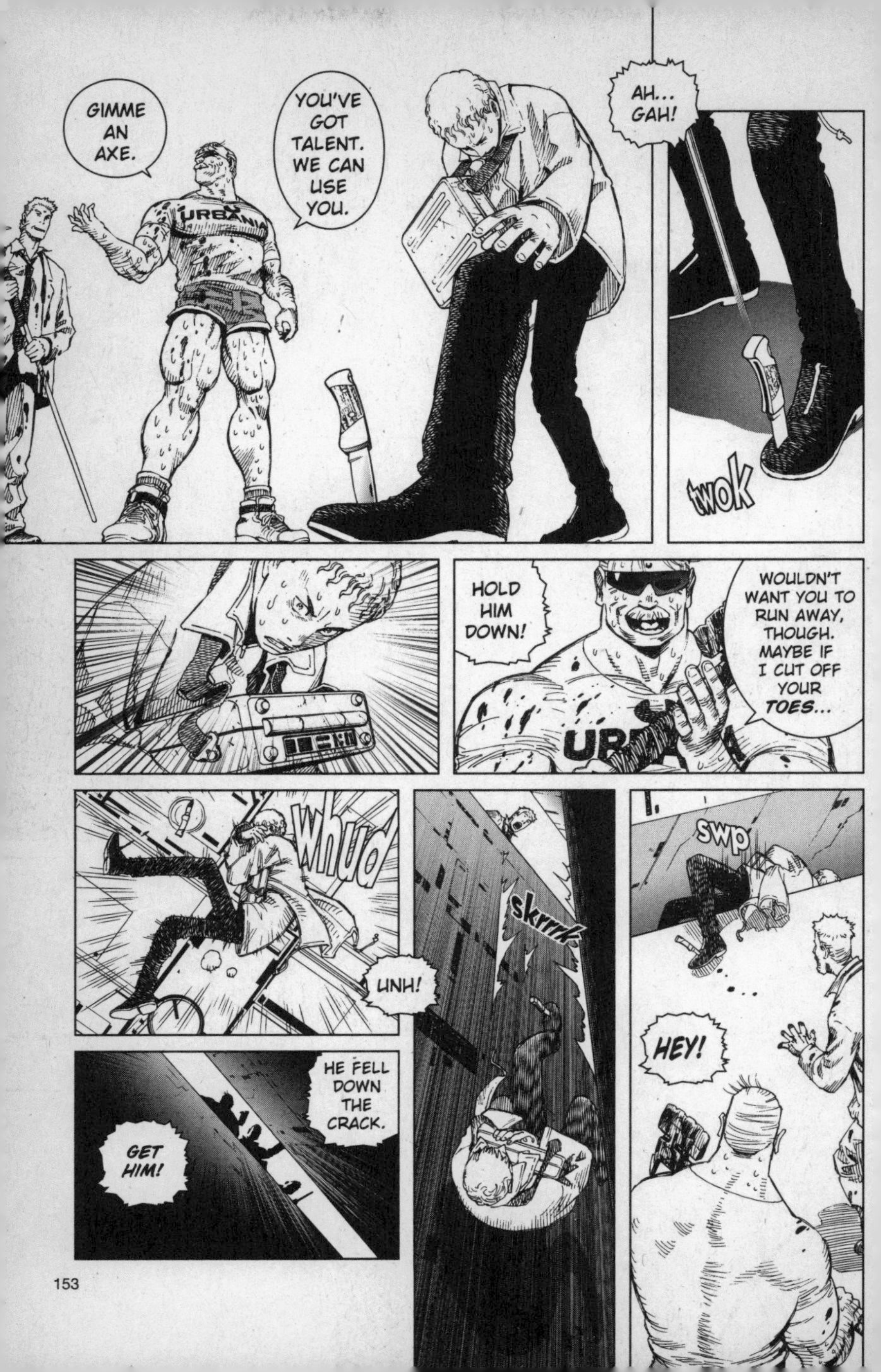
GIMME AN AXE.
YOU'VE GOT TALENT. WE CAN USE YOU.
AH... GAH!
twok
HOLD HIM DOWN!
WOULDN'T WANT YOU TO RUN AWAY, THOUGH. MAYBE IF I CUT OFF YOUR *TOES...*
whud
UNH!
HE FELL DOWN THE CRACK.
GET HIM!
skrrrk
swp
...
HEY!

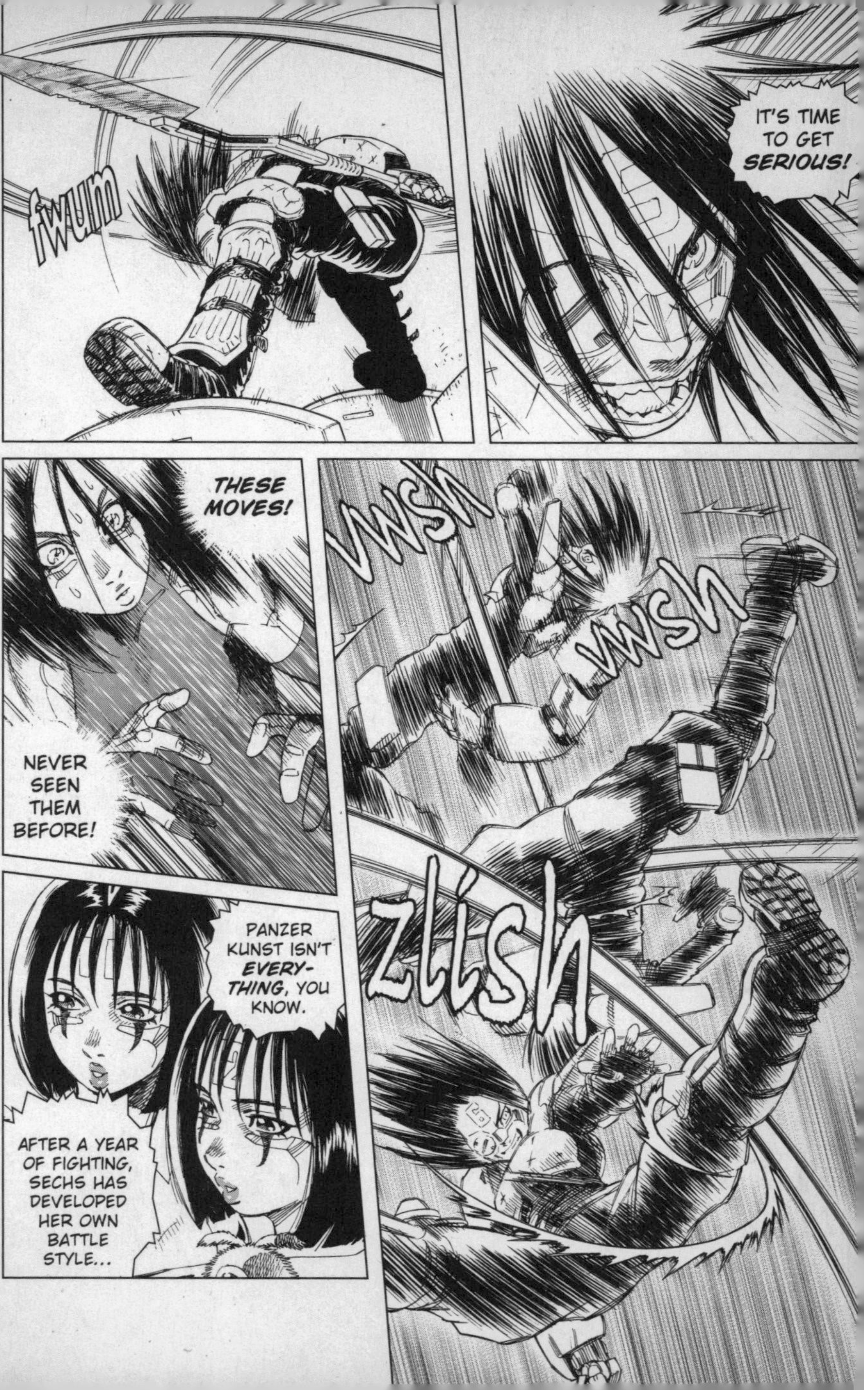
IT'S TIME TO GET SERIOUS!
fwum
vwsh
vwsh
zlish
THESE MOVES!
NEVER SEEN THEM BEFORE!
PANZER KUNST ISN'T EVERY-THING, YOU KNOW.
AFTER A YEAR OF FIGHTING, SECHS HAS DEVELOPED HER OWN BATTLE STYLE...

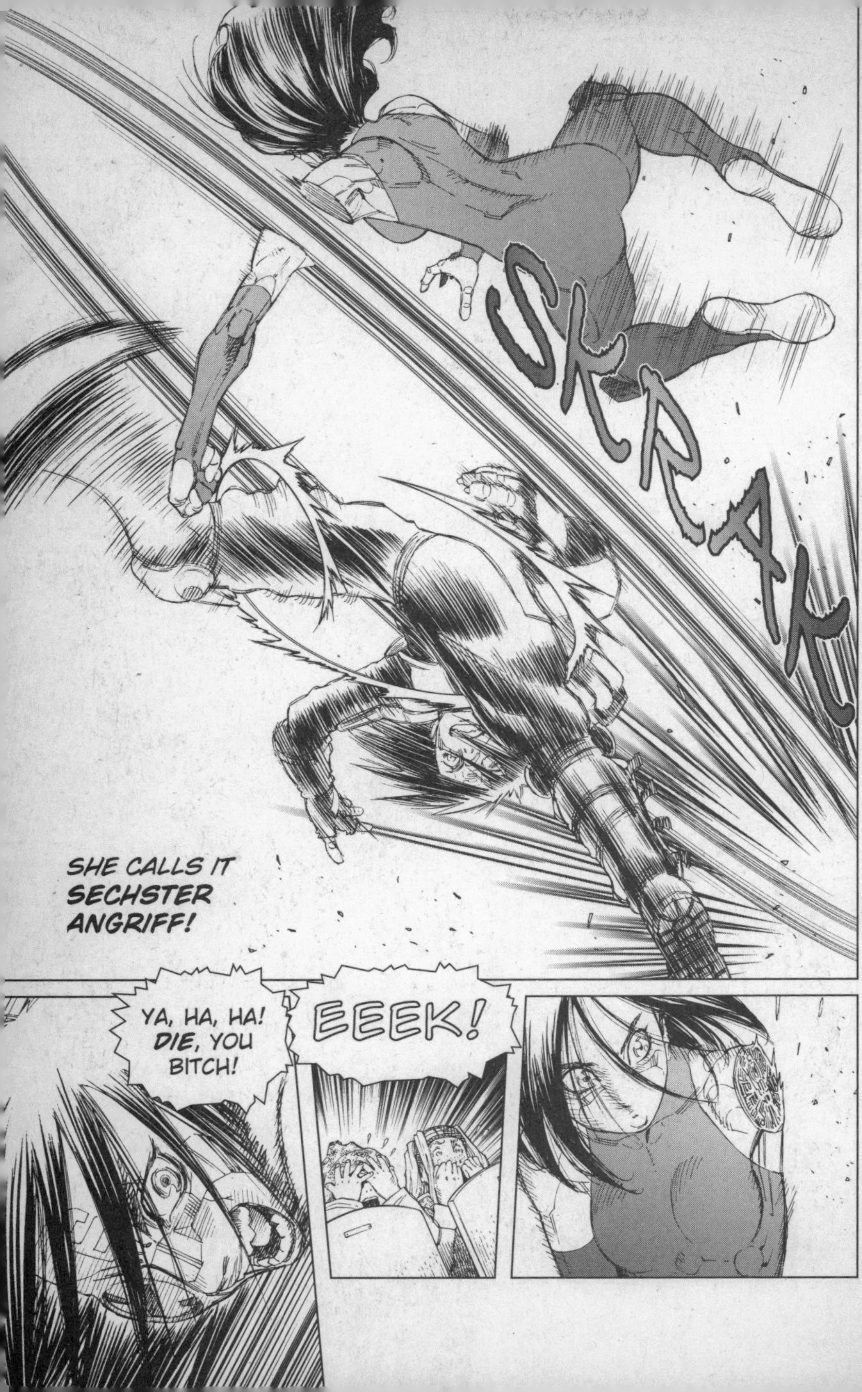
SKRAK
SHE CALLS IT SECHSTER ANGRIFF!
EEEK!
YA, HA, HA! DIE, YOU BITCH!

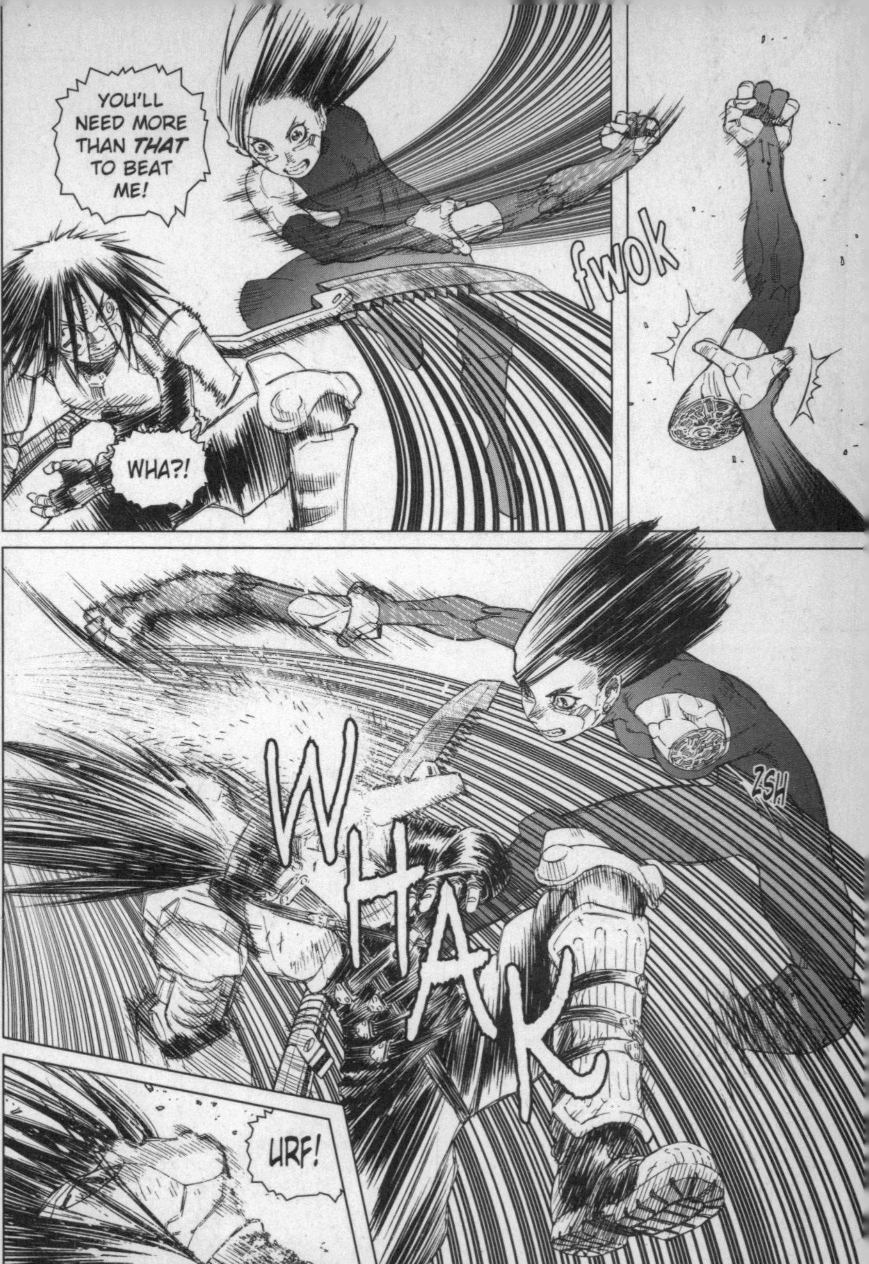
YOU'LL NEED MORE THAN *THAT* TO BEAT ME!
fwok
WHA?!
ZSH
WHAK
URF!

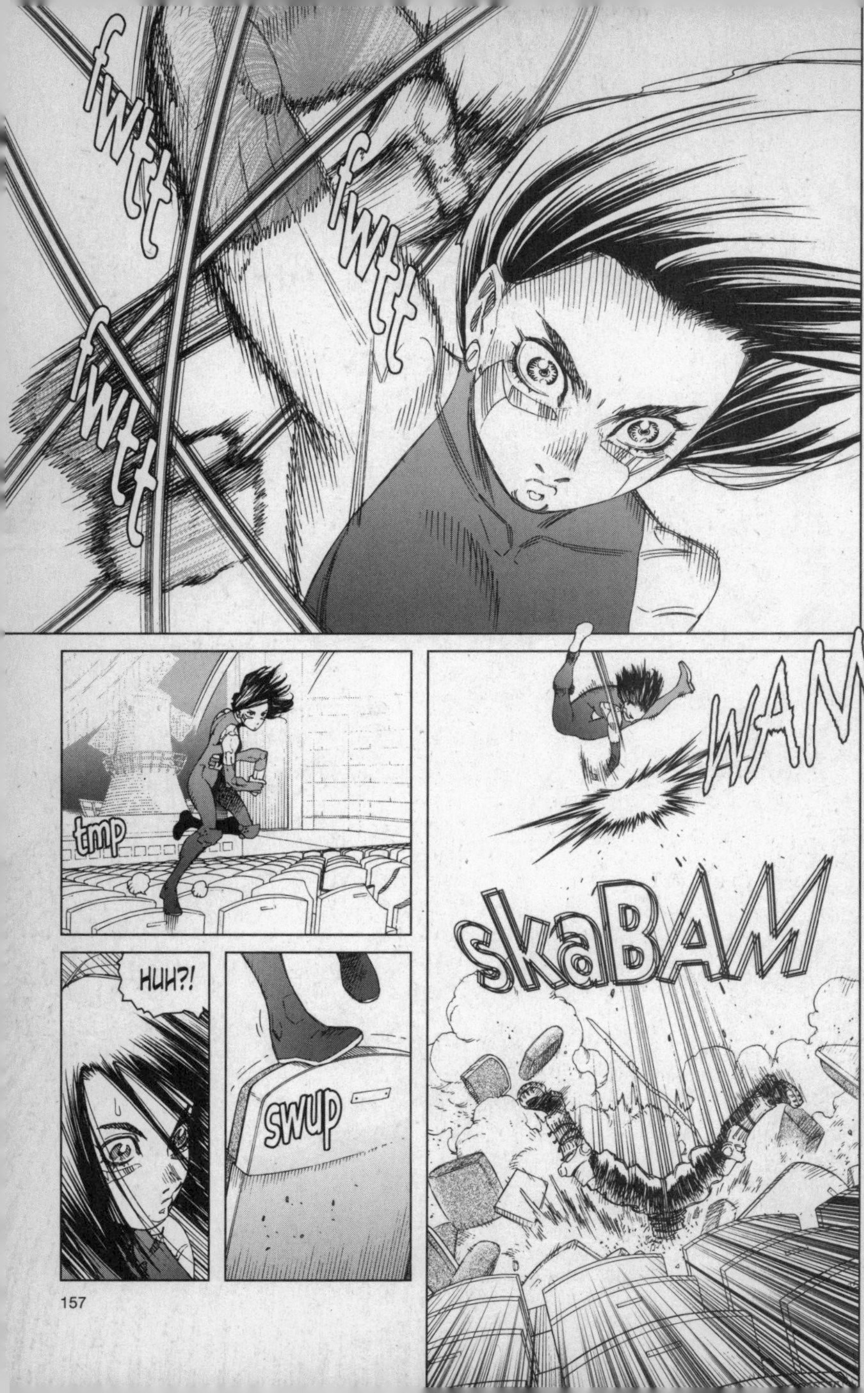
fwtt
fwtt
fwtt
tmp
HUH?!
swup
WAM
skaBAM

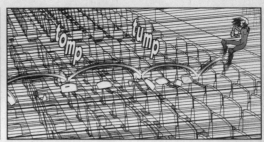

Lomp *lump*

wmp

jing!

SWEET! THEY DON'T CALL YOU "ORIGINAL" FOR NOTHING!

shwp

YOU GOT HER TO SEVER YOUR ARM SO YOU COULD USE IT AS A WEAPON!

MONO-
MOLECULAR
WIRE!*

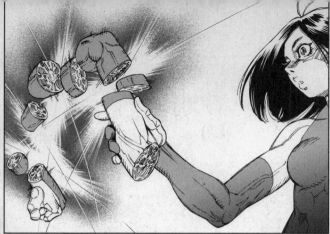

WATCH
YOUR STEP
THERE,
ORIGINAL!

LOSING THAT
ARM HAS
COMPLETELY
UNBALANCED
YOUR NIFTY
NEW BODY!

YOU
GUYS
STAY
OUTTA
THIS!

*Mono-molecular wire: TUNED standard issue equipment. 2 microns thick, with a tensile strength of 2.4 tons, this wire is one long cylindrical molecule, held together by the powerful covalent bonds between atoms.

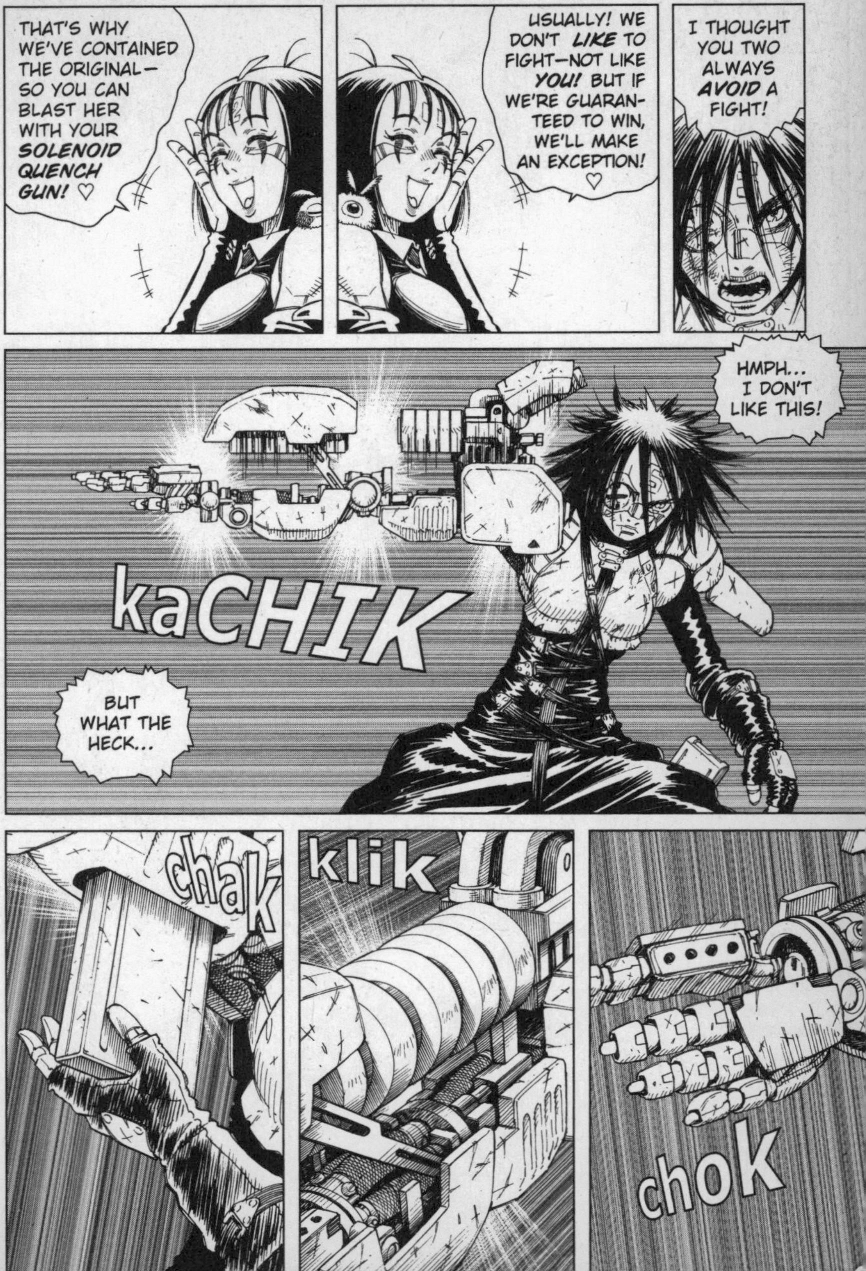
I THOUGHT YOU TWO ALWAYS AVOID A FIGHT!
USUALLY! WE DON'T LIKE TO FIGHT—NOT LIKE YOU! BUT IF WE'RE GUARAN-TEED TO WIN, WE'LL MAKE AN EXCEPTION! ♡
THAT'S WHY WE'VE CONTAINED THE ORIGINAL—SO YOU CAN BLAST HER WITH YOUR SOLENOID QUENCH GUN! ♡
HMPH... I DON'T LIKE THIS!
kaCHIK
BUT WHAT THE HECK...
chok
klik
chak

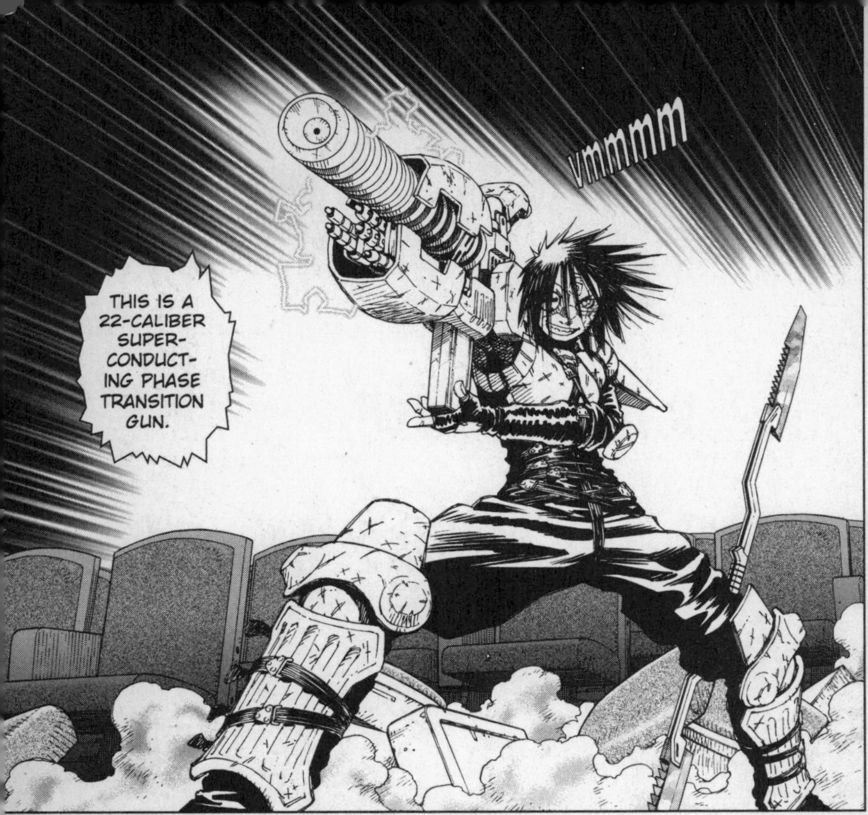
VMMMM
THIS IS A 22-CALIBER SUPER-CONDUCT-ING PHASE TRANSITION GUN.
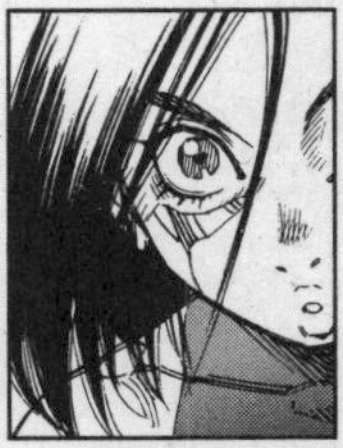
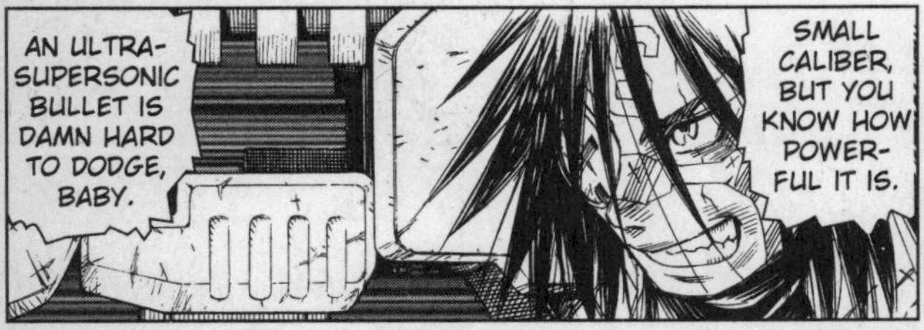
SMALL CALIBER, BUT YOU KNOW HOW POWER-FUL IT IS.
AN ULTRA-SUPERSONIC BULLET IS DAMN HARD TO DODGE, BABY.
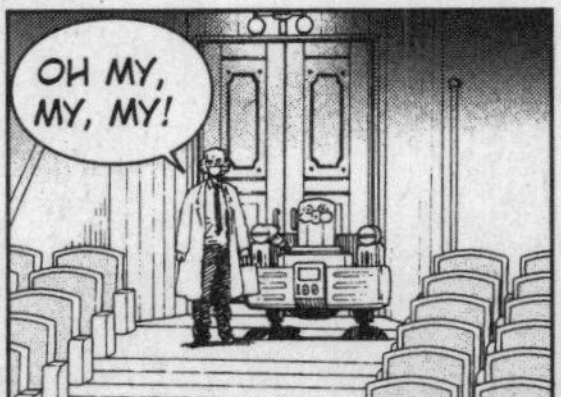
OH MY, MY, MY!
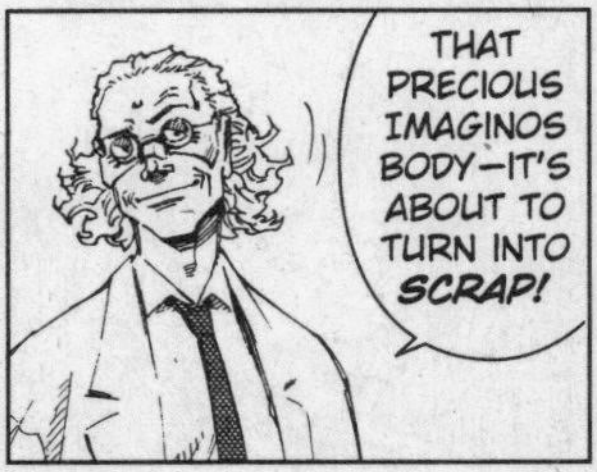
THAT PRECIOUS IMAGINOS BODY—IT'S ABOUT TO TURN INTO *SCRAP!*
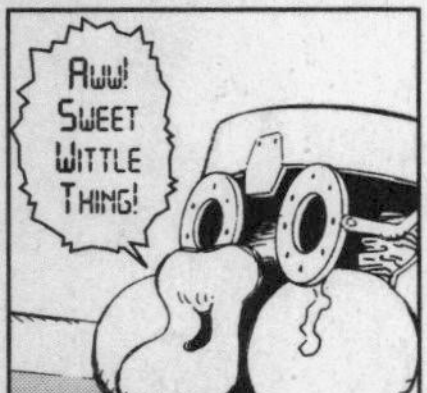
AWW! SWEET WITTLE THING!

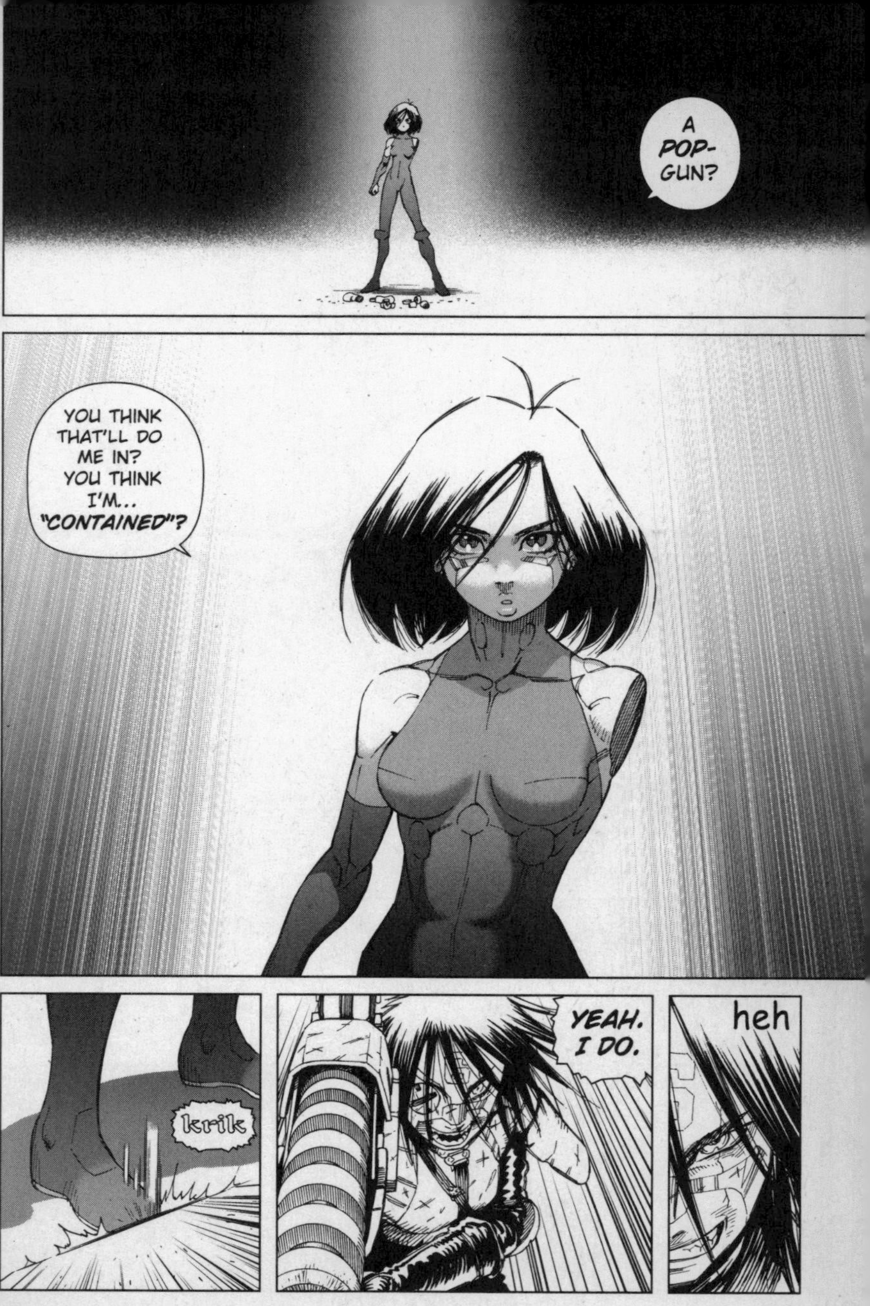
A POP-GUN?
YOU THINK THAT'LL DO ME IN? YOU THINK I'M... "CONTAINED"?
krik
YEAH. I DO.
heh

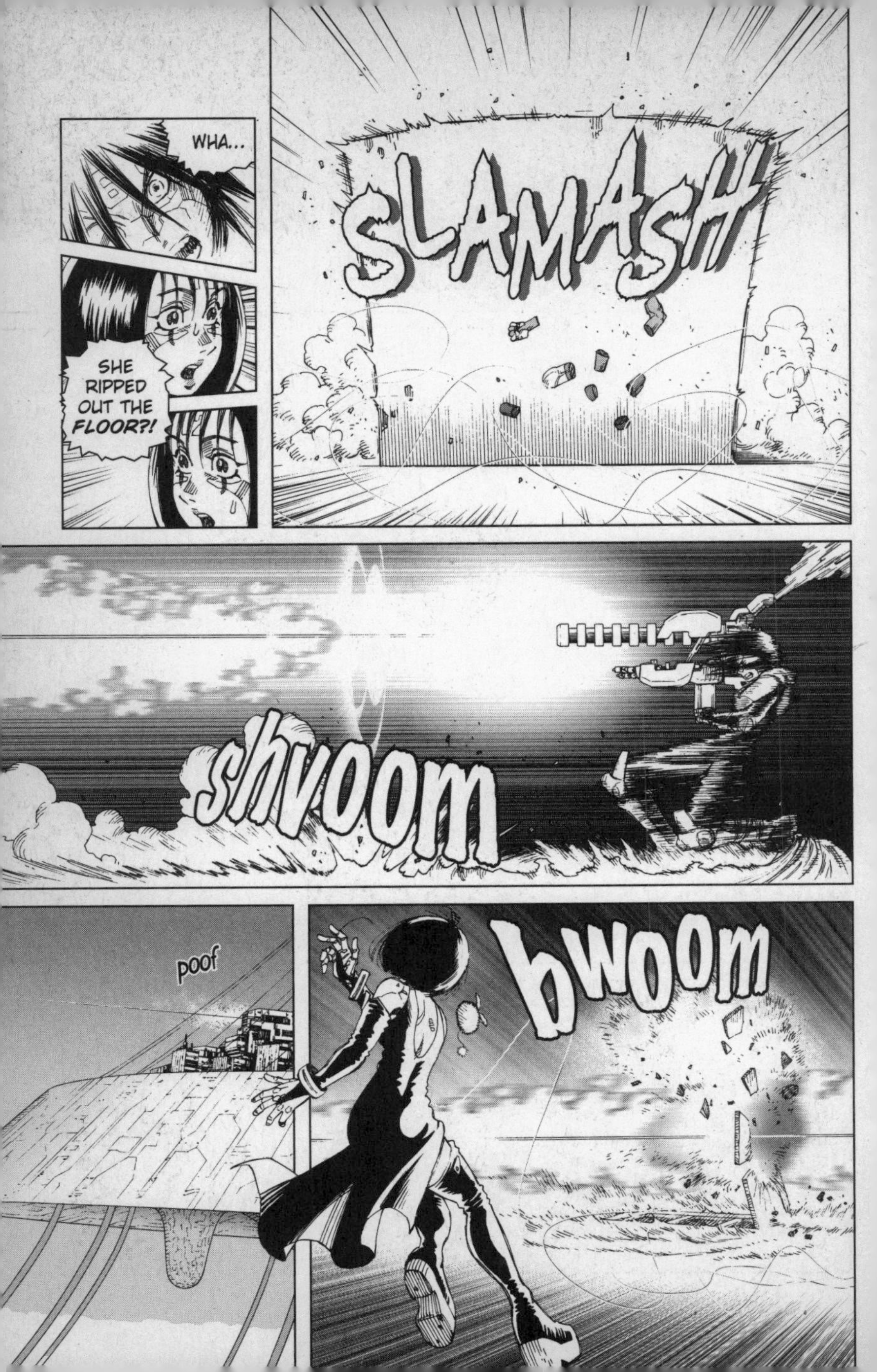
SLAMASH
WHA...
SHE RIPPED OUT THE FLOOR?!
shvoom
bwoom
poof

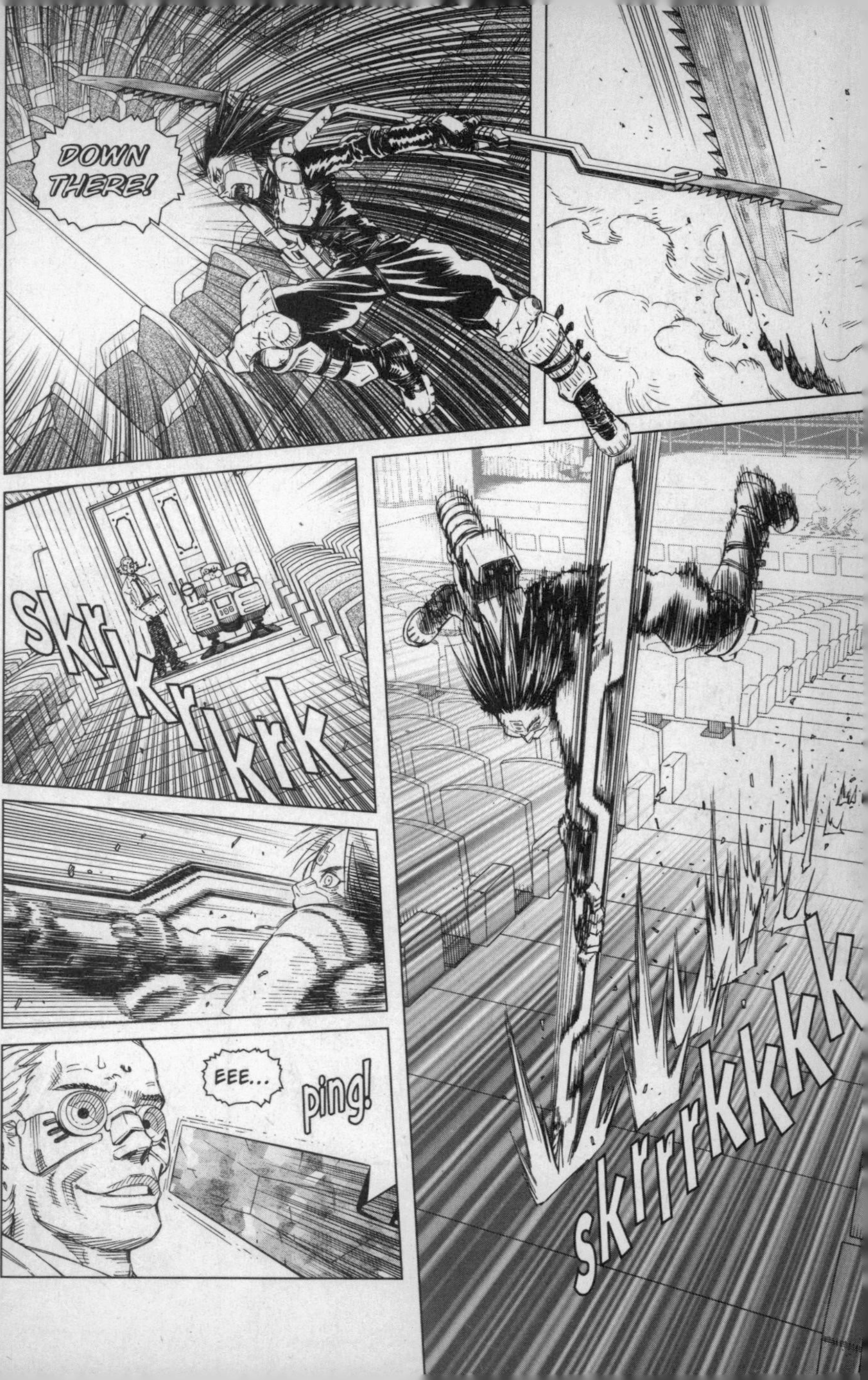
DOWN THERE!
skrkrkrk
EEE...
ping!
skrrrkkkk

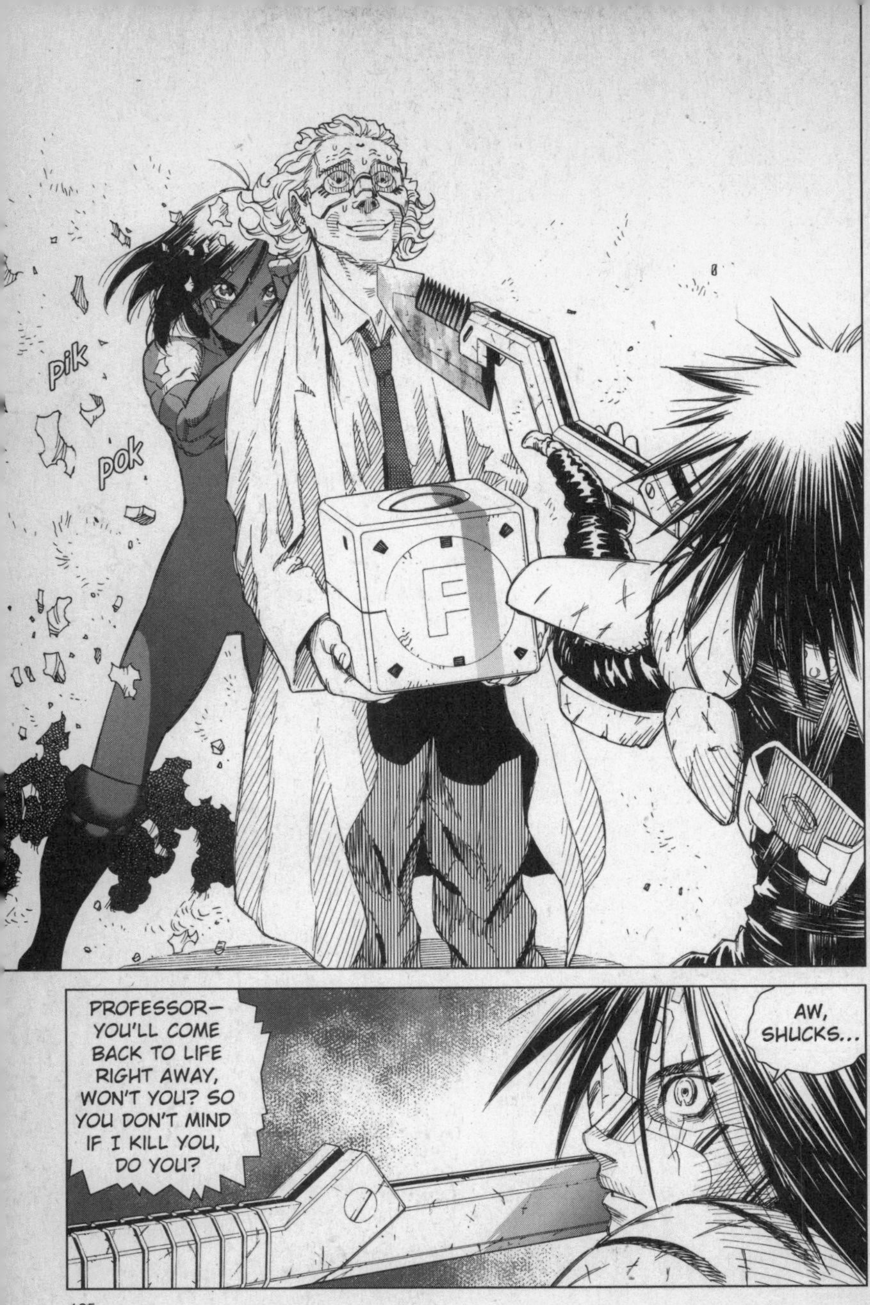
pik
pok
PROFESSOR— YOU'LL COME BACK TO LIFE RIGHT AWAY, WON'T YOU? SO YOU DON'T MIND IF I KILL YOU, DO YOU?
AW, SHUCKS...

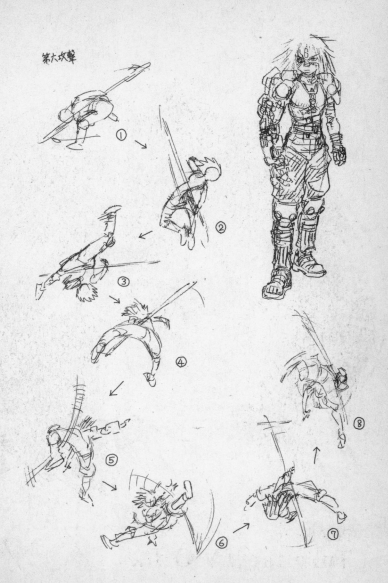

第六攻擊

①
②
③
④
⑤
⑥
⑦
⑧

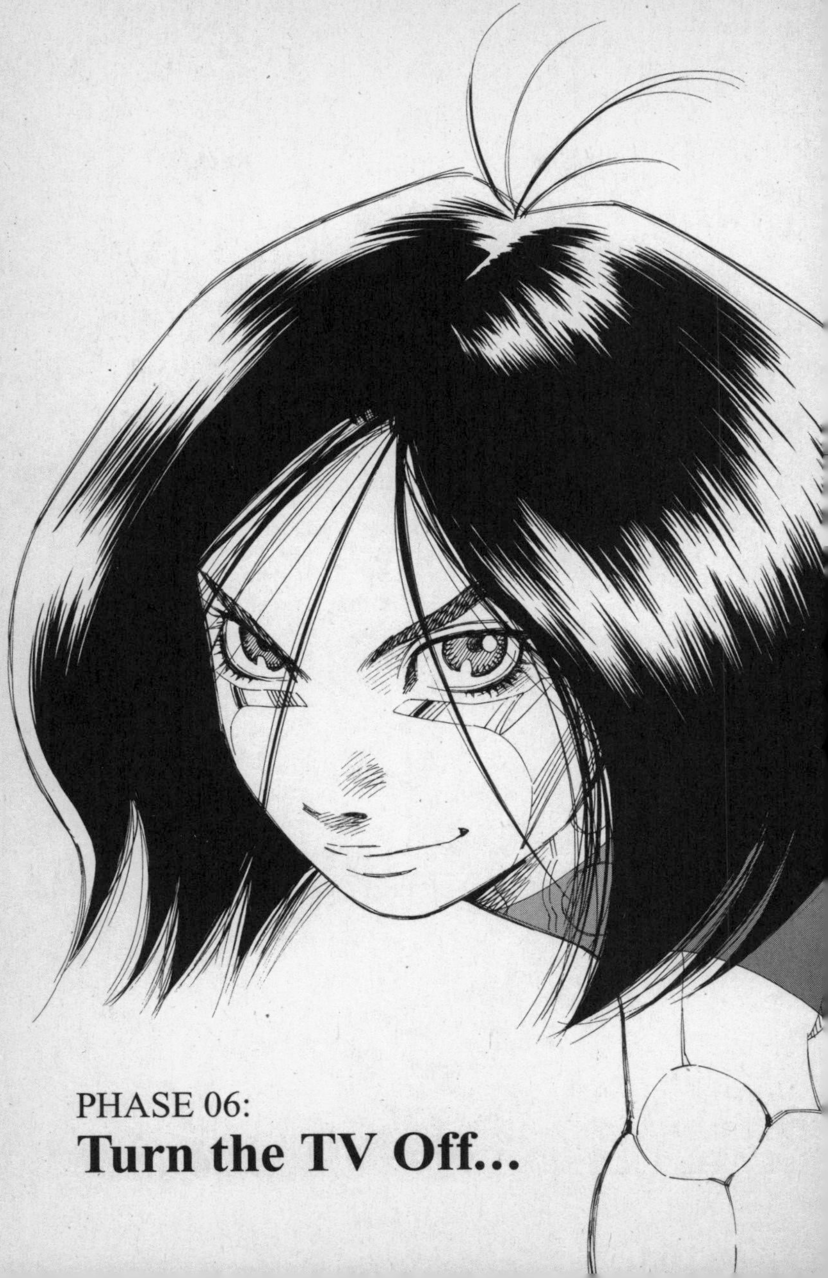

PHASE 06:

Turn the TV Off...

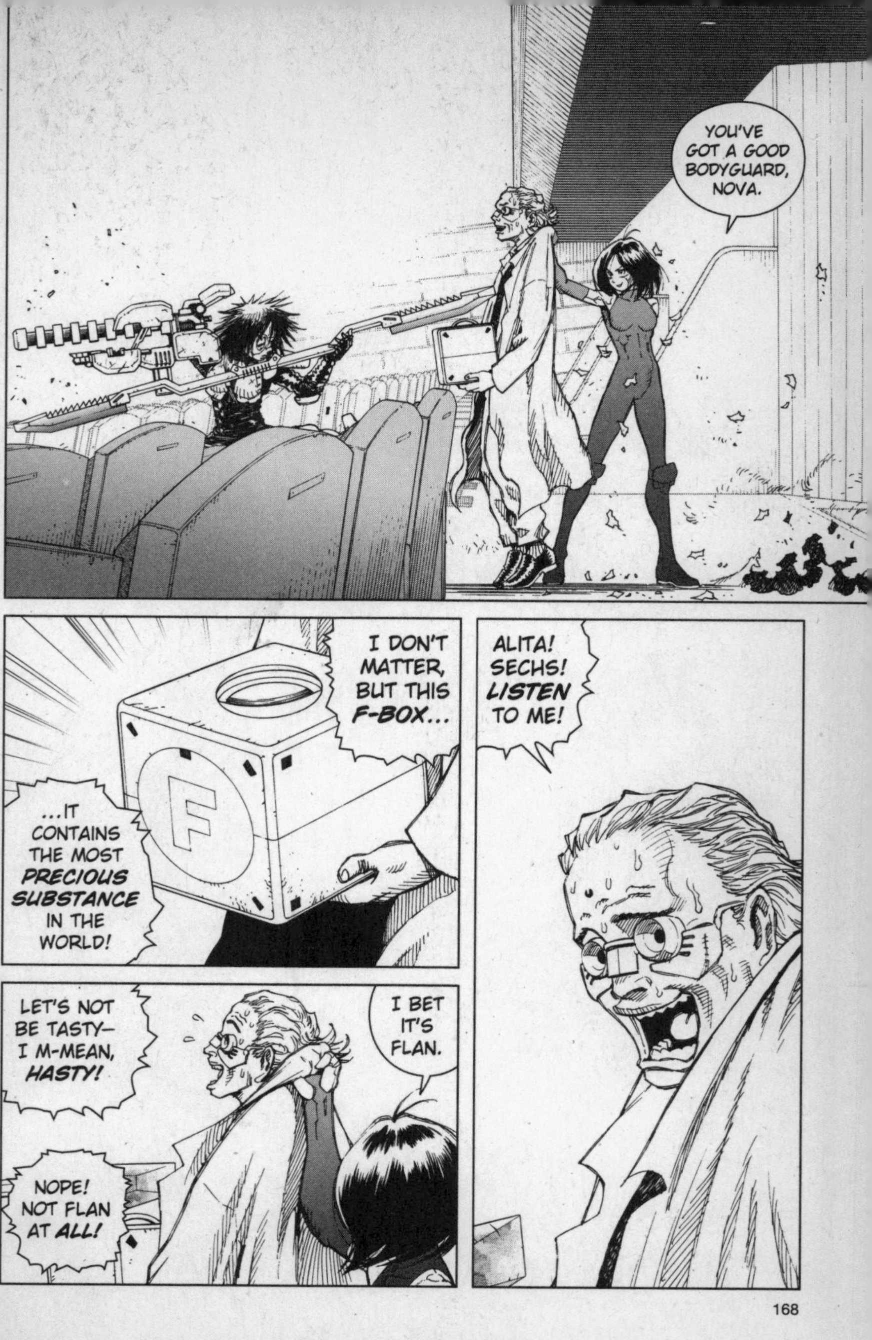
YOU'VE GOT A GOOD BODYGUARD, NOVA.
ALITA! SECHS! *LISTEN* TO ME!
I DON'T MATTER, BUT THIS *F-BOX*...
...IT CONTAINS THE MOST *PRECIOUS SUBSTANCE* IN THE WORLD!
I BET IT'S FLAN.
LET'S NOT BE TASTY— I M-MEAN, *HASTY!*
NOPE! NOT FLAN AT *ALL!*

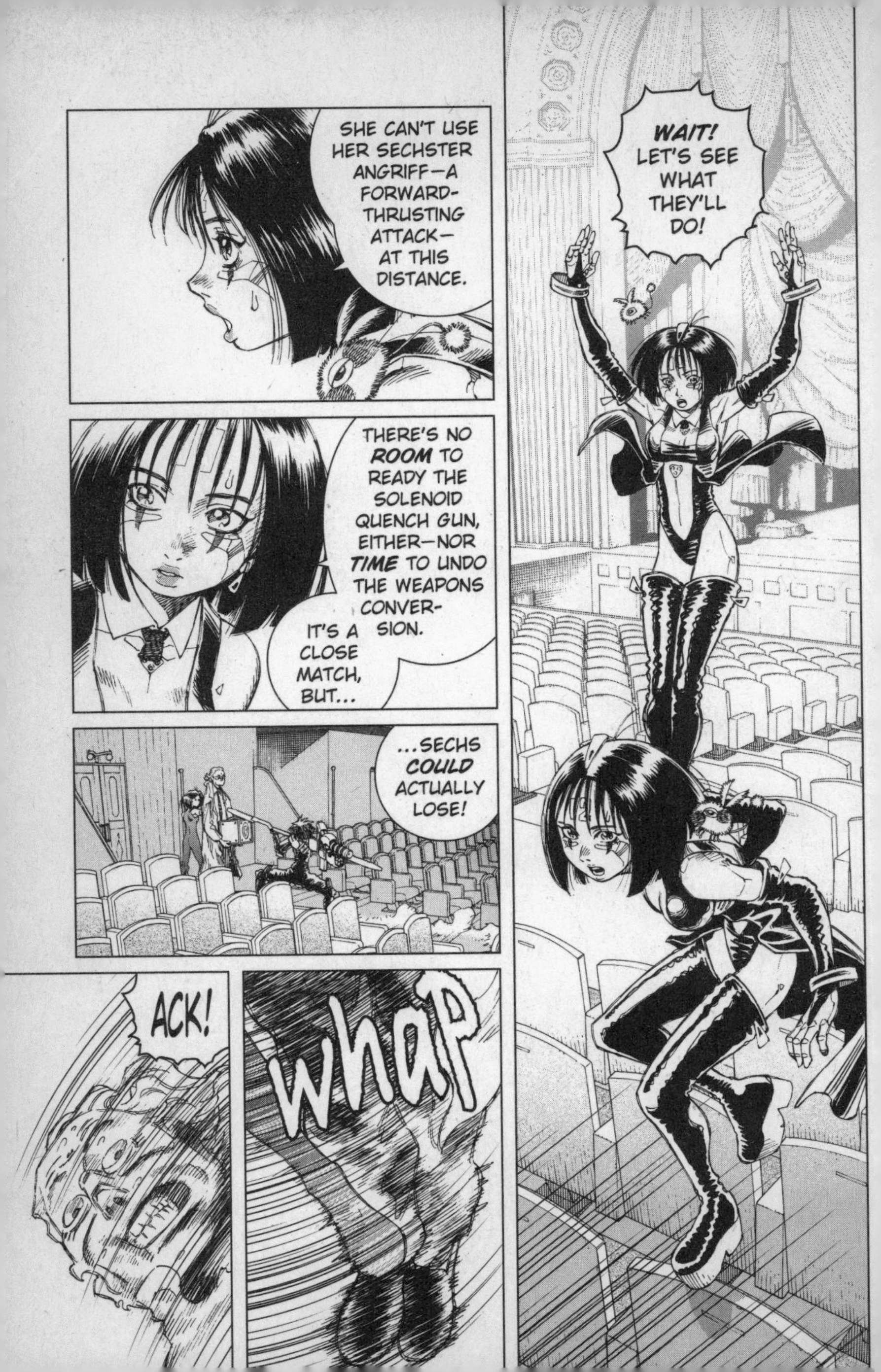
WAIT! LET'S SEE WHAT THEY'LL DO!
SHE CAN'T USE HER SECHSTER ANGRIFF—A FORWARD-THRUSTING ATTACK—AT THIS DISTANCE.
THERE'S NO ROOM TO READY THE SOLENOID QUENCH GUN, EITHER—NOR TIME TO UNDO THE WEAPONS CONVER-SION.
IT'S A CLOSE MATCH, BUT...
...SECHS COULD ACTUALLY LOSE!
whap
ACK!

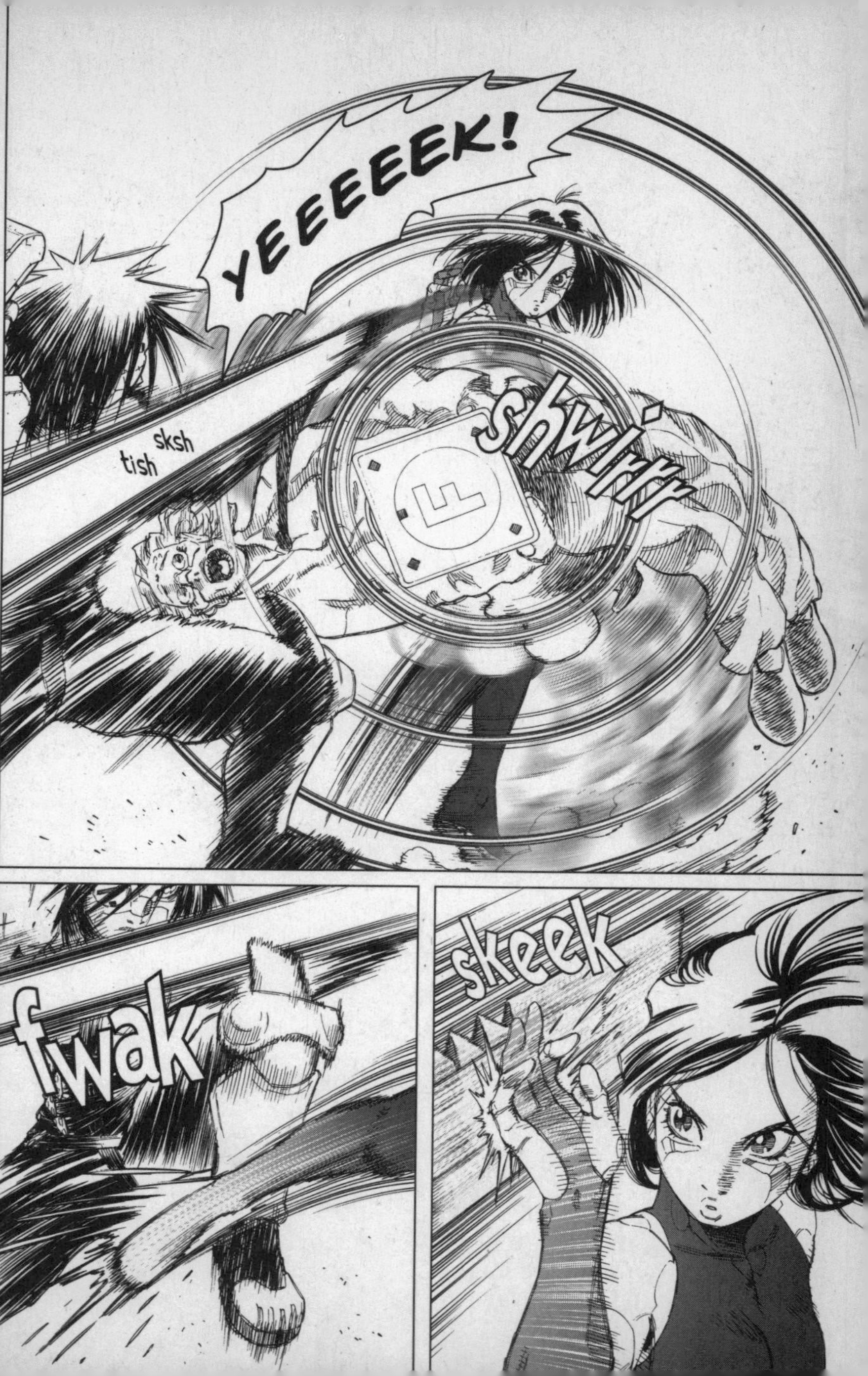
YEEEEEK!
shwirry
sksh
tish
skeek
fwak

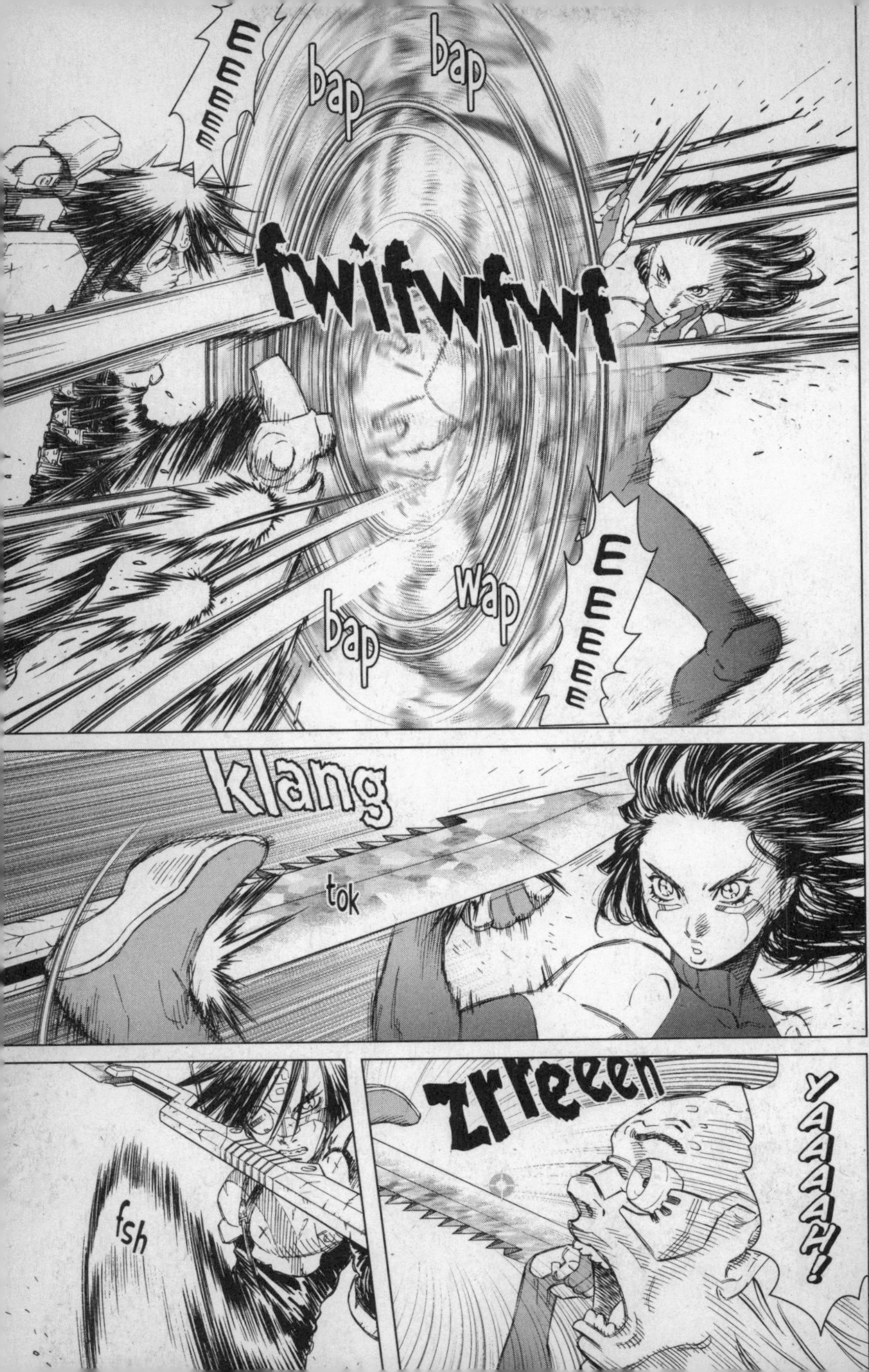
bap
bap
EEEEEE
fwifwfwf
EEEEE
wap
bap
klang
tok
YAAAAH!
zrreeen
fsh

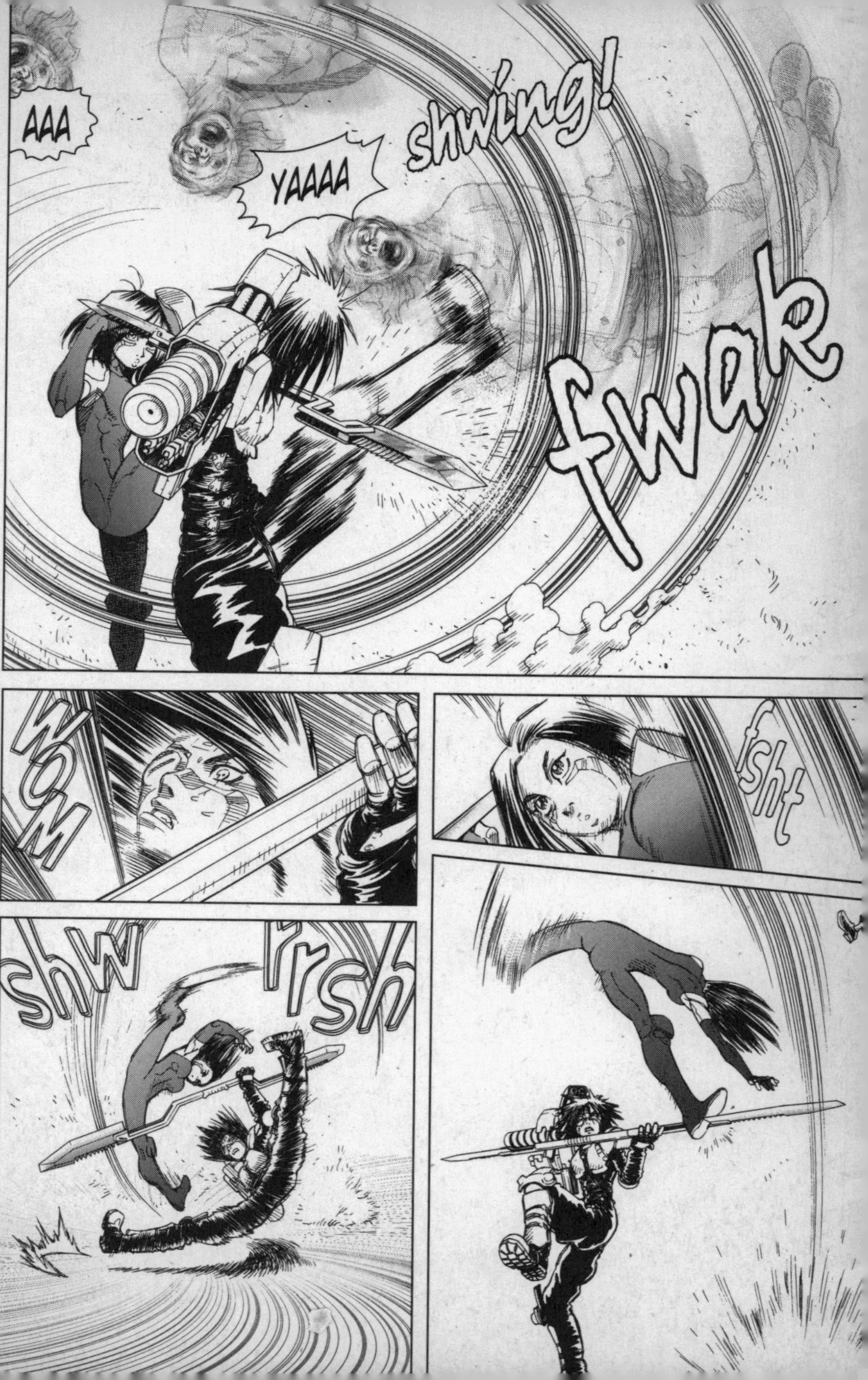
shwing!
YAAAA
AAA
fwak
fsht
WOM
shw
rrsh

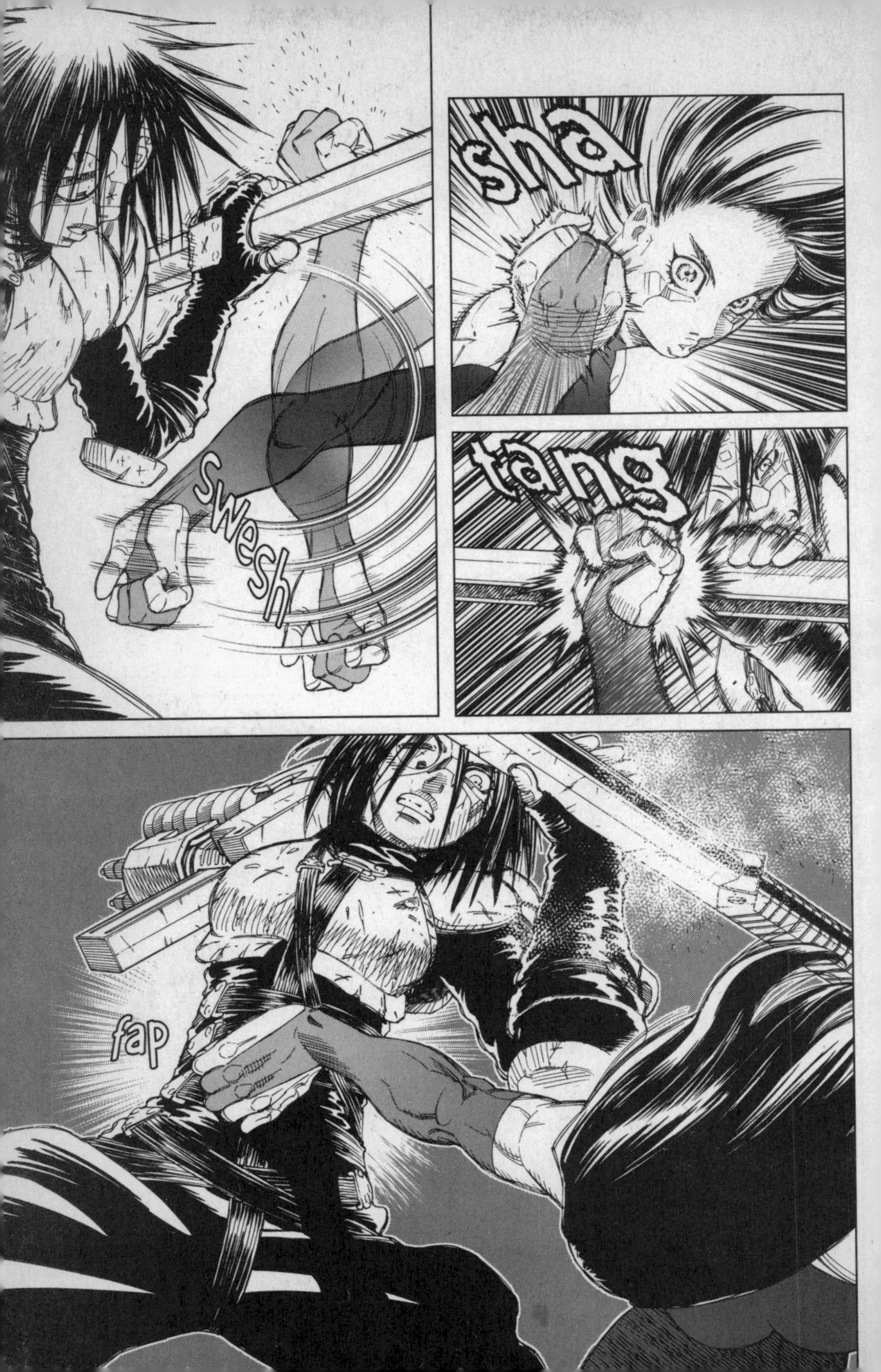
sha
tang
swesh
fap

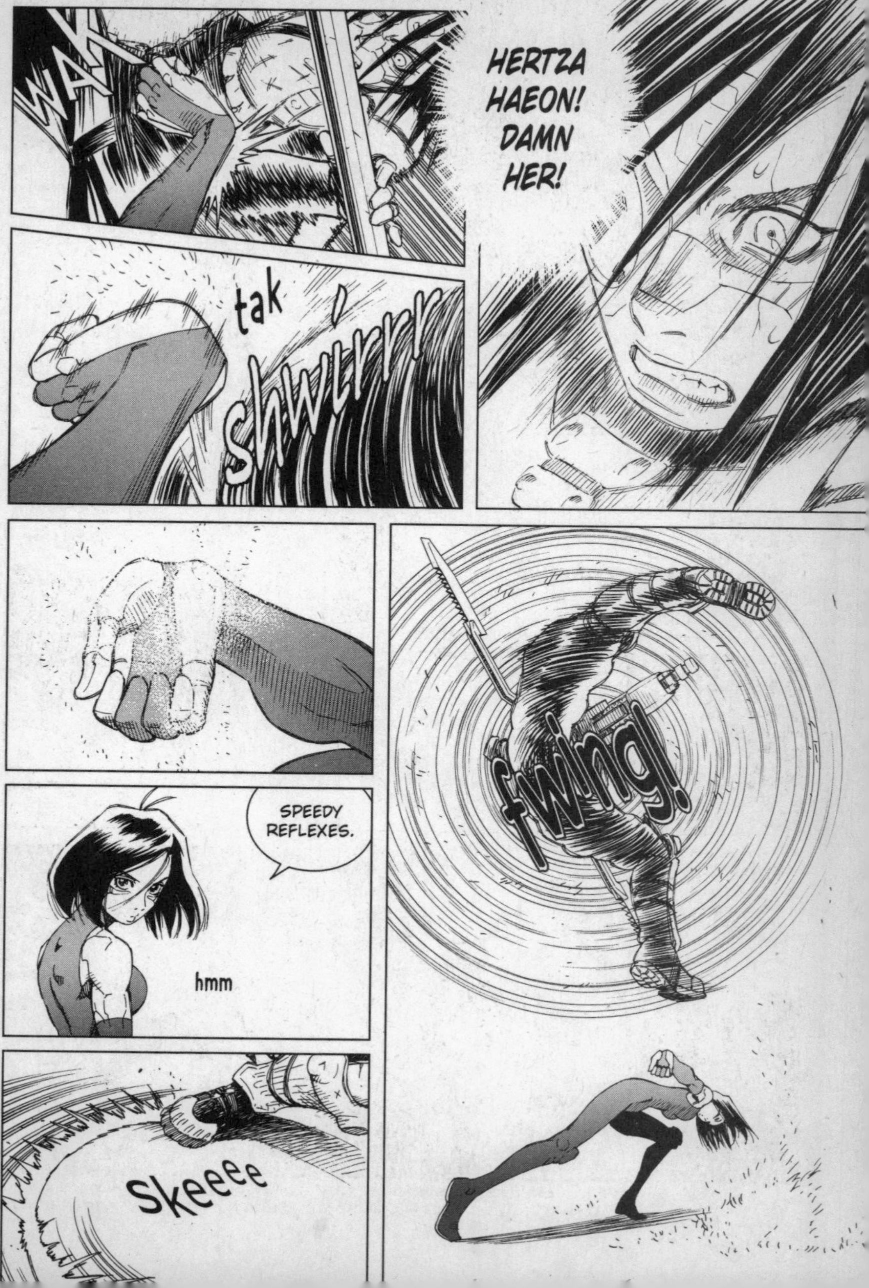
WAK
tak
shwirrr
HERTZA HAEON! DAMN HER!
SPEEDY REFLEXES.
hmm
Skeeee
fwing!

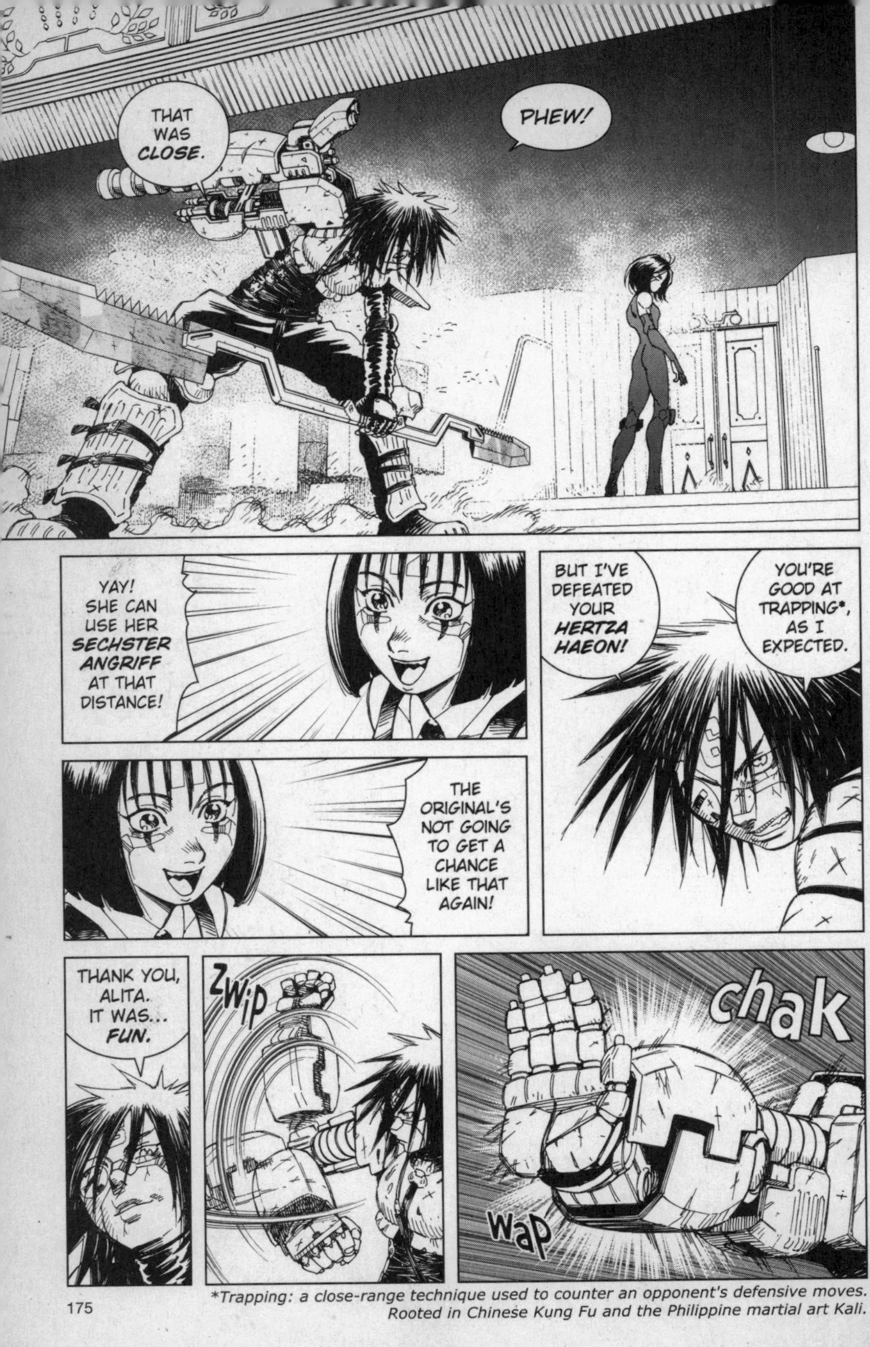
THAT WAS CLOSE.
PHEW!
YAY! SHE CAN USE HER SECHSTER ANGRIFF AT THAT DISTANCE!
THE ORIGINAL'S NOT GOING TO GET A CHANCE LIKE THAT AGAIN!
BUT I'VE DEFEATED YOUR HERTZA HAEON!
YOU'RE GOOD AT TRAPPING*, AS I EXPECTED.
THANK YOU, ALITA. IT WAS... FUN.
ZWIP
chak
wap

*Trapping: a close-range technique used to counter an opponent's defensive moves. Rooted in Chinese Kung Fu and the Philippine martial art Kali.

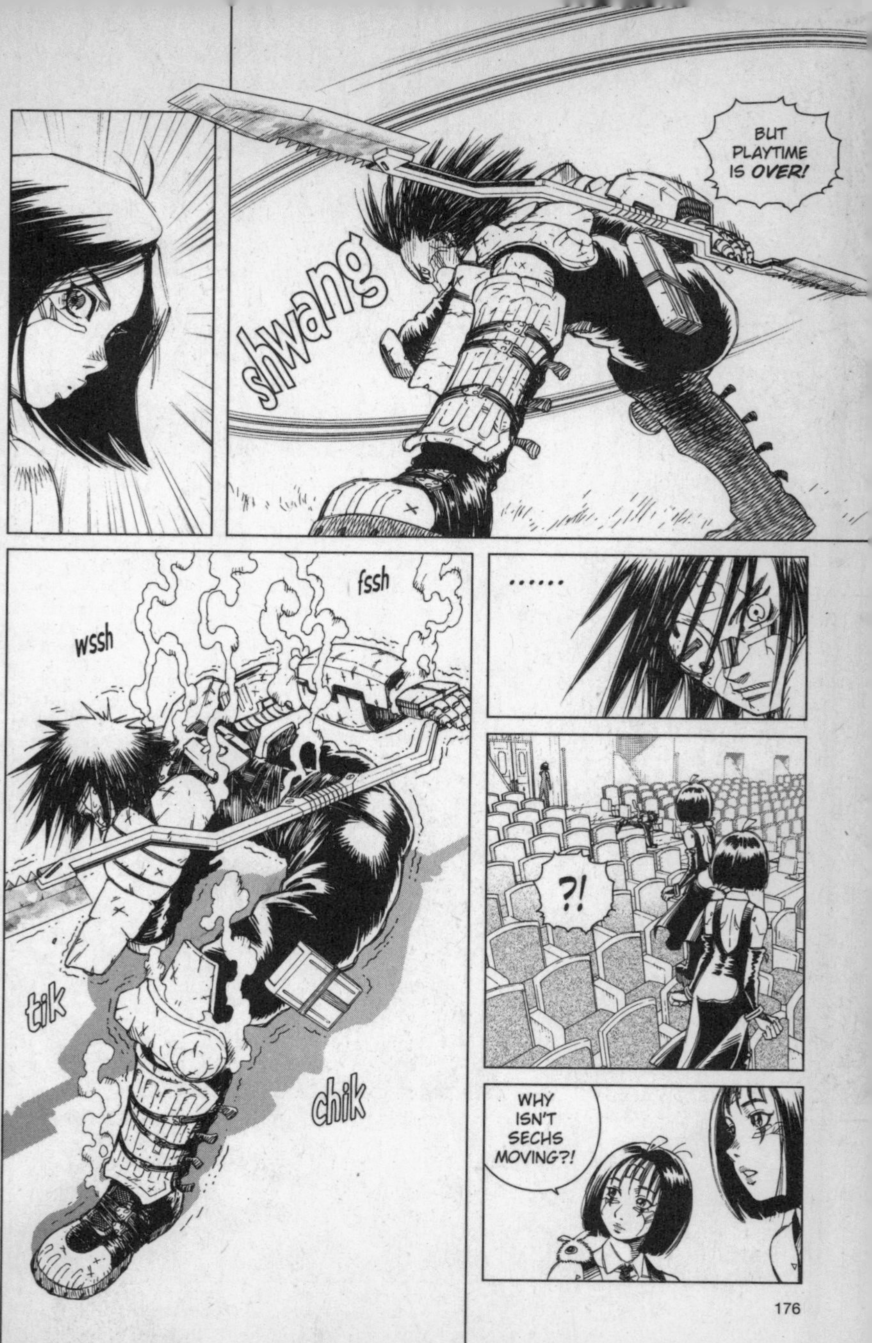
shwang
BUT PLAYTIME IS OVER!
wssh
fssh
tik
chik
......
?!
WHY ISN'T SECHS MOVING?!

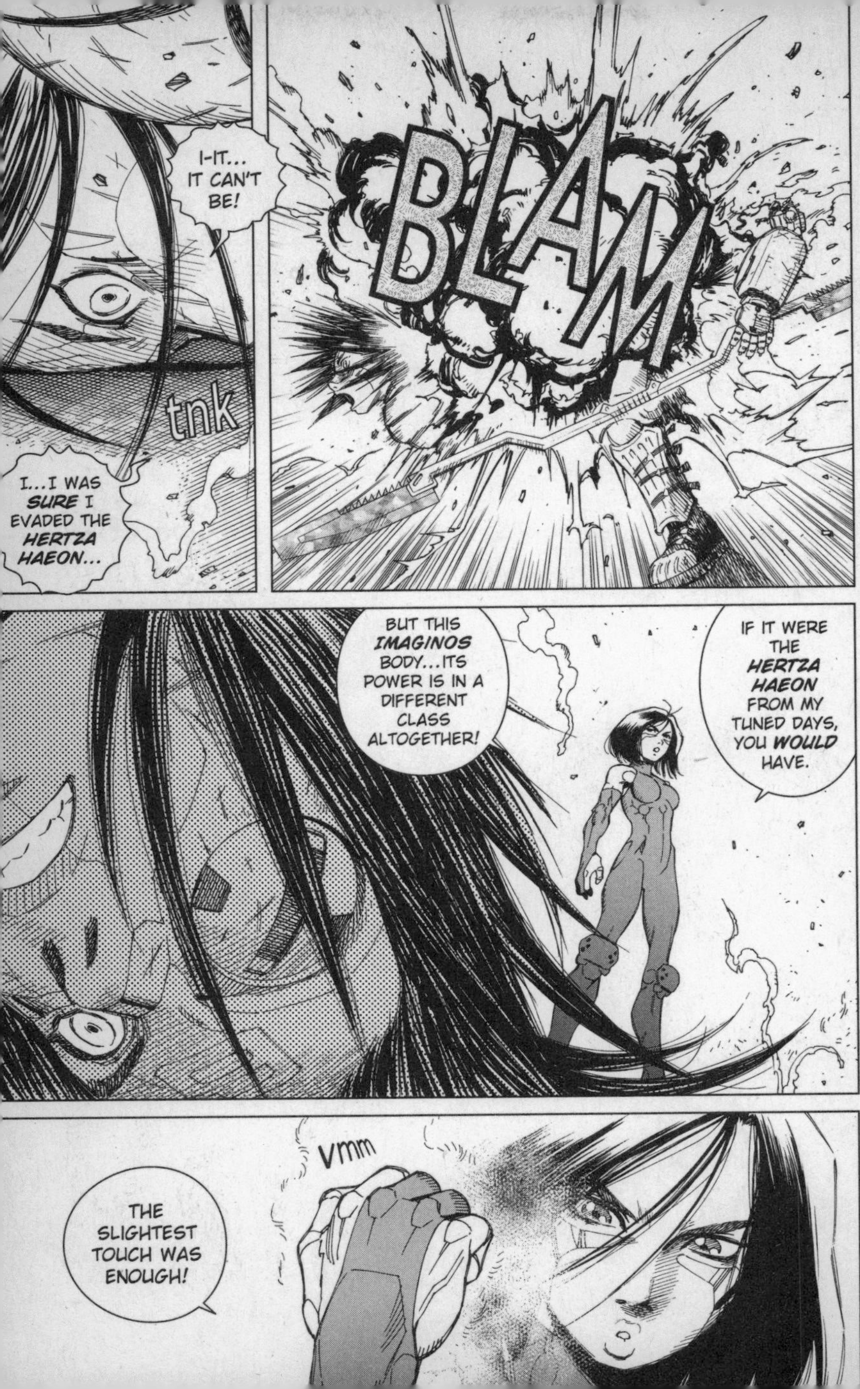
BLAM
I-IT... IT CAN'T BE!
tnk
I...I WAS SURE I EVADED THE HERTZA HAEON...
IF IT WERE THE HERTZA HAEON FROM MY TUNED DAYS, YOU WOULD HAVE.
BUT THIS IMAGINOS BODY...ITS POWER IS IN A DIFFERENT CLASS ALTOGETHER!
VMM
THE SLIGHTEST TOUCH WAS ENOUGH!

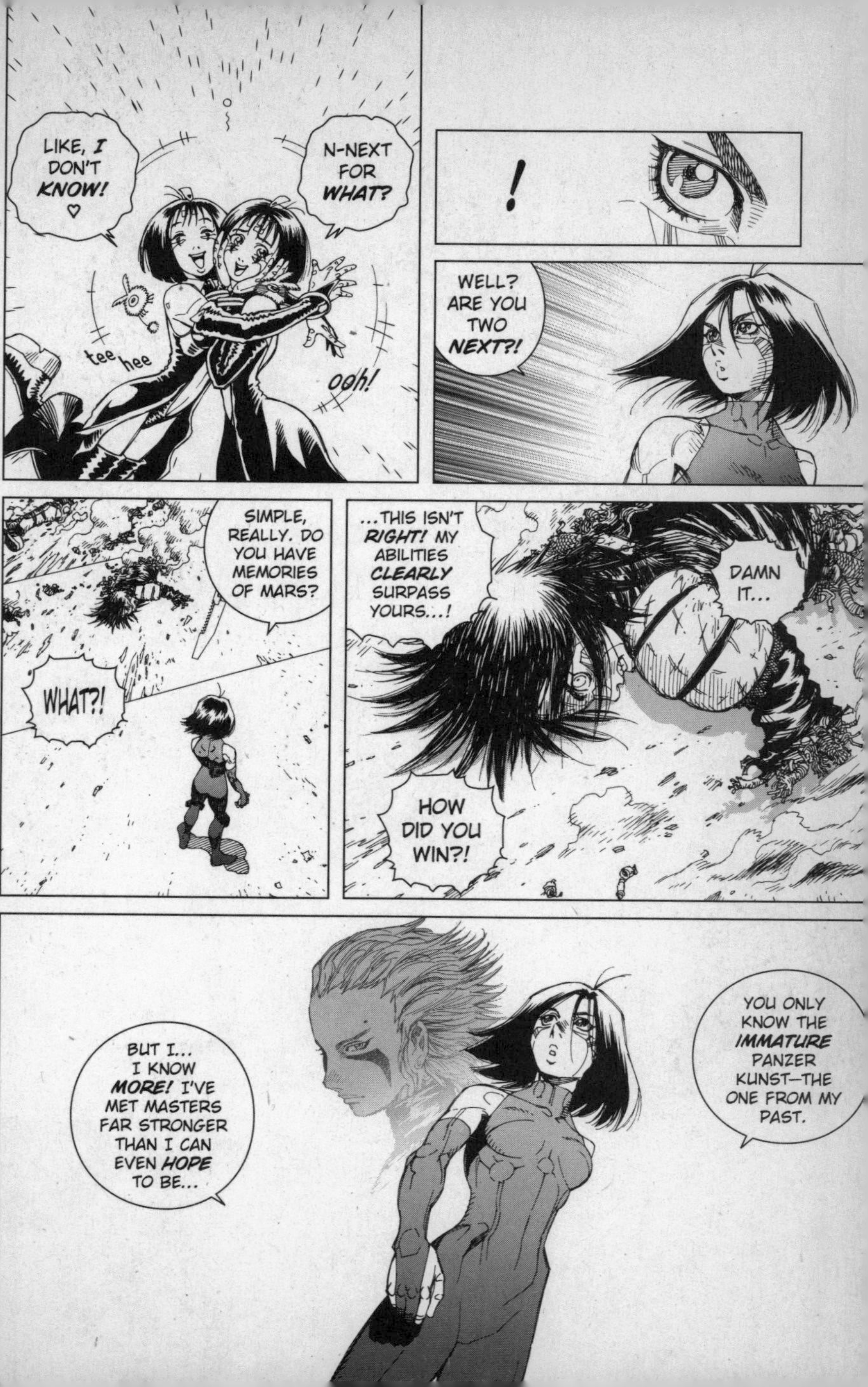
!
WELL? ARE YOU TWO NEXT?!
N-NEXT FOR WHAT?
LIKE, I DON'T KNOW! ♡
ooh!
tee hee
DAMN IT...
...THIS ISN'T RIGHT! MY ABILITIES CLEARLY SURPASS YOURS...!
HOW DID YOU WIN?!
SIMPLE, REALLY. DO YOU HAVE MEMORIES OF MARS?
WHAT?!
YOU ONLY KNOW THE IMMATURE PANZER KUNST—THE ONE FROM MY PAST.
BUT I... I KNOW MORE! I'VE MET MASTERS FAR STRONGER THAN I CAN EVEN HOPE TO BE...

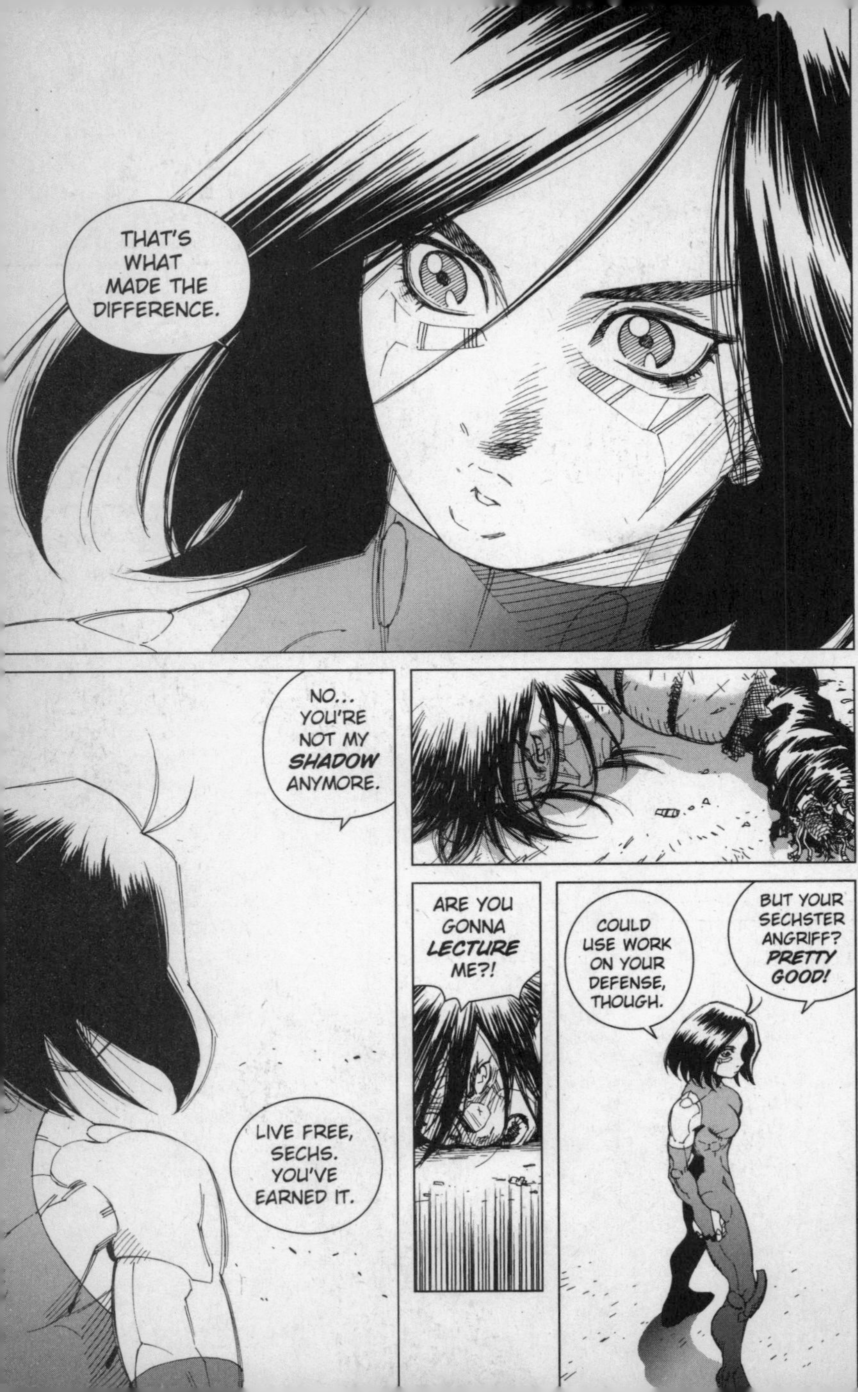
THAT'S WHAT MADE THE DIFFERENCE.
BUT YOUR SECHSTER ANGRIFF? PRETTY GOOD!
COULD USE WORK ON YOUR DEFENSE, THOUGH.
ARE YOU GONNA LECTURE ME?!
NO... YOU'RE NOT MY SHADOW ANYMORE.
LIVE FREE, SECHS. YOU'VE EARNED IT.

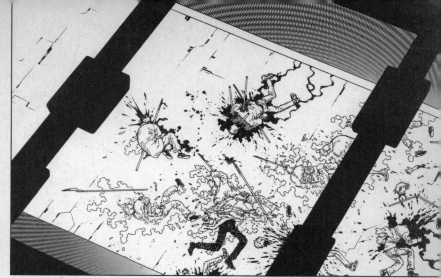

THEY'RE
ALL...

...ALL...
IDIOTS...

skmp

FFU

FFH

skmp

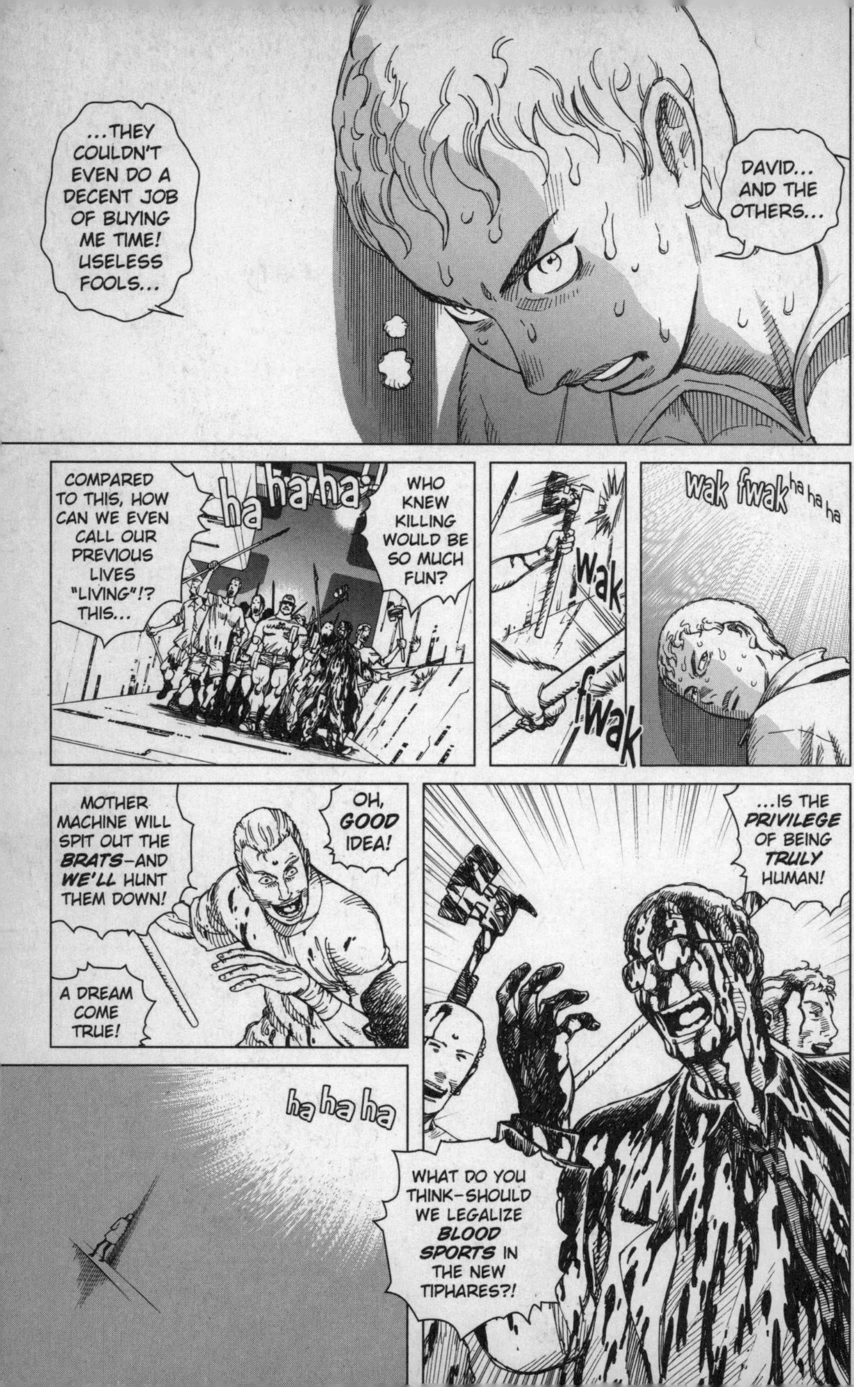
DAVID... AND THE OTHERS...
...THEY COULDN'T EVEN DO A DECENT JOB OF BUYING ME TIME! USELESS FOOLS...
wak fwak ha ha ha
wak
fwak
WHO KNEW KILLING WOULD BE SO MUCH FUN?
ha ha ha!
COMPARED TO THIS, HOW CAN WE EVEN CALL OUR PREVIOUS LIVES "LIVING"!? THIS...
...IS THE ***PRIVILEGE*** OF BEING ***TRULY*** HUMAN!
WHAT DO YOU THINK—SHOULD WE LEGALIZE ***BLOOD SPORTS*** IN THE NEW TIPHARES?!
OH, ***GOOD*** IDEA!
MOTHER MACHINE WILL SPIT OUT THE ***BRATS***—AND ***WE'LL*** HUNT THEM DOWN!
A DREAM COME TRUE!
ha ha ha

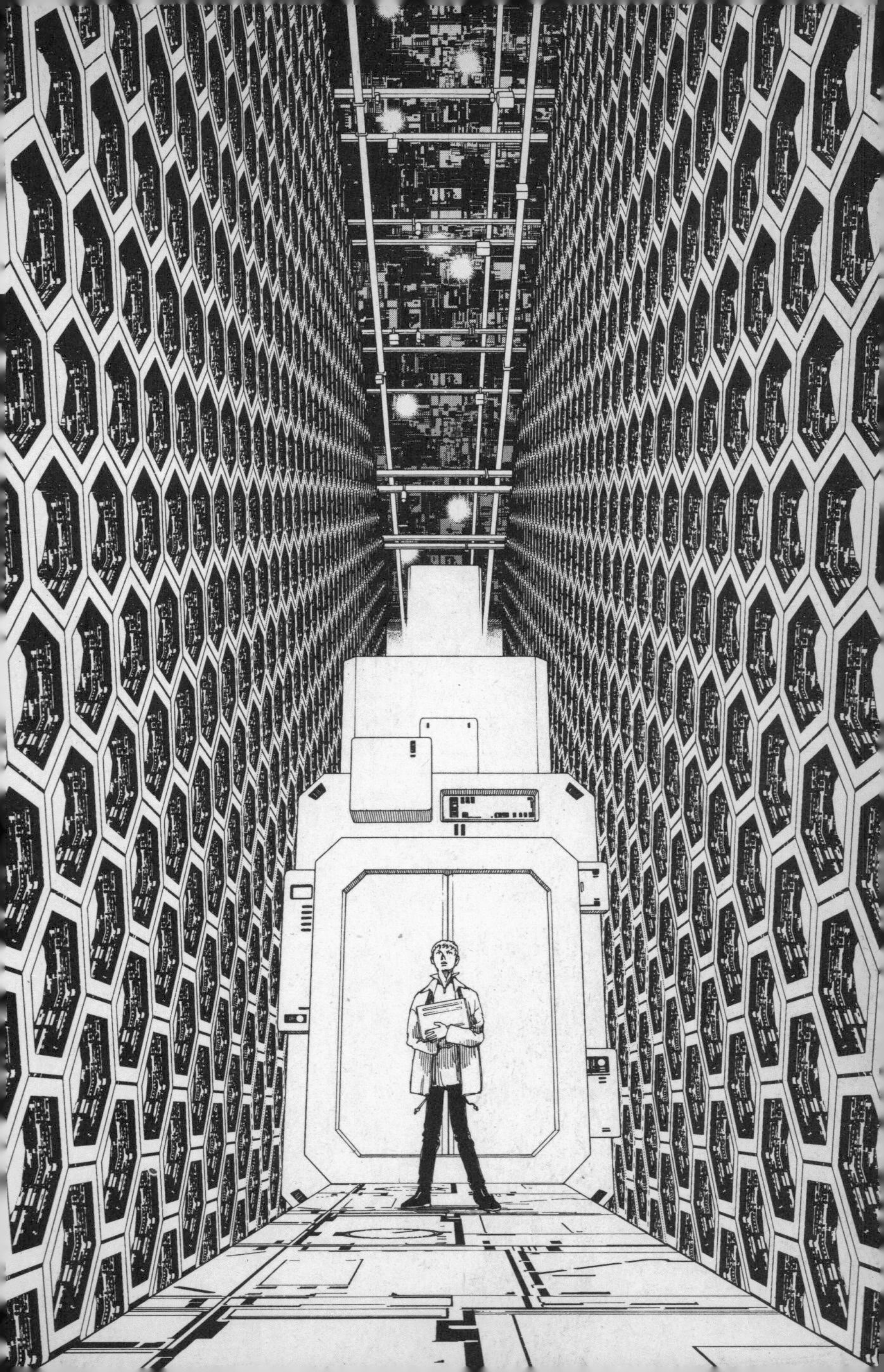

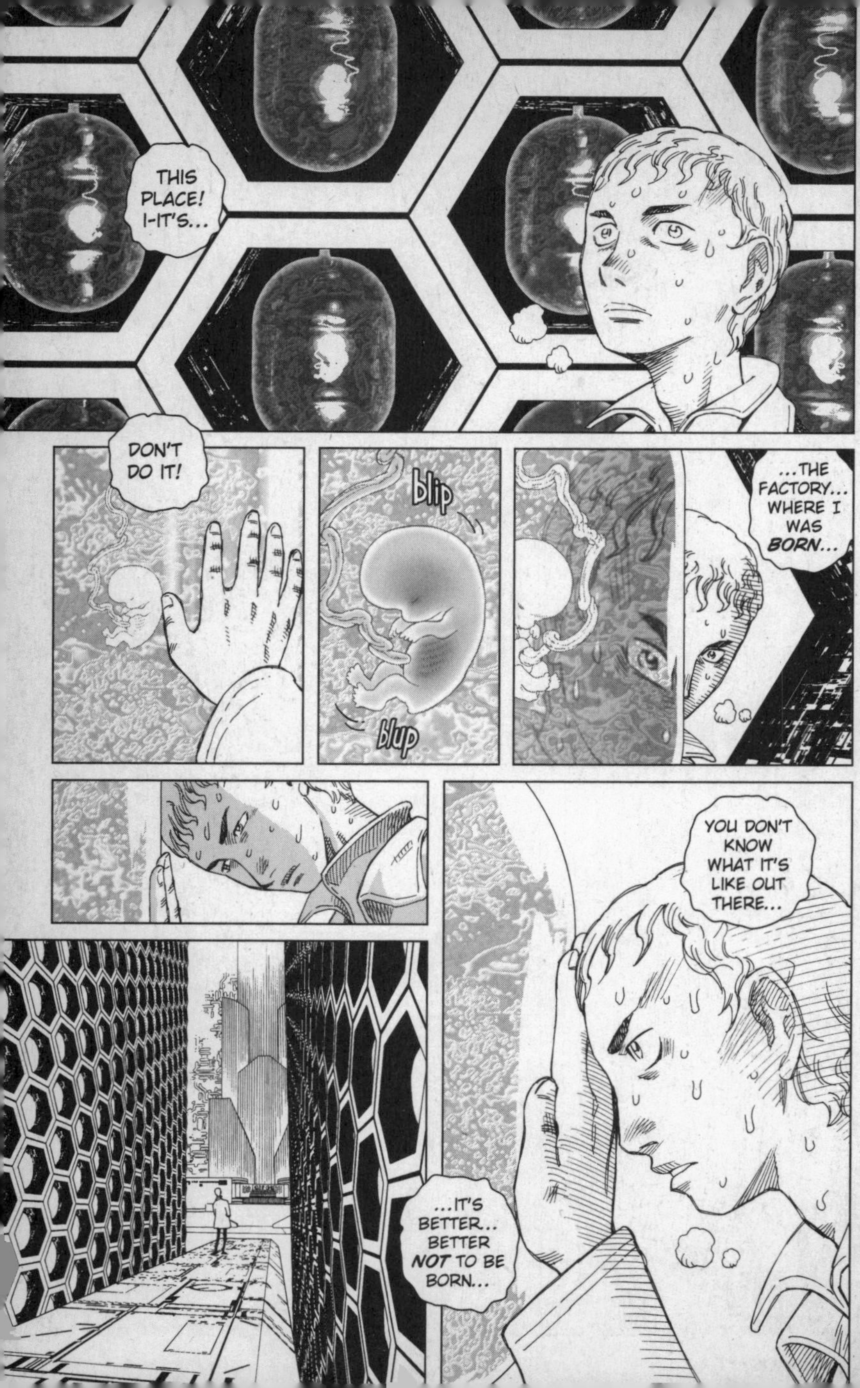
THIS PLACE! I-IT'S...
...THE FACTORY... WHERE I WAS *BORN*...
blip
blup
DON'T DO IT!
YOU DON'T KNOW WHAT IT'S LIKE OUT THERE...
...IT'S BETTER... BETTER *NOT* TO BE BORN...

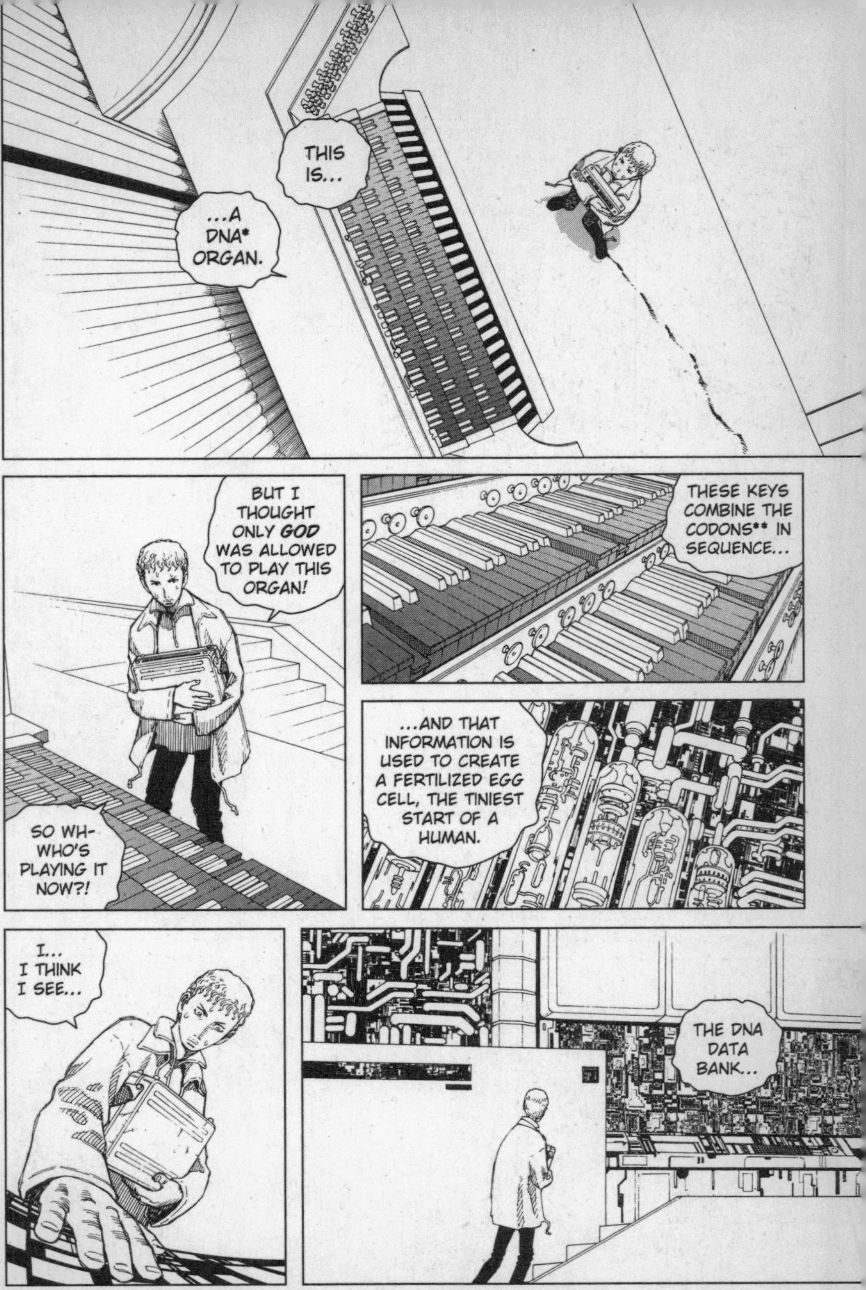
THIS IS...
...A DNA* ORGAN.
BUT I THOUGHT ONLY **GOD** WAS ALLOWED TO PLAY THIS ORGAN!
SO WH-WHO'S PLAYING IT NOW?!
THESE KEYS COMBINE THE CODONS** IN SEQUENCE...
...AND THAT INFORMATION IS USED TO CREATE A FERTILIZED EGG CELL, THE TINIEST START OF A HUMAN.
I... I THINK I SEE...
THE DNA DATA BANK...

**DNA: deoxyribonucleic acid, a polymer that encodes an organism's genetic attributes in a series of four nucleotides (adenine, guanine, thymine, and cytosine).*

***Codon: a triplet code of three adjacent nucleotides is the basic unit of the genetic code. Like the I Ching, there are 64 sequences in all.*

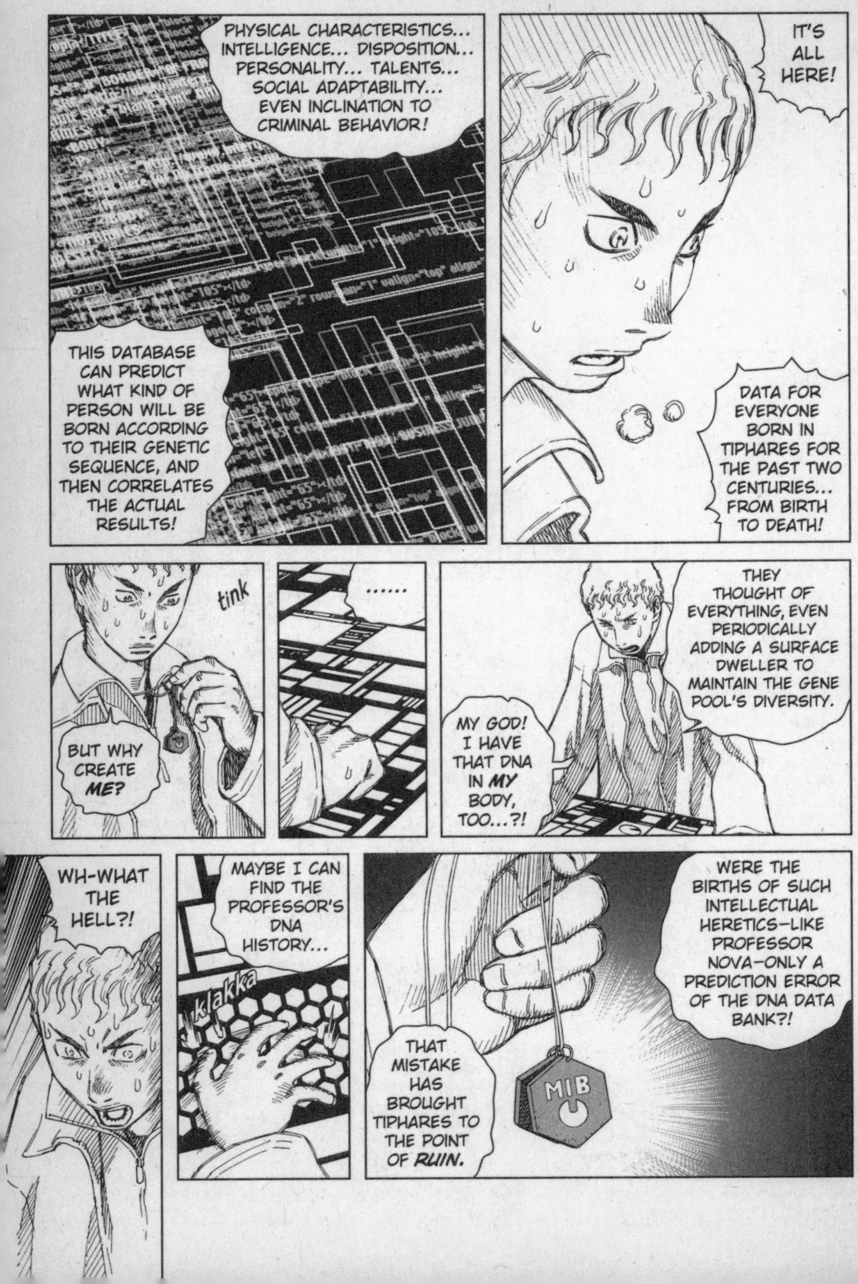
PHYSICAL CHARACTERISTICS... INTELLIGENCE... DISPOSITION... PERSONALITY... TALENTS... SOCIAL ADAPTABILITY... EVEN INCLINATION TO CRIMINAL BEHAVIOR!
THIS DATABASE CAN PREDICT WHAT KIND OF PERSON WILL BE BORN ACCORDING TO THEIR GENETIC SEQUENCE, AND THEN CORRELATES THE ACTUAL RESULTS!
IT'S ALL HERE!
DATA FOR EVERYONE BORN IN TIPHARES FOR THE PAST TWO CENTURIES... FROM BIRTH TO DEATH!
tink
BUT WHY CREATE *ME?*
......
THEY THOUGHT OF EVERYTHING, EVEN PERIODICALLY ADDING A SURFACE DWELLER TO MAINTAIN THE GENE POOL'S DIVERSITY.
MY GOD! I HAVE THAT DNA IN *MY* BODY, TOO...?!
WH-WHAT THE HELL?!
MAYBE I CAN FIND THE PROFESSOR'S DNA HISTORY...
klakka
WERE THE BIRTHS OF SUCH INTELLECTUAL HERETICS—LIKE PROFESSOR NOVA—ONLY A PREDICTION ERROR OF THE DNA DATA BANK?!
THAT MISTAKE HAS BROUGHT TIPHARES TO THE POINT OF *RUIN.*
MIB

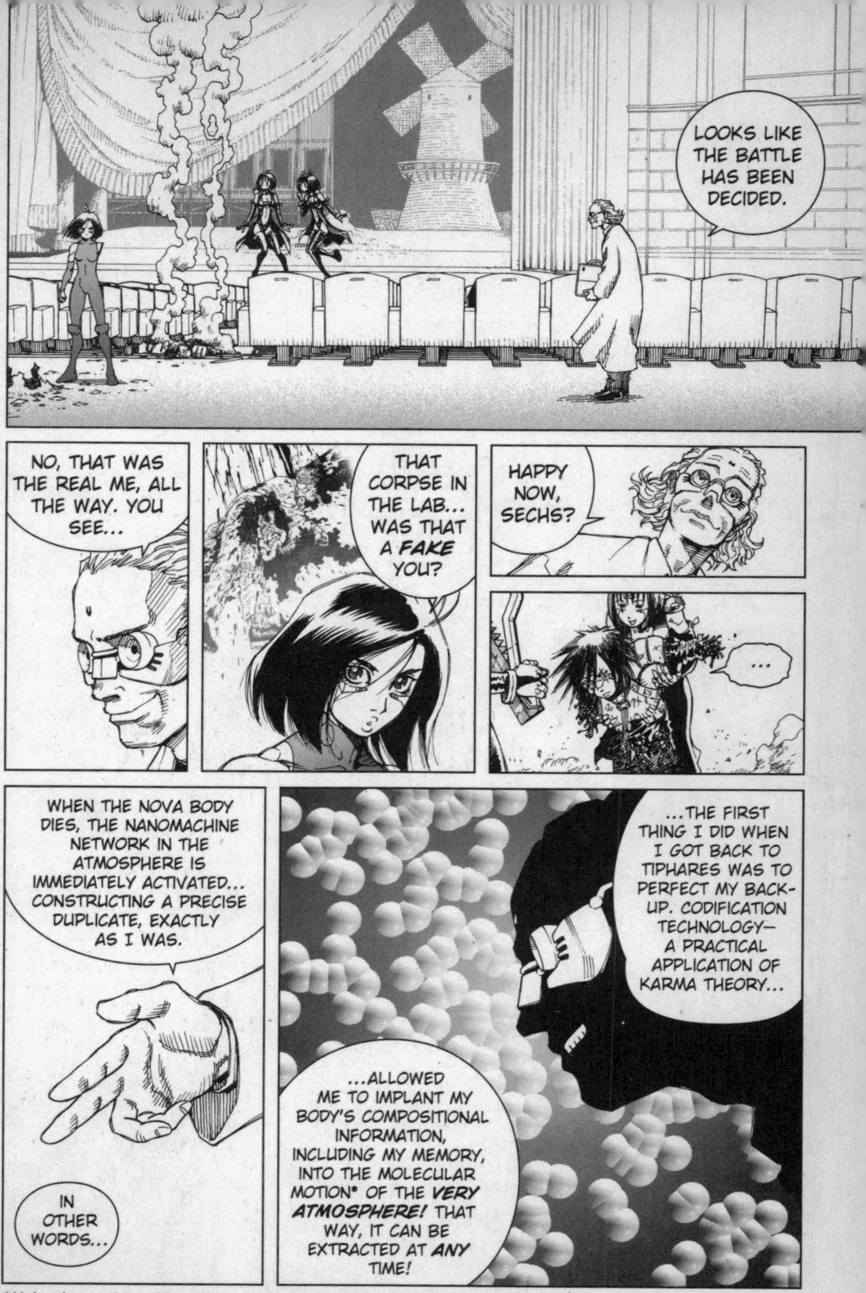
LOOKS LIKE THE BATTLE HAS BEEN DECIDED.
HAPPY NOW, SECHS?
...
THAT CORPSE IN THE LAB... WAS THAT A ***FAKE*** YOU?
NO, THAT WAS THE REAL ME, ALL THE WAY. YOU SEE...
...THE FIRST THING I DID WHEN I GOT BACK TO TIPHARES WAS TO PERFECT MY BACK-UP. CODIFICATION TECHNOLOGY— A PRACTICAL APPLICATION OF KARMA THEORY...
...ALLOWED ME TO IMPLANT MY BODY'S COMPOSITIONAL INFORMATION, INCLUDING MY MEMORY, INTO THE MOLECULAR MOTION* OF THE ***VERY ATMOSPHERE!*** THAT WAY, IT CAN BE EXTRACTED AT ***ANY*** TIME!
IN OTHER WORDS...
WHEN THE NOVA BODY DIES, THE NANOMACHINE NETWORK IN THE ATMOSPHERE IS IMMEDIATELY ACTIVATED... CONSTRUCTING A PRECISE DUPLICATE, EXACTLY AS I WAS.

**Molecular motion: although it appears as random noise, atomic-level movement can contain information. Sorted and codified, an infinite variety of signals could be extracted.*

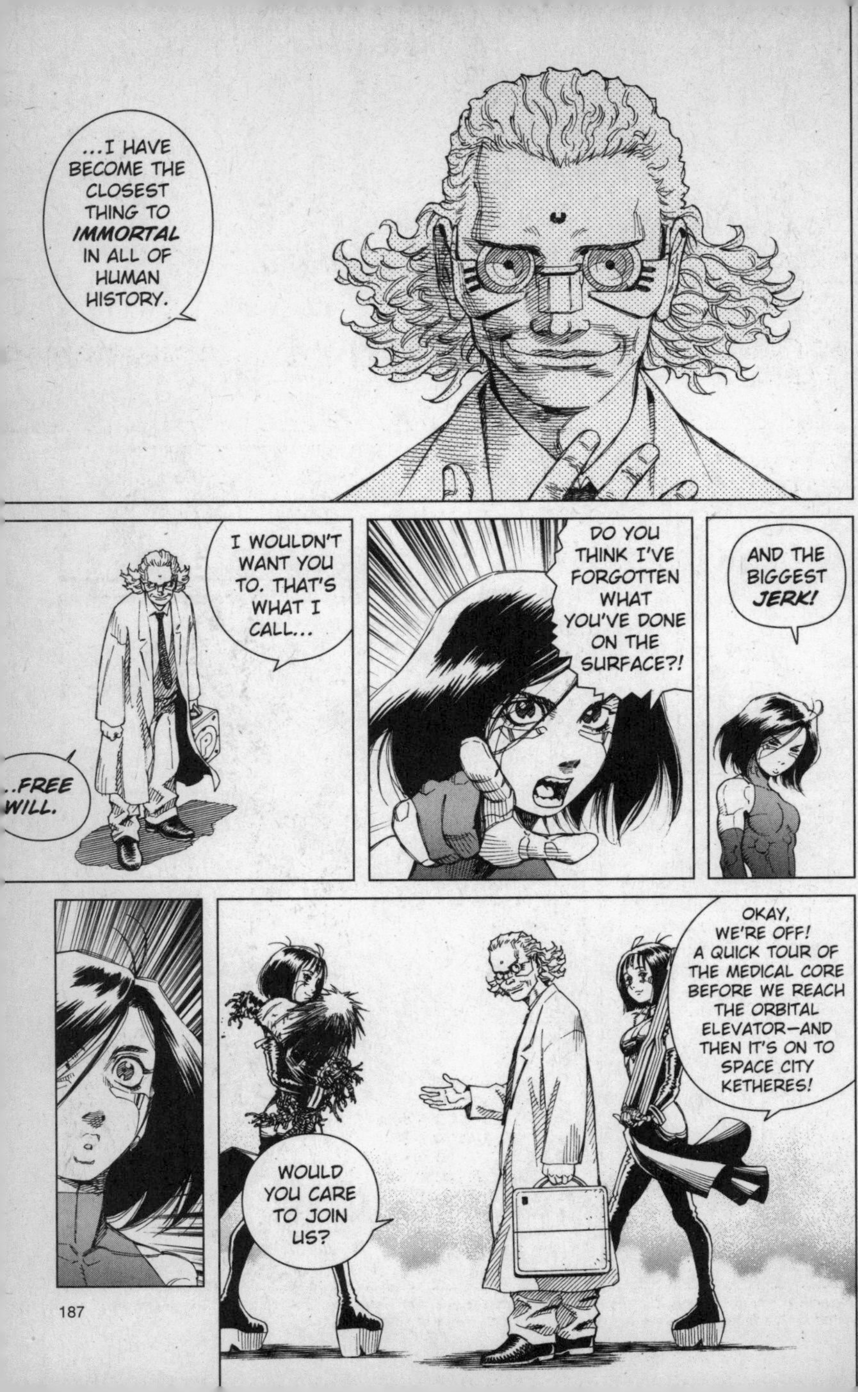
...I HAVE BECOME THE CLOSEST THING TO *IMMORTAL* IN ALL OF HUMAN HISTORY.
AND THE BIGGEST *JERK!*
DO YOU THINK I'VE FORGOTTEN WHAT YOU'VE DONE ON THE SURFACE?!
I WOULDN'T WANT YOU TO. THAT'S WHAT I CALL...
..FREE WILL.
OKAY, WE'RE OFF! A QUICK TOUR OF THE MEDICAL CORE BEFORE WE REACH THE ORBITAL ELEVATOR—AND THEN IT'S ON TO SPACE CITY KETHERES!
WOULD YOU CARE TO JOIN US?

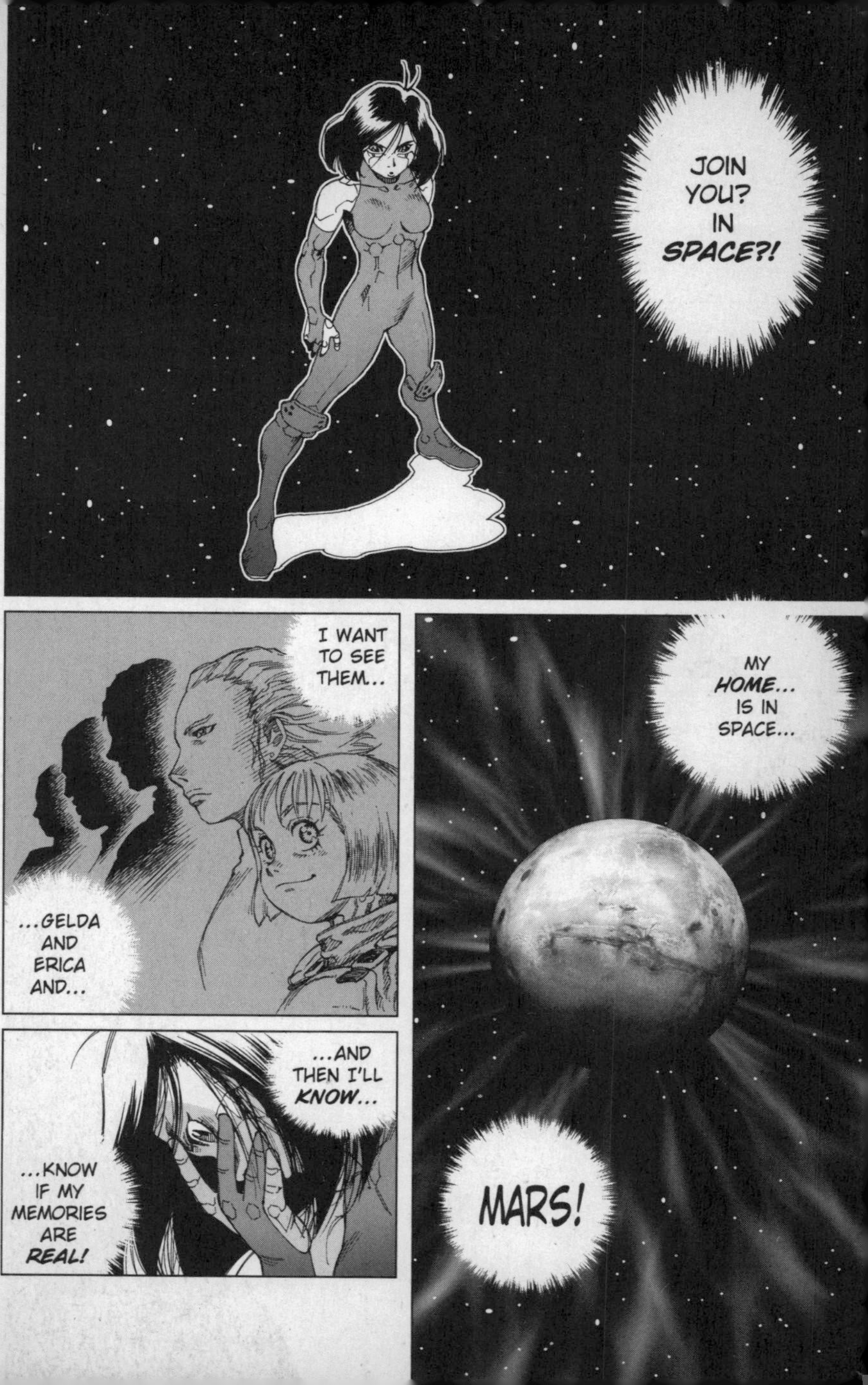
JOIN YOU? IN SPACE?!
I WANT TO SEE THEM...
...GELDA AND ERICA AND...
...AND THEN I'LL KNOW...
...KNOW IF MY MEMORIES ARE REAL!
MY HOME... IS IN SPACE...
MARS!

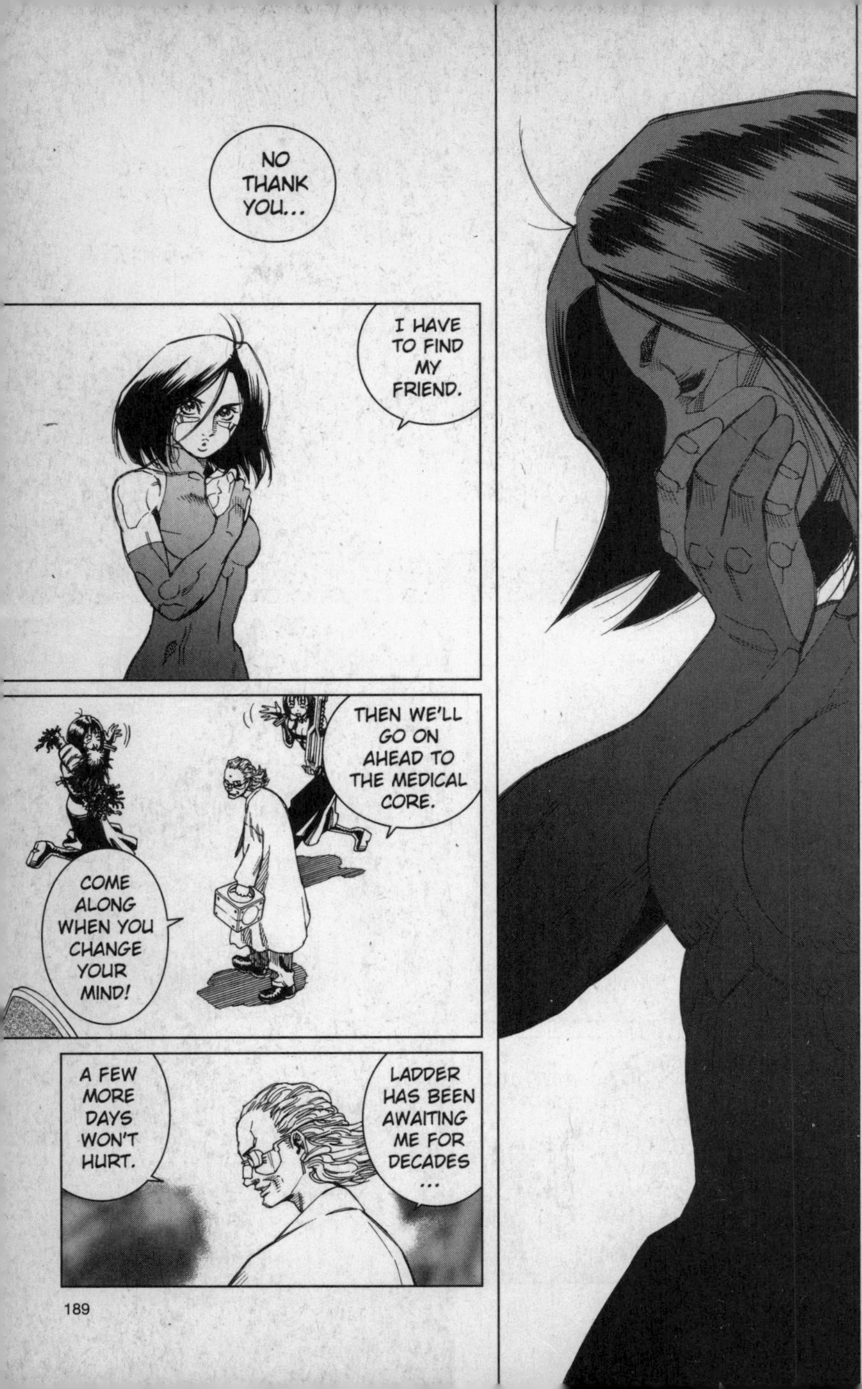
NO THANK YOU...
I HAVE TO FIND MY FRIEND.
THEN WE'LL GO ON AHEAD TO THE MEDICAL CORE.
COME ALONG WHEN YOU CHANGE YOUR MIND!
LADDER HAS BEEN AWAITING ME FOR DECADES ...
A FEW MORE DAYS WON'T HURT.

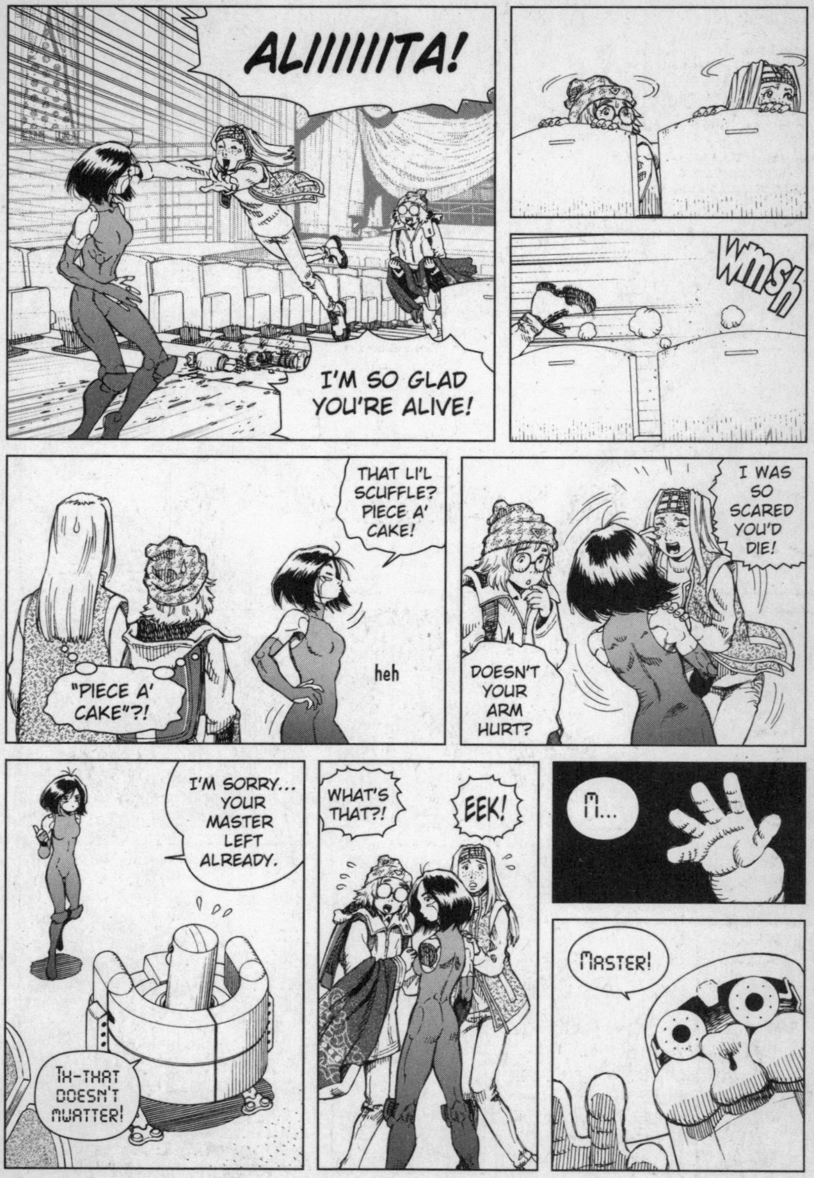
WMSH
ALIIIIIITA!
I'M SO GLAD YOU'RE ALIVE!
I WAS SO SCARED YOU'D DIE!
DOESN'T YOUR ARM HURT?
THAT LI'L SCUFFLE? PIECE A' CAKE!
heh
"PIECE A' CAKE"?!
M...
MASTER!
EEK!
WHAT'S THAT?!
I'M SORRY... YOUR MASTER LEFT ALREADY.
TH-THAT DOESN'T MWATTER!

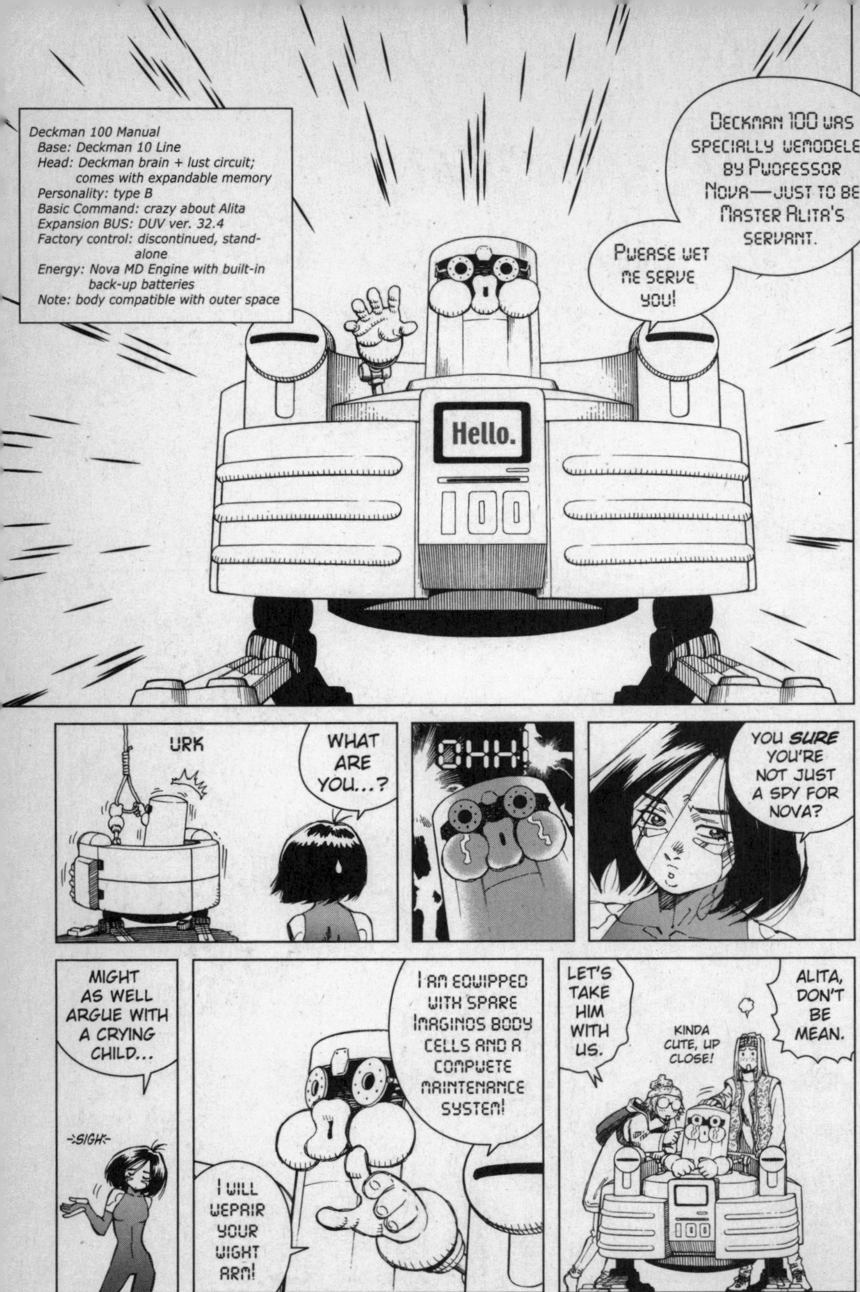

DECKMAN 100 WAS SPECIALLY WEMODELED BY PWOFESSOR NOVA—JUST TO BE MASTER ALITA'S SERVANT.
PWEASE WET ME SERVE YOU!
Deckman 100 Manual
Base: Deckman 10 Line
Head: Deckman brain + lust circuit; comes with expandable memory
Personality: type B
Basic Command: crazy about Alita
Expansion BUS: DUV ver. 32.4
Factory control: discontinued, stand-alone
Energy: Nova MD Engine with built-in back-up batteries
Note: body compatible with outer space
Hello.
100
YOU SURE YOU'RE NOT JUST A SPY FOR NOVA?
OHH!
WHAT ARE YOU...?
URK
ALITA, DON'T BE MEAN.
LET'S TAKE HIM WITH US.
KINDA CUTE, UP CLOSE!
100
I AM EQUIPPED WITH SPARE IMAGINOS BODY CELLS AND A COMPWETE MAINTENANCE SYSTEM!
I WILL WEPAIR YOUR WIGHT ARM!
MIGHT AS WELL ARGUE WITH A CRYING CHILD...
-SIGH-

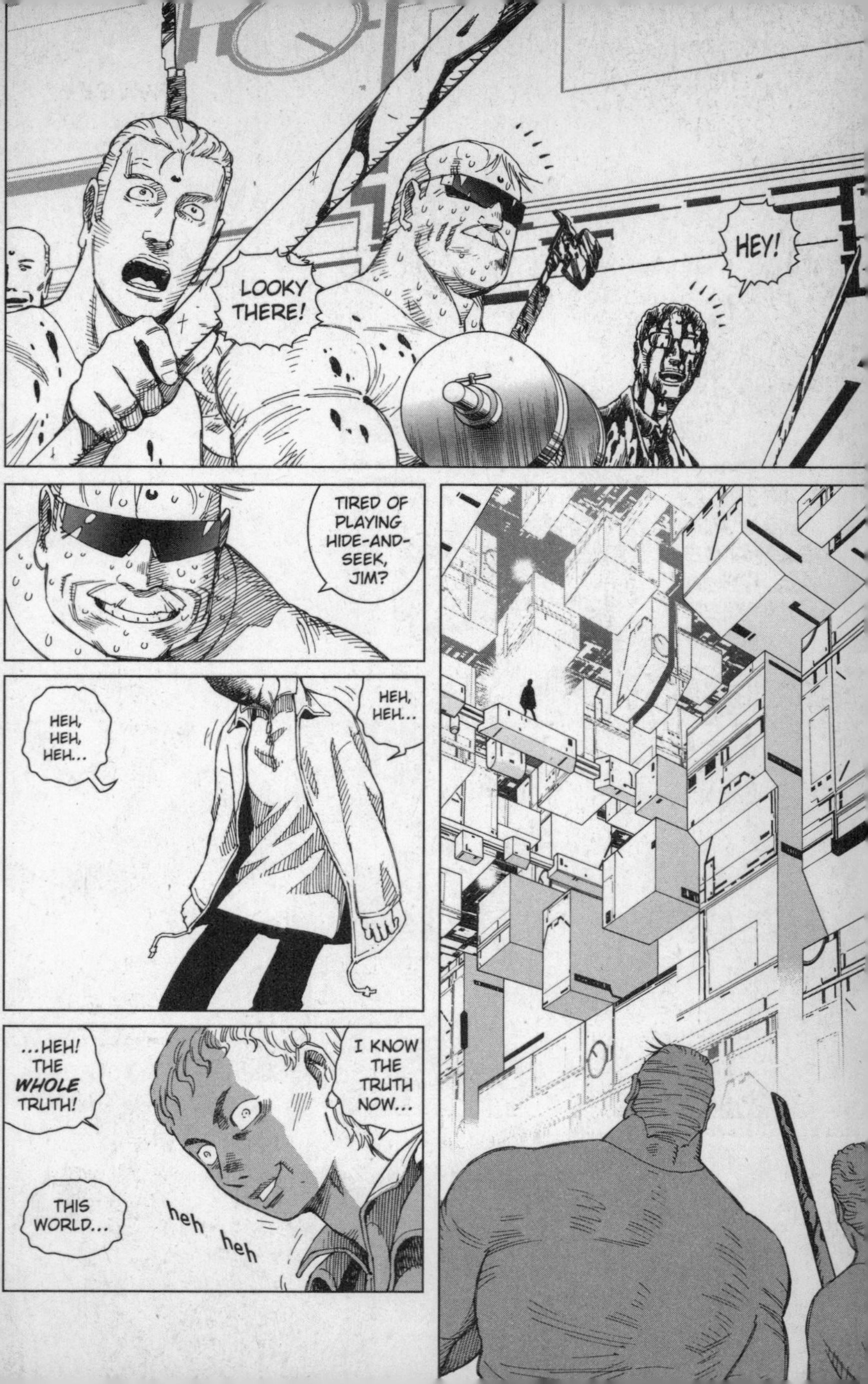
HEY!
LOOKY THERE!
TIRED OF PLAYING HIDE-AND-SEEK, JIM?
HEH, HEH...
HEH, HEH, HEH...
I KNOW THE TRUTH NOW...
...HEH! THE WHOLE TRUTH!
heh heh
THIS WORLD...

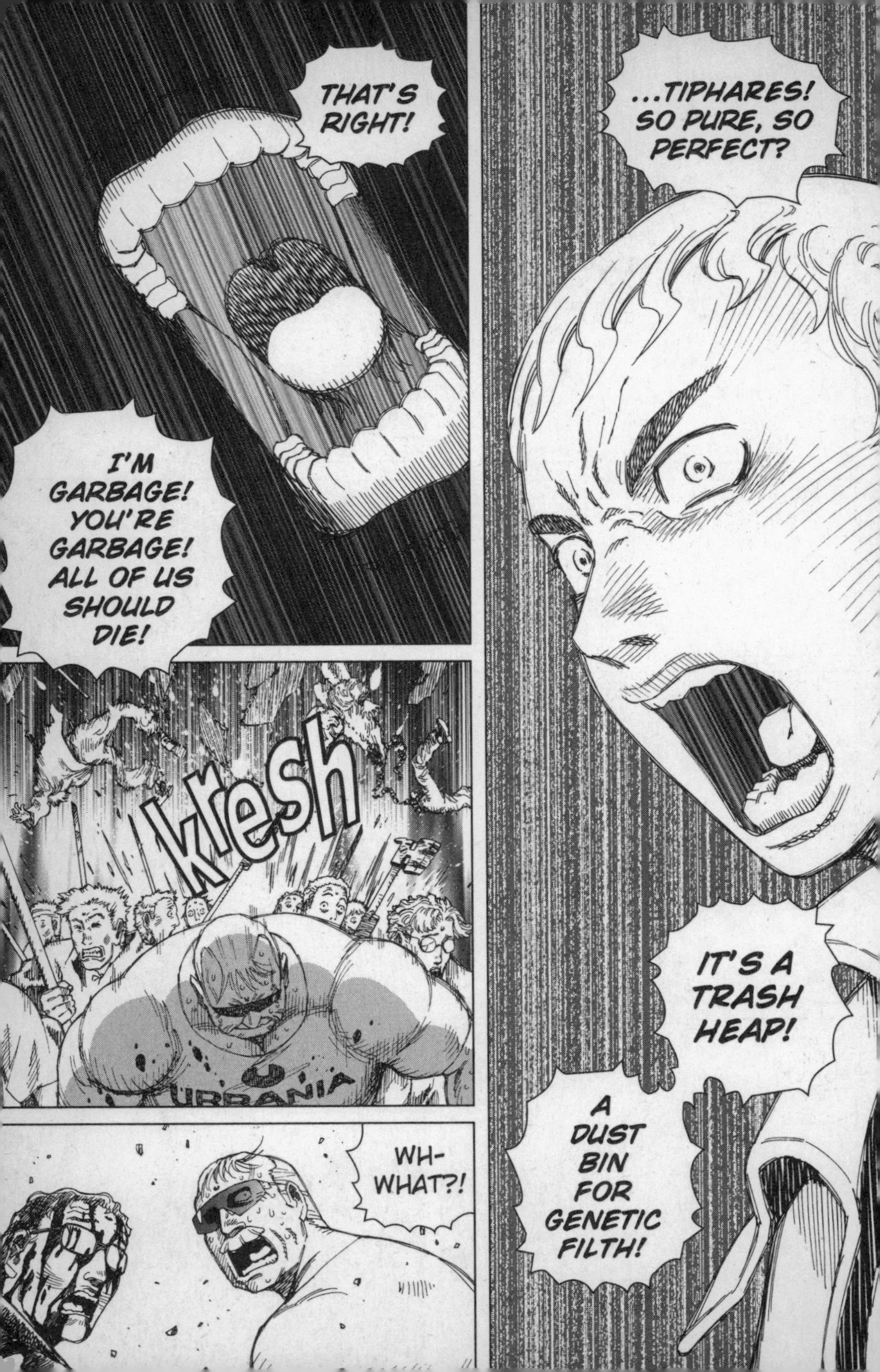
THAT'S RIGHT!
I'M GARBAGE! YOU'RE GARBAGE! ALL OF US SHOULD DIE!
kresh
URBANIA
WH- WHAT?!
...TIPHARES! SO PURE, SO PERFECT?
IT'S A TRASH HEAP!
A DUST BIN FOR GENETIC FILTH!

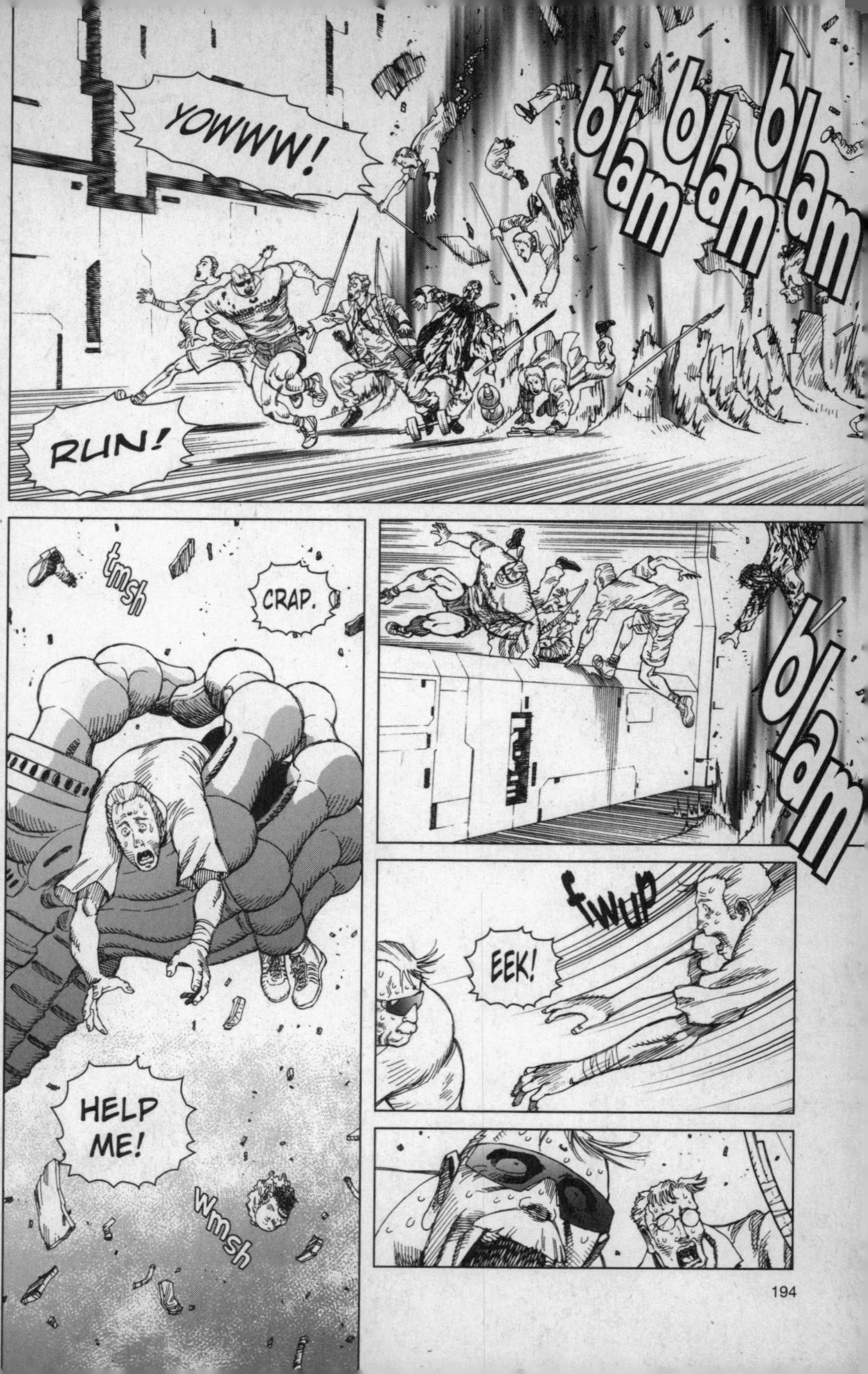

blam blam blam
blam blam blam
YOWWW!
RUN!
blam blam
fwup
EEK!
CRAP.
tmsh
HELP ME!
wmsh

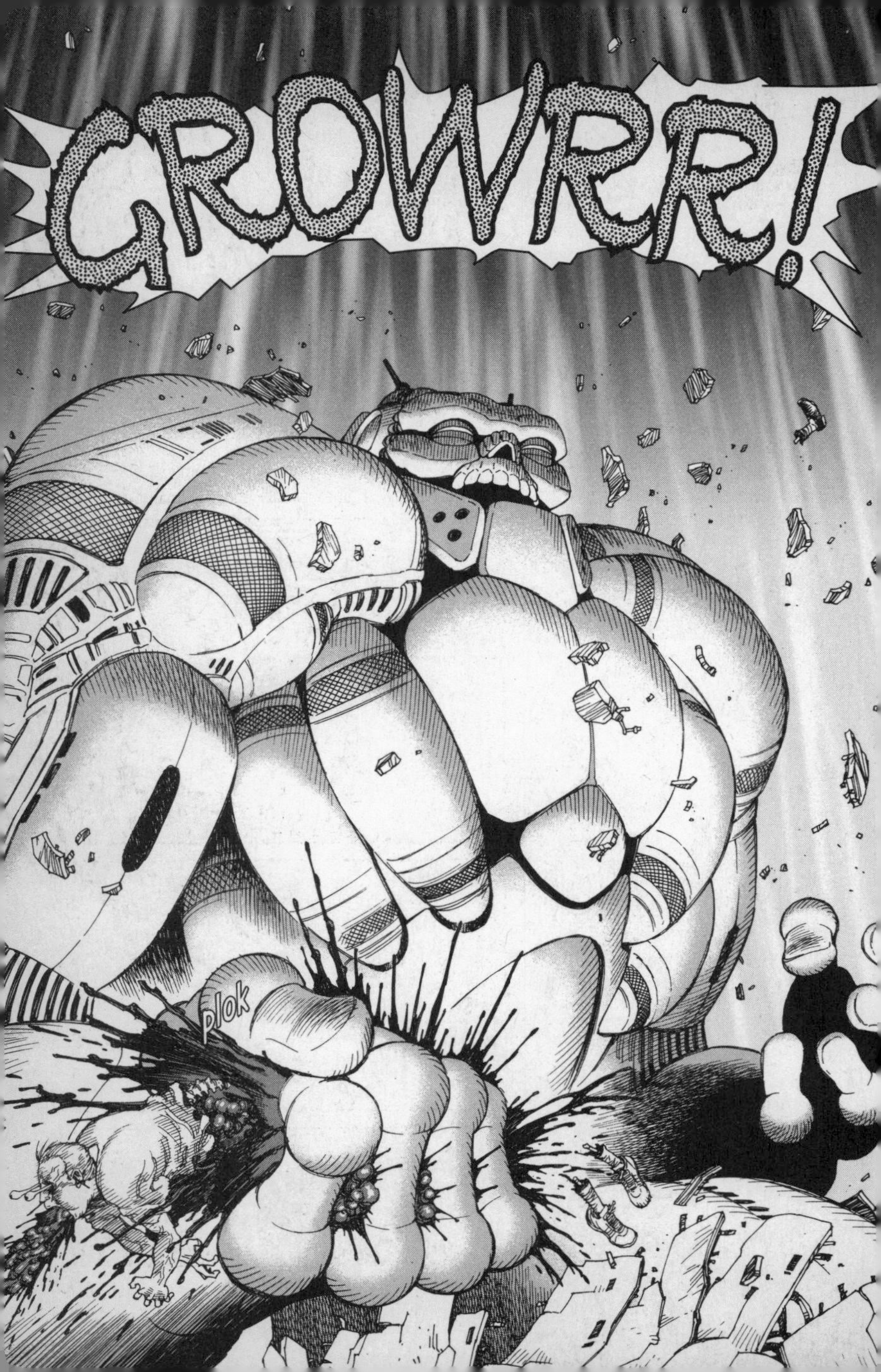
GROWRR!
plok

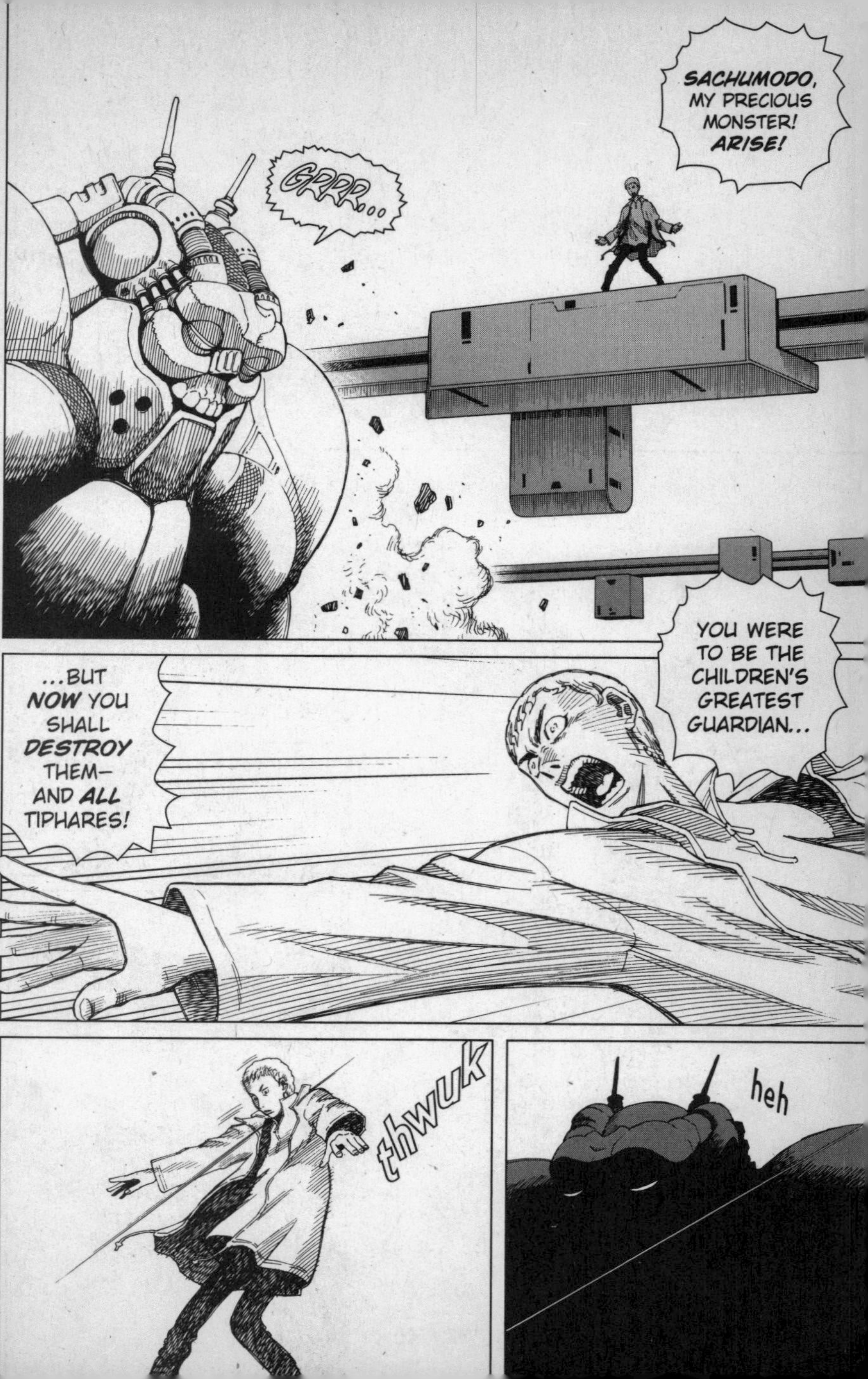
SACHUMODO, MY PRECIOUS MONSTER! ARISE!
GRRR...
YOU WERE TO BE THE CHILDREN'S GREATEST GUARDIAN...
...BUT NOW YOU SHALL DESTROY THEM— AND ALL TIPHARES!
heh
thwuk

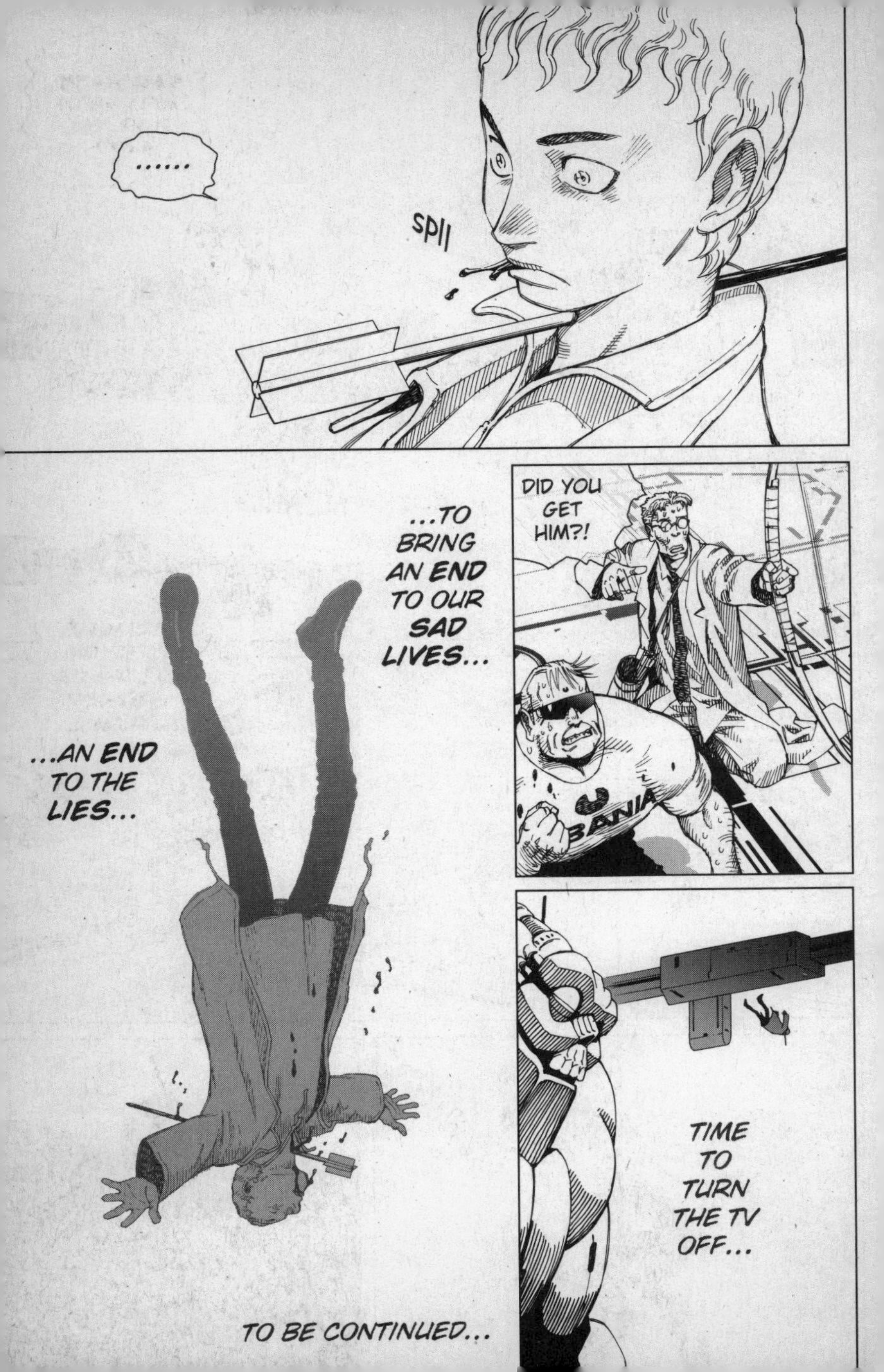
......
SPLI
DID YOU GET HIM?!
TIME TO TURN THE TV OFF...
...TO BRING AN END TO OUR SAD LIVES...
...AN END TO THE LIES...
BANIA

TO BE CONTINUED...

EDITOR'S RECOMMENDATIONS

After my first day of employment as an editor at **Viz**, in August of 1994, I came home and gleefully exclaimed, "Guess what I did on my first day at my new job? I spent the whole day reading about a female cyborg fighting a brain-sucking monster! I can't believe I'm getting paid for this!"

My job training had begun with reading the first few volumes of YUKITO KISHIRO'S ***Battle Angel Alita*** in preparation for editing the rest of the series. It's been nine years now; I'm still at **Viz**, had a couple promotions, and I'm happy to say that with the continuation of the ***Alita*** saga with ***Last Order***, I'm still reading about that female cyborg and monsters who, if they aren't sucking brains *per se*, are certainly doing them and their concomitant bodies some serious damage.

Which is what some pundits and parents would say reading manga and comics in general does to your brain.

So why am I still here? Precisely because of sophisticated, complex, philosophical, emotional, humorous, and exquisitely drawn stories like ***Alita*** that never fail to entertain and stimulate my unsucked, undamaged brain!

Annette Roman

Annette Roman
Battle Angel Alita editor

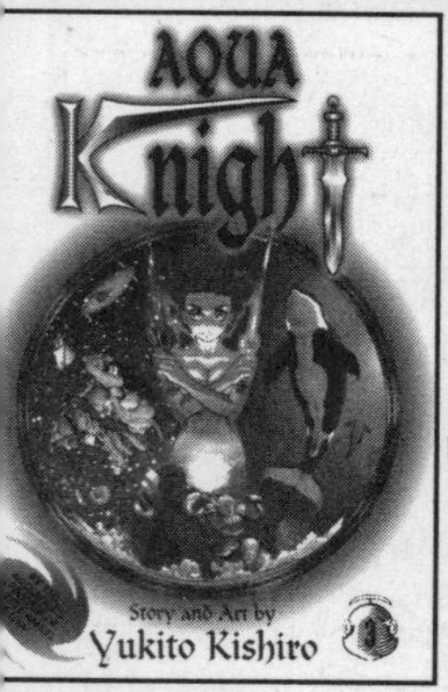
AQUA
Knight
Story and Art by
Yukito Kishiro

Aqua Knight: This fantasy tale ›y ***Alita*** creator **Yukito Kishiro** lso stars a female heroine and mad genius, but is a tad more ghthearted and quirky. Set on water world where Aqua ;nights ride the high seas on he backs of orca steeds.

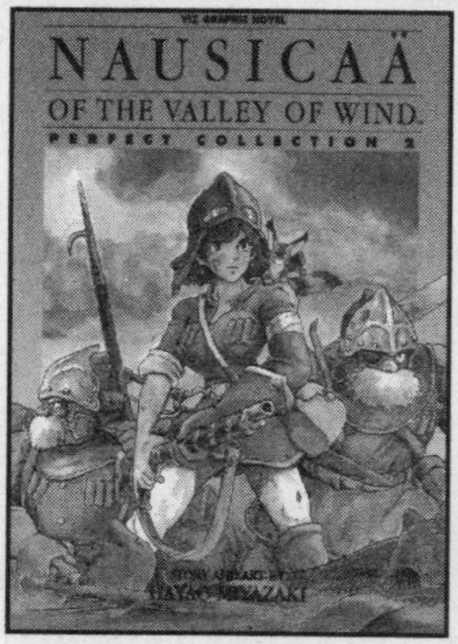
VIZ GRAPHIC NOVEL
NAUSICAÄ
OF THE VALLEY OF WIND
PERFECT COLLECTION 2
HAYAO MIYAZAKI

• ***Nausicaä of the Valley of Wind***: Another strong heroine in another ravaged world... The hand-drawn (no tone!) classic masterpiece and plea for world peace by HAYAO MIYAZAKI, the brilliant director of ***Spirited Away***, winner of the **2002 Academy Award** for **Best Animated Feature.**

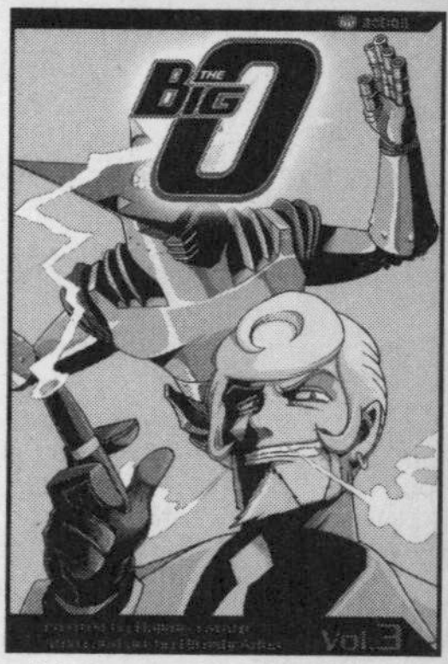
THE BIG O
Vol.3

• ***The Big O***: A post-something world with amnesia! A robot girl in search of her identity! *Film noir* wry humor and snappy dialogue!

LOVE MANGA?   LET US KNOW!

☐ Please do NOT send me information about VIZ Media products, news and events, special offers, or other information.

☐ Please do NOT send me information from VIZ Media's trusted business partners.

Name: _____

Address: _____

City: _____ **State:** _____ **Zip:** _____

E-mail: _____

☐ **Male** ☐ **Female**   **Date of Birth** (mm/dd/yyyy): ___ / ___ / _____   (Under 13? Parental consent required)

What race/ethnicity do you consider yourself? (check all that apply)

☐ White/Caucasian ☐ Black/African American ☐ Hispanic/Latino

☐ Asian/Pacific Islander ☐ Native American/Alaskan Native ☐ Other: _____

What VIZ title(s) did you purchase? (indicate title(s) purchased) _____

_____

What other VIZ titles do you own? _____

_____

Reason for purchase: (check all that apply)

☐ Special offer ☐ Favorite title / author / artist / genre

☐ Gift ☐ Recommendation ☐ Collection

☐ Read excerpt in VIZ manga sampler ☐ Other _____

Where did you make your purchase? (please check one)

☐ Comic store ☐ Bookstore ☐ Grocery Store

☐ Convention ☐ Newsstand ☐ Video Game Store

☐ Online (site:_____) ☐ Other _____

How many manga titles have you purchased in the last year? How many were VIZ titles?
(please check one from each column)

MANGA

- ☐ None
- ☐ 1 – 4
- ☐ 5 – 10
- ☐ 11+

- ☐ 11+

How much influence do special promotions and gifts-with-purchase have on the titles you buy?
(please circle, with 5 being great influence and 1 being none)

1 2 3 4 5

Do you purchase every volume of your favorite series?

☐ Yes! Gotta have 'em as my own ☐ No. Please explain: ____________________

What kind of manga storylines do you most enjoy? **(check all that apply)**

- ☐ Action / Adventure
- ☐ Comedy
- ☐ Fighting
- ☐ Artistic / Alternative
- ☐ Science Fiction
- ☐ Romance (shojo)
- ☐ Sports
- ☐ Other ____________________
- ☐ Horror
- ☐ Fantasy (shojo)
- ☐ Historical

If you watch the anime or play a video or TCG game from a series, how likely are you to buy the manga? **(please circle, with 5 being very likely and 1 being unlikely)**

1 2 3 4 5

If unlikely, please explain: ____________________

Who are your favorite authors / artists? ____________________

____

What titles would like you translated and sold in English? ____________________

____

THANK YOU! Please send the completed form to:

VIZ media

NJW Research
42 Catharine Street
Poughkeepsie, NY 12601

Your privacy is very important to us. All information provided will be used for internal purposes only and will not be sold or otherwise divulged.